THE GOLDEN LETTERS

THE GOLDEN LETTERS

The Three Statements of Garab Dorje,
the first teacher of Dzogchen,
together with a commentary by
Dza Patrul Rinpoche
entitled "The Special Teaching of the
Wise and Glorious King"

Foreword by
NAMKHAI NORBU RINPOCHE

Translation, Introduction and Commentaries by
JOHN MYRDHIN REYNOLDS

Snow Lion Publications
Ithaca, New York USA

Snow Lion Publications
P.O. Box 6483
Ithaca, New York 14850 USA
Tel: 607-273-8519

ISBN 1-55939-050-6

Library of Congress Cataloging-in-Publication Data

Garab Dorje.
    [Tshig gsum gnad brdeg. English]
    The golden letters : the three statements of Garab Dorje, the first teacher
of Dzogchen, together with a commentary by / Dza Patrul Rinpoche,
entitled: the special teaching of the wise and glorious King ; foreword by
Namkhai Norbu Rinpoche ; translated with introduction and commentaries
by John Myrdhin Reynolds. -- 1st ed.
        p. cm.
    Includes bibliographical references and index.
    ISBN 1-55939-050-6
    1. Rdzogs-chen (Rñiṅ-ma-pa)   I. Reynolds, John Myrdhin, 1942-
II. O-rgyan-'jigs-med-chos-kyi-dbaṅ-po, Dpal-sprul, b. 1808. mKhas pa sri
rgyal po'i khyad chos' grel pa dang bcas pa. English.   III. Title.
BQ7662.4.G3613   1996
294.3'923--dc20   96-7519
                                                                        CIP

Contents

Preface

First of all, I wish to thank Namkhai Norbu Rinpoche, who first made clear to me the crucial importance of these three statements of Garab Dorje for the understanding of Dzogchen as a whole (Potter Valley, California, 1980); and for his invaluable help in translating the present texts, especially the *'Das-rjes*. I also extend my thanks to Rinpoche for writing a foreword to this book. Moreover, I am grateful for the transmissions I have received on the Patrul Rinpoche text, the translation of which is also found in this book, from several masters of the Nyingmapa tradition, notably H.H. Dudjom Rinpoche, Lama Gonpo Tsedan Rinpoche, and Lama Tharchin Rinpoche.

I translated this Patrul Rinpoche text, known as the *mKhas-pa sri rgyal-po'i khyad-chos*, "The Special Teaching of the Wise and Glorious King," which is among the best-known commentaries in Tibetan on these three statements, while I was living at Baudha in the Kathmandu valley of Nepal (Spring 1978). My thanks go to Ani Lodro Palmo for having kindly provided me with a copy of this text, bringing it with her from Tashi Jong in Himachal Pradesh. Over many cups of tea in the early morning hours at the Bir Hotel, during the course of several days, I completed the translation. But then I set it aside for several years. In the meantime I came to read several other translations of the same text by Sogyal Rinpoche, by Tulku Thondup, and by Keith Dowman. A few years ago, I took out my translation once again and revised it somewhat, bringing it into line with my revised translations of Tibetan Buddhist technical terms. When I considered the translation for publication, it was suggested that I include with it a translation of the *'Das-rjes*, which is said to represent the actual text of Garab Dorje's last testament. This effort was inspired by my program of going back to the original texts of the Dzogchen tradition, and not just relying on the expositions, excellent as they may be, of more recent masters of that tradition, which is generally the case among the Tibetans themselves.

This latter text, unlike the work of Patrul Rinpoche, turned out to be written in a difficult Tibetan language, being exceedingly terse and elliptical, rather like college lecture notes. Moreover, the presentation of Thekchod (*khregs-chod*) and Thodgal (*thod-rgal*) were mixed up together in the text, instead of being rigidly separated, as is the case with the later Terma tradition. During the course of three afternoons at a retreat in Jamestown, Colorado (July 1987), Namkhai Norbu Rinpoche generously provided several hours during which we went over the translation of this text. The results of this will also be seen in the interlinear commentary and notes which follow the translation. Because of the linguistic difficulties of the text and the necessity of interspersing the translation of the root text with the notes (*mchan*) found in the Tibetan, as well as with some additional phrases in parentheses supplied by the translator in order to facilitate the reading and understanding of the text, I decided that the best method would be to provide a running and rather free translation uninterrupted by the notes, and to follow this with a strictly literal translation along with an interlinear commentary where necessary.

For a justification of my method of translation, first developed in a seminar on the translation of Buddhist technical terms with Professor Edward Conze in 1967–68 (University of Washington, Seattle), see the section entitled "Note on the Translation of Dzogchen Technical Terms." A glossary of Dzogchen terms in Tibetan and English is provided at the back of the book, but the explanations of why I translate certain Tibetan terms in the way I do will be found in the notes and commentaries. I leave these out of the texts of the translations themselves in order not to burden the reader. This book is primarily a presentation of the teachings of Dzogchen found in these two texts, rather than a philological or historical study of the origins of the Dzogchen tradition. There exist a number of biographical or hagiographical accounts of the life of Garab Dorje preserved in the Nyingmapa tradition and they do not agree in all details. So, by way of biography I have included here only one translation: the account of Garab Dorje found in the *Lo-rgyus chen-mo* of Zhangton Tashi Dorje (1097–1167) contained in the *Bi-ma snying-thig* collection of Longchen Rabjampa (vol. 7, pt. III). This is probably one of the oldest extant accounts of the historical career of Garab Dorje. I also make reference to the account found in the *'Dra 'bag chen-mo* (author unknown), the famous biography of Vairochana the translator, which has been in existence since at least the thirteenth century, but which contains material which is much older. I also include here, of interest to practitioners, a short Guru Sadhana (*bla-sgrub*) for Garab Dorje written by Khyentse Chokyi Lodro Rinpoche (1896–1959). The transmission for this sadhana was graciously given by Sogyal Rinpoche during his visit to the spring retreat at Merigar, Italy, in April 1985.

Since many of the extant early texts for the Dzogchen tradition come from the tenth and eleventh centuries of our era, some modern scholars propose that Dzogchen was actually invented at that time by certain unscrupulous Nyingmapa and Bonpo Lamas. According to this argument, these Lamas, wishing to have their unorthodox doctrines accepted by Tibetans generally, attributed these texts to certain early heroic historical figures, especially to Padmasambhava and Vimalamitra in the eighth century. However, this theory falls into an error common among academic scholars whose knowledge is limited to the study of written texts, where it is assumed that an idea or a practice did not exist until it was written down in some text. This approach, of course, overlooks and disregards the importance of oral tradition (*snyan brgyud*) with regard to spiritual teachings. The reality of oral tradition I have experienced for myself first-hand during years of residence among Tibetan Lamas in India and Nepal. Accordingly, I have no doubt that the Dzogchen teachings go back to the eighth century in Tibet with Padmasambhava, Vimalamitra, and Vairochana, just as is claimed in the tradition, and most likely before that to India and to Uddiyana. Dzogchen was not something created *ex nihilo* in the tenth century. Certain manuscripts from the Tun Huang library of the tenth century prove its existence at that time. Even if it could be definitively shown, however, that Dzogchen as an independent movement first came into existence in the tenth century with Nubchen Sangye Yeshe (gNubs-chen sangs-rgyas ye-shes), Shenchen Luga (gShen-chen klu-dga'), and others, this two-hundred-year gap between the eighth and the tenth centuries would make no difference with respect to the universal truth of the Dzogchen teachings as a path to liberation and enlightenment. Spiritual truth transcends history. I allude to some of these philological and historical problems in the section entitled "Historical Origins of Dzogchen," but a fuller consideration of the problems involved must be left for a later discussion.

All translations from Tibetan are mine, except where otherwise indicated. Foreign words found in the text are Tibetan, unless otherwise indicated. Tibetan words in transliteration according to the Wylie system are contained within parentheses or italicized without parentheses; the initial root letters of Tibetan personal names and text titles are capitalized. Tibetan words spelled according to English pronunciation are not italicized. Also, common Sanskrit words are not italicized. In the translations, my interpolations and explanations are placed in parentheses. Brackets indicate a note in Tibetan inserted into the original Tibetan text.

Finally, in terms of the preparation of this book for publication, I wish to thank my editor Michael Taylor for his extensive editorial suggestions and comments; my thanks are also extended to Arthur Mandelbaum, Bob Kohut, Charles Stein, Andrea Loseries-Leick, Tina Smith, and Andy Lukianowicz for proofreading the manuscript and making many useful suggestions. Furthermore, my special thanks also go to Brooke Henley for patiently typing this manuscript onto disk and to Robert Knight for his efforts with regard to inputting the text on computer.

Although the entire text of this book, *The Golden Letters*, was written and completed in 1990, the publication of the book was delayed for almost four years due to circumstances beyond my control relating to the original publisher. I am therefore grateful to Snow Lion Publications for bringing out the book. Furthermore, because the book has been so long delayed, the "Historical Origins of Dzogchen" section does not deal with any new scholarly works in the field that have appeared since 1990. I apologize for this. Nevertheless, it is my hope, as the translator, that the translations of the Dzogchen texts found herein will be of some use to those modern practitioners who travel this ancient path.

Vajranatha (John Myrdhin Reynolds)
Freehold, New Jersey, January 1995

Foreword

by Namkhai Norbu Rinpoche

All of the teachings concerning the path of Ati Dzogchen may be subsumed under the three topics of the Base, the Path, and the Fruit. Similarly, the texts that teach matters relating to these three topics are generally known as the Three Series of Dzogchen teachings.[1]

Now, with regard to these Three Series, initially all of the teachings relating to the Path of Ati Dzogchen were revealed as a single and unified whole by the first great human teacher of Dzogchen, Garab Dorje,[2] to his close personal disciples. Foremost among them was the great master Manjushrimitra,[3] and it was he who collected together the original Dzogchen teachings. Making a written redaction of the precepts, he divided them into these Three Series. Thus, we may ask, what were the criteria for organizing the teachings in this way? On the occasion when the teacher Garab Dorje realized the purified Body of Light,[4] he bestowed upon Manjushrimitra, who was the principal disciple in the retinue of that master, "The Three Vajra Verses."[5] These verses are considered to represent the Last Testament[6] of the master wherein he condensed the very pith of all the teachings belonging to the Path of Dzogchen into their essential points. In a perfect and inexhaustible manner, these Three Vajra Verses of the Last Testament embody the very heart of the essential points of the Base, the Path, and the Fruit, respectively. Just as butter is the pure product of milk, these Three Statements[7] bring out the intended meaning of all of the teachings belonging to the Path of Dzogchen. Therefore, these Three Statements represent a veritable key for opening the great door to the goal of all of the profound Upadeshas of the essential points expounded in Dzogchen. Because of encompassing everything connected with Dzogchen, these Three Vajra Verses of the Last Testament provide the rationale for the division of the Dzogchen teachings into the Three Series.

Some Tibetan scholars, however, although they have entered with sincere devotion into the teachings of the Path of Dzogchen have given out to their students that these Three Series of Dzogchen teachings, namely, Semde, Longde, and Upadesha,[8] are quite dissimilar in terms of their views and their tenets.[9] They assert that the teachings contained within the Three Series originated at some earlier time, when it was understood that three distinct views existed within the Dzogchen tradition. However, the different viewpoints[10] held by these scholars, even though they were formulated in accordance with the general principles of their respective systems,[11] actually presented Dzogchen idiosyncratically. There is nothing here that was established in reality, and this procedure deviated substantially from the intention of the real meaning of Dzogchen. It is clear that these speculations represent the fantasies of the individual scholars, who merely pursued an intellectual analysis. On occasion, it is proper to differentiate the teachings of Dzogchen into these Three Series and to indicate that they refer, respectively, to the Base, the Path, and the Fruit of Dzogchen Yet in terms of the Primordial Natural State of Ati Dzogchen,[12] there is actually complete freedom from falling into any partiality and, hence, from insisting on making such categorical distinctions. Accordingly, there is nothing whatsoever (regarding the Natural State of Dzogchen) that requires the kind of confirmation of philosophical position[13] established by way of (the threefold process of) refutation, demonstration, and rebuttal[14] as employed by these scholars.

Because there exists an infinity of different temperaments and personalities among sentient beings, (it goes without saying that) there equally exist various different means and methods that can be employed to introduce them directly to the Primordial State of Dzogchen.[15] It is not necessary to speak of all of them here. However, when a particular individual is about to enter into the practice of Dzogchen, there exists an appropriate method to be employed for this. As regards the individual, three different kinds of activities correspond to the three gates of body, speech, and mind, respectively. Thus, the master, taking into consideration the disciple's individual experiences of the three gates (of body, speech, and mind), gives an appropriate direct introduction to the Primordial State of Ati,[16] by way of employing various different methods and means. For example, he may explain to the disciple that the nature of the mirror possesses an innate disposition that is clear, pure, and stainless[17] in its quality and that, therefore, the things (placed before the mirror) arise as reflected images in it. On the basis of this analogy or example,[18] an understanding (with regard to the meaning) arises (in the disciple) that the experiences of phenomena are similar to the reflections seen in a mirror.

All of the many teachings concerning the path of Ati Dzogchen that the Supreme Teacher Garab Dorje revealed to his human disciples may be classified, in brief, into three types: Tantra, Agama, and Upadesha.[19] Traditionally, it is said that there exist some 6,400,000 Tantras within Ati Dzogchen. Furthermore, it is recorded (in the *sGra thal-'gyur Tantra*[20] and elsewhere) that these teachings of Dzogchen are found in many different inhabited world-systems throughout the great universe. It is obvious, however, that there would be no purpose for the existence of so many teachings of Ati Dzogchen in our own limited human world here.

The Ati Dzogchen teachings that do exist here (in our human world) are present due to the good fortune of our own (individual and collective) meritorious karma. The most important of them are such root Tantras[21] as the *Byang-chub kyi sems kun-byed rgyal-po'i rgyud* (the great Root Tantra of the Dzogchen Semde Series), the *kLong-chen rab-'byams rgyal-po'i rgyud* (the great Root Tantra of the Dzogchen Longde Series), and the *sGra thal-'gyur rtsa-ba'i rgyud* (the great Root Tantra of the Dzogchen Upadesha Series), as well as their explanatory Tantras[22] and various kinds of Upadeshas and Tantras,[23] both large and small. According to the *sGra-thal-'gyur*, the Dzogchen Tantras hold particular importance in thirteen great star systems[24] (one of which is our own.) Within the multitude of Tantras belonging to Ati Dzogchen present throughout the great vast expanse of the universe,[25] there is found one group of texts that reveals the very nectar of the profound meaning. In addition, there exist various kinds of Agamas, or philosophical texts that represent abridgements of these Tantras. Furthermore, there are various kinds of Upadeshas that expound straightforwardly the rather particular experiences of the individual Vidyadharas who have attained realization (of the practice of Dzogchen). This is certain.

However, some Tibetan scholars routinely maintain that, since these Dzogchen Tantras do not actually display the ten topics that ordinarily characterize a Tantra,[26] these texts therefore do not fully possess the requisite characteristics of a Tantra. Generally speaking, it is required that a given Tantra exhibit all ten topics of a Tantra. This is the view of the Path of Transformation, otherwise known as the Secret Mantra system. However, there is nothing whatsoever (in these ten topics) specifically belonging to the system of Ati, which is the path of self-liberation[27] as opposed to the viewpoint[28] of the path of transformation. Therefore, it is certain that the absence of the ten topics should not be an impediment to these texts' being considered Tantras. Furthermore, in the *Byang-chub kyi sems kun-byed rgyal-po* and in other great root Tantras of Ati, the ten topics are not found. So, if the ten topics do not occur in this principal Tantra, one should not expect to find them elsewhere (in other acknowledged Dzogchen Tantras).

Again, certain Tibetan scholars, such as Drigung Paldzin,[29] maintain that the doctrine of Dzogchen itself is not authentic and that the root texts, whether Tantra, Agama, or Upadesha, such as, for example, the Dzogchen Tantra *Kun-byed rgyal-po*, were composed by Tibetan scholars of a later time. On such occasions, when there arise attempts to call into question the authenticity of Dzogchen by claiming that the original texts from ancient times were fabricated and hence are not genuine (Buddhist scriptures), it is like a dark dense cloud of wrong thoughts (obscuring the clarity of the mind). By contrast, realized scholars (of the Nyingmapa tradition) belonging to both ancient and recent times, such as, among others, the great Kunkhyen Longchen Rabjampa[30] and Sogdogpa Lodro Gyaltsan,[31] employing the sunlight of reason and scriptural citations, have excellently clarified these matters.

Moreover, in our own time, a number of old texts (relevant to this issue and dating from the eighth through tenth centuries CE) have been found at Tun Huang in China. Among them was the Agama entitled the *Rig-pa'i khu-byug*,[32] which is a root text of Dzogchen, together with a short commentary on its intent, both translated from the language of Uddiyana by the great Tibetan translator Vairochana. Furthermore, (among the Tun Huang discoveries) there was found a second Dzogchen text, entitled *sBas-pa'i rgum chung*, written by the Dzogchen master Buddhagupta,[33] together with a commentary on the intent of its difficult essential points. In addition, with them was found another text, where the Primordial State of Ati[34] is ultimately realized by way of the perfection process of the meditation deity Shri Vajrakilaya.[35] So one can see that, clearly, these three texts found at Tun Huang attest to the authenticity of Dzogchen.

Furthermore, the Dzogchen teachings first appeared here in Tibet even earlier (than the eighth century), that is to say, during the time of Triwer Sergyi Jyaruchan,[36] the king of Zhang-zhung. From his time until the present some 3600 years have elapsed. The Teacher of Bon, Shenrab Miwoche,[37] was the first to teach Dzogchen (to humanity) which, at that time, was known as "the Bon of the Perfect Mind."[38] He did this in Olmo Lung-ring in Tazig (Central Asia), and later the Dzogchen teachings spread from there to the country of Zhang-zhung, which lay to the west of Central Tibet.[39] Then, in the time of the Tibetan king Songtsan Gampo,[40] the practitioner of Bon from Zhang-zhung Gyerpung Nangzher Lodpo[41] was invited to reside in Tibet, and there he taught the Tantras of the *Zhang-zhung snyan-rgyud*.[42] Thus, it is clear from the history found in the *Zhang-zhung snyan-rgyud* that it was this master who first inaugurated the custom of teaching Dzogchen in Central Tibet.[43]

After that, in the time of the Tibetan king Tisong Detsan,[44] Padmasambhava, the great master from Uddiyana, was invited to visit the country of Tibet. Thus, for Central Tibet, it was he who first opened the door (to the Tibetans) of the Dharma of the Great Secret Mantra Vajrayana, and, in particular, he introduced the Mahayoga, the Anuyoga, and the Atiyoga teachings among them. He caused these teachings, known as the Three Series of Yogas of the Inner Tantras, to be spread far and wide throughout Tibet.

However, some scholars (that is, Bonpos) entertain the notion that, even though the great master Padmasambhava did indeed come to Central Tibet (in the eighth century), it was Gyerchen Nangzher Lodpo, the disciple of Tapihritsa, who first introduced the tradition of teaching Dzogchen in Tibet. Furthermore, they assert that it was the Teacher of Bon, Shenrab Miwoche, who was the original Supreme

Teacher of Dzogchen. Indeed, from the most ancient times there had existed the teaching of certain cycles of Dzogchen (in Central Asia), this teaching being known as "the Bon of the Perfect Mind."[45] Therefore, they conclude that the teaching of Dzogchen must have existed even before the Supreme Teacher Garab Dorje appeared in the country of Uddiyana. But for some scholars possessing limited sectarian views, the very notion that the teaching of Dzogchen could have existed before the advent of Garab Dorje is not an agreeable idea. Be that as it may, it is certain that the Supreme Teacher Garab Dorje (is indeed an historical figure and that) he actually taught the many expositions of the Dzogchen teachings, which are incontrovertibly among the most vast and profound Tantras, Agamas, and Upadeshas of Ati that are extant at the present time and preserved in the Nyingmapa tradition. These (authentic teachings of Garab Dorje) are known as the the the Three Series of Dzogchen[46] already cited above.

However, (also in the Nyingmapa tradition,) it is inappropriate to think that the Dzogchen teachings did not exist at a time earlier than Garab Dorje. Even before the advent of this Supreme Teacher, the Dzogchen teachings had not become exhausted and, thus, were not disappearing (from the world). According to the Dzogchen Tantras, there have appeared (in our world) the Twelve Teachers of Dzogchen.[47] The earliest among them appeared in most ancient times at the very beginning of our world, even before the advent of the Teacher of Bon, Shenrab Miwoche (who appeared in Olmo Lungring). Because the histories of the Dzogchen teachings revealed by these Twelve Teachers is completely known (from the Dzogchen Tantras), this implies that there existed an even more ancient source for the Dzogchen taught by Shenrab Miwoche.[48]

Then, in the eighth century of our era, the great master Padmasambhava expounded the seventeen Supremely Secret Tantras of the Dzogchen Nyingthig[49] to the hosts of Dakinis, including the Tibetan princess from the Kharchen clan, Yeshe Tsogyal.[50] Together with the *kLong-gsal*, and along with the secret instructions and the supplementary teachings,[51] these texts comprise a total of eighteen texts (representing the Root Tantras of the Dzogchen Upadesha Series). Thereupon Padmasambhava, together with the Kharchen princess (Yeshe Tsogyal) revealed, on the one hand, the exceedingly vast Upadeshas,[52] which were the Tantras (mentioned above), and, on the other hand, the great Master himself revealed the profound

Condensed Upadeshas[53] in the form of his own compositions, setting them down separately in writing and compiling a catalogue[54] enumerating them.

Then, at a later time, the daughter of King Tisong Detsan, Lhacham Padmasal,[55] having died (at the age of eight), the great Master drew the syllable NRI with vermillion ink on the breast of her corpse. By means of his miraculous powers, he recalled her consciousness[56] and restored her to life. Thereafter he conferred upon her the initiation for the *gSang-ba mkha'-'gro snying-thig*; and then gave her the secret initiatory name of Padma Letreltsal.[57] Having placed a casket containing the texts of the *mKha'-'gro snying-thig* on the crown of the young girl's head, he expressed this heartfelt aspiration: "At a future time, may you meet again with this teaching of mine, and may it come to benefit sentient beings."

Subsequently, he concealed these Tantras, which are exceedingly vast Upadeshas,[58] (the eighteen Tantras mentioned above,) as treasures at the lionlike rock in lower Bumthang[59] (in Bhutan); and he concealed the profound Condensed Upadeshas[60] at Danglung Tramograg[61] in Dwagpo (in South Tibet). Centuries later, the monk Tsultrim Dorje[62] was recognized as the reincarnation of the princess Lhacham Padmasal. Subsequently, having become known as Padma Letreltsal,[63] he obtained possession of the catalogue of these hidden treasure texts. It was he who extracted the treasure texts of the *mKha'-'gro snying-thig* from Danglung Tramodrag in Dwagpo and thereafter caused the teaching of the Nyingthig to be widely promulgated. (Later the remaining texts of this cycle were recovered in Bumthang by his successor and reputed reincarnation, Longchen Rabjampa.)

Furthermore, the great master Vimalamitra taught the profound instructions for the Nyingthig to Nyang Tingdzin Zangpo.[64] There being no other appropriate disciples at that time, he concealed the texts at the Gegung of Chimphu[65] near Samye Monastery. Vimalamitra then departed for (the five-peaked mountain of Wu-tai Shan in) China. When he was fifty-five years old, Nyang Tingdzin Zangpo erected the temple of Zhwai Lhakang at Uru[66] and concealed there the texts of the instructions (that is, the Explanatory Tantras),[67] which he had received from Vimalamitra, in the crevices between the pillars above the door. However, he transmitted the aural lineage[68] to his disciple Dro Rinchenbar.[69] In turn, Dro Rinchenbar transmitted them to Be Lodro Wangchug;[70] and he, in his turn, explained and transmitted them to the elder Dangma Lhungyal.[71] In accordance with a prophecy coming from Zhwai Gonpo[72] (that is, from Damchan Dorje Legpa, the guardian deity into whose protection the temple had been entrusted by Nyang Tingdzin Zangpo), Dangma Lhungyal discovered the Terma texts concealed there. He, in turn, transmitted them to Chetsun Senge Wangchug.[73] Thereafter Chetsun encountered the actual visible manifestation of Vimalamitra's Body of Light,[74] and for some period of years he relied upon these encounters (for receiving revelations of the Nyingthig teachings, now known as the *lCe-btsun snying-thig*.) Thus, he was given the guidebook[75] for the discovery of the treasure texts concealed at Chimphu. He extracted these profound treasures, and since he practiced them, in his 125th year, he himself demonstrated the method for appearing as the Body of Light. All of this is clearly indicated in the histories of the Dzogchen Nyingthig.

Prior to this, the great Vidyadhara Vimalamitra compiled the distilled essence of the Dzogchen Nyingthig into five series[76] of written texts: "The Golden Letters" (*gSer yig-can*), "The Copper Letters" (*Zangs yig-can*), "The Variegated Letters" (*Phra yig-can*), "The Conch Shell Letters" (*Dung yig-can*), and "The Turquoise Letters" (*gYu yig-can*). The most important among these texts set down in writing by the master Vimalamitra himself is "The Golden Letters" collection, and within this collection the most important text is the *rDo-rje'i tshig gsum*, "The Three Vajra Verses," which represents the Last Testament[77] of the Supreme Teacher of Dzogchen, Garab Dorje himself. This text is one of the Four Posthumous Teachings of the Vidyadharas.[78] These Four Posthumous Teachings are as follows:

1. *Tshig gsum gnad du brdeg-pa*, "The Three Statements That Strike the Essential Points" (or "The Three Vajra Verses"), the Last Testament of the Supreme Teacher Garab Dorje;
2. *sGom nyams drug-pa*, "The Six Meditation Experiences," the Last Testament of the Master Manjushrimitra;
3. *gNyer-bu bdun-pa*, "The Seven Nails," the Last Testament of the Master Shrisimha;
4. *bZhags thabs bzhi-pa*, "The Four Methods of Establishing Absorption," the Last Testament of the Master Jñanasutra.

Collectively these texts are known as the *Rig-'dzin gyi 'das-rjes rnam-pa bzhi*, "The Four Posthumous Teachings of the Vidyadharas."

"The Three Vajra Verses" embodies the life essence[79] of all the Dzogchen teachings and it further represents the ultimate realization of the essential points of the profound Dharma (of Dzogchen).[80] Therefore, for those disciples who are sincerely devoted to the Dzogchen teachings, it is necessary to know that this text contains a very special Upadesha that must be securely kept in the core of one's heart.

On the occasion of this present book, *The Golden Letters*, Vajranatha (John Myrdhin Reynolds), who is not only a learned scholar and translator, but a Ngagpa sincerely devoted to actual practice of the Primordial Yoga of Dzogchen, has translated this original text of Garab Dorje from the Tibetan into the English language. This translation will most certainly increase the auspicious portion of the meritorious karma of those disciples who have supreme aspiration for the Yoga of Dzogchen. I am delighted by this, and together with scattering offerings of the flowers of thanksgiving, I earnestly pray that this text, which reveals the very heart of the teaching, will completely remove the intellectual darkness of disciples and become a great cause for the benefit and happiness of infinite numbers of living beings.

At Merigar, on the eighth day of the third month of the year of the iron-sheep (1991), this was written by Chögyal Namkhai Norbu. [Translated by John Myrdhin Reynolds.]

Introduction

THE PRIMORDIAL ORIGIN OF DZOGCHEN

The Nyingmapa school preserves the oldest traditions of Mahayana Buddhism in Tibet and was established in the eighth century of our era by the Uddiyana tantric master Guru Padmasambhava, the Indian scholar-monk and abbot Shantirakshita, and the Tibetan king Tisong Detsan. Within this Nyingmapa tradition, Dzogchen is said to represent the quintessential teaching of the Buddha. The Tibetan term *Dzogchen* (*rdzogs-pa chen-po*, Skt. *mahāsandhi*) has usually been translated into English as the Great Perfection. This teaching is so called because it is complete and perfect (*rdzogs-pa*) in itself, with nothing lacking, and because there exists nothing higher or greater (*chen-po*) than it. Because it is regarded as the culmination of all preceding vehicles (Skt. *yāna*), or paths to enlightenment found within the Sutra and Tantra systems, it is also known as *Atiyoga*, the ultimate yoga. However, Atiyoga is at times interpreted as a variant of the Sanskrit term *Ādiyoga* (*gdod-ma'i rnal-'byor*), "the Primordial Yoga." This latter term refers to what is truly the Great Perfection: the Primordial State of the individual. This primordially pure state (*ka-dag*) of enlightenment, embodying the Base, the Path, and the Fruit simultaneously (*gzhi lam 'bras-bu gsum*), is truly the state of inherent Buddhahood known as the Bodhichitta. Transcending all time and conditioning, this state is at the core of every living being. In view of this, the Nyingmapa Lamas do not regard Dzogchen as just another set of beliefs, or a system of philosophical assertions, or a collection of texts, or some sect or school. Rather, Dzogchen refers to the direct introduction to and the abiding in this Primordial State of enlighten-

ment or Buddhahood that has been ever-present from the very beginning like the sun in the sky, even though its radiant face has been
obscured by the clouds of ignorance (*ma rig-pa*, Skt. *avidyā*).[1]

Indeed, throughout the history of Tibet, the practitioners of
Dzogchen have not been strictly limited to the Nyingmapa school.
Moreover, a Dzogchen system identical in meaning, but of independent lineage, is found preserved within the Bonpo tradition of Tibet,
namely, the oral tradition from Zhang-zhung (*zhang-zhung snyan
rgyud*).[2] Generally, in the view of the practitioners of Dzogchen, who
may belong to any Tibetan school, whether Buddhist or Bonpo, the
ultimate goal of the spiritual path is the realization of this intrinsic
Buddhahood in the context of one's immediate daily life, rather than
the establishing of another philosophical school. That realization is
known as the Great Perfection.

According to the Nyingmapa tradition of Tibet, Garab Dorje (Skt.
Prahevajra)[3] was the first human teacher of the Dzogchen precepts.
We say human because, traditionally, Dzogchen is said to have been
taught previously to certain nonhuman beings in other dimensions
of existence. Indeed, one early account refers to thirteen other star-
systems where the Dzogchen teachings are said to have been propagated.[4] Furthermore, Garab Dorje is said to have been born not in
India but in the long-vanished country of Uddiyana (O-rgyan) that
lay somewhere to the northwest of India, probably in modern-day
Pakistan or Afghanistan. It is believed that Garab Dorje received the
transmission of the Dzogchen precepts (*bka'*, "the word") directly
from Vajrasattva, the Sambhogakaya aspect of the Buddha, while
the former was in a state of transcendent consciousness. Vajrasattva
(rDo-rje sems-dpa') was not a historical manifestation of the Buddha; rather, he represents the principle of Buddha enlightenment
which is beyond the cycle of conditioned existence (Skt. *saṃsāra*),
beyond all time and history. Thus, in terms of the tradition, the revelation of the Buddha Dharma was not limited to the lifetime of the
historical Buddha Shakyamuni, also known by his personal name,
Siddhartha Gautama, who probably lived in northern India in the
sixth century BCE (or even earlier, according to the chronological
calculations of the Tibetans). Vajrasattva is not merely one Buddha
in a long series of Buddhas, but he is the archetype of eternity, existing beyond profane space and time, dwelling at the center of the
mandala of all existence. Out of him emanate all of the historical

Buddhas or Nirmanakayas who have appeared from time to time throughout the history of our planet. In this sense, Garab Dorje is also considered to be an emanation of Vajrasattva, and, in fact, in the Nyingmapa tradition he is given the designation Tulku (*sprul-sku*) or Nirmanakaya, which means "emanation body."[5]

According to the traditional account, at the very beginning of time Vajrasattva directly received the transmission of Dzogchen, or Atiyoga, from the Adibuddha, the Primordial Buddha Samanta-bhadra (Kun tu bzang-po), who is the ultimate Dharmakaya aspect of Buddhahood. As such, Samantabhadra is beyond conception by the finite intellect and beyond expression in mere words or symbols, being without limitation and all-pervading like infinite space. Vajrasattva received the teachings from Samantabhadra directly in a mind-to-mind fashion, that is, instantaneously without a word being spoken. This represents the Mind Transmission or the direct mind-to-mind transmission of the Buddhas (*rgyal-ba dgongs brgyud*). In this marvelous and miraculous manner, the teachings emerged spontaneously out of the Absolute, the unmanifest Dharmakaya level, coming into manifestation on the Sambhogakaya level. But this all occurred in a state of total purity, undefiled by any limitations or by any obscurations, whether intellectual, psychic, or material. In turn, Vajrasattva, the timeless eternal aspect of Buddhahood, communicated the Dzogchen precepts through symbolic means, with only a few words intervening, to certain august individuals, both human and divine, who are known as Vidyadharas (*rig-'dzin*), "those who have realized knowledge of the Primordial State." At first this occurred in various worlds and dimensions existing above and beyond the human world. Among these nonhuman Vidyadharas was Garab Dorje in his previous divine incarnation. This process represented the symbolic transmission to the Vidyadharas (*rig-'dzin brda brgyud*).

Having previously existed as a Deva or god in a certain heaven-world among the stars, then, under miraculous circumstances, events including an immaculate conception and a virgin birth to a Buddhist nun,[6] Garab Dorje was reborn on earth in the country of Uddiyana. Thus he represented a Nirmanakaya, or historical aspect of Buddha-hood. Although the principle of Buddhahood is in itself transmundane and atemporal, the Sambhogakaya Buddha continuously emanates out of its infinite potentiality countless Nirmanakaya Buddhas that incarnate as human beings on the earth plane within time and history in order to save humanity from the prison of Samsara by means of the Dharma teachings and so lead it to liberation and enlightenment. In the course of his earthly manifestation and activity, Garab Dorje transmitted the Dzogchen teachings to various Dakini disciples (both human and nonhuman),[7] and most especially to his principal disciple, the scholar Manjushrimitra. He did this telepathically and symbolically, but he chiefly accomplished it by way of oral explanations. Manjushrimitra, in turn, transmitted the precepts to his chief disciple, Shrisimha, and the latter, on different occasions, bestowed them upon Jnanasutra, Vimalamitra, Padmasambhava, and the Tibetan translator Vairochana. This process, proceeding downward from Garab Dorje, represents the oral transmission to various persons (*gang-zag snyan brgyud*). Thus, we have three principal types of transmission for the Dzogchen precepts: direct, symbolic, and oral.

THE PLACE OF DZOGCHEN IN BUDDHIST TEACHING

The Nyingmapas, "The Ancient Ones," comprise the oldest school of Buddhism in Tibet and follow in practice the Old Tantras, which were translated in the early period of the diffusion of the Dharma (*snga dar*) from the seventh to the ninth centuries.[8] In the view of the Lamas belonging to the Nyingmapa tradition, Dzogchen represents the genuine and authentic teaching of the Buddha. It is *Buddhavachana*, "the Word of the Buddha," but this Word, or Logos (*bka'*), derives not so much from the historical Buddha Shakyamuni as from his atemporal, transhistorical archetype, Vajrasattva, through the mediation of Garab Dorje. But how do these precepts relate to the more well-known traditional teaching of the Buddha?

All schools of Tibetan Buddhism are in agreement that the teachings of the Lord Buddha may be classified into the Trikaya, or the Three Vehicles to enlightenment (*theg-pa gsum*). These are the Hinayana, the Mahayana, and the Vajrayana. However, the Nyingmapas elaborated this threefold classification into their own special system of classification where they speak of nine successive vehicles to enlightenment (*theg-pa rim dgu*).

The Hinayana (*theg-pa dman-pa*), or the Lesser Vehicle, according to the Nyingmapas, consists of two distinct vehicles: (1) the Shravakayana (*nyan-thos kyi theg-pa*), "the Vehicle of the Listeners or Disciples," and (2) the Pratyekabuddhayana (*rang sangs-rgyas kyi theg-pa*), "the Vehicle of the Solitary Buddhas."

These Hinayana teachings all pertain to the threefold training in higher morality, higher meditation, and higher wisdom. The goal of this path of training is the attainment of the status of an Arhat, or perfect saint, "one who has vanquished and cut off all impure passions." This path is delineated in the scriptures preserved in the Hinayana schools, namely, the Sutras (*mdo*), or philosophical discourses of the Buddha, and the Vinaya (*'dul-ba*), or monastic discipline. A Shravaka (literally, a listener) differs from a Pratyekabuddha in that he or she must first hear the teachings of the Dharma from another. A Pratyekabuddha, abandoning all contact with humanity for a life of absolute solitude, discovers the teachings on his or her own. However, their levels of realization are similar.

The Mahayana (*theg-pa chen-po*), or the Greater Vehicle, is known in the Nyingmapa classification as the third vehicle to enlightenment, namely, (3) the Bodhisattvayana (*byang-chub sems-dpa'i theg-pa*), "the Vehicle of the Bodhisattvas."

These Mahayana teachings, in which the Lord Buddha reveals that the inherent nature of all phenomena is shunyata (emptiness, insubstantiality, lack of any inherent nature or existence), are found in the Sutras, or philosophical discourses of the Buddha, preserved in the Mahayana schools. Here the practitioner is called a Bodhisattva (*byang-chub sems-dpa'*), that is to say, a heroic individual (*sems-dpa'*) who is bent on attaining the enlightenment (*byang-chub*) of a Buddha. He or she seeks liberation from Samsara, not for his or her own salvation alone, but for the sake of benefiting all sentient beings and freeing them from the sorrows experienced within cyclical existence. The goal here is not that of the Arhat, who is concerned only with his or her own personal salvation, but that of complete Buddhahood. Only a Buddha can bring about the universal salvation of all living beings. The ground or basis (*gzhi*) of the Mahayana is the original Buddha-nature inherent within every sentient being. This is called the Tathagatagarbha (*de-bzhin gshegs-pa'i snying-po*), a term which means the embryo or seed (*snying-po*, Skt. *garbha*) of a future Buddha or Tathagata (*de-bzhin gshegs-pa*). The path (*lam*) of the Mahayana consists of the practice of the six perfections (*pha-rol tu phyin-pa drug*) during innumerable lifetimes extending over the course of three immeasurable cycles of time. The six perfections are those of generosity (*sbyin-pa*), morality (*tshul-khrims*), patience (*bzod-pa*), vigor (*btson-'grus*), meditation (*bsam-gtan*), and wisdom (*shes-rab*). Since the path consists of these six, the Mahayana is also known as the Paramitayana, or the Vehicle of the Perfections. The goal or fruit (*'bras-bu*) of the Mahayana is the realization of the Two Bodies of the Buddha, namely, the Rupakaya (*gzugs-sku*), or Form Body, and the Dharmakaya (*chos-sku*), or Reality Body. The practice of the first five perfections represents the accumulation of merit (*bsod-nams kyi tshogs*), which culminates in the realization of the Rupakaya. This Rupakaya, or Form Body, is therefore quite unique to each individual Buddha, since its realization depends on the vows and actions of that individual while he or she was still on the path as a Bodhisattva. On the other hand, the Dharmakaya is realized through the accumulation of wisdom (*ye-shes kyi tshogs*) by means of the practice of the perfection of wisdom. The Dharmakaya is identical for all who have realized Buddhahood. Because the teachings expounding the principles of the Mahayana are found in the Sutras or discourses delivered at Vulture Peak and elsewhere, this path is also known as the Sutra system (*mdo lugs*). Because each stage of one's spiritual development has its own definitive characteristics (*mtshan-nyid*), it is also known as the Lakshanayana (*mtshan-nyid theg-pa*), or Vehicle of Definitive Characteristics. And because the Sutras speak of Buddhahood as having a cause (*rgyu*, Skt. *hetu*), namely, the Tathagatagarbha, the Mahayana is additionally known as the Hetuyana (*rgyu'i theg-pa*), or Causal Vehicle. Both the Hinayana and the Mahayana are said to have been revealed some 2500 years ago in northern India by the historical Buddha Shakyamuni.

The Vajrayana (*rdo-rje theg-pa*), or the Diamond-like Vehicle, is subdivided in the Nyingmapa system into six classes of Tantras, each being an independent and sufficient vehicle to enlightenment, namely, Kriya Tantra, Charya Tantra, Yoga Tantra, Mahayoga Tantra, Anuyoga Tantra, and Atiyoga Tantra. The Vajrayana is so called because the inherent original nature of the individual is said to be like a diamond (*rdo-rje*, Skt. *vajra*): unchanging, indestructible, translucent. The teachings of the Vajrayana are found in esoteric texts known as Tantras (*rgyud*). Because the Tantras deal with the transmutation of energy, and energy manifests as sound, and sound employed this way is called mantra, this path of the Tantras is also known as the Mantrayana and as the Mantra system (*sngags lugs*). The esoteric doctrines found therein are known as the Secret Mantras (*gsang sngags*).

Although the approaches of the Sutra system and the Mantra system are in no way contradictory, it is said that the Mantra system, being the higher, includes within itself the lower Sutra system. Nevertheless, the Mantra system, or Vajrayana, differs from the Mahayana Sutra system in four principal ways: (i) the practice of the Tantras is easier because no arduous austerities are required; (ii) the results are quicker, and one may attain liberation within a single lifetime; (iii) the Tantras contain a greater number and variety of methods suited to different individuals; and (iv) a keener and more penetrating intelligence is required in tantric practice.

There are three classes of Tantra that are considered lower and are consequently known as the Outer Tantras (*phyi rgyud*): Kriya Tantra, Charya Tantra, and Yoga Tantra.

(4) The Kriya Tantrayana (*bya-ba'i rgyud kyi theg-pa*), "the Vehicle of the Kriya Tantra," emphasizes the performance of external rituals. The Sanskrit term *kriyā* (*bya-ba*) in this context means "ritual activity."

(5) The Charya Tantrayana (*spyod-pa'i rgyud kyi theg-pa*), "the Vehicle of the Charya Tantra," equally emphasizes external ritual and internal meditation. The Sanskrit term *caryā* (*spyod-pa*) in this context means "conduct" or "behavior." Charya Tantra is also known as Upaya Tantra, where the Sanskrit *upāya* (*thabs*) is "method," and as Ubhaya Tantra, where *ubhaya* (*gnyis-ka*) means "both"; that is, it links both Kriya Tantra and Yoga Tantra. Whereas its activity is the same as Kriya Tantra, its view is the same as Yoga Tantra. In this and in the preceding vehicle, the practitioner visualizes the deity (*yi-dam*) in the sky before him- or herself and prays to and petitions this deity in order to receive its blessings (*byin-rlabs*) of inspiration and wisdom. In the case of Kriya Tantra this is done in the manner of a servant approaching his or her master or lord and is similar to the attitude of conventional devotional religion. In the case of Charya Tantra, this is done in the manner of a friend making a request of an intimate friend. This is similar to the attitude of devotional mysticism.

(6) The Yoga Tantrayana (*rnal-'byor gyi rgyud kyi theg-pa*), "the Vehicle of the Yoga Tantra." Here Yoga (*rnal-'byor*) means "union" or "unification." In Yoga Tantra, as with the two previous vehicles, the practitioner begins by visualizing the deity in the sky before him- or herself, invoking its blessings of inspiration and wisdom in the same way. But subsequently, one enters into a mystical union with the de-

ity by dissolving oneself (one's empirical being) into the state of emptiness and then remanifesting in a purified body of light, actually becoming the deity in one's meditation. This experience is known as divine pride (*lha'i nga-rgyal*). Thus, one comes to realize within oneself all of the qualities and attributes of that particular deity.[9] The methods of purification employed in these Outer Tantras are very exacting and complex, and thus they principally represent the path of purification (*sbyong lam*). These Tantras are said to have been revealed by Vajrasattva, the esoteric archetypal form of the Buddha.

Then there are three classes of Higher Tantra, known also as the Inner Tantras (*nang rgyud*): Mahayoga, Anuyoga, and Atiyoga. The Higher Tantras are said to have been revealed by the Primordial Buddha Samantabhadra. In terms of these Higher Tantras, the ground or basis of the Vajrayana is the human body. The path of the Vajrayana is the practice of the generation process (*bskyed-rim*, Skt. *utpattikrama*) and the practice of the perfection process (*rdzogs-rim*, Skt. *sampannakrama*). In the course of the generation process one visualizes oneself as the divine form of the deity and one's environment as the pure field of the mandala of that deity, that is, its dimension in time and space. It is by means of this generation process that the practitioner purifies the propensity for rebirth in the desire world (Skt. *kāmadhātu*), that is to say, within the six destinies of rebirth among the Devas or gods, the Asuras or titans, the human beings, the animals, the Pretas or hungry ghosts, and the denizens of the hot and cold hells. In the course of the perfection process, the practitioner visualizes the psychic channels (*rtsa-ba*) and the psychic energies (*rlung*) within the body of him- or herself as the deity. Here the impure energies of the passions (*nyon-myongs pa'i rlung*, Skt. *kleśavāyu*), are purified and transformed into the pure energies of knowledge (*ye-shes kyi rlung*, Skt. *jñānavāyu*). By means of this latter process the propensity to be reborn in the form worlds (Skt. *rūpadhātu*) among the long-lived gods of the higher mental planes is purified. As described in the Tantras, the Vajrayana, which is the path of the Mahasiddhas, or great adepts, represents an actual alchemical process wherein the energies of the base passions are transmuted within the vessel of the physical and subtle bodies into the elixir of primordial awareness or gnosis (*ye-shes*, Skt. *jñāna*). It is this alchemical elixir that bestows life eternal. Therefore, it is not necessary to renounce and suppress the passions, as is the case with the practice of the Sutra system. The method specific to the Sutra system is the path of renunciation (*spong lam*), whereas the method specific to the Tantras is the transformation (*sgyur-ba*) of energy. For this reason, the texts speak of Tantra as the path of transformation (*sgyur lam*).

The goal or fruit of the Vajrayana is the realization of the Three Bodies of the Buddha, or Trikaya (*sku gsum*). Here the Form Body is twofold: (1) the Sambhogakaya (*longs-sku*), the Body of Perfect Bliss, which manifests in Akanishtha (*'og-min*), the highest plane of existence, and nowhere else; and (2) the Nirmanakaya (*sprul-sku*), the Body of Emanation, which manifests on the physical and astral planes within time and history.[10] Whereas the Sambhogakaya manifests to the vision of only highly evolved spiritual beings, the great Bodhisattvas, the Nirmanakayas appear to countless beings throughout the universe whose vision is still impure and obscured by their passions and intellectual limitations. Nevertheless, because this fruit is already present in the individual from the very beginning, albeit obscured, the Vajrayana is said to already contain the fruit and is therefore called the Phalayana (*'bras-bu'i theg-pa*), or Fruitional Vehicle.

(7) The Mahayoga Tantrayana (*rnal-'byor chen-po'i theg-pa*), "the Vehicle of the Great Union," emphasizes the Utpattikrama (*bskyed-rim*), or generation process. This is very elaborate and involves the visualizing of many deities and mandalas. Mahayoga is divided into the Tantra section (*rgyud-sde*) and the Sadhana section (*sgrub-sde*). In general Mahayoga corresponds to the Anuttara Tantra of the newer schools of Tibetan Buddhism, and in particular to the Father Tantras (*pha rgyud*), which emphasize the male aspect of enlightenment.

(8) The Anuyoga Tantrayana (*rjes su rnal-'byor gyi theg-pa*), "the Vehicle of the Further Union," emphasizes the Sampannakrama (*rdzogs-rim*), or perfection process. This corresponds in many ways to the Mother Tantra (*ma rgyud*) class of the Anuttara Tantra, which emphasizes the female aspect of enlightenment. However, unlike the Anuttara Tantra, Anuyoga has two distinct styles or methods of visualization: the gradual and the instantaneous. In the Anuyoga also are found elaborate visualizations of deities and mandalas, but here more emphasis is placed on the practice of the esoteric yoga of the psychic channels and energies (*rtsa rlung*). Properly, in the Tantra system, after dissolving the visualization back into the state of emptiness, out of which it originally arose at the commencing of the

process of tantric transformation, one then enters into a state of contemplation (*mnyam-bzhag*, Skt. *samāhita*). In the Anuttara Tantra of the newer schools this state is known as Mahamudra (*phyag-rgya chenpo*), "the Great Symbol." However, in the Anuyoga system, this stage, which represents the culmination of the process of transformation, is known as Dzogchen. Some very old texts testify to this, indicating that in the early period Dzogchen was thought to be what lay beyond the generation process (*bskyed-rim*) and the perfection process (*rdzogs-rim*), as a state that is *rdzogs-chen*, or totally perfected.

(9) The Atiyoga Tantrayana (*shin tu rnal-'byor gyi theg-pa*), "the Vehicle of the Ultimate Union," is otherwise known as Dzogchen, "the Great Perfection." In the Nyingmapa system, the ninth vehicle, known as Atiyoga or Dzogchen, is classified as a Tantra. However, Dzogchen also exists on its own terms, independent of the methods of Tantra. Here its practice does not require any prior process of transformation into a deity residing in the pure dimension of the mandala, as is the case with Mahayoga or Anuyoga. Rather, the practice begins where Tantra leaves off, that is to say, Dzogchen begins with the state of contemplation. Thus Dzogchen is classified as a vehicle on its own account, and not merely as the concluding state of the process of transformation, as is Mahamudra, for example. In the Nyingmapa system, Dzogchen is regarded as the highest peak (*yang rtse*) attained by all spiritual paths and as the culmination of all the preceding vehicles or yogas.

Dzogchen has a methodology all its own which distinguishes it from other vehicles, and so it is not just an extension or continuation of the Tantra system. The proper method of the Sutra system is the path of renunciation, as exemplified by the practice of taking vows, the proper method of the Lower Tantras is the path of purification, as exemplified by the many types of practices for cleansing impure karmic vision; and the proper method of the Higher Tantras is the path of transformation, as exemplified by the process of transforming oneself, both externally and internally, into the deity in the pure dimension of the mandala of that deity. Here in the Higher Tantras, the impure karmic vision (*ma dag las snang*) that afflicts the ordinary ignorant sentient being is not only cleansed, but actually transformed into the pure vision (*dag snang*) of the wisdom and gnosis of an enlightened being. The ordinary sights of the world are no longer ordinary, but pure visions of deities and mandalas. The ordinary sounds of the world are no longer ordinary, but the pure sounds of mantras. The ordinary thoughts and memories of one's mind are no longer ordinary, but the pure contemplations or samadhis of an enlightened being or Buddha. However, the proper method of Dzogchen is not transformation, but the path of self-liberation (*grol lam*), and herein lies its uniqueness.

All of these methods of practice found in the Three Vehicles, or in the Nine Vehicle system of classification, are quite distinct in terms of their approach to the spiritual path. This may be seen in the metaphor of the poisonous plant. The first type of practitioner, one who follows the method of the Hinayana Sutras, tries to avoid the poisonous plant found obstructing his or her path. This approach represents the path of renunciation. The second type of practitioner, one who follows the methods of the Mahayana Sutras and the Lower Tantras, tries to apply an antidote to the poison of the plant with which he or she has come into contact while on the path. This second approach represents the path of purification. This universal antidote to the poisons of the world is the meditation on shunyata, the insubstantiality of all phenomena. The third type of practitioner, one who follows the Higher Tantras, tries to alchemically transform the poison found in the plant into the nectar of gnosis or enlightened awareness. This third approach represents the path of transformation. This poisonous plant symbolizes all the passions and negativities which afflict one's mind in Samsaric existence. But these do not represent the method proper to Dzogchen. The practitioner of Dzogchen does not try to avoid, or apply an antidote to, or transform this poison. In Dzogchen there is nothing to be renounced and nothing to be transformed. Properly speaking, Dzogchen has its own method, called self-liberation (*rang grol*), where, within the individual's meditation practice, thoughts are allowed to self-liberate as soon as they arise. The texts translated below deal with this last method, called the path of self-liberation (*rang grol lam*).

THE THREE SERIES OF DZOGCHEN TEACHINGS

In terms of the path, there exist three series of teachings (*rdzogs-chen sde gsum*) into which the original texts of Dzogchen have been classified. The first of these is the Semde, or Mind Series (*sems-sde*, Skt. *citta-varga*). Here the word *mind* (*sems*) refers not to one's ordinary

thought process, which exists in time and is conditioned by antecedent causes, but to the nature of mind (*sems-nyid*), which exists beyond time and conditioning. In the Dzogchen Semde texts this nature of mind is usually called the Bodhichitta (*byang-chub kyi sems*).
The meaning of Bodhichitta in this context, referring to the Primordial State of the individual, is therefore quite different from that found
in the texts belonging to the Sutra system. But on the whole, the
Dzogchen Semde teachings provide a rather intellectual approach, a
step-by-step explanation of how to enter into the state of contemplation (*rig-pa*). This explanation is similar to that found in the Mahamudra system of Gampopa, which is prominent in the Kagyudpa
school. In both cases, the practice is divided into four stages called
yogas (*rnal-'byor bzhi*).[11] The extant texts of the Dzogchen Semde
series were transmitted to Tibet by the translator Vairochana and by
the master Vimalamitra.

Second, there is the Longde, or Space Series (*klong-sde*, Skt.
abhyantara-varga) where everything is much more direct, immediate,
and spacious in its approach to contemplation. Literally, *klong* means
"a vast expanse of space." The four stages in Longde practice are
known as the four signs (*brda bzhi*), but these occur simultaneously
rather than sequentially as do the four stages of yoga in Semde. The
extant texts of the Dzogchen Longde were all transmitted to Tibet by
the translator Vairochana, in particular the Vajra Bridge precepts (*rdo-
rje zam-pa*). Vairochana had received the transmissions of the Semde
and the Longde in India from the Dzogchen master Shrisimha.

Third, there are the extraordinary teachings of the Upadesha Series, or the Secret Instruction Series (*man-ngag gi sde*, Skt. *upadeśa-
varga*). These teachings assume that one already knows how to enter
into the state of contemplation, and so they give much practical advice on and many methods for continuing in the state of contemplation. These teachings are also known as Nying-thig (*snying-thig*, Skt.
citta-tilaka), which means "the essence of the mind," from *snying-po*
(mind) and *thig-le* (essence).[12] The Nying-thig teachings were originally transmitted to Tibet by Guru Padmasambhava and Mahapandita Vimalamitra, both of whom had earlier been disciples of the
master Shrisimha in India. Both of the texts translated below belong
to the Upadesha Series of teachings.

From the viewpoint of the Nying-thig teachings, the original state
of the individual, one's inherent enlightened nature, is seen as being

primordially pure and spontaneously self-perfected (*lhun-grub*). These two aspects of the state are realized in the two divisions of Nying-thig teaching and practice, namely, Thekchod and Thodgal. The term *Thekchod* (*khregs-chod*) literally means "cutting loose (*chod*) the bundle (*khregs*)," much as a woodman might cut loose the ties binding a bundle of sticks he has brought with him from the forest. In the case of the individual, this bundle is all one's emotional and intellectual tensions and rigidities that keep one imprisoned in a self-created cage and prevent one from realizing one's intrinsic freedom. The principal point in Thekchod is to relax all these tensions of body, speech, and mind that obscure our inherent Buddha-nature, which has been primordially present as the Base (*ye gzhi*). In Thekchod practice, one settles into a state of contemplation without being distracted for a moment from the view of the primordial purity of our inherent nature. As the master Garab Dorje said, "Whatever is produced in the mind is unobstructed like the clouds in the sky. Having understood the meaning of the complete identity of all phenomena (in terms of their essence which is emptiness), then when one enters into this (state of contemplation) without following them, this is the true meditation." Through the practice of Thekchod, one comes to understand and be totally familiar with the state of contemplation.

Then, through the practice of Thodgal, one develops this state of contemplation through the medium of vision. The term *Thodgal* (*thod-rgal*, Skt. *vyutkrāntaka*) literally means "direct" (*thod-rgal du*) in the sense of an immediate and instantaneous transition from one location to another, where there is no intervening interval of time. Thus some would translate it as "leap over," but it is much more immediate than leaping about. And also here, when we say "vision" (*snang-ba*), we are not speaking about visualization (*dmigs-pa*), which, for example, is much used in Tantra. Visualization is a process which involves the working of the mind. However, with Thekchod we have moved into a dimension beyond the mind, and, with Thodgal, one continues in this direction. Rather than visualizations created by the mind, we are talking about an integration with vision, with whatever arises spontaneously to vision while the practitioner is in the state of contemplation. Therefore, the mastery of contemplation through the practice of Thekchod is an immediate prerequisite to the practice of Thodgal. Otherwise, there exists the danger of becoming caught up in one's visions, becoming distracted by them and believing them to be an objective reality. Indeed, it was precisely this attachment to one's impure karmic visions that got the individual caught up in Samsara in the first place.

Whereas the principle of Thekchod is the primordial purity of everything, the principle of Thodgal is their spontaneous self-perfection. By contrast, the method in Tantra is to transform one's impure karmic vision (such as we experience at this very moment as human existence) into pure vision, which is how an enlightened being sees the external world. Thus one visualizes oneself as a deity in the pure dimension of the mandala, and through repeated sadhana practice in retreat one makes this experience into something real and concrete. However, in Dzogchen there is no transforming of impure phenomena into pure phenomena, because whatever phenomena may manifest to the senses are perfect just as they are. They are spontaneously perfected (*lhun rdzogs*) because they are manifestations of the nature of mind (*sems-nyid kyi snang-ba*), of the potentiality of the inexhaustible energy (*rtsal*) of the mind. In the Dzogchen teachings, the nature of the mind is likened to a mirror, and phenomena are like the reflections seen in that mirror. Whether these reflections are good or bad, beautiful or ugly, pure or impure, they in no way modify or limit the nature of the mirror. It is the same with one's own nature of mind.

The ultimate fruition of the practice of Thodgal is the realization of the Rainbow Body of Light (*'ja'-lus*), so that one no longer needs to undergo the process of death and rebirth. All of the original masters of the Dzogchen tradition in India, at the end of their earthly teaching careers, manifested this Body of Light (*'od lus*). These masters—Garab Dorje, Manjushrimitra, Shrisimha, and Jnanasutra, after dissolving their gross physical body into pure radiant energy (a process known as *ru-log*, or "reversal," where the physical elements of the material body are dissolved into the corresponding colored lights), then subsequently reappeared in the dimension of the sky as bodies of light in order to bestow their last testaments (*zhal 'chems*) upon their respective senior disciples. Such a last testament gave in succinct verses the very heart-essence of the master's teaching, which had now been realized in his own personal experience. This was an Upadesha, not a scholastic exposition. Upon hearing these precepts, the disciple instantly attained a vast and profound understanding equal to that of the master. These last testaments were known as the posthumous teachings of the Vidyadharas (*Rig-'dzin gyi 'das-rjes*). In the case of Garab Dorje, this last testament, his posthumous teaching (*'Das rjes*), is known as "The Three Statements That Strike the Essential Points" (*Tshig gsum gnad du brdeg-pa*). In Dzogchen the essential point (*gnad*) is the state of contemplation, that is, the state of immediate intrinsic awareness.[13]

According to the Nyingmapa tradition, the quintessential meaning of the entire corpus of Dzogchen teaching coming from the Adibuddha Samantabhadra himself and contained in some sixty-four million verses in Tantras, Agamas, and Upadeshas are found in these three succinct statements. There exist a number of large scholastic commentaries in many volumes by later masters of the Nyingmapa tradition elaborating on these three statements. But one of the most immediately accessible commentaries, and nowadays one very widely known among Tibetan Dzogchen practitioners, is the text by the nineteenth-century Dzogchen master Dza Patrul Rinpoche (1808–1887) entitled the *mKhas-pa shri rgyal-po'i khyad chos*, "The Special Teaching of the Wise and Glorious King." The translation of both the root text and its auto-commentary will be found below. This is followed by a translation of another text which, according to tradition, represents the actual last testament of the master Garab Dorje. This text is found in a collection entitled the *Bi-ma snying-thig*, compiled in the fourteenth century by the famous Dzogchen master and Nyingmapa scholar Longchen Rabjampa (1308–1363). One of the principal purposes of both of these texts is to provide the practitioner with a direct introduction (*ngo-sprod*) to Dzogchen, the Primordial State.

PART ONE:

The Three Statements That Strike the Essential Points

The Three Statements That Strike the Essential Points
(Tshig gsum gnad du brdeg-pa)

by Garab Dorje

I. ཉོ་རང་ཐོག་ཏུ་སྤྲད།།

NGO RANG THOG TU SPRAD
(pronounced *ngo rang t'og tu tray*)
One is introduced directly to one's own nature.

II. ཐག་གཅིག་ཐོག་ཏུ་བཅད།།

THAG GCIG THOG TU BCAD
(pronounced *t'ag chig t'og tu chay*)
One definitively decides upon this unique state.

III. གདེང་གྲོལ་ཐོག་ཏུ་བཅའ།།

GDENG GROL THOG TU BCA'
(pronounced *deng drol t'og tu cha*)
One continues directly with confidence in liberation.

A Short Commentary on the
Three Statements of Garab Dorje

by H. H. Dudjom Rinpoche

I. As for the direct introduction to one's own nature: This fresh immediate awareness of the present moment, transcending all thoughts related to the three times, is itself that primordial awareness or knowledge (*ye-shes*) that is self-originated intrinsic Awareness (*rig-pa*). This is the direct introduction to one's own nature.

II. As for deciding definitively upon this unique state: Whatever phenomena of Samsara and Nirvana may manifest, all of them represent the play of the creative energy or potentiality of one's own immediate intrinsic Awareness (*rig-pa'i rtsal*). Since there is nothing that goes beyond just this, one should continue in the state of this singular and unique Awareness. Therefore, one must definitively decide upon this unique state for oneself and know that there exists nothing other than this.

III. As for directly continuing with confidence in liberation: Whatever gross or subtle thoughts may arise, by merely recognizing their nature, they arise and (self-)liberate simultaneously in the vast expanse of the Dharmakaya, where Emptiness and Awareness (are inseparable). Therefore, one should continue directly with confidence in their liberation.

Translated by Vajranatha
Baudhnath, Nepal, 1978

The Special Teaching of the Wise and Glorious King

by Patrul Rinpoche

THE ROOT TEXT

Homage to the Guru.
The view is Longchen Rabjampa: "the infinite great vast expanse";
The meditation is Khyentse Odzer: "the light rays of wisdom and love";
And the conduct is Gyalwe Nyugu: "the fresh sprouts of future Buddhas."
Anyone who practices wholeheartedly in this way
Will surely attain Buddhahood within a single lifetime without striving after it;
And even if one does not (accomplish the practice), one's mind will surely enjoy happiness.
A-la-la!

I.
As for the view of Longchen Rabjampa (the infinite great vast expanse),
There exist three statements that strike the actual essential points (of the practice).
First, allow one's own mind to settle into a relaxed state
Without thoughts, neither diffusing nor concentrating them.

While in this condition, a state of equanimity and complete
   relaxation,
Suddenly utter *PHAT!* which strikes the thought (that has arisen)
Forcefully and abruptly.
EMAHO (how marvelous)!
There remains nothing else except a sharp startled awareness;
This startled awareness is directly penetrating.
Nothing arises that impedes it; it is indescribable.
One should recognize this as the immediate intrinsic Awareness
   which is the Dharmakaya itself.
This direct introduction to one's own nature is the first essential point.

II.
Whether (thoughts) are proliferating or remaining in a calm state,
   this is perfectly all right.
Whether there arises desire or anger, happiness or sorrow,
At all times and on all occasions,
One should hold to the recognition of the Dharmakaya which has
   been recognized previously.
Reuniting the Clear Lights of the Mother and of the Son,
One should allow oneself to settle into a state of indescribable
   Awareness.
Whether there arise experiences of the calm state, or of pleasurable
   sensation, or of clarity, or of thoughts proliferating, shatter them
   again and again
With the sudden explosive uttering of this syllable *PHAT!* that
   unites skillful means and wisdom.
Thereupon there will be no difference between the state of even
   contemplation and what is realized subsequently;
And there will be no distinction between a meditation session and
   the nonsession (afterwards).
One should continuously remain in the state where they are
   inseparable.
Nevertheless, if one is unable to attain stability in this,
Then having renounced all worldly entertainments, it is important
   to meditate
And divide one's practice into discrete sessions.
At all times and on every occasion,

One should continue in the state of this single Dharmakaya
And one should discover that there is nothing other than this.
Thus, directly discovering this single state is the second essential
    point.

III.
At that time, whatever desires or aversions, whatever happiness or
    sorrow,
Whatever discursive thoughts may suddenly arise,
(While remaining) in the state of recognizing them, one does not
    follow after them.
Since one holds to the recognition of the Dharmakaya on the side
    of liberation,
Then, for example, like drawing pictures on the water,
There is no discontinuity between the self-arising (of thoughts) and
    their self-liberation.
(Therefore) whatever arises (in the mind) becomes the food for
    empty naked Awareness (and is consumed);
Whenever movements (of thought occur), they represent the
    creative energy of the king who is the Dharmakaya;
Without leaving a trace, (these thoughts) are self-purified.
A-la-la!
The way of their arising will be the same as previously,
But the particularly crucial essential point is the way in which
    (thoughts and experiences) are liberated.
Without this latter, meditation will merely represent a path of
    erroneous delusions.
But if one possesses this (essential point), then nonmeditation is
    truly the state of the Dharmakaya.
Therefore, directly continuing with confidence in (self-)liberation is
    the third essential point.
With regard to this view, which embraces these three essential
    points,
The meditation that links together wisdom and compassion,
As well as the conduct in general of the Sons of the Victorious
    Ones, act as friends (to the view and support it).
Even if all of the Buddhas of the three times deliberated together,
There would exist no higher teaching than this.

The creative energy of intrinsic Awareness, which is the Treasure
   Master of the Dharmakaya,
Brought forth this treasure from out of the vast expanse of
   wisdom.
But this is not like extracting ore from the rocks of the earth;
Rather, it represents the last testament of Garab Dorje himself;
It is the spiritual essence of the three transmission lineages
And should be given to the sons of one's heart and sealed.
Its meaning is profound and spoken from the heart.
It represents my heartfelt advice, being the essential point of the
   real meaning.
This essential point of the real meaning should not be allowed to
   disappear,
Nor should one allow this secret instruction to be profaned!
This is "The Special Teaching of the Wise and Glorious King."

THE COMMENTARY [1]*

Prologue

Homage to my benevolent Root Guru, he who possesses unequaled
compassion. Here I shall explain a little of the method of practice
associated with the essential points represented by the view, the
meditation, and the conduct.

First, since my own Guru in his essence fully embodies and unifies within himself the totality of the Three Jewels, so by doing homage to him alone, one is actually paying homage to all of the sources
of refuge simultaneously. Thus it says (in the root text): "Homage to
the Guru" [2].

Moreover, as for the real meaning, which I shall explain here (regarding the following lines): If one practices wholeheartedly, having
first become aware that all of one's Gurus, both one's own Root Guru
as well as the Gurus belonging to all of the lineages of transmission
which one has received, are, in fact, inseparable from one's own mind,
then all three—the view, the meditation, and the conduct—are com-

---

*Bracketed numbers in this chapter refer to sections of the translator's com-
mentary, which begins on page 65.

bined and included within the practice. Hence, I must explain here that the view, the meditation, and the conduct correspond precisely to the real meaning of the names of my own personal masters, both my Root Guru and the Gurus of my lineage of transmission [3].

First, the view is one's own awareness that all of the infinity of appearances occurring in both Samsara and Nirvana, however many there may be, are wholly perfected (from the very beginning) within the vast expanse of the Tathagatagarbha, which is the Dharmadhatu itself, free of all conceptual elaborations. Thus, since there exists an awareness of this real meaning, it says (in the root text): "The view is Longchen Rabjampa" (where this name literally means "the infinite great vast expanse").

Then, with respect to this view, which in its own nature is free of all conceptual elaborations: (On the one hand, the view) is systematically established by means of discriminating wisdom (Skt. *prajñā*) and insight (Skt. *vipaśyanā*) on the side of wisdom and emptiness. And then, (on the other hand,) it abides (and continues) evenly and one-pointedly in contemplation, where it is inseparably united with the skillful means of concentrated peaceful calm (Skt. *śamatha*), and therefore, (this represents the side) of great loving compassion. Since there exists here this meditation that links together both emptiness and compassion in this way, therefore it says in the text: "The meditation is Khyentse Odzer" (which literally means "the light rays of wisdom and love").

Then, while in a state where one possesses equally such a view and such a meditation, one comes to practice wholeheartedly the six perfections for the benefit of others in accordance with the proper method of the Bodhisattvas, who represent the fresh sprouts (that will grow into) future Buddhas. Since this is the conduct and behavior (in question), it says in the text: "The conduct is Gyalwe Nyugu" (which literally means "the fresh sprouts of future Buddhas").

The individual who practices wholeheartedly, having a view and a meditation and a conduct such as this, is described as one who truly possesses good fortune. Hence it says (in the root text): "Anyone who practices wholeheartedly in this way . . ." [4].

And furthermore, having relied upon a secluded hermitage (as the site of retreat practice), if one is able to renounce the activities of this world and practice one-pointedly, then in this present life one will become liberated into the original Base, which has been primordially pure from the very beginning. Thus, it says in the text: ". . . will surely attain Buddhahood within a single lifetime without striving after it."

Similarly, even though one may not accomplish this, still if one turns the mind toward a view, a meditation, and a conduct such as this, then, even in this present life, one will become aware of all negative conditions (being transformed, so as to) carry one farther along the path; and although remaining preoccupied with the activities of everyday life, one will not produce so many expectations and anxieties, while thereafter (in future rebirths) one will go from one happy existence to another. Hence, it says in the text: "And even if one does not (accomplish the results of practice), one's mind will enjoy happiness. A-la-la!"

The First Essential Point

Now I shall explain step by step the view, the meditation, and the conduct that possess such benefits as those (cited above). First, I want to explain extensively the method for practicing the view. Thus, it says in the text: "As for the view of Longchen Rabjampa (the infinite great vast expanse)" [5].

Furthermore, by way of the actual secret instructions that pertain to these three statements that strike the essential points of the practice, one cuts off (at the root) the very vitality possessed by delusions. Hence, it says in the text: "There are three statements that strike the actual essential points of the practice."

First there is the method for introducing the individual to the view that had not been introduced previously. In general, according to the Lakshanayana, one systematically establishes the view by means of various authoritative scriptural traditions and by reasoning. Again, according to the usual approach of the Secret Mantra system, having relied upon the knowledge of the example which is indicated during the third initiation, one is introduced to actual knowledge of primal awareness in the fourth initiation. There exist many systems for this. However, here the method of the Holy Gurus of the Siddha Lineage is to introduce directly (the nature of mind) by way of the dissolving of all mental activities.

Furthermore, at those times when the confused and turbulent waves of deluded thoughts (overwhelm the individual), gross discursive thoughts that pursue and follow after their objects will come to obscure the true face of the nature of mind. Thus, even though one has been introduced previously to it, one will not recognize (the nature of mind). For that reason, one must first allow those gross discursive thoughts (to settle down and the mind) to become clear. So, it says in the text: "First, allow one's own mind to settle into a relaxed state . . ." [6].

Nevertheless, one's own mind, when it is allowed simply to settle down without making any attempt to modify it, becomes in itself just that knowledge or primal awareness which is the Clear Light. Since one's natural condition cannot be understood by way of a process of conceptual fabrications, in order that one may indicate to oneself this spontaneously born primal awareness that is in no way fabricated or contrived, it says in the text (that one shall remain) "without thoughts, neither diffusing nor concentrating them."

When the individual is only a beginner, even though the mind may continue in a natural self-settled state, still, as part of this calm state, it will not be possible to transcend a condition of attachment to experiences (arising in meditation), such as pleasurable sensations, clarity, and the absence of thoughts. Thus, it says in the text (that one should proceed) "while in this condition, a state of equanimity and complete relaxation. . . ."

In order to free oneself from envelopment by attachments to experiences such as these (cited above), and in order to reveal the unadorned natural condition of naked intrinsic Awareness which is in no way obstructed by anything that arises, it says in the text that one should "Suddenly utter *PHAT!* which strikes the thought (that has arisen)" [7].

This interrupts the flow of thoughts, and, since it is critically important to shatter one's meditation, which has been deliberately created by mental activity, it is necessary to utter the sound *PHAT!* forcefully and abruptly. So, it says in the text: ". . . forcefully and abruptly. How marvelous!"

And it is at the moment when one is freed from all conceptions, such as thinking, "This is a thought" or "This is mind," that one in fact becomes liberated. Hence, it says in the text, "There remains nothing but a sharp startled awareness."

In this state of the Dharmakaya, which is freed from all such conceptual thoughts, the directly penetrating naked Awareness remains just as it is, a knowledge or primal awareness that has transcended the mind (that is to say, it has transcended all mental activity). So it says in the text: "This startled awareness is directly penetrating."

Moreover, it is directly penetrating in this way because it transcends all limitations (and dualities), such as creation and cessation, existence and nonexistence, and so on. This self-existent state that transcends all objects of thought and all efforts of speech and mind represents the essential point of an indescribable primal awareness or knowledge. Therefore, it says in the text: "Nothing arises that impedes it; it is indescribable."

The real meaning of this essential point is that this immediate intrinsic Awareness that remains as the Base is in fact the Dharmakaya itself. And since primordial purity devoid of all conceptual elaborations is the real view properly belonging to the Path of the Yogins, until one has recognized just this (immediate intrinsic Awareness), even though one may meditate and practice continually, one will not pass beyond a view and a meditation that has been merely fabricated by one's own intellectual activities. Therefore, (one's view and one's meditation) will be as distant from the actual path of the natural Great Perfection as the earth is from the sky. And in them (this view and this meditation,) there will exist nothing of the essential point of the cycle of practice of the Clear Light, which is, in fact, nonmeditation. So, it is crucially important to first recognize just this (point of intrinsic Awareness). Therefore, it says in the text: "One should recognize this as the immediate intrinsic Awareness which is the Dharmakaya itself" [8].

The real meaning of this is the first of the three statements that strike the essential points. If there were no direct introduction (to immediate intrinsic Awareness) by means of the view, there would exist no cause for continuing in the state (of Awareness) by means of meditation. Therefore, it is very important to be introduced to the view at the very beginning. Furthermore, once the individual is introduced to this primal awareness (this knowledge or gnosis) which is self-existing and present within oneself (from the very beginning), it will no longer be something that must be sought after somewhere else (outside of oneself). Since this is not a matter of producing something in the mind that had not existed there previously, it says in the text: "This direct introduction to one's own nature is the first essential point."

The Second Essential Point

Now I shall explain extensively the method of practicing the meditation [9]. If one settles oneself into a state of meditation that is like the continuous flowing of a river, and at all times remains without attempting to create or stop anything or trying to develop thoughts or to calm them down, then this represents the real nature of the Dharmakaya [10]. When thoughts begin to proliferate and develop, one should just continue in this condition of inherent creative energy or potentiality of primal awareness. Therefore, it says in the text: "Whether (thoughts) are proliferating or remaining in a calm state, this is perfectly all right."

Moreover, from the power of the creative energy or potentiality of thoughts in the mind arise the various passions, such as anger and desire, which represent the Truth of Origination, as well as reactive feelings, such as happiness and sorrow, which represent the Truth of Suffering. Yet if one is aware that the inherent nature of all of these discursive thoughts is just the Dharmata itself, then they will be transformed into the state of the Dharmakaya. Therefore, it says in the text (that one should remain in this awareness continuously,) "Whether there arises desire or anger, happiness or sorrow."

Moreover, in general, even though one is directly introduced (to immediate intrinsic Awareness) by means of the view, when one falls again (into distraction) into the ordinary profusion of erroneous delusory (thoughts), without being able to sustain oneself in the state by means of meditation, then one will become fettered once more to Samsara by this arising of discursive thoughts in one's own stream of consciousness. Thus, the Dharma and one's own mind-stream having gone (their own separate ways), one will become no different than an ordinary (deluded) individual. Thus, it is necessary that one never become separated from this totally self-settled state of nonmeditation. Hence, it says in the text: "At all times and on all occasions . . ."

Similarly, whether thoughts are developing or remaining quiet and still, it should not be the case that one is trying to subjugate each individual thought (as it arises) by means of a particular antidote. Rather, whenever thoughts and passions arise, the unique and sufficient antidote to liberate each one of them is the mere recognition of that singular view which was introduced previously. Hence, it says in the text: "One should hold to the recognition of the Dharmakaya which was recognized previously."

Furthermore, even though some thoughts and passions may be produced, when one comes to recognize that they (these thoughts and passions) are not in any way different from the primal awareness of the Dharmakaya (the gnoses or knowledges emanating from it) and that the inherent nature of these discursive thoughts is in actuality the Clear Light of the Dharmakaya, then that (condition) is known as the Mother Clear Light, which abides as the Base. Recognizing it by means of the view, the Clear Light of one's own awareness, which has been directly introduced by the Guru previously, is then known as the Clear Light of the Path of practice. Remaining in this self-same state where the Clear Light of the Base and the Clear Light of the Path become inseparable is known as the meeting of the Clear Light of the Son with the Clear Light of the Mother. Hence, the text refers to "reuniting the Clear Lights of the Mother and of the Son" [11].

In this fashion, having recollected the Clear Light that was recognized by means of the view, one settles into the state (of contemplation), trying neither to create nor to stop anything, neither accepting nor rejecting anything with respect to the thoughts and passions that arise from the play of the creative energy (of the mind). Since this is the principal essential point here, it says in the text: "One should allow oneself to settle into a state of indescribable Awareness."

When beginners continue for a long time in the state (of contemplation) in that way, their true and natural face will become obscured and concealed by experiences of pleasurable sensation, clarity, and nondiscursiveness, or the absence of thoughts. Therefore, having freed oneself from those veils represented by experiences such as these, one uncovers the naked face of one's (original) awareness, so that the knowledge will become visible within oneself. And somewhere it was said: "The Yogin becomes better by destroying his meditation, just as the mountain stream becomes better by falling steeply from above." Hence, it says here in the text: "(Whether there arise experiences) of the calm state, or of pleasurable sensation, or of clarity, or of thoughts proliferating, shatter them again and again."

Furthermore, if one inquires into how one is to destroy them in this way, then at the time when these experiences of calmness or of pleasurable sensation or of clarity are produced, like a bolt of lightning (striking them from the sky), one must shatter into fragments these layers of attachment with the ferocious sound of *PHAT!* This forceful sound *PHAT!* unites *PHA*, the letter of skillful means that represents the accumulating of merit, and *TA*, the letter of discriminating wisdom that cuts through (all delusions). Therefore, it says in the text (to shatter them) "with the sudden explosive uttering of this syllable *PHAT!* which unites skillful means and wisdom" [12].

Similarly, without being separated from the essential point of these experiences, at all times and in every way, one continues in this indescribable directly penetrating Awareness. And because of this, there is no difference in the condition of meditation between the state of even contemplation and the period of subsequent realization. Therefore, it says in the text: "Thereupon there will be no difference between the state of even contemplation and what is realized subsequently" [13].

For this reason, there do not exist different meditations for the period of the actual meditation session and for the period of activity that follows afterwards. Thus it says in the text: "And there will be no difference between the meditation session and the nonsession (afterwards)."

That great meditator who is actually not meditating is the Yogin in whom effulgent and self-existent primal awareness or knowledge is like the continuous flowing of a river. Moreover, in that individual there exists not even so much as a hair-tip of a cause for meditation, nor is he or she for any moment distracted. As it was said somewhere: "Neither have I ever meditated, nor have I ever been separated from meditation. Thus I have never departed from the real meaning of nonmeditation." Since this is the actual meaning here, it says in the text: "One should continuously remain in this state where they are inseparable."

Similarly, if one has become a pure container for the real significance of the path of the natural Great Perfection, that is to say, the type of individual who is capable of being liberated instantly upon merely hearing (the teaching), then all thoughts and appearances are totally liberated into the Base, and whatever arises is immediately transformed into the state of the Dharmakaya. Thus, there exists no meditator and no meditation (when the individual is in that condition). However, those less fortunate individuals who pursue the gradual approach and who fall under the power of deluded thoughts must meditate until they are able to realize some stability (in the practice). Thus, it says in the text (that one must practice) "nevertheless, if one is unable to attain stability in this."

Moreover, with respect to this meditation, when one has perfected the accumulation of the causes of concentration (Skt. *dhyāna*), experiences (in meditation certainly) will be produced. But (on the other hand), no matter how long a time one may meditate in the midst of worldly entertainments and distractions, no experiences (in meditation) will be produced. Thus it says in the text: "Having renounced worldly entertainments, it is important to meditate."

Also with regard to this meditation, even though there exists no actual difference in terms of practice between the state of even contemplation and the period of subsequent realization, nevertheless, if one has not gotten hold of the state of contemplation first, one will not be able to integrate the primal awareness of one's experiences in meditation with what is subsequently realized. Thus, even though one may try to make one's daily activities into the path itself, the deviations of falling away from one's innate disposition and of irregular habits will arise. Hence, it says in the text: "And divide one's practice into discrete sessions."

Similarly, having divided one's practice into discrete sessions, one should practice in a way that relies upon fixating the mind (upon some object of meditation), so as to continue in the essence of contemplation. However, when one comes to integrate this with the ordinary daily activities during the period subsequent to meditation, if one does not know how to preserve (the state of contemplation) continuously, one will not be capable of controlling secondary conditions by means of this antidote. Rather, one will be led astray by these secondary causes, including (any distracting) thoughts that may arise, and so one will fall back again into being merely an ordinary (confused) individual. Therefore, it is very important to maintain and continue in this directly penetrating primal awareness or knowledge during the period that follows (the meditation session). Hence, it says in the text: "At all times and on every occasion . . ."

Moreover, at such a time, it is not necessary for the individual to search about for any other meditation. While in the state of contemplation, a condition that is inseparable from the view of the

Dharmakaya, all of one's thoughts and actions continue as usual without any deliberate calculations on one's part or any attempts at creating or stopping anything. Thus, it says in the text: "One should continue in the state of this single Dharmakaya" [14].

Practicing in this way represents the yoga that is both natural and free from conceptual elaborations; it is the yoga where peaceful calm (Skt. *śamatha*) and higher insight (Skt. *vipaśyanā*) are inseparably united. Thus, one can continue in the spontaneously born and unfabricated state of the Dharmata. This is at the heart of every practice found in the Tantras belonging to the Secret Mantra Vajrayana. It is the actual gnosis or knowledge indicated in the fourth initiation. It is the special teaching which is the wish-granting gem of the Siddha Lineage. And because it is the unexcelled state of every individual included within the lineages of the Mahasiddhas who have previously attained realization in India and in Tibet, whether they belong to the Old School (Nyingmapa) or to the New Schools (Sarmapa), we should decide definitively (upon this single point) with absolute conviction. However, if one thirsts after the water of other secret instructions, it is like having an elephant at home, but searching for its tracks elsewhere in the dense forest. Having let oneself become trapped in a cage of mind-made fabrications, one will find that one has no time for liberation. So, it is absolutely necessary for the individual to decide definitively with intelligence (upon this single essential point) with respect to the practice. Hence, it says in the text: "And one should discover that there is nothing other than this."

Similarly, having discovered that the Dharmakaya is Buddhahood itself experienced as naked primal awareness, which is self-existing and never deluded, one continues in just that way. This is the second secret statement relating to the essential points of practice. Since this is extremely important, it says in the text: "Thus, directly discovering this single state is the second essential point."

The Third Essential Point

Now, at those times, if one does not have confidence in the method of (self-)liberation and merely lets oneself meditate, relaxing into a calm state of mind, then one will not transcend that deviation represented by rebirth in the higher worlds. Therefore, one will not be able to control the secondary causes of anger and desire, the activities of our samskaras (impulses) will not be interrupted, and the mind will lack confidence in one's discovery. Therefore, (confidence in the method of self-liberation) is very important [15].

Furthermore, whether there arise strong desire for an object that one wants or strong aversion toward an object that one does not want; or delight over acquiring riches, harmonious conditions, and enjoyments; or feelings of sorrow over disharmonious conditions, evils, illnesses, and so on, since whatever arises at that time merely represents the manifestations of the creative energy of intrinsic Awareness, it is very important to recognize primal awareness (gnosis or knowledge) as the very basis of liberation. Hence it says in the text: "At that time, whatever desires or aversions, whatever happiness or sorrow . . ."

Otherwise, if the liberation of thoughts as soon as they arise is not made the essential point of practice, then whatever is produced (in the mind), including the entire undercurrent of thoughts deriving (unnoticed) from the mind, will accumulate (endless) future karma for the individual in Samsara. Since one should continue liberating any thoughts that are produced without a trace remaining behind, whether they are gross or subtle, this being the essential point (of the practice), the text refers to "whatever discursive thoughts may suddenly arise."

Therefore, with respect to whatever discursive thoughts may be produced, without letting them become an undercurrent of proliferating delusions or letting them become a tangled net of memories created by mind, we should recognize the nature of those thoughts that arise while remaining in a state that is inseparable from self-occurring natural mindfulness. It is necessary to continue in this state, where one allows them to liberate as soon as they arise without following after them. This is just like drawing pictures on (the surface) of the water. Hence, it says in the text: "(While remaining) in the state of recognizing them, one does not follow after them" [16].

However, at that time, if one does not purify discursive thoughts by way of self-liberation, then merely recognizing these discursive thoughts as such will not interrupt the current of erroneous delusory activities (of the mind). But, having previously recognized primal awareness and continuing in that state, these discursive thoughts are purified without leaving a trace behind, since, simultaneous with their recognition, one beholds their faces (or natures) nakedly. Thus, with respect to the importance of this essential point, the text says: "Since one holds to the recognition of the Dharmakaya on the side of liberation . . ."

For example, just as at the very moment when one draws a picture on the water, the drawing itself disintegrates—the drawing (of the picture) and its dissolving being simultaneous—so the producing of a discursive thought and its (self-)liberating become simultaneous. There exists neither an interruption nor a discontinuity between its self-arising and its self-liberation. Thus, it says in the text: "as, for example, like drawing a picture on the water."

Therefore, the essential point of the practice is that, no matter what thoughts arise, they be allowed to enter (freely) into their arising without trying to suppress them or prevent them from arising in any way, and also that whatever thoughts may arise be carried along through the process of purifying them into their natural state, (by allowing them to freely dissolve back into the empty state out of which they originally arose). Hence, it says in the text: "There is no discontinuity between the self-arising (of thoughts) and their self-liberation."

In that way, discursive thoughts are purified through the creative energy of the Dharmakaya. Thus, whenever thoughts arise, they arise (inherently) purified by way of the inherent potentiality of the presence of intrinsic Awareness. However gross may be the thoughts produced (in the mind) giving expression to the five passions, that much stronger and clearer will be the awareness present at their liberation. Thus, it says in the text: "Whatever arises (in the mind) becomes the food for naked empty Awareness."

Any discursive thoughts that may occur will arise as the inherent potentiality of the directly penetrating nature of immediate intrinsic Awareness itself. Because one continues (in that state) without accepting or rejecting anything (that arises as thought), the very moment thoughts arise, they become liberated and they do not proceed anywhere beyond the state of the Dharmakaya. Thus, it says in the text: "Whenever movements of thought occur, they represent the creative energy of the king who is the Dharmakaya."

Because thoughts in the mind, being but forms of ignorance and delusion, are purified within the vast expanse of the Dharmakaya, any movements of thoughts that do occur (afterwards) arise in the same vast expanse of the unceasing Clear Light and are devoid of any inherent existence. Hence, it says in the text: "Without leaving a trace, these thoughts are self-purified. A-la-la!" [17].

When one habitually practices for a long time, continually carrying on along the path in this way, then discursive thoughts will arise as the meditation itself; and since the boundaries between the calm state and the movements of thought have collapsed, no harm or injury will come to the calm state. Therefore, it says in the text: "The way of arising will be the same as previously" [18].

Discursive thoughts in themselves represent the potentiality or play of creative energy (of the mind), whether as happiness or sorrow, or as hope or fear. And even though, (for the Yogin,) the way in which these thoughts arise is similar to (the process) found in the minds of ordinary (deluded) individuals, still, (for the Yogin,) this is not the same as the experience of ordinary individuals where the latter attempt either to create or to suppress (thoughts); and in consequence, by accumulating the activities of the samskaras, they come under the external domination of anger and greed. (In contrast to this,) the Yogin achieves the liberation (of thoughts precisely) at the very moment of their arising. (Here there are three degrees of liberation.) First, liberation is by means of recognizing thoughts (as soon as they arise), which is like encountering a person whom one has met before. Second, thoughts are liberated by themselves (as soon as they arise), which is like a snake unknotting itself. And finally, thoughts are liberated without benefit or harm (occurring to one's state of contemplation), which is like a thief entering an empty house. Because the Yogin possesses this very essential point with respect to the way of liberating thoughts, it says in the text: "But the particularly crucial essential point is the way in which thoughts are liberated" [19].

Somewhere it was said: "Although one may know how to meditate, but does not know how to liberate thoughts, why is this not like the levels of absorption (Skt. *dhyāna*) of the Devas?" If one's meditation lacks this very essential point of the method of liberating thoughts, and one places confidence only in concentration (Skt. *dhyāna*) within a calm state of mind, this will represent the deviation of dwelling in the dhyanas, or levels of absorption, which comprise the higher worlds [15].

Those who consider merely recognizing the calm state or the movement of thought as being sufficient are no different from the ordinary person afflicted with erroneous and delusory thoughts. And even though such an individual may entertain various notions such as "emptiness" and "Dharmakaya," which are confirmed by way of conceptual fabrications created by the intellect, when he or she encounters adverse circumstances, this individual will not be capable of maintaining his or her composure because the inherent ineffectiveness of such antidotes becomes plainly evident. Therefore, it says in the text: "Without this latter, meditation merely represents a path of erroneous delusions."

As for "liberation through bare attention," or "liberation upon arising," or "self-liberation," or whatever other name may be applied to it, this method of liberation, which purifies discursive thoughts through self-liberation without leaving even a trace behind, is the singular and unique essential point that was revealed as the extraordinary special teaching of the natural Great Perfection. If one possesses (in the practice) this essential point, then no matter what passions and discursive thoughts are produced, they arise solely within the Dharmakaya. Thus, deluded erroneous thoughts are purified into primal awareness or knowledge, and adverse circumstances now arise as one's helpful friends. The passions are transformed into the path itself, and having purified them into a calm state without abandoning Samsara, the individual is liberated from bondage to both Samsara and Nirvana. One goes beyond (all limitations) into a state where there is nothing left to do, where one is free from all efforts to accomplish anything whatsoever. Hence, it says in the text: "But if one possesses this (essential point), then nonmeditation is truly the state of the Dharmakaya" [20].

But if one does not have confidence in such a procedure for liberating thoughts, then, even though one may proclaim proudly that one's view is higher and that one's meditation is deeper, there will truly be no benefit to one's mind, nor will (one's view and meditation) serve as antidotes to the passions. Consequently, this is not the correct path. But if one possesses the essential point of (the simultaneity of) the self-arising and the self-liberation of thoughts, then it will be impossible not to liberate one's stream of consciousness from

the bonds of dualism, even if one does not have so much as a hand-
ful of the higher view or so much as a dust speck's worth of the
deeper meditation. It is as if one were to go to an island of gold and,
once there, even though one searched for ordinary rock and soil, one
did not find any; so in the same way, whenever discursive thoughts
are produced, whether one is in a calm state or in a condition of the
movement of thoughts, even though one searches for one's delusions with their inherent characteristics, one shall not find them. This
alone is the measure which determines whether or not one's practice
is proceeding in accordance with the essential point. That is why it
says in the text: "Hence, directly continuing with confidence in (self-)
liberation is the third essential point" [21].

Conclusion

These three points are the unerring essentials that alone are sufficient to carry the individual into the state of directly penetrating
Awareness, which represents (the unification of) the view, the meditation, the conduct, and the fruit of the natural Great Perfection. Therefore, (this pertains not only to the view) this is also the Upadesha or
the secret instruction relating to the meditation and to the conduct.
Nevertheless, according to the general Dharma methodology of those
who follow the scriptural systems, the objects of the intellect which
are knowable are evaluated in terms of the criteria of the various
traditions. However, I do not want to consider this matter systematically here, because when one understands (in direct personal experience) this manifest naked primal awareness, that experience itself
will become the view, namely, the gnosis or primordial knowledge
that is immediate intrinsic Awareness. Thus, the view and the meditation become identical (in essence) and have a single taste. Nor would
it be a contradiction to say that all three essential points represent
the practice of the view. Hence, the text says, "With regard to this
view which embraces these three essential points . . ." [22].

   This practice, being the summit of the Nine Vehicles (to enlightenment), is the unerring essential point of the path of the state of
primordial purity which is the natural Great Perfection. Just as when
a king goes forth it is not possible that the hosts of his entourage fail
to follow him, so, in the same way, the essential points of the paths
of all the (lower) vehicles will accompany Dzogchen as its loyal

helpers and attendants who support it in every way [23]. Moreover, at the time when one encounters directly the true face of the self-originated light of discriminating wisdom as primordially pure awareness, this discriminating wisdom (Skt. *prajñā*), which is born of the power of meditation, will blaze up, becoming a vast expanse of wisdom like (the mountain-born) rivers rushing forth in the spring season [24]. And as well, the innate disposition of emptiness, having arisen as the great compassion, becomes a compassion which loves all beings universally and impartially. Since this refers to the Dharmata, it speaks in the text of "the meditation which links together wisdom and compassion" [25].

In the same way, at the time when the essential point of the Path, wherein emptiness and compassion are united, becomes manifest, then the oceanlike activities of the Sons of the Victorious One included within the path of the six perfections will arise as one's own inherent potentiality or energy, just as is the case with the sun and its rays. As such activities are related to the accumulation of merit, then whatever one does will become of benefit to others. And, moreover, one's actions will become loyal friends who help (intrinsic Awareness) without their deviating from the correct view and falling into some selfish pursuit of their own personal peace and happiness. Thus, it says in the text: "As well as the conduct in general of the Sons of the Victorious One, act as friends (to the view and support it)" [26].

These three then—the view, the meditation, and the conduct—represent (in their unity) the principal state of all the Buddhas who have come forth in the past, who are present here and now, and who will come forth in the future. Thus, it says in the text: "Even if all the Buddhas of the three times deliberated together . . ."

(This unification of the view, the meditation, and the conduct) is truly the victorious summit of all of the vehicles (to enlightenment), as well as the essential point of the path of the Nyingtik Dorje Nyingpo, "the diamondlike heart of the essence of the mind." Because there exists nothing higher than this quintessence of the fruit, it says in the text: "There would exist no higher teaching than this" [27].

Moreover, since the actual meaning expressed in this teaching represents the very nectar of the Upadesha (the secret oral instructions) of the transmission lineage, this composition expressed in a few words here must surely arise through the creative energy of my own intrinsic Awareness. This being the case, it refers in the text to "the creative energy of intrinsic Awareness which is the treasure master of the Dharmakaya."

Even though I myself have not personally had any experience of the real meaning of these teachings by means of discriminating wisdom in meditation, nevertheless, all of my doubts have been thoroughly annihilated by means of discriminating wisdom through hearing the inerrant oral teachings of my own Holy Guru. Having set these down systematically by means of the discriminating wisdom that reflects upon things, I have arranged this composition accordingly. Thus the text indicates that it has "brought forth this treasure from out of the vast expanse of wisdom." But since these teachings are not like some common worldly treasure that merely removes our poverty temporarily, it says in the text: "But this is not like extracting ore from the rocks of the earth" [28].

These three essential points relating to the view are known as "The Three Statements That Strike the Essential Points." At the time when he was passing into Nirvana, from the center of a great mass of light in the sky, the Nirmanakaya Prahevajra (Garab Dorje) transmitted (these secret instructions) to the Arya Manjushrimitra. Because this was the very Upadesha wherein their states of contemplation became inseparably united, it says in the text: "It represents the last testament of Garab Dorje himself."

By virtue of having practiced the essential point of the real meaning of these three instructions here, the omniscient King of the Dharma (Longchen Rabjampa), having manifested the state where all phenomena are extinguished in the primordial purity, attained manifest perfect Buddhahood. (He had received in full the direct mind-to-mind transmission of the Victorious Ones.) Then, having manifested his Wisdom Body (Skt. *jñānakāya*) to the Vidyadhara Jigmed Lingpa (Khyentse Odzer), in the manner of the symbolic transmission of the Vidyadharas, he (Longchenpa) bestowed upon him his blessings. Then, the latter (Jigmed Lingpa) bestowed upon my own benevolent Root Guru (Gyalwe Nyugu) the oral transmission from mouth to ear. Having received in full this direct introduction to the instructions, he then actually encountered (in his personal experience) the Dharmata. And so, here above are the instructions which I heard in the actual presence of this glorious protector of beings, (my precious Root Guru). Hence, it says in the text: "It is the spiritual essence of the three transmission lineages" [29].

This Upadesha, which is like highly refined melted gold, is in truth the essence of the mind. I am reluctant to reveal it to persons who do not practice; but to those individuals who would cherish these teachings as much as their own lives and who, having practiced the essential points, might attain Buddhahood within a single lifetime, I would not hesitate to reveal them. Hence, it says in the text, "and should be given to the sons of one's heart and sealed."

"Its meaning is profound and spoken from the heart. It represents my heartfelt advice, being the essential point of the real meaning. This essential point of the real meaning should not be allowed to disappear, nor should one allow this secret instruction to be profaned!" [30].

This completes my brief treatise, which elucidates some of the special teaching of the Wise and Glorious King. May this represent meritorious karma!

This translation of the mKhas-pa shri rgyal-po'i khyad-chos, *together with its auto-commentary by Dza Patrul Rinpoche, was made by Vajranatha at the great stupa of Baudhnath in Nepal in the spring season of 1978 and subsequently revised in 1985.*

SARVA MANGALAM

Commentary on "The Special Teaching of the Wise and Glorious King" by the Translator

PROLOGUE

1. Title of the Text

Following the conventions of Indian Buddhism in the Sanskrit language, a Tibetan Buddhist text is not really complete unless the root text (*rtsa-ba*), often written in verse, is accompanied by a commentary (*'grel-ba*), either written by the author or by some later scholar in the same tradition. In Tibetan a stanza of four lines is called a *sho-lo-ka*, from the Sanskrit *śloka*, each line in Tibetan having seven or nine syllables. The commentary which accompanies the root text is usually written in prose, as is the case here. Both the root text and its commentary were written by Dza Patrul Rinpoche (rDza dpal-sprul rin-po-che, O-rgyan 'jigs-med chos kyi dbang-po, 1808–1887). (For the biography of Patrul Rinpoche, see p. 297.)

Every Tibetan Buddhist text properly has three parts: (I) the introductory or preliminary section (*sngon-'gro*); (II) the principal section (*dngos-gzhi*), which constitutes the main body of the text; and (III) the concluding section (*rjes*). The preliminary section contains (1) the title (*mtshan*); (2) the verses of offering (*mchod brjod*); and (3) the statement of the author's purpose (*dam-bca'*) in writing the text.

Tibetan tradition distinguishes between individuals possessing three levels of capacity in terms of understanding, namely, superior capacity (*dbang-po rab*), intermediate capacity (*dbang-po 'bring-po*), and inferior capacity (*dbang-po tha-ma*). Thus, with respect to understanding the meaning of the text, the individual of superior capacity will immediately understand the contents of the entire text merely by hearing the title alone. The individual of intermediate capacity, upon hearing the title, will understand to what category or classification the text belongs. The individual of inferior capacity will only hear the words of the title and will require a full explanation.

Traditionally in Tibet, the individual did not just walk into a monastery, select a book off the shelf at random, and begin reading. Rather, the student required permission and authorization of a qualified Lama or master before reading and studying a religious book. Such a scriptural authorization, or *lung*, took the form of the Lama reading the text aloud to the student or students. This style of transmission reflects the tradition that the Buddhist teachings were first transmitted orally from master to disciple. Only at a later time were these teachings written down in the form of texts. Thus, in the opening section of every Buddhist Sutra it says, "Thus I have heard at one time . . ." The individual speaking here is Ananda, the personal attendant of the Buddha, who was present at the Lord Buddha's every discourse and committed all of them to memory. In Tibet, usually this *lung* was given at an exceedingly rapid rate, in a kind of singsong chanting. Depending on the length of the text, the *lung* might require many days and many cups of thick salty butter tea. When the *lung* was completed, it might be followed by an explanation, or *tri* (*khrid*), of the meaning of the text. This was often quite necessary, because a root text in Tibetan is frequently found to be composed in a highly terse and concise language. Moreover, it is generally assumed by the author that the reader is already familiar with the scholastic tradition to which the text belongs. Frequently the root text serves more as an aid to memory, a collection of brief mnemonic verses, than as a detailed presentation of the teaching. Thus, a Buddhist religious or philosophical text is not just casually read by the aspiring student and then put aside— rather, the individual is taught the text by a Lama teacher. And one's Lama, in turn, has received the *lung*, or scriptural authorization, for the text from his own master, and so on, back in time to the original author. This receiving of the oral transmission is considered to be very important in the Tibetan tradition.

The title of the text we have here is *mKhas-pa shri rgyal-po'i khyad-chos 'grel-pa dang bcas-pa*, "The Special Teaching of the Wise and Glorious King," together with the commentary. A full title of a text in Tibetan will first give the literary cycle to which the text belongs (if any), then the subject matter of the text at hand, and finally the title of the particular text. But here the title is a bit short, and the first two parts are omitted. *mKhas-pa* means "learned" or "wise," and *shri* (*śrī*) is a Sanskrit word (Tib. *dpal*) meaning "glorious." *rGyal-po* is "king," and *khyad-chos* means "a special teaching." The Buddhist teaching, or Dharma (*chos*), consists of scriptural tradition (*lung*, Skt. *āgama*), handed down generation after generation, and of actual understanding (*rtogs-pa*, Skt. *avabodhi*), which derives from one's own meditation practice and direct personal experience. This *khyad-chos* or special teaching represents the latter, the actual understanding of the Dharma. Such a special teaching belongs to the fruitional Vajrayana, the highest classification of the Buddhist teachings.

"The Wise and Glorious King" in the title apparently refers to the Dharmakaya Samantabhadra, the ultimate source of the Dzogchen teachings; to Garab Dorje (Skt. Prahevajra), the first human teacher of Dzogchen according to the Nyingmapa tradition; and also to the lineage of Gurus of the author (cited in the text), who represent for him the quintessential view, meditation, and conduct of the Dzogchen teaching. (For the traditional account of the life of Garab Dorje, see p. 179.) At the time of his passing into Nirvana, Garab Dorje revealed himself within a sphere of light (*thig-le*) of rainbow colors, and, in his last testament, he summarized for his disciple Manjushrimitra the essential meaning of Dzogchen in three brief statements (*tshig gsum*). These three statements strike (*brdeg-pa*) the nail, or the essential point (*gnad*), on the head, and hence they are known as the *Tshig gsum gnad du brdeg-pa*, "The Three Statements That Strike the Essential Points." The essential points are the view, the meditation, and the conduct. A full translation of this text will be found in Part One. It is contained in a larger work known as the *Rig-'dzin gyi 'das-rjes*, "The Posthumous Teachings of the Vidyadharas," found in the *Bi-ma snying-thig* collection of Longchen Rabjampa. (See bibliography.) The root text and its auto-commentary, both by Patrul Rinpoche, elaborate on the meaning of these three statements.

2. Invocation: Homage to the Guru

Following the title, we find the verses of offering, which may be either an invocation in Sanskrit beginning *Namo*, "homage to," and/ or a number of verses in Tibetan. These verses pay respect to the Gurus, the Buddhas, the Bodhisattvas, and so on, and invoke their blessings. In this text the invocation reads simply, "Homage to the Guru."

The Sanskrit word *guru*, "master," that is to say, a spiritual teacher and guide who acts as a catalyst for the spiritual development, transformation, and awakening of the disciple, is translated into Tibetan as *bla-ma*. This word is interpreted by tradition to mean *bla*, "superior," and *ma*, "one who is." Or again, it may be interpreted as *bla*, "soul," and *ma*, "mother," because the Lama is like a mother to the soul of the disciple, nurturing this soul and guiding it to liberation and enlightenment. In the Vajrayana it is said that the Guru, or master, is even more important than the Buddha because there is no liberation or enlightenment without the direct introduction given by the Guru. In fact, there would be no Buddhas at all if there were no Gurus. Furthermore, the historical Buddha lived long ago and is not visible today, whereas it is the Guru who actually transmits Dharma to the disciple in the present. For this reason, the practitioner on the spiritual path first pays respect to the Guru before anyone else.

The Tibetan word for doing homage (*phyag 'tshal*) is also the word indicating the offering of a prostration to a superior authority. In terms of approaching the Dharma, the best way of paying homage to the master is to possess and cultivate the correct view and to continue in that view, integrating it into whatever practice one does, as well as into the activities of everyday life. Here the view referred to is Dzogchen and no lesser view. But "the view" (*lta-ba*) is not just some sectarian viewpoint arrived at by way of reasoning and analysis. An ordinary view may easily be altered or even abandoned because of some new argument or source of information. Rather, as we have pointed out previously, it is "a way of seeing" (*lta-ba*). In terms of Dzogchen, it is a way of seeing with naked Awareness (*rig-pa gcer mthong*), where one's vision is unobstructed and unobscured by conceptual constructions fabricated by the mind. In Samsara our vision in space has become distorted and warped because of the weighty presence of past karma.[1] Thus, cultivating the view of Dzogchen represents the best service to the Guru. The next best method is to practice the generation process and the perfection process belonging to the tantric method of transformation, where one visualizes the meditation deity and recognizes that this manifestation is identical in its essence with one's own Root Guru. The next best method of paying homage to the Guru is to come into his presence and offer him money and service.

In both the root text and the author's auto-commentary, the author pays homage to his Root Guru (*rtsa-ba'i bla-ma*), whose kindness and compassion toward him are unequaled. Traditionally, three kinds of Gurus are distinguished. First there are those masters from whom one has received teachings and who has given one guidance along the path. They are known as *'dren-pa'i bla-ma*, "masters who provide guidance." One may have many of these masters throughout one's lifetime. In one way or another, to a greater or to a lesser extent, drawing on their own knowledge and experience, they have pointed out the way to the disciple and have given him or her advice and encouragement along the path. But it is only the disciple who can walk that path. The master cannot do this for the disciple, no matter how great his or her knowledge and power. As Buddha Shakyamuni himself said, "I can but show you the way. You yourself must walk the path."

Then there are the various Gurus in the lineages of transmissions (*brgyud-pa'i bla-ma*) one has received in this present life. These lineages extend back in time over generations of masters and disciples to the original source of enlightenment. These lineages of transmission (*brgyud-pa*) are like high-tension electric wires strung across pylons spanning the countryside, bringing electric power to many distant cities from a single hydroelectric generating plant located in the mountains. In the same way, these lineages of transmission bring the blessings of spiritual power and inspiration from the original transcendent source, the Buddha, or from another enlightened being who manifested in the time of the beginning, to all disciples living in the present day who follow the teachings.

Finally, there is the Root Guru, who is that master or masters, whether male or female, bestowing upon the disciple the most important empowerments or initiations (*dbang*) which ripen one's stream of consciousness (*rgyud smin*), and the most essential explanations, which liberate one's mind (*sems grol*). More than anyone else, it is this Root Guru who is the guide indicating the way and who acts as the catalyst in the alchemical process of the spiritual awakening of the disciple. In this regard, the Root Guru referred to in the text is Jigmed Gyalwe Nyugu ('Jigs-med rgyal-ba'i myu-gu), the Root Guru of Patrul Rinpoche.

Moreover, the Root Guru has three aspects: outer, inner, and secret. The Outer Guru (*phyi'i bla-ma*) is that master who, in his or her physical presence, gives the individual practitioner teaching and introduces one to the nature of one's own mind. The Inner Guru (*nang gi bla-ma*) is one's own personal meditation deity with whom one identifies oneself in any practice and also upon awakening from sleep in the morning. The deity is felt to reside always in one's heart or always to be seated above the crown of one's head. The Secret Guru (*gsang-ba'i bla-ma*) is Samantabhadra (Kun tu bzang-po), the Primordial Buddha (Skt. Ādibuddha), who is in reality one's own primordially enlightened state, one's inherent Buddha-nature. Thus, in doing homage to the Guru and in making prostrations before him or her, we are not paying homage to some external authority or to some God outside of ourselves; but rather we are recognizing and acknowledging our own inherent Buddhahood which has been there from the very beginning at the very core of our being. And this is our True Guru.

According to the Sutra system, the entrance to the spiritual path is marked by taking refuge in the Three Jewels, that is, the Buddha, the teacher, the Dharma, the teaching, and the Sangha, the community of practitioners who follow the teaching. To these Three Jewels, the Tantra adds a fourth refuge: the Guru. In terms of Tantra and Dzogchen, the Guru represents the manifest embodiment of all of the Three Jewels, so that by taking refuge in the Guru, all refuges are simultaneously realized.

The way in which the practitioner maintains and develops a direct connection with the Guru (*bla-ma*), who is the source of transmission by way of empowerment and teaching, is the practice of Guru Yoga (*bla-ma'i rnal-'byor*). This term means the unification of Body, Speech, and Mind (*lus ngag yid*) with the state of the body, speech, and mind (*sku gsung thugs*) of the master. From the viewpoint of Dzogchen, no matter what practice one does, one must link that practice with Guru Yoga. In this way, the transmissions that we have received, including the introduction to our own Primordial State, are maintained and enhanced. In this way, the Root Guru and the Lineage Gurus remain inseparably connected with our own mind, infusing our stream of consciousness with their blessings of inspiration and knowledge. Among all practices found in Tantra and Dzogchen, that of Guru Yoga is the most important and essential. And when we practice Guru Yoga properly, according to our author, we thereby unify our view, meditation, and conduct.

3. The View, the Meditation, and the Conduct as the Author's Three Masters

Any path of spiritual practice and development may be considered in terms of view, meditation, and conduct, or action. The author points out that these three correspond to the three statements of Garab Dorje. And in the Dzogchen perspective, it should be recalled, the view is even more important than meditation, because if the view is not pure and correct, then one's meditation and one's conduct, no matter how well intentioned, will deviate off-center and lead the practitioner into increasing difficulties. Thus, from the very outset, as practitioners, we must spend much time examining our view and coming to understand the view of Dzogchen in terms of our direct experience.

Here in the text, the author unifies his view, meditation, and conduct by making them correspond to the three Gurus in his lineage with whom he feels a very direct and personal connection. We can do no better than follow his example. And here also, Patrul Rinpoche makes a play on the names of these Gurus. His view is that of Longchen Rabjampa (kLong-chen rab-'byams-pa, Dri-med 'od-zer, 1308–1363). This great fourteenth-century master of Dzogchen collected together most of the early Nyingthig teachings of the Dzogchen Upadesha Series that were attributed to Padmasambhava and Vimalamitra. He systematized these teachings in his famous commentarial and exegetical works found in the famous *mDzod bdun*, or "Seven Treasures." In Tibetan Longchenpa's name translates as "the infinite (*rab-'byams*) great (*chen-po*) vast expanse of space (*klong*)"; and so his view is an infinite great vast expanse.

Patrul Rinpoche's meditation practice is that of Jigmed Lingpa
('Jigs-med gling-pa, 1730–1798), otherwise known as Khyentse Odzer
(mKhyen-brtse'i 'od-zer). The illustrious eighteenth-century master
of Dzogchen also made a systematic presentation of the Dzogchen
Nyingthig teachings and practices, thus completing the work of
Longchenpa. This synthesis is known as the *Longchen Nyingthig*
(*kLong-chen snying-thig*), "The Essence of the Mind of Longchenpa."
Jigmed Lingpa's alternative name, Khyentse Odzer, means in translation "the light rays (*'od zer*) of wisdom (*mkhyen-pa*) and love (*brtse-
ba*)"; and so his meditation is veritably the light rays of wisdom and
love.

The behavior or conduct of Patrul Rinpoche is that of Jigmed
Gyalwe Nyugu ('Jigs-med rgyal-ba'i myu-gu), whose earthly career
abundantly exemplified the compassionate activity of the Bodhisattva, in terms of the practice of the six perfections. He was the Root
Guru of Patrul Rinpoche. In translation the name of this master means
"the fresh sprouts (*myu-gu*) of (future) Jinas (*rgyal-ba*)." Jina is an
epithet of the Buddha meaning "the Victorious One," and this has
reference to the Lord Buddha's decisive victory over Mara, the demon of ego delusion. The "fresh sprouts" refer to the Bodhisattva,
that is, one who is on the way to the realization of Buddhahood.
In other contexts, the Bodhisattva is known as a Jinaputra, "a child
of the Victorious One"; and so his or her conduct is that of the fresh
sprouts who will be future Buddhas, that is to say, the great
Bodhisattvas.

4. Promise to the Reader: the Benefits of Practice

Following the invocation or verse of offering in a Tibetan text, traditionally there will be found the author's promise to his readers, in-
forming us of the subject matter of the text in question and perhaps
also of his purpose in writing it. He may elaborate on this, citing
what benefits will come to the reader from the reading of the text.
Having informed us of his view, meditation, and conduct, Patrul
Rinpoche goes on to promise that "Anyone who practices (Dzogchen)
wholeheartedly in this way will surely attain Buddhahood within a
single lifetime without straining after it; and even if one does not
practice, one's mind will enjoy happiness." *A-la-la* is an expression
of delight.

THE FIRST ESSENTIAL POINT

5. The Essential Point of the View

Direct Introduction

Part one considers the first essential point, that is to say, the view symbolized by the master Longchenpa, which corresponds to the first statement of Garab Dorje: "the direct introduction." Instruction in Dzogchen always begins with such a direct introduction. The entering into the Sutra system, the path of renunciation, is marked by the taking of vows that restrict one's negative behavior, particularly those actions which inflict harm and injury upon others. The entering into the Tantra system, the path of transformation, is marked by receiving initiation (*dbang*, Skt. *abhiṣeka*). The entering into Dzogchen, however, is by way of direct introduction. By means of direct introduction one may come to understand the real meaning of initiation, which is not just some sort of ceremony. Initiation is, in fact, a transmission. In the Tantra system, initiation begins at the Kriya Tantra level and progressively becomes more elaborate in terms of ceremony with the Higher Tantras. In the Anuttara Tantras, we find the method of the four initiations (*dbang bzhi*). By receiving the vase initiation, we are empowered to practice the visualization of the deity (*bskyed-rim*); by receiving the secret initiation, we are empowered to practice the yoga of the channels and energies (*rtsa rlung*); and by receiving the wisdom initiation, we are empowered to practice the perfection process. Within the fourth initiation (*dbang bzhi-po*), there will be found little or no ceremony, yet there exists some explanation in words; and for this reason it is also known as the word initiation (*tshig dbang*). In the Nyingmapa system, this fourth initiation is effected by way of the initiating master or Vajracharya (*rdo-rje slob-dpon*) entering him- or herself into the state of contemplation (direct transmission), displaying certain symbolic objects (symbolic transmission), and then giving an explanation in a few words (oral transmission). Thus, these three types of transmission occur simultaneously. According to the Anuttara Tantra, this word initiation empowers us to practice the Mahamudra; but, as pointed out above, this final state beyond transformation in Mahayoga Tantra and Anuyoga Tantra is called Dzogchen, the state of total perfection. However, both Mahayoga and Anuyoga represent the Tantra system, the path of transformation. In Dzogchen *per se*, no formal ritual initiation is required for entering into the practice. But what is absolutely prerequisite for Dzogchen practice is the direct introduction to the Primordial State.

The author proceeds to explain extensively the method for practicing the view (*lta-ba nyams su len tshul rgyas-par 'chad*). We have been directly introduced to the state of contemplation and then, through regular practice (*nyams-len*), we will come into a direct experience (*nyams-myong*) of the state. Thereby we will proceed to develop a genuine and authentic understanding regarding Rigpa, immediate intrinsic Awareness, which is the knowledge found in the state of contemplation.

Entering into Sutra, Tantra, and Dzogchen

Generally, in the Sutra system, which is also known as the Lakshanayana, vehicle of definitive characteristics, the view is established by means of citations from scriptural authority and by means of logical analysis (*dpyad-pa*, Skt. *vicāra*), that is, through reasoning and inference. Here the author uses the term *lung rig* to indicate this, where *lung* means "scripture" and *rig* (or *rig-pa*) means "reasoning." In the Sutra system generally, *rig-pa* simply means "intelligence," but the same term has a very special usage in the Dzogchen context; so that the two usages, Sutra and Dzogchen, should not be confused. In the Sutra system, we speak of three sources of valid knowledge (*mtshan-ma*, Skt. *pramāna*):

1. valid knowledge from direct perception (Skt. *pratyakṣa-pramāna*),
2. valid knowledge from reasoning or inference (Skt. *anumāna-pramāna*),
3. valid knowledge from scripture or trustworthy authority (Skt. *āgama-pramāna*).

For example, we may be introduced to the view by the master saying, "Everything is emptiness (shunyata)," which is the view of the Madhyamika school (*dbu-ma-pa*), or "Everything is mind (*sems*, Skt. *citta*)," which is the view of the Yogacharin, or Chittamatrin, school (*sems-tsam-pa*). He may also present many reasoned arguments in support of these contentions. If one hears such statements, learns them in the classroom, or reads them in books, certainly one is introduced to the nature of reality to a certain extent, but it remains rather intellectual and is not at all immediate experience. However, there exist other methods for introducing the nature of mind more directly.

Then, in the Tantra system of the Secret Mantra Vajrayana (*gsang sngags rdo-rje theg-pa*), we find the four initiations (mentioned above). In the course of the third initiation, known as the wisdom initiation, we are introduced to an exemplary knowledge (*dpe'i ye-shes*), or a knowledge by way of example, in the form of a female partner called a Yogini or Dakini. Symbolically, her presence is indicated with the picture of a naked dancing woman with a green scarf draped over her shoulders. Then, relying upon this exemplary experience, in the fourth initiation we receive from the master a brief explanation regarding the nature of mind. In this way, we are introduced to a real knowledge (*don gyi ye-shes*), which is the actual meaning.

Thus, as practitioners we engage the Sutra system by way of rational analysis and scriptural authority, and we enter into the Tantra system through initiation. But these represent the methods of Sutra and Tantra, respectively, and not that of Dzogchen. According to the system of the superior practitioners, the Lineage of the Siddhas (*sgrub brgyud*, Skt. *siddha-paramparā*), and here this means those individuals practicing Dzogchen, the proper procedure is to introduce the practitioner directly to the state of contemplation by way of first dissolving one's mental activities (*sems kyi yal-ba ngo-sprod-pa*). If one observes the mind and searches for where a thought (*rnam-rtog*) arises, where it remains, and where it goes, no matter how much one researches and investigates this, one will find nothing. It is this very "unfindability" (*mi rnyed*) of the arising, the abiding, and the passing away of thoughts which is the greatest of all finds. Thoughts do not arise from anywhere (*byung sa med*), they do not remain anywhere (*gnas sa med*), and they do not go anywhere (*'gro sa med*). They do not arise from inside the body, nor do they arise from outside the body. They are truly without any root or source (*gzhi med rtsa bral*). Like the clouds in the sky, they arise only to dissolve again. Thoughts arise out of the state of emptiness and return again into this state of emptiness, which represents pure potentiality. We only have to observe our mind to discover this for ourselves. And this shunyata, this state of emptiness, is in fact the very essence of the mind (*sems kyi ngo-bo stong-pa nyid*).

6. Beginning the Practice: Fixation and Learning to Relax

The first thing incumbent on the novice Dzogchen practitioner (*dang-po-pa*) is to learn to relax (*lhod-pa*), because, if we do not relax right at the very beginning, we will find ourselves too charged up with psychic energy, and the resulting flood of thoughts will overwhelm our consciousness. We will find ourselves endlessly distracted (*g.yeng-ba*). When the surface of our mind is distracted and disturbed by confused and turbulent waves of delusory thoughts (*'khrul rtog gi rba-rlabs 'tshub-pa*), those gross discursive thoughts which pursue and follow their objects (*yul gyi rjes su 'brang-ba'i rnam-rtog rags-pa*) will obscure and conceal the true face of the nature of mind (*sems nyid kyi rang zhal bsgribs*), just as a thick layer of clouds might obscure and hide the face of the sun in the sky. Thus, even if Rigpa, the intrinsic awareness of the nature of mind, is introduced to us at this time, we will not recognize it, and the introduction will not be realized. Under such circumstances, self-recognition (*rang ngo shes-pa*) will be very difficult. So, in order to facilitate this introduction, these gross discursive thoughts must be allowed to settle down and clarify of themselves (*rags-pa'i rnam-rtog dangs gzhug*), so that our mind becomes calm and clear. This is like allowing the sediment that has clouded the turbulent waters to settle, so that the lake or river becomes clear and limpid. This preliminary process of calming the mind is known as Shamatha (*zhi-gnas*), and this must be accomplished first before the introduction is attempted.

In order to relax the mind and discover a calm state (*gnas-pa*) where thoughts no longer distract us, it is necessary that we practice fixation (*gtad-pa*) of mind on some object of meditation (*dmigs bcas*). Any object that does not strain our attention is suitable, but in the Dzogchen tradition, especially in the Dzogchen Semde, we fixate on the visualization of the white Tibetan letter *A* (ཨ), suspended in space in front of us. If the mind is afflicted with agitation (*rgod-pa*), the visualization of the letter should be lowered; but if it is lulled by drowsiness (*bying-ba*), the letter should be raised. Otherwise, the white letter *A* may be kept at the usual eye level, at a comfortable distance out in space. We assume the usual meditation position on a comfortable seat, the essential point for the body being to hold the spinal column straight and upright. Then we visualize the white *A* while sounding "Ahh..." slowly and repeatedly. In this way, our attention, our energy, and the visualization are all integrated, and this integration aids our concentration. Fixating acutely on the white letter A does not allow any space for distracting thoughts to arise. After fixating acutely, then we relax a bit, and this will allow thoughts to arise again. That thoughts arise does not matter, so long as our attention is kept focused on the A and we do not follow these thoughts. We should not strain ourselves during this practice; rather, we should give ourselves lots of space and practice for short sessions only.

When we feel accomplished and familiar with practicing fixation with an object, then we can proceed to fixation without an object (dmigs med). Here we remove the visualization of the white A in front and simply fixate our attention on the same location in space, which is now empty.

If we try to deliberately suppress thoughts, we will find that this method will not succeed. First, this is so because the arising of thoughts is a natural function of the mind. It is not that a calm state of mind without any thoughts is something good, while the presence of thoughts is something bad. It is an error to think in this way, further obstructing the process with judgments and evaluations. Both the calm state and the movement of thoughts ('gyu-ba) are merely experiences (nyams) that we have in meditation. In our practice we should not be attached to such experiences, neither accepting nor rejecting them (spang blang med-pa). These experiences are simply allowed to be themselves, and if there is no intervention or interference with them by the mind, they will dissolve again of their own accord into their own original condition (rang sor zin). This original condition is the state of shunyata, or emptiness (stong-pa nyid).

Second, if our mind does try to interfere and thrust these thoughts below the threshold of consciousness, they will simply absorb an amount of energy equivalent to the effort exerted to repress them. And even if they are effectively repressed, they will be charged with sufficient energy to cause us disturbances in the future, though we may no longer consciously recognize their influence. It is here that fixation of mind works indirectly, because the energy of attention is focused elsewhere than on these potentially distracting thoughts. By focusing our conscious attention on some specific object of meditation, no room remains for distracting thoughts to arise and they receive no new charge of energy.

Therefore, relaxation is the key to Dzogchen practice, and, for this reason, Dzogchen is also known as "the great relaxation" (*lhod-pa chen-po*), that is to say, it represents a profound state of total relaxation. This is also the meaning of the term *Thekchod*, as indicated previously. (See the introduction above.) Dzogchen does not involve some sort of effort like body-building, a kind of mental muscle development, nor the acquisition of some skill we do not at present possess. Rather, it is a matter of relaxing all of our tensions or rigidities of body, speech, and mind that cause us disturbance and distraction. Having relaxed our tensions totally, this allows what is already present from the very beginning to manifest of itself, freely and spontaneously. It is all very simple, almost too simple. That is why it is not easily understood. Normally we expect that on the spiritual path we will be instructed to do something, given some rules, and exhorted to strive to improve ourselves and become better than before. But this is not the way of Dzogchen. We are told only to relax and to be aware. There is nothing dull or drowsy or sleepy about contemplation. It is a state of being totally relaxed, but totally alert (*lhug-pa*). This is also the reason why the path of Dzogchen is characterized as being effortless (*rtsol med*).

When our mind is simply allowed to settle down on its own without interference, without our making any attempt to change or modify it (*rang sems ma bcos-par bzhag-pa*), then the gnosis or knowledge (the primal awareness) which is the Clear Light dawns (*'od gsal-ba'i ye-shes shar-ba*), just as when the clouds dissipate, the shining face of the sun is revealed in the sky. This natural condition (*gnas-lugs*) cannot be understood by any method involving conceptual fabrications (*bcos-ma'i lam gyis gnas-lugs ma rtogs-pa*). At the time of the practice of contemplation, no amount of analysis, reasoning, or argument will be able to help us in any way. Such efforts will only result in erecting additional conceptual constructions which imprison us further. In order to indicate this spontaneously born primal awareness or knowledge, which is in no way fabricated or contrived (*ma bcos lhan skyes-pa'i ye-shes*), the text speaks of a state "without discursive thoughts, neither diffusing nor concentrating them" (*mi spro mi bsdo rnam-rtog med*).

7. Shattering Thoughts and Experiences: Startled Awareness

Attachment to Experiences

When one is a beginner (*dang-po-pa*) and commences this practice, even if one's mind may continue in this natural self-settled state (*sems rang bzhag gnyug-ma'i ngang bskyangs*) which is contemplation, it will not be possible for us to transcend attachments to experiences (*nyams zhen*) in our meditation. These are chiefly experiences of pleasurable sensation (*bde-ba'i nyams*), experiences of clarity (*gsal-ba'i nyams*), and experiences of nondiscursiveness, or the absence of thoughts (*mi rtog-pa'i nyams*). When these meditation experiences occur and we allow ourselves to become attached (*zhen-pa*) to them, what can we do? In order to free ourselves from envelopment in attachments to experiences (*nyams zhen gyi sbubs dang bral*), and in order to reveal the unadorned natural condition of naked intrinsic Awareness, which is in no way obstructed by anything that arises (*rig-pa gcer-bu zang ma thal byung gi gnas-lugs rjen-par ston-pa*), that is, in order to realize that state of *gnas-lugs* (the natural mode of existence) which is free of being attired in any conceptions whatsoever— we suddenly utter a thought-shattering PHAT! (*thol byung blo rdeg PHAT*). That PHAT shatters the thought that has just arisen, like a bolt of lightning splitting apart a great tree.

This action interrupts the flow and continuity of our thoughts (*rnam-rtog gi rgyun thag gcod-pa*). This forceful (*drag*) and intense (*ngar thung*) PHAT is extremely important because it shatters our meditation that has been created and constructed by our mental activity (*blo byas kyi sgom-pa 'jig-pa*), that is to say, having such thoughts as "This is Rigpa!" or "This is mind!" (*sems 'di yin*), and so on. In this way, we are freed from all conceptions (*gza' gtad thams-cad dang bral-ba*), and thus we become actually liberated from them (*grol-ba mngon du gyur-pa*). And in its wake all that remains is a sharp startled awareness (*had-de-ba*).

Mind and the Nature of Mind

Crucial to the understanding of all this is the fundamental distinction made in Dzogchen between the nature of mind and the mind or thought process, that incessant flow of discursive thoughts which continually arise into consciousness. In his introduction, the master likens our nature of mind to a highly reflective mirror, having the characteristics of clarity, purity, and limpidity; and all of our thoughts, emotions, impulses, feelings, sensations, and so on, are like the reflections in this mirror. Intrinsic awareness, the state of immediate presence, is like the capacity of this mirror to reflect whatever is set before it, whether it be good or bad, pure or impure, beautiful or ugly. And just as these reflections in no way change or modify the nature of the mirror, so in no way do the discursive thoughts that arise in the mind change or modify the nature of mind. When integrated into the knowledge of this intrinsic awareness, we live in the condition of the nature of the mirror. But lacking awareness and remaining in ignorance, we live in the condition of the reflections, thinking that whatever arises before our consciousness is somehow real and substantial. These reflections, originally having the nature of rainbow light, because of ignorance and obscurations gradually come to appear solid and opaque, becoming the material world surrounding us. We become attached to these phantoms or holographic projections that represent the beginningless cycle of existence we know as Samsara. All of this comes about because of a lack of knowledge or gnosis. Nevertheless, in both cases, whether there exists the pure vision of Nirvana or the impure karmic vision of Samsara, it is the same nature of mind that knows them. Similarly, it is the same mirror that reflects all the objects set before it, whether these objects reflected are beautiful like Nirvana or ugly like Samsara. There is no change in the nature of mind, just as there is no change in the nature of the mirror, and thus we say that this state is primordially pure. When the Dzogchen teachings speak of the Primordial State or the Base (*ye gzhi*), it is precisely this nature of mind, existing in the condition of being just as it is (*ji bzhin nyid*), that is meant. It is a state beyond time and beyond conditioned existence; it is a state beyond the mind and beyond both Samsara and Nirvana.

If this were not the case, we would not have the possibility of attaining the enlightened state of Buddhahood, no matter how many endless kalpas of time we practiced the Dharma, accumulating vast stocks of meritorious karma and wisdom. In the ultimate sense, we cannot become other than what we already are in essence. But because Buddhas have manifested in countless world-systems since time without beginning, and not just on our planet Earth, it is clear that the potentiality for the realization of Buddhahood is universal and, indeed, represents the potentiality inherent in all living beings. However, our Buddhahood is not something merely potential, as it is according to the Sutra system, but, in the view of Dzogchen, it is primordially present (*ye rdzogs*). It has already been realized and become fully manifest right from the very beginning as our nature of mind, although, up until now, prior to our being introduced to it, it has gone unrecognized through an infinite series of lifetimes.

Semdzin Exercises

To bring this distinction between the nature of mind and mind into our immediate experience is the function of the Rushan exercises ('*khor 'das ru shan phye-ba*). Also, in the Dzogchen Upadesha Series there exist another series of exercises, known as Semdzin (*sems 'dzin*), which serve this same purpose. Many Semdzin will be found in Semde and Longde texts, but the list of twenty-one Semdzin found in the *Nyi-zla kha-sbyor Tantra* is much used in the Dzogchen Upadesha system. Longchenpa also explains these Semdzin at some length, although his explanation is somewhat different from that found in the above Tantra.[2] Literally, the term *sems 'dzin* means "to hold or fixate ('*dzin-pa*) the mind (*sems*)."

According to Longchenpa, the Semdzin are divided into three categories of seven exercises. The first group enables the practitioner to find him- or herself in a calm state, and thus the exercises are similar to the practice of Shamatha. When one abides in the calm state, one can clearly discern what is the movement of thoughts and precisely distinguish that from the calm state as such. The exercises in the second group enable the practitioner to discover the relationship between body and mind. And those in the third group enable one to discover the nature of one's own condition.

The first exercise in the first category involves fixating on a white Tibetan letter *A* on the tip of one's nose. Linking the letter with one's breathing, it goes out into space with each exhalation and returns to the tip of the nose with each inhalation. This fixation inhibits the arising of extraneous thoughts, as explained previously. However, the second exercise in the same category involves the sounding of the syllable *PHAT!* which instantly shatters one's thoughts and attachments. Symbolically, the two parts of the syllable indicate the two aspects of enlightenment, that is, *PHA* signifies Means (*thabs*) and *TA* signifies Wisdom (*shes-rab*). This syllable is also much used in Chod (*gcod*), the practice of cutting through attachments to the ego. It is this Semdzin exercise which Patrul Rinpoche employs here to provide a direct introduction to the knowledge of Rigpa. It blocks temporarily the flow of our thoughts, and we find ourselves in a state of emptiness and clarity.

First, we must relax and not follow any thoughts that arise. On the other hand, we should not make any attempt to block them. Having relaxed, we find that gradually our breathing slows and the flow of our thoughts similarly slows down, since our thoughts ride on our psychic energy (correlated with our breathing), like a rider on a horse. We fixate our attention on some object like the white letter *A* or just on a location in space. Our eyes do not move because movement of the eyes will also induce the arising of thoughts. At first our fixation is acute and there is no room remaining for thoughts to arise, but then, when we relax this fixation a little, thoughts arise once more. When they do, we sharply and abruptly sound *PHAT!* For example, when we are sitting quietly, lost in reverie, and someone behind us without warning suddenly fires a gun, we are shocked and startled, so much so that our thought process itself is interrupted and comes to an abrupt halt for a few moments. This state in which we find ourselves is called *had-de-ba*, "startled awareness." But this condition of *had-de-ba* is not Rigpa, the state of contemplation. This state of shock is only an experience. However, through this experience we can come to some understanding and sense of what Rigpa means. This question of discovering the state of Rigpa is like the problem of trying to explain sweetness to someone who has never tasted something sweet, like sugar.

The State of Startled Awareness

In the state of contemplation, we are freed from all conceptions (*gtad-so dang bral-ba*) and find ourselves in the state of the Dharmakaya (*chos-sku'i ngang na*), that is, in a directly penetrating naked Awareness (*zang-thal rjen-pa'i rig-cha*) that remains just as it is, a knowledge or primal awareness that has transcended the mind (*sems las 'das-pa'i ye-shes ji bzhin-par bzhugs-pa*). This state of shock or startled awareness is directly penetrating (*had-de-ba la zang-thal-le*). It is beyond the mind because at that moment the mind is not functioning. The habitual flow of thoughts has been interrupted and halted momentarily, and we find ourselves in an alert, startled state where there are no thoughts. There are no thoughts, yet there is awareness. This is certainly not a state of unconsciousness, even though no thoughts are present. But if we utter *PHAT!* and do not integrate awareness and emptiness, making them inseparable (*rig stong dbyer med*), then the exercise will be of no use and this *had-de-ba* will not differ from a kind of experience of thoughtlessness (*mi rtog-pa'i nyams*). We become lost in mere experience and miss the mark which is Rigpa.

8. A Transparent and Unobstructed State of Knowledge

Rigpa and the Prajnaparamita

The transparent, unimpeded, and unobstructed state of knowledge or primal awareness (*ye-shes zang-thal*) that follows in the wake of *PHAT* is just itself and nothing else. It transcends all extremes or limitations of existence and nonexistence, as well as of creation and cessation (*skye 'gag yod med la sogs-pa'i mtha' las 'das*). It is a self-existing state which transcends all objects of thought and all efforts of speech and mind (*ngag dang yid kyi rtsol rtog gi yul las 'das-pa'i rang gnas*). It represents the essential point of an inexpressible primal awareness (*ye-shes brjod bral*). As stated in the *Prajnaparamita Sutra*, "The Perfection of Wisdom is inconceivable by the intellect and inexpressible in words (*blo 'das brjod bral*)." It is not produced, and it does not cease (*skye 'gags med-pa*). Its nature is like space. We cannot point out this emptiness because it is intangible and is not a concrete object. We cannot say that space comes from somewhere and that it departs for somewhere else. But whereas the nature of mind is like space, it is not a mere nothing, because it has the character of luminous clarity and illuminates everything within Samsara and Nirvana.

In the Sutra system, the Prajnaparamita is called the Mother of all the Buddhas of the Three Times. And in the Dzogchen perspective, Rigpa is identical with the Prajnaparamita. It is the Mother of all the Buddhas because, without our relying upon this state of immediate intrinsic Awareness, we could not realize Buddhahood at all. Instead, we would remain ignorant sentient beings caught up in the beginningless cycle of transmigration. This is the essential point. This Awareness abides as the Base which is the Dharmakaya, and this intrinsic Awareness is present as the core of our being even now. This state is primordially pure and free of all conceptual elaborations (*spros bral*). If we recognize this state and settle into it, this is the correct practice of Dzogchen. But if we do not recognize it, then our mind will continue to erect thought constructions, and these structures arise about us like the walls of a prison, limiting and confining our space until we feel suffocated. As it says in Jigmed Lingpa's *gNas-lugs rdo-rje tshig rkang*, "Aside from having this *rig-pa* not lose its own spot, nothing else is necessary."

The Base

This immediate intrinsic Awareness which abides as the Base (*gzhir gnas kyi rig-pa*) is the Dharmakaya itself. In his direct introduction, the master likens the Base (*gzhi*) to the empty open dimension of the infinite sky, while Rigpa, its capacity for awareness, is like the sun shining in the sky. The energy or potentiality of this Awareness (*rig-pa'i rtsal*), its knowledge or gnosis (*ye-shes*), is like the countless rays of sunlight that illuminate all things in the world. This is very easy to see on a clear cloudless day, as in the case of arid Tibet. But on various days (that is, during our various different lifetimes or incarnations experienced in Samsara) the sky may be filled with clouds from horizon to horizon. The sun is there in the sky, shining all the time, but because of the thick layers of clouds, the face of the sun is invisible to us down here below, and we do not recognize its presence. Yet, if the sun were not there above the clouds, all of the world about us would be in total darkness. Without the light of the sun penetrating through the cloud layers, we could see nothing at all. It is the same with our inherent Buddha-nature. The mark of its presence is that we exist as sentient beings possessing awareness and consciousness. Without its presence, there would be no awareness and consciousness. This presence has existed in the universe from the very beginning, like a great vast expanse of space. It is inseparably bound up with sentient existence and did not come into being at some particular historical moment in time, nor was it made by some Creator God. In its own essence, it transcends time and conditioning. If this Buddha-nature had not been present from the very beginning, even before the so-called "big bang," the sound of creation which brought the universe into existence, there would exist no consciousness or awareness at all in this universe. Awareness did not come into being out of existence, but existence came into being out of awareness.

The Bodhichitta

The Base of all existence is our own Primordial State, which is our inherent Buddha-nature. In the Dzogchen texts there exist many different designations for this Primordial State, but especially in the Dzogchen Semde Series, it is called the Bodhichitta, as pointed out above. Here Bodhichitta does not mean what it does in the Sutra system, that is to say, "the thought of enlightenment" or the resolute intention to attain Buddhahood for the sake of liberating all sentient beings. We must always be careful not to translate, or rather mistranslate, Dzogchen texts in terms of Sutra and Tantra. Each level, whether Sutra, Tantra, or Upadesha, has its own specific viewpoint and methodology, even where the Tibetan words at face value appear to be the same. We must look to the meaning and not just to the words, in order to avoid problems and confusions. In general, the thrust of Dzogchen is ontological, rather than epistemological, as was the case with the Indian Buddhist philosophers of the Madhyamika and Chittamatra schools. (See Part Three, "Historical Origins of Dzogchen.")

In the Dzogchen context, the Sanskrit word *bodhicitta* is translated into Tibetan as *byang-chub kyi sems*. This Tibetan word is interpreted as follows: *byang* means "pure" from the very beginning, that is, *ka-dag*, or "primordially pure," and *chub* means "perfected," that is, *lhun-grub* or "spontaneously self-perfected." Finally, *sems* means not "mind," the conditioned thought process, but *sems-nyid*, "the nature of mind." This primordial purity and this spontaneous perfection exist in inseparable unity (*ka-dag lhun-grub dbyer-med*) as the two aspects of a single Primordial State that is Buddhahood.

Essence, Nature, and Energy

This Primordial State, the Base, is an inseparable unity, but in order to speak about its manifestation, we distinguish three aspects (*chos gsum*): its Essence (*ngo-bo*), its Nature (*rang-bzhin*), and its Energy (*thugs-rje*). In the Sutra system, the Tibetan word *thugs-rje* translates the Sanskrit word *karuṇā*, "compassion"; but in the Dzogchen context it means the "Energy" of the Primordial State. This Energy is uninterrupted, unobstructed (*ma 'gags-pa*), and all-pervasive (*kun khyab*) throughout existence. The Essence of mind, which is primordial purity, is emptiness, and this is the Dharmakaya. Its Nature is clear luminosity (*gsal-ba*), which is spontaneous self-perfection, and this is the Sambhogakaya. Its Energy is unobstructed and all-pervading (*ma 'gags kun khyab*), which represents the inseparability of emptiness and luminosity (*gsal stong dbyer med*), and this is the Nirmanakaya. These three aspects of the Primordial State, which is Buddhahood, are known as the Trikaya of the Base (*gzhi'i sku gsum*).

The Trikaya

In the Sutra system and in the Tantra system, we translate Trikaya (*sku gsum*) as the Three (*gsum*) Bodies (*sku*) of the Buddha, these being the Dharmakaya, the Sambhogakaya, and the Nirmanakaya. These refer to three ontological levels of the manifestation of Buddhahood as the principle of enlightenment. The Nirmanakaya manifests in time and history on the material, etheric, astral, and mental planes of conditioned existence (Samsara). Thus, the texts speak of the manifestations of the Nirmanakaya as being uncertain (*ma ngespa*) because they may manifest at various times and at various places. However, the Sambhogakaya only manifests in eternity beyond time and history at the center and summit of existence called Akanishtha (*'og-min*), "nothing higher." This Sambhogakaya is said to possess five certainties (*nges-pa lnga*) of transcendent Place (*gnas*), Time (*dus*), Teacher (*ston-pa*), Audience (*'khor*), and Doctrine (*chos*). It does not manifest anywhere other than Akanishtha, the center of all existence and the source of all being. It does not appear anywhere in the course of time and history, but dwells solely in the timeless moment of eternity. And it only manifests as the Supreme Teacher (individually as Vajrasattva or collectively as the Five Dhyani Buddhas), expounding only the highest, most esoteric teachings of the Mahayana and the Vajrayana to an exalted celestial audience consisting of only Great Bodhisattvas who have attained the seventh through the ninth stages of their spiritual evolution. The Dharmakaya also possesses certainties, but it transcends all location in time and space, and it is all-pervasive, beyond all limitations and forms, beyond conceptions by the intellect or expression in words. The only proper description of the Dharmakaya is a profound silence.

But in the Dzogchen context, these terms have a more specialized usage peculiar to Dzogchen. In the Sutra and Tantra systems, the Trikaya, the Three Bodies of the Buddha, represent the Fruit or the goal realized at the end of the spiritual path. But in the Dzogchen view, they are fully present right from the very beginning, inherent in the Base of the Primordial State as its Essence, Nature, and Energy. The Dharmakaya is the open spaciousness and profound emptiness of the nature of mind, the Sambhogakaya is its clear luminosity, and the Nirmanakaya is its all-pervasive inexhaustible energy.

In the Sutra system, we speak of the Base as being our inherent Buddha-nature, the Tathagatagarbha, "the embryo of Buddhahood," which is like the seed out of which the great tree of Buddhahood will grow in the future. It is Buddhahood in potential. But, because it only represents a potentiality, the Path is also necessary. Although the result exists as potentiality in the seed or the cause, nevertheless, many secondary causes or conditions (*rkyen*, Skt. *pratyaya*) are necessary in order to bring about the manifestation of the Fruit. We must practice the six perfections, accumulating meritorious karma and wisdom for countless lifetimes extending over three immeasurable kalpas, in order to attain the realization of Buddhahood. These activities are like the secondary factors necessary to cultivate and nourish this seed, such as water, fertile soil, the proper season, and so on, so that the seed will germinate and grow. And the Fruit is the manifestation of the Trikaya, which is like the fruits growing on the adult tree at harvest time. In other words, there exists a path or process that takes us to a goal, the realization of Buddhahood.

But all of this is quite otherwise in Dzogchen, for here the Base is the Trikaya, the Path is the Trikaya, and the Fruit is the Trikaya. We do not go anywhere at all, because we have already arrived at the goal before starting out on the path. It is like searching our whole life throughout the world for a great treasure, then finding it has been concealed within our own house all along. But if this is so, why must we do any practice at all? Because, although Buddhahood is primordially present as the nature of mind, we do not recognize this and habitually look for it elsewhere. Although there is this single Base, there exist two Paths, the path of delusion ('*khrul lam*) and the path of liberation, and consequently there exist two Fruits, ordinary deluded sentient beings (*sems-can*) and enlightened Buddhas (*sangs-rgyas*). The clouds must first be dispelled before we can behold the face of the sun. This is the point of practice on the path.

These three aspects of the Base also correspond to the components in the word *bodhicitta* in its Tibetan translation—*byang chub sems*—and this may be tabulated as follows:

BYANG Purity	CHUB Perfection	SEMS Mind
NGO-BO Essence	RANG-BZHIN Nature	THUGS-RJE Energy
STONG-PA NYID Emptiness	GSAL-BA Clarity	MA 'GAGS-PA Unobstructedness
KA-DAG Primordial Purity	LHUN-GRUB Spontaneous Perfection	DBYER-MED Inseparability
CHOS-SKU Dharmakaya	LONGS-SKU Sambhogakaya	SPRUL-SKU Nirmanakaya

The Real View Is the State of Primordial Purity

Primordial purity, which is free of all conceptual elaborations (*ka-dag spros bral*), is the real view (*don gyi lta-ba*) properly belonging to the Path of the Yogins (*rnal 'byor lam*), that is to say, Dzogchen. However, even though we practice the meditation, unless we recognize Rigpa we will not go beyond a view and a meditation that are merely ideas fabricated by our own intellectual activities (*blo byas bcos-ma'i lta sgom las mi 'da'-ba*). Therefore, our view and our meditation will be far from the actual path of Dzogchen, the natural Great Perfection (*rang-bzhin rdzogs-pa chen-po'i lam*). In that case, we will find nothing here of the essential point of the cycle of practice of the Clear Light which is nonmeditation (*bsgom med 'od gsal gyi 'khor-lo'i gnad med-pa*). It is called nonmeditation because contemplation transcends the working of the mind.[3] Therefore, the matter immediately at hand is to recognize this intrinsic Awareness which is the actual manifest state of the Dharmakaya (*chos-sku'i rig-pa ngos zungs shig*).

This is the real meaning of the essential point (*gnad don*) that is the first statement of Garab Dorje. If there were no introduction to Rigpa by means of the view, then there would exist no cause for continuing in the state of Rigpa by means of meditation. We would only sit there and merely create more thought constructions and more conceptions, forever erecting around ourselves an invisible cage, and we would never come to perceive our intrinsic freedom. We must go beyond this, go beyond the mind, in order to discover our freedom. There exists not even so much as an atom of discursive thought in the state of contemplation. Therefore, we must be introduced to the real view at the very beginning of the path. Once we are introduced to this knowledge, this primal awareness that is self-existent and ever-present within ourselves (*rang gnas kyi ye-shes rang las gnas-pa nyid*), we will no longer seek elsewhere outside of ourselves for the real meaning. It is not a matter of producing something in our minds which had not existed there previously. This is the significance of the first statement of Garab Dorje.

THE SECOND ESSENTIAL POINT

9. Discovering a Single State of Awareness

A Single Definitive Decision

The second statement speaks of arriving at a single definitive decision or discovery (*gcig thag-bcad-pa*). But in the case of Dzogchen, this is not something that we decide intellectually. On the basis of secondhand information or on the basis of faith alone, an individual may indeed come to a decision, but, if we have not discovered for ourselves what is at bottom the principle, this decision is something that is ultimately false. Perhaps on the basis of detailed and expert information we come to a decision about the nature of some mysterious object, but we have not seen it for ourselves. When new information arrives, we must revise or change our decision as to its nature. However, if we have actually discovered something through our own personal experience, then there is no question of coming to a decision intellectually because we have already determined for ourselves its real condition.

The Tibetan word *thag-bcad-pa*, literally, "to cut the rope," means "to decide or to make a decision." But this is not really the meaning of the term here in the Dzogchen context. When we are making a decision, we are using our mind or intellect. We consider the evidence or accept matters on faith, and then we come to a decision, intelligent or otherwise, thinking, "It is like this." But this decision, for the above reasons, is never final or conclusive or certain. It is always something tentative, subject to revision. For practical purposes in daily life, this is usually sufficient. But once we have seen the situation for ourselves, having been introduced to it by a master who is quite familiar with it him- or herself, then we come to possess not a tentative knowledge, but a certain knowledge (*nges shes*). Thus, in the Dzogchen context, *thag-bcad-pa* means to determine something decisively and definitively through direct, firsthand personal experience.

However, even though we have been introduced to a direct knowledge of this mysterious object, later our friends may disparage what we say about it and cast doubts on our account. Furthermore, so-called experts and other learned scholars may make counterassertions based on their vast erudition, and so we may come to doubt our own original face-to-face encounter with that mysterious object. It is the same with our direct introduction to Rigpa or the state of contemplation. More and more doubts arise in our mind as we listen to these experts discuss the matter and as we read their books and monographs. We come to doubt our own experience. We have been conditioned by our culture, our society, and our education to defer to these so-called "authorities," for we are repeatedly told that they know the real situation by virtue of their higher education and professional training, and we do not. But with Dzogchen, it is not a matter of the scientific experts in their white coats or of the priests in their maroon robes and fancy Chinese silk brocade hats alone knowing the real situation. Quite the contrary, Dzogchen is something to which every living individual has immediate access.

As the freshness of the memory of our first encounter with this mysterious object fades, doubts naturally arise, and we begin to speculate and to reinterpret matters. Thus a single introduction is not sufficient for continuing on the path, and faith alone will not carry us through. Having once been introduced to the state, we then must practice in order to have this experience of Rigpa again and again. For example, suppose that before we departed and returned to our everyday mundane life, the master gave us a copy of the key to the room where that mysterious object is kept, so that we could return whenever we desired to that dark room on our own, open it, turn on the light for a moment, and look again at that mysterious object. We can do this again and again at any time of the day or night we wish, and gradually we discover how to keep the light turned on for longer and longer periods of time. Again we can experience for ourselves the sight, sound, smell, taste, and touch of this object. We can investigate it from every angle to our heart's content, so that we have no doubt whatsoever as to its nature. And so, when we leave the room where it is kept, no doubts remain with us regarding this mysterious object. We have discovered it for ourselves and have definitively determined its nature. Even though our friends continue to laugh at us and the experts and authorities debate and disagree with us, we are no longer intimidated. For we have a certain knowledge of this mysterious object which cannot be doubted, because we have an immediate and continuing access to the source of knowledge. This is how it is with the state of Rigpa. And this is the significance of the second statement. (Namkhai Norbu Rinpoche repeatedly explains the significance of this second statement as "not remaining in doubt" [*the-tshom med-pa*]; however, this is not the literal translation of the Tibetan, but an explanation or gloss on it.)

Once we have been introduced to the view, the way to develop this view is through the practice of meditation. Whereas the first series of Dzogchen teachings, the Semde, or Mind Series, is principally concerned with the direct introduction to Rigpa, the second series, known as the Longde, or Space Series, is principally concerned with coming to a definitive determination by way of discovering this single state of Rigpa within a large variety of experiences that can be induced by employing different types of methods. Thus, in the Dzogchen Longde system we find an equally large variety of methods and techniques of practice provided. Having discovered this single and unique state of immediate intrinsic Awareness within all of these varied and different experiences, then we will entertain no more doubts as to its nature.

Experiences in Meditation

In the course of our meditation practice, we will have many experiences. First, through the practicing of Shamatha, or calming the mind by means of fixating our attention on an object of meditation (*dmigs-bcas, mtshan-bcas*), and later by fixating it simply on a location in space (*dmigs-med, mtshan-med*), we discover a calm state. However, this experience of a calm state without any disturbing thoughts (*mi rtog-pa*, Skt. *nirvikalpa*) is not in itself intrinsic Awareness or Rigpa. It is only a meditation experience. If a mere blank state of mind, one devoid of all thoughts, actually represented contemplation (Skt. *samādhi*), then our lying drunk on the ground in an unconscious stupor would be enlightenment, because no thoughts are arising in the

mind. Or again, a cow standing in a pasture lush with grass, con-
tentedly chewing her cud, would be enlightened because her mind
is utterly blank at that time. On the contrary, such a state is only a
dull blankness or neutral state (*lung ma bstan*) and not contemplation. It is an experience. All meditation systems found throughout
the world, whether Buddhist or Hindu, ancient or modern, have
methods for arriving at this calm state. Instruction in these methods
has become a large business enterprise in the West at this time. But
to think that contemplation merely consists of a state where no
thoughts arise (*mi rtog-pa*) is a serious error, because then we are de-
nying the inherent creative energy or potentiality (*rang rtsal*) of the
mind.

It is the natural function of the mind to give rise to thoughts. This
rtsal, "power, energy, potentiality," is only an expression of the spontaneous energy of the mind. Thus, the process of our development
in meditation (*bsgom-pa*, Skt. *bhāvanā*) does not stop with Shamatha,
"quiescence," or the realization of a calm state devoid of thoughts;
but after attaining this calm state, we proceed to a detached observa-
tion of the movement of thoughts. This second process is known as
higher insight, or Vipashyana (*lhag-mthong*, Pali *vipassana*). For example, Shamatha is like the calm surface of a mountain lake when
the winds of distraction have ceased to blow, whereas Vipashyana is
like our watching the fish swimming about in the clear waters of the
depths of the lake.

But neither of these two moments, neither the calm state nor the
movement of thoughts, represents Rigpa. It is very important to grasp
this point in order to understand the meaning of Dzogchen, as against
some other systems of meditation practice. Rigpa is a third factor: it
can be discovered in either of these two experiences, the calm or the
movement. Rigpa is not the experience itself, but the immediate
awareness of that experience. Again, it is like the example of a single
mirror and the infinity of reflections reflected in it. This immediate
awareness is the one thing, the single thing (*gcig*), that is discovered
in whatever experiences arise for us. These experiences are diverse
(*sna-tshogs*), occurring in uncountable variations, but this presence
or immediate Awareness, is unique and ever the same. It is the capacity of the nature of mind. It is, as we have already said, like the
capacity of the clear, pure, and limpid surface of the mirror, the unre-
stricted and unlimited capacity of the mirror to reflect everything.

This immediate presence is the one thing we must discover everywhere, so that we come to live in the nature of the mirror and not in the reflections.

Although our experiences are infinite in variety, in the Dzogchen teachings we conventionally speak, in terms of our meditation practice, of three kinds of experiences, namely, experiences of pleasurable sensation, experiences of clarity or luminosity, and experiences of nondiscursiveness or the absence of thoughts. Furthermore, the individual has three dimensions or aspects to his or her existence, namely, body, speech, and mind. Body (*lus*) means both our physical body proper and also its interaction with our material environment. The experiences of pleasurable sensation are more related to our body, our dimension of physical existence. Sensations may also be neutral or painful, but in terms of our meditation practice, it is easier for us to work with pleasurable sensations. Speech (*ngag*) means not only the sounds we make with the voice, but the whole dimension of the energy of the individual. This includes breathing and the circulation of psychic energy throughout the body. Experiences of clarity or luminosity are more related to this dimension of our existence. Finally we have our dimension of mind (*yid*), and experiences of nondiscursiveness or emptiness are more related to this level.

10. Remaining in Contemplation or Falling into Distraction

A State of Meditation Like the Continuous Flow of a River

In this section of his auto-commentary, Patrul Rinpoche provides an extensive explanation of the methods of meditation practice (*sgom-pa nyams su len tshul rgyas-par 'chad-pa*). Here he says that the practitioner should settle into a state where meditation is like the continuous flowing of a river (*ngang bzhag chu-bo'i rgyun gyi sgom-pa*). "Continuous" (*rgyun*) means uninterrupted. Thoughts arise and dissolve again without our making any attempt to create or stop them. When acute fixation is relaxed a little, thoughts begin to develop and diffuse (*'phro-ba*). Instead of trying to suppress or otherwise interfere with them, we recognize them to represent the continuous display of the inherent creative energy of primal awareness (*ye-shes kyi rang rtsal du skyong-ba*). However, we are not distracted (*ma g.yeng-ba*) by these thoughts and we do not follow them. In the state of contemplation, whether thoughts are diffusing (*'phro*) or quiescent (*gnas*), this is perfectly all right, because both of them represent this inherent energy and we continue in contemplation. The arising of discursive thoughts and the passions represent the Truth of Origination (*kun 'byung gi bden-pa*) among the Four Holy Truths expounded by the Buddha; but becoming attracted and attached to them, so that feelings of attachment and aversion arise, leading to expectations and frustrations, represents the Truth of Suffering (*sdug-bsngal gyi bden-pa*). As the master Tilopa said, "The problem is not that thoughts arise in the mind, but that we become attached to them." If we become attached, then whatever experiences arise, whether these be pleasurable or painful, will possess the nature of Samsara. But, if we recognize these thoughts and passions as just being the creative play (*rtsal*) of the mind, they will simply manifest in the open unobstructed space of the state of the Dharmakaya (*chos-sku'i yo-langs*, i.e., *chos-sku'i ngang*), and there will be neither benefit nor harm for the individual.

Falling Again into Delusion

But even though we may have been introduced to the correct view, if we fall again into the ordinary profusion of delusory thoughts, being unable to sustain the state of contemplation by means of meditation (*sgom-pas ngang ma 'khyongs-par 'khrul 'byams tha-mal du shor na*), we will again find ourselves helplessly caught up in the dream world of Samsara by the arising of thoughts in our continuum of consciousness. In that case, although we call ourselves Yogins or practitioners (*rnal-'byor-pa*), we will in no way differ from an ordinary deluded individual in worldly life. Therefore, in our practice we should never be separated from that great or total self-settled state of nonmeditation (*mi bsgom-pa rang bzhag chen-po*) which is called contemplation. This contemplation (*ting-nge 'dzin*) is called great (*chen-po*) because it is total, all-embracing, and continuous under all circumstances. It is self-settled (*rang bzhag*) because it is natural and spontaneous. It is nonmeditation (*bsgom med*) because the state of contemplation lies beyond the mind and the workings of the mind. With Rigpa there is no creating by the mind of some state of meditation or visualization. Rigpa is beyond the mind and beyond meditation.

Nevertheless, even though we may encounter the view by way of a direct introduction, if we do not practice meditation, we will remain caught up in Samsara—the cyclic process of creating thoughts by the mind. This process will carry us around and around endlessly.

With each discursive thought (*rnam-rtog*) arising in the mind, we come to identify ourselves with it. Thus, we have as many I's or selves as we have thoughts arising in the mind, and we find ourselves reborn again and again with the arising of each new thought. In this sense, we suffer death and rebirth not only when our physical body dies but from moment to moment with the arising and passing away of each thought with which we identify ourselves. Therefore, Samsara is a process that is with us at every moment.

Meditation as an Antidote

In terms of the method employed in meditation, whether thoughts are developing (*'phro*) or quiet and still (*gnas*), we do not need to apply any particular antidote (*gnyen-po*, Skt. *pratipakṣa*). By contrast, in the meditation methods found in the Sutra system, when some negative emotion or passion arises in the mind, the practitioner applies a particular antidote to counteract its influence. For example, if a monk should chance to see a beautiful naked woman at her bath and as a result a thought of lust arises in his stream of consciousness, he should immediately visualize her as being a skin bag filled with blood, guts, pus, and other foul substances in order to overcome any attachment to the sight of her. This practice is known as Ashubha-bhavana, or meditation on the repulsive. Or if he should momentarily experience a thought of anger, he should counter this by cultivating thoughts of loving-kindness, a process known as Maitri-bhavana. This is the way in which an antidote is applied, a kind of allopathic medicine, but this is not the method of Dzogchen. In terms of Dzogchen, when negative thoughts and passions arise, all antidotes are rendered superfluous by our settling into the state of Rigpa. The single and sufficient antidote is Awareness, and this antidote is like a panacea that cures all ills.

11. The Mother and the Son Clear Light

In our meditation practice, we recognize that whatever thoughts and passions arise represent the energy or potentiality of Rigpa manifesting. This Rigpa is like the sun in the sky, and its energy is like the rays of the sun. We recognize that the inherent nature of all these discursive thoughts (*rnam-rtog de dag gi rang-bzhin*), no matter how diverse they appear, is, in fact, the actual Clear Light of the Base, which is none other than the Dharmakaya, the Great Mother. And this nature or source is called the Mother Clear Light that abides as the Base (*gzhi gnas ma'i 'od gsal*). The Clear Light is, in reality, their natural condition or mode of being (*gnas-lugs*), the way in which thoughts exist naturally. And this Mother is something universal, rather than being individual, in the sense that, although many different individual Buddhas manifest throughout time and space, they all participate in a single Dharmakaya that transcends all dualities and pluralities.[4] We come to recognize the Clear Light by means of the view to which we have been previously introduced by the master, who indicates it to us, saying, "This is the Clear Light of your own Rigpa, your state of intrinsic Awareness." This individual Clear Light to which the master introduces us and which we experience again and again in our meditation experience throughout our lifetime, is known as the Clear Light of the Path (*lam gyi 'od gsal*) rather than the Clear Light of the Base (*gzhi' 'od gsal*). This luminosity met with on the path is also known as the Son Clear Light (*bu'i 'od gsal*), in contrast to the Mother Clear Light (*ma'i 'od gsal*). This son or child is like a small spark of the totality of the Clear Light. For example, it is said to be no more than a small butter lamp held up against the midday sun that is the source of all light. The Son, the Clear Light of the Path, is experienced in our meditation practice during our lifetime, but the Mother, the Clear Light of the Base, is met with at the moment of death when the Clear Light dawns at the onset of the Bardo of Reality.

In the Dzogchen tradition, three Bardos or intermediate states (*bardo*, Skt. *antarābhava*) are distinguished with respect to death and rebirth:

    1. the Bardo of Dying (*'chi-kha'i bar-do*),
    2. the Bardo of Reality (*chos nyid bar-do*), and
    3. the Bardo of Existence (*srid-pa'i bar-do*).

The Mother Clear Light manifests at the beginning of the second Bardo before the visions of the Peaceful and Wrathful Deities arise. In terms of our everyday experience, the Bardo of Dying corresponds to the process of falling asleep, and the Bardo of Reality corresponds to the momentary manifestation of the Clear Light before the onset of the dream state, whereas the dream state itself corresponds to the Bardo of Existence. But unless we practice contemplation during our lifetime, the manifestation of the Clear Light will occur so swiftly and instantaneously that we will fail to recognize it.[5] But if we do practice contemplation during our working state, then, when we die, we will be prepared. At the moment of death, when the Clear Light dawns, we will recognize it, and we will have the possibility of instantly liberating into the Dharmakaya. This is the highest type of Phowa (*'pho-ba*), or transference of consciousness. This moment, when the Clear Light of the Path and the Clear Light of the Base merge and become inseparably united (*gzhi lam gyi 'od gsal gnyis dbyer-med du gyur-ba*), is spoken of as the meeting of the Mother Clear Light and the Son Clear Light (*ma bu 'phrad-pa*). This is like a child recognizing his own beloved mother after a long separation due to his wandering off and becoming lost.

For example, in ancient times, a candidate for initiation into the Mysteries was led through a series of dark chambers, virtually a labyrinth, beset by terrifying sounds and ominous presences. And then in the adytum, the final chamber, there was a sudden illumination. The enthroned hierophant tells the candidate, "Behold the light, my child! It is your own being and nature." Just this *epopteia*, or sudden illumination, is the introduction to the Clear Light that is one's own original nature. The course of the initiation in the ancient Mystery Religions simulates the experience of death and rebirth and leads the candidate into what lies beyond, so that one no longer need fear death. This initiatory process may be compared to the *Tibetan Book of the Dead*.

Through our practice of contemplation, we become familiar with the Clear Light of the Path. The Clear Light of the Base (the Dharmakaya) is the source or matrix from which springs forth thoughts and emotions as the representatives of its inherent creative energy. Like the hierophant of the Mysteries, the master introduces the light of the path, and we follow this light in our practice. Thus, eventually we come to discover, in a moment of illumination and self-recognition, a knowledge or gnosis that is not just exemplary (*dpe'i ye-shes*), but one that is actual (*don gyi ye-shes*). We discover the Clear Light of our inherent Buddha-nature, the Tathagatagarbha, which has been present within us from the very beginning, since time without beginning. The master has previously introduced us to this luminous inherent awareness, and by means of this view of the Clear Light, we come to recognize ourselves (*sngar bla-mas ngo-sprad-pa'i rang rig 'od gsal kyi lta-bas rang ngo-shes-pa*). Thus we come to realize the ultimate initiation, and this takes us beyond Tantra, the process of transformation.

12. Rediscovering an Immediate Naked Awareness

Shattering Again the Thoughts and Experiences

If our meditation is coming smoothly and we find ourselves in a clear state, that is fine; but if not, it is better to break the meditation, relax for a few minutes, and rest. Nothing will be gained by forcing ourselves; striving too hard is a fault of meditation, just as not striving at all is a fault. If we strive too hard, difficulties will arise and our mind will not become clear when we try to force it. We will become tired and bored, and our mind itself will rebel against the meditation practice. So it is better to practice only for brief periods of time, keeping meditation sessions (*thun*) short. When beginners practice contemplation for a long period of time, usually experiences begin to arise. At this time it is better to break the meditation and rest, and only afterwards resume the practice; otherwise, we will find ourselves becoming attached to these experiences in meditation. They then become like veils progressively concealing the naked face of Rigpa.

To rediscover an immediate naked Awareness (*rig-pa rjen-pa*), we must destroy the conventional mental structures which enclose us and thereby break or shatter our meditation. There is a great danger that we will become attached to our meditation experiences, especially those that are luminous and blissful, such as visions of celestial paradises. We become distracted and lost in our experiences, so that our state of contemplation is terminated and we find ourselves again caught up in the dreamworld of Samsara. So once again we can employ the semdzin *PHAT!* Like a bolt of lightning it shatters the clouds. Here the text speaks of four kinds of attachments to experiences in meditation that are dispelled by this *PHAT*:

1. blissful experiences (*bde-ba*),
2. luminous experiences (*gsal-ba*),
3. the calm state (*gnas-pa*), and
4. the proliferating and diffusing of thoughts ('*phro-ba*).

In this way, we can destroy all attachments and thereby continue in the state of contemplation.

The State of Directly Penetrating Awareness

In meditation, no matter what may occur in terms of experience, we must rely on this essential point of continuing in an indescribable, directly penetrating Awareness (*brjod med kyi rig-pa zang-thal-le-ba*) without being distracted. The word *zang-thal* (or *zang-thal-le-ba*) means "directly penetrating" in an unimpeded fashion, as, for example, when a Siddha passes his phurba dagger effortlessly through solid rock, meeting no resistance, or like light passing through a clear transparent crystal.

First, we must establish contemplation by means of Shamatha practice as described previously, in order to discover Rigpa or immediate presence in the calm state within each session of practice. Then, this same immediate Awareness is taken into the movements of thought. Finally, there arises no difference between the calm state and the movement of thoughts, because a single unique state of immediate Awareness is present. This is Rigpa. But as practitioners we do not stop there. The purpose in Dzogchen is not to develop Rigpa so as to restrict it to meditation sessions only, and then, in between meditation sessions (*thun mtshams*), to return to our usual distracted and deluded states of consciousness. Rather, the purpose is to develop a directly penetrating immediate Awareness (*rig-pa zang-thal*) in terms of whatever we are doing under whatever circumstances. The aim is to take Rigpa out of our meditation sessions and bring it into all the activities of our daily life. Having discovered Rigpa in the calm state and the movement of thoughts, we now take it into the physical movements of our body, beginning with very simple movements, such as moving the head, the hands, and so on, without losing this immediate presence. Later we take it into more complex movements, such as walking or dancing, and yet we remain in the state of contemplation all the while. (A Siddha or adept will be able to speak and to think rationally, and yet remain in the state of contemplation [samadhi] without being distracted.) Gradually all barriers will be broken down; this immediate awareness is brought into every activity of body, speech, and mind. For the first time, we become fully awake, instead of being a sleepwalker. This is something extremely radical. We are now living in the mirror and no longer living in the reflections. Now there is no difference between the state of even contemplation (*mnyam-bzhag*, Skt. *samāhita*) in the meditation session and our condition upon re-entering normal consciousness and everyday life when the meditation session is completed, the latter being known as postmeditation or the subsequent realization (*rjes thob*, Skt.

pṛṣthalabdha). When contemplation is extended into all areas of life, it is known as total contemplation or Maha-samadhi (*ting-nge 'dzin chen-po*).

Vipashyana Meditation

This process of taking awareness progressively into movement in terms of body, speech, and mind is known in Dzogchen as Vipashyana (*lhag-mthong*), which literally means "higher insight." Here the meaning of Vipashyana is different than in the Sutra system. In Dzogchen, this higher (*lhag-par*) insight (*mthong-ba*) is not simply a matter of watching the fish swim about in the clear waters of the lake, or of watching them leap out of the water from time to time, the metaphor frequently employed in the Sutras. Rather, when a fish suddenly leaps out of the water, we find ourselves no longer a detached observer on the shore of the lake, as we did in the Shamatha practice. Now we find that we are the fish. We have integrated with it, and there is no difference between the observer and what is observed. We have become the vision; the outer and the inner have integrated, transcending duality. So Vipashyana becomes a process of integrating immediate awareness into movement. In this integration there is no distance or difference between awareness and the movement. The movement is awareness, and awareness is the movement. We do not decide on some action and then move; that is dualistic existence, and in that condition we are obstructed and limited. Rather, we integrate and actually become the movement. This movement is spontaneous, without thought or intention. But this movement is not blind or unconscious; it is totally alive and aware. The dancing of the Vidyadharas is not only the spontaneous play of energy; it is also "the dance of awareness."

In terms of action, Dzogchen is not limited by any rules; therefore, no action is forbidden as such. Rather, Dzogchen practice aims at bringing immediate Awareness into every action, and the manifestation of that intrinsic Awareness is one's true will. Awareness and intention are not at war with each other but are integrated. In the state of contemplation, the Bodhichitta compassion is natural and spontaneous; it is not contrived or created by mind. But this is true only when we are in the state of contemplation. The state of Rigpa is beyond karma and its consequences, beyond good and evil, but our ordinary dualistic consciousness is most definitely not. Being primordially pure, Rigpa is beyond selfish motivations, and all its actions are spontaneously self-perfected. All this is true of contemplation, but if we merely claim to be a Siddha, announcing proudly, "I am in a state of Rigpa!" and do as we like, following every impulse and indulging all transient desires, we merely delude ourselves and will suffer the karmic consequences. To think we are in the state is not the same as actually being in the state. The only rule in Dzogchen is to be aware. Dzogchen teaches us to take responsibility for our actions, and this is what awareness means. We are always aware of what we do and also of the consequences that each action entails. Integration with movement is not at all the same as attachment, for the latter represents a lack of awareness.

Intellectualism and Mental Analysis

Some scholars have claimed that Dzogchen is inherently anti-intellectual. True Dzogchen is not something that can be discovered through historical scholarship or philosophical speculation, because it is a state beyond the mind and beyond cause and effect. It cannot be conceived by the finite intellect or expressed in words. Dzogchen, the Primordial State of the individual, must be discovered through a direct introduction by a master and then developed through meditation practice. It cannot be found through conventional intellectual means, such as reasoning and philosophizing about the nature of the absolute, and so on. It lies in experience, not speculation. But once this state is introduced and then discovered again and again in our meditation experience, Dzogchen does not demand that we cannot talk or write intelligently about this state. However, philosophical discussion of Rigpa should not be confused with Rigpa itself. It is not an idea. To make it so is to confuse the finger pointing at the moon with the moon.

Nor again, is mental analysis (*yid dpyad*) the meditation practice proper to Dzogchen. However, this does not mean that reason and analysis should not be used when necessary and appropriate. Even while in a state of contemplation (samadhi), the Siddha has the capacity to move, to speak, to think, to reason, to do whatever is necessary. But, unlike ordinary sentient beings, the Siddha does so with total awareness. The Siddha is not just blissful and spaced-out, barely aware of his or her surroundings, as if intoxicated from smoking hashish. Nonetheless, these activities of thinking and speaking, and so on, do not represent the principle; they are only the reflections in the mirror. The center of balance of the Siddha, no matter in what direction he or she moves, is Rigpa. For this reason one is called a Vidyadhara or Rigdzin (*rig-pa 'dzin-pa*), that is, "one who holds ('*dzin-pa*) to immediate Awareness (*rig-pa*)." This is how the realized individual or Siddha differs from an ordinary person, who perpetually lives off-balance and off-center. In the activities of the Siddha, everything moves from a single center of gravity, this unique state of immediate intrinsic Awareness. One moves like a skillful dancer through a crowded hall, never stumbling, never colliding with another; yet one is totally aware in every movement and flows gracefully through the spatial patterns in the hall.

A Dzogchenpa like Longchen Rabjampa may be a scholar and may write many learned philosophical treatises on Dzogchen, such as his *Seven Treasures* (*mDzod bdun*), but this is not the principal concern. Dzogchen is not a philosophy like other philosophies, any more than is Zen. Indeed, it is possible to present Dzogchen philosophically, but the method proper to Dzogchen is not philosophical analysis and the system-building of metaphysics. However, it is an error to say that Dzogchen rejects or disparages the intellect and intellectual activity. The intellect is useful and necessary. It is a tool, but in Dzogchen it is not the principle; Rigpa is the principle. Reason has its uses and should be used when appropriate, but it also has its inherent limitations. Rigpa is the "intelligence" that is beyond reason (*dpyad-pa*) and beyond the intellect (*blo-gros*). The aim of all Dzogchen practice is to be aware and undistracted, and to act intelligently and responsibly in every situation. The Siddha always moves from this higher or true center. In the state of contemplation, both reason and intuition operate at maximum efficiency. Dzogchen is a state cleared of all obscurations arising from the unconscious existence of the individual, both those obscurations deriving from this present life and those from all past lives. It is a state lying at the center of one's being that is characterized by emptiness—that is, a total openness and lack of obstruction and limitation, so that all possibilities exist simultaneously within it—as well as by clarity, meaning not only a clear luminosity, but "intelligence."

13. Contemplation and Subsequent Realization

Thus, in terms of Dzogchen practice, there is ultimately no difference or separation between the meditation session and the postmeditation period (*thun dang thun mtshams dbye-ba med*). There is no difference between the state of even contemplation and the subsequent realization afterwards (*mnyam-bzhag rjes-thob tha-dad med*). In terms of Rigpa, they are the same. Thus, nonmeditation (*bsgom med*) is the great meditation (*bsgom-pa chen-po*). Within Rigpa, there is no meditation, and yet Rigpa is the supreme meditation. While in the state of contemplation, the practitioner is not meditating and yet never abandons meditation. For the Siddha in Mahasamadhi, there is not even so much as a hair-tip of meditation or mental activity or distraction. Thoughts may arise, even proliferate and develop, but the Siddha is not distracted by them, and, in this way, his or her meditation becomes like the continuous flow of a river.

There exist different kinds of disciples according to whether their capacities are superior, intermediate, or inferior. The individual of superior capacity has a predisposition for the practice of contemplation because of having heard the teachings and practiced them in past lives. Thus, in this present life, when one hears the teachings and is directly introduced, one understands immediately, just as Manjushrimitra did when he first encountered Garab Dorje. Such a disciple is the most suitable vessel for the teachings. When the view of Thekchod is expounded to such an individual, he or she immediately understands and instantly cuts through all tensions and rigidities. And in terms of his or her Thodgal practice, the first stage, the direct perception of Reality (*chos-nyid mngon-sum*), encompasses the realization of the other stages of vision simultaneously. Here we are speaking of the four stages in the practice of vision (*snang-ba bzhi*). (See the commentary for "The Last Testament of Garab Dorje," line 30.) All thought (internal) and appearances (external) are immediately liberated into the Base as they arise, into the state where awareness and luminosity are inseparable (*rig gsal dbyer med*). They are like waves on the surface of the ocean, rising and falling, and there exists no problem in this. Here there is neither meditation nor nonmeditation. But such an individual of superior capacity is very rare.

An individual of intermediate capacity, upon hearing the teachings from a master, comes to recognize that no matter what appearances may arise, they merely represent the creative energy of the Dharmakaya. But those who do not understand this, those being individuals of inferior capacity, must follow a more gradual approach, since they may easily fall under the sway of delusory appearances (*'khrul snang*). They must practice regularly in order to attain some stability (*brtan-pa thob*) in their practice of contemplation.

However, if we complete the accumulation of the causes of concentration, or dhyana (*bsam-gtan gyi rgyu tshogs*), such causes as an isolated, remote, quiet place, a comfortable seat, no excitement, no coming and going of others, and so on, then experiences in meditation are bound to be produced. But this will not be the case if we are distracted. Thus, it is very important to abandon all worldly entertainments, if we are to attain success in meditation (*'du 'dzi spang nas sgom-pa gces*).

Although ultimately, there will be no difference, in terms of the practice of contemplation, between the state of even contemplation and the subsequent realization (*mnyam rjes kyi nyams len tha-dad du med*), if we do not first master contemplation (*mnyam bzhag*) and establish it on its own proper ground in the meditation session, making it firm and stable, we will not be able to take it into the period of subsequent realization. And thus, we will not be able to transform all of our activities into the path. Irregular meditation habits (*spyi 'byams*) will leave us with deviations (*gol-sa*) where we fall away from our center or innate disposition (*gshis shor gyi gol-sa*). Therefore, it is necessary for beginners to divide their practice of meditation into discrete sessions. During the meditation session, we should stabilize our contemplation, so that we can continue in its essence, take it into our activities after the session, and continue in this directly penetrating knowledge or gnosis (*ye-shes zang-thal*).

14. The Unique State of the Dharmakaya

Therefore, it is not necessary to search for any other kind of meditation practice. While remaining in the view of the Dharmakaya (*chos-sku'i lta-ba*), that is to say, in the state of contemplation, our thoughts and our actions nevertheless continue to manifest. But they do so spontaneously and without any deliberate effort on our part to stop or to create anything (*dgag sgrub med-par chad chod yad yud du skyong*). We continue naturally in the unique state of the Dharmakaya (*chos-sku gcig-po'i yo-langs bskyang*). And when we practice this natural yoga which is free of conceptual elaborations, where Shamatha and Vipashyana are inseparable (*zhi lhag dbyer med spros bral gnyug-ma'i rnal 'byor*), everything becomes unfabricated and spontaneous (*ma bcos lhan-cig skyes-pa*) and we continue in the inherent state of Reality (*chos nyid kyi rang ngo skyong-ba*). Generally, we can translate the Sanskrit term *dharmatā* (*chos nyid*) as "Reality," that is to say, "the state of being just what it is" (*ji bzhin nyid*).

The practice is known as the wish-granting gem of the Siddha Lineage. As it says in the *gNas-lugs rdo-rje tshig rkang* of Jigmed Lingpa, "Apart from this practice of all the Buddhas of the three times, there exists no other method." Once we have come to the discovery of this essential point that is Rigpa, then there is no need to return to the visualization practices (*bskyed rim*) of the Tantra system and to the practices of the Sutra system, such as mental analysis and so on. We need not make shopping tours of the spiritual supermarkets, searching for still more practices. However, if we understand the principle of Dzogchen, which is Rigpa, then we can utilize all other methods, of both the Sutra system and the Tantra system, whenever they prove useful to us. But we practice all of these other methods from the Dzogchen point of view, linking each of them with the Guru Yoga practice in order to integrate and maintain our transmissions of the teachings. All of the teachings belonging to the other vehicles to enlightenment are different ways eventually leading to the discovery of the Dharmakaya. They are but different paths leading up the mountainside; however, Dzogchen already finds itself at the summit of the mountain, because it represents the view of the Dharmakaya. It is the highest pinnacle of all the paths or vehicles to enlightenment. Therefore, it is not necessary to retrace our steps down the slope of the mountain in order to find any other path. All of the practices taught by the Buddha Shakyamuni actually represent various means for finding this single unique state of immediate intrinsic Awareness. Through these means, we come to discover the Dharmakaya within ourselves. But if we hanker for other teachings and look elsewhere than within ourselves and start doing practices that are less than our original understanding and capacity, then we are like an old woman having much gold in her house, yet living in poverty because she does not recognize it. Or again, we are like a beggar wandering from place to place who arrives at a hearth made of gold stones, and yet he sits there begging copper pennies from all who pass his way. If we pursue practices involving the workings of the mind, required in both Sutra and Tantra, we will only build an invisible cage of meditation around ourselves. This invisible cage will become a prison for us, and we will then not exercise our intrinsic freedom. So we must come to a definitive decision through self-discovery that there is nothing else aside from this practice of immediate Awareness. Once we have discovered for ourselves that the Dharmakaya is Buddhahood itself, experienced as naked primal awareness or gnosis that is self-existing and never deluded (*chos-sku rang gnas kyi ye-shes rjen-pa 'khrul med myong-ba'i sangs-rgyas su blo thag-bcad*), we can continue in the practice of contemplation without being afflicted with any doubts. That is the essence of the second statement of Garab Dorje.

THE THIRD ESSENTIAL POINT

15. Continuing in the State of Contemplation

The Method of Self-Liberation

The third statement of Garab Dorje relates to our continuing in the state of contemplation, where whatever arises in the mind self-liberates. Having been directly introduced to Rigpa, and having removed all doubts with regard to it through effectively practicing meditation, we are then able to continue confidently (*gdengs bca'-ba*) in the state of self-liberation (*rang grol*). For example, in order to learn how to swim, we must first be introduced to the water by an experienced swimmer and shown how to move our limbs, so that we do not sink into the water. Thereafter we need to practice a variety of swimming techniques. Now that we know how to swim, the only remaining problem is how to swim the distance over a period of time. That is the question considered here. The final statement of Garab Dorje is connected with the Upadesha Series of Dzogchen teachings. The Dzogchen Upadesha texts generally assume that we have already been introduced to Rigpa and that we already know how to enter into the state of contemplation. Therefore, these Upadesha texts principally offer advice on how to continue in this state. The method here is to throw the student into the water immediately; he or she will either sink or swim.

Rigpa, or immediate intrinsic Awareness, has been liberated from the very beginning; it is primordially liberated (*ye-grol*). The word *confidence* (*gdengs*) in this context refers to a confidence in the process that liberates discursive thoughts (*rnam-rtog grol*) as they arise. At the time of stabilizing meditation and settling into contemplation, we become free of all notions of subject and object, and, thus, thoughts

are no longer grasped at nor apprehended; they are allowed to liberate by themselves into their own original condition, which is the state
of emptiness. But, if we do not have confidence in this method of
self-liberation (*rang grol lam*), and only meditate, relaxing ourselves
into a calm state of mind and continuing to practice Shamatha as
before, then we will not go beyond merely attaining rebirth in the
higher worlds, the mental planes of the Rupadhatu. Such a practice
and such a result only represents a deviation (*gol-sa*).

The Dhyanas and the Samapattis: Rebirth in the Higher Worlds
    Generally, the term *Dhyana* (*bsam-gtan*) can be translated as "con-
centration," but it also means a level of concentration attained in
meditation practice. If we should die at a moment when we are absorbed in a particular level of concentration (Skt. *dhyāna*), we will
find ourselves reborn at the corresponding mental plane, also called
Dhyana, of the Rupadhatu, or form world. This is the case when we
are concentrating on an object of meditation, but if we are practicing
concentration without an object, then we find ourselves reborn on
the higher mental planes of cosmic consciousness, the Samapattis of
the Arupadhatu, or formless world. For example, if we master the
First Dhyana in meditation practice, then we can attain rebirth among
the Brahma gods dwelling on the three lowest mental planes of the
Rupadhatu, namely, Brahmakayika, Brahmapurohita, and Mahabrahma. These subtle mental planes belonging to the Brahmaloka lie
far above the higher astral planes of the Kamadhatu, or desire world,
where the Devas or gods who dwell there are still dominated by
sensual desires (Skt. *kāma*). The Brahmas are not afflicted by sensual
desires and passions, but only by more subtle and refined intellectual impulses. They inhabit very subtle mental bodies possessing
great auras of light, and these are much more splendid, attenuated,
and refined than the etheric and astral bodies possessed by the Devas
inhabiting the Kamadhatu. Nevertheless, the Brahmalokas represent
a conditioned state of existence and therefore belong to Samsara.
Although existence within a Brahmaloka is of exceedingly long
duration, calculated in millions of human years, it is not eternal
and everlasting.
    According to the tradition preserved in the *Abhidharmakosha* of
Vasubandhu (3 cen. CE), the standard Abhidharma and cosmological text studied in Tibet, there exist six Devalokas, or levels of the
astral plane, inhabited by the Devas or gods: Chatur-maharajika,

Trayatrimsha, Yama, Tushita, Nirmanarati, and Paranirmitavasha-
vartin. These six Devalokas, comprising the divine part of the
Kamadhatu, are depicted as heaven-worlds and celestial paradises.
Then, in ascending order, the same text lists some seventeen
Brahmalokas, or mental planes, which correspond to the four
Dhyanas (Pali *jhana*), or levels of concentration in meditation. To the
First Dhyana correspond the three lowest Brahmalokas: Brahma-
kayika, Brahmapurohita, and Mahabrahma; to the Second Dhyana
correspond the three intermediate Brahmalokas: Parittabha,
Apramanabha, and Abhasvara; to the Third Dhyana correspond the
next highest Brahmalokas: Parittashubha, Apramanashubha, and
Shubhakritsna; and to the Fourth Dhyana correspond the seven highest Brahmalokas, known as the Shuddhavasa Brahmalokas, "the Pure
Abodes." In ascending order, they are Anabhraka, Punyapravesha,
Brihatphala, Avriha, Atapa, Sudrisha, Sudarshana, and Akanishtha.
This last heaven-world or Brahmaloka is the Samsaric Akanishtha
and is not to be confused with the Supernal Akanishtha at the center
of all existence, which is the abode of the Sambhogakaya. These seventeen Brahmalokas comprise the Rupadhatu, or form world, so
called because all of the Brahmas have subtle, though visible, forms
that are glorious bodies of light.

By means of the mastery of the higher Dhyanas, known as
Samapattis, or absorptions, the practitioner can attain rebirth on one
of the four planes of cosmic consciousness belonging to the
Arupadhatu, or formless world, which lie beyond the Brahmalokas
of the Rupadhatu. These four dimensions of cosmic consciousness,
in ascending order, are Akashanantya, "infinite space," Vijnana-
nantya, "infinite consciousness," Akinchanya, "nothing whatever,"
and Naivasanjnanasanja, "neither perception nor nonperception."
These dimensions are called "formless" (*gzugs med*, Skt. *arūpa*) because one's consciousness is diffused throughout space, and although
one possesses a type of extremely subtle mental body, it is something lacking a visible form. Many religious traditions consider the
attaining of these Samapattis, or levels of cosmic consciousness (a
common experience of mystics throughout the world), as tantamount
to realizing Godhood or attaining union with God. These mystical
experiences are characterized by bliss (*bde-ba*), luminosity (*gsal-ba*),
and spaciousness or nondiscursiveness (*mi rtog-pa*), reminiscent of
the Satchitananda formula of the Upanishads. Nevertheless, these

Samapattis are not Rigpa. They are merely mystical experiences characterized by bliss, light, lack of spatial limitations, and so on. They are conditioned states of consciousness (Skt. *samskrta-dharma*), and as such they are impermanent and not eternal. They do not constitute the ultimate goal, which is unconditioned existence (Skt. *asamskrta-dharma*).[6]

Thus, a rebirth among the long-lived gods, or the angels in heaven, does not represent ultimate salvation or liberation from Samsara, in the light of the Buddhist teachings. The states of the gods and angels are conditioned states of consciousness brought about by antecedent causes, and when their stocks of meritorious karma are exhausted, they will find themselves reborn elsewhere. For example, at one time ages ago, we (humanity) existed for millions, even billions of human years, in a state of cosmic consciousness. Then, from our originally exalted existence in bliss and light as Brahma gods in the Abhasvara Brahmaloka, "the pure dimension of clear light," we fell and found ourselves reborn as the new humanity on the surface of this planet earth. This is the Buddhist Myth of Genesis.[7] Thus, to practice meditation or Shamatha-bhavana, and master the Dhyanas solely in order to seek rebirth in the heaven-worlds among the Devas and the Brahmas, belonging to the higher astral planes and the mental planes, respectively, represents a deviation. A deviation (*gol-sa*) is a falling away from the center, or a going astray from the spiritual path.

Moreover, even though we master these Dhyanas through our Shamatha practice, we will not find ourselves able to control the secondary causes (*rkyen*) that give rise to the samskaras, that is, the unconscious impulses that erupt as conscious emotions such as anger and desire, in our stream of consciousness. Nor will we develop confidence in our discovery of Rigpa. For example, we may visit countless times the dark room where a mysterious object is kept because we now possess our own copy of the key to the room. But no matter how many times we visit that room, this is not the same as being able to take that mysterious object out into the sunlight and carry it with us wherever we may go in the world. To be able to do so would inspire unquestioned confidence. We would no longer be keeping contemplation locked up in our meditation sessions.

Knowledge as the Basis of Liberation

To continue with confidence in contemplation is to be like a mighty lion, the king of beasts, who fearlessly strolls throughout the jungle at a leisurely pace. In this way, without any attachment or aversion, we must recognize that whatever arises (*gang shar*) is truly the manifestation of the creative energy of Rigpa (*rig-pa'i rtsal*). This knowledge or gnosis (*ye-shes*) is the very basis of liberation. Similarly, in the Gnostic tradition in the West it is knowledge (Gk. *gnosis*) that brings salvation and not faith or belief (Gk. *pistis*); for faith, whether or not enforced by the Church and by scriptural authority, is still only provisional, and ultimately it represents ignorance. We have faith (*dad-pa*) in the teachings and in the possibility of liberation and enlightenment until we come into possession of an immediate knowledge (or gnosis) of this through our direct experience. Salvation is realized only through this direct knowledge; it does not come through some Church or Dharma center that claims to mediate between the individual and a higher reality and to dispense salvation to its members. All claims by priest and church to possess a monopoly on the means to salvation are false and merely serve to beguile and manipulate those on the path. A church or a monastery or a Dharma center, like any social institution, is conditioned and impermanent. These institutions only represent means, whether useful or not; they are not the goal. The real Community of the Saints, the Arya Sangha, transcends any earthly institution, for the latter is always historically, socially, and culturally conditioned.

16. Recognizing the Nature of Thoughts and Experiences

If we do not have confidence in this path to liberation, confidence in the self-liberating of discursive thoughts as soon as they arise in the mind, and do not make it the essential point of our practice, then we will fall once again under the multifarious potentiality of the mind (*rig-pa'i rtsal lhung-ba*); we will find ourselves once more living in the reflections and the ever-changing phantasmagoria of the dream of Samsara. And soon we will find ourselves overwhelmed by the undercurrents of thought (*'og 'gyu'i rnam-rtog*), which lie like water hidden by the tall grass of the bog in the moorlands. Once again, we find ourselves trapped, continuing to accumulate karma, and transmigrate in Samsara. If, however, our thoughts, whether gross or subtle, are self-liberated without a trace, in the same way as the clouds dissipate in the sky, then we will not generate any fresh karma. So whenever thoughts arise, they should not be allowed to become an undercurrent of proliferating delusions (*'og 'gyu 'khrul 'byams*).

Otherwise, we will become entangled in a net of memories created by the mind (*blos byas 'jur dran*). But rather, we must continue in a state of self-occurring natural mindfulness (*rang babs gnyug-ma'i dran-pa*) and never be separated from that. In this way, we come to recognize the nature of whatever thoughts arise (*rnam-rtog ci shar rang ngo shes-par byas*). The key here is recognition (*ngo shes-pa*). When thoughts arise, we turn our attention to them, recognize them for what they are, and without following them, allow them to remain in their own native condition (*rang sor zin*) and dissolve of their own accord. This is like meeting someone on a crowded street whom we have met before. We greet each other and then go our separate ways. This is the essential point of practice, and this method is known as *gcer-grol*, "liberation through bare attention."

In the present context, *dran-pa*, which ordinarily means "memory" and "to remember," means "mindfulness" (Skt. *smṛti*, Pali *sati*). Mindfulness is the balanced poise of Rigpa, ready to direct the attention of recognition to any thought that arises above the horizon. This is said to be like a hunter patiently waiting in concealment, his bow and arrow ready for the deer to emerge out of the forest. He is waiting, but his mind is alert and mindful, in no way distracted, even if he must wait for hours. If he becomes distracted, then he will miss his target when the deer appears. To a certain extent, this attention and process of recognition is mind-work, like recognizing a familiar face in a crowd or a hunter spotting a deer among the trees. But when a thought arises, if we think, "Oh, a thought has arisen; I must liberate it!" this is a fault in practice. The recognition must be nearly automatic and instantaneous, and then one allows the thought to liberate by itself. We remain in contemplation the whole time and do not fixate on or otherwise interfere with the thought. We let it go its own way without following it. It will then vanish of its own accord. We allow thoughts to dissolve in the sky of the mind without leaving a trace behind (*rjes med*). We have only to observe the clouds dissipating in the sky to get a feel for this process. Thoughts in the mind dissipate in the mind; they are no more substantial than the morning mist.

This is how we continue in the practice at the beginning. But if we do not follow through with the process, if we do not purify our thoughts by means of self-liberating them, but only recognize them as thoughts, then we will not succeed in interrupting the current of delusory activity of the mind (*rnam-rtog ngos shes-pa tsam gyis 'khrul-pa'i las rgyun mi chod-pa*). This would be like finding ourselves in a lucid dream. We recognize the dream as a dream, and yet we remain caught up in the dream. In that case, it is easy to slip again into unconsciousness, mistaking the dream for something real. So, first we recognize each thought as a thought, seeing its real face nakedly (*gcer mthong*), without conceptions or the activity of the intellect intervening. We recognize the knowledge (*ye-shes*) that we had met previously (*sngon 'dris kyi ye-shes de nyid ngos bzung*), the knowledge that knows thoughts to be empty, and yet knows that they are manifestations of energy, and we remain in that state (*ngang la bzhag-pa*). But simultaneously with this recognition (*ngos bzung*), we allow the thought to self-liberate by itself, dissolving into its original condition of emptiness and pure potentiality without leaving a trace behind. Thus, this recognition and this liberation must occur together.

17. Meditation and Self-Liberation

When we remain in the state of contemplation, even though thoughts arise, they have no capacity or power to distract us and injure our contemplation. Thoughts may arise just as they did before, because this is the natural activity of the mind, but their liberation is not the experience of the ordinary person, but that of the Yogin. For the yogin, when thoughts arise, they do not come under the sway of judgment or other mental processes. They remain only "ornaments" (*rgyan*) of the nature of mind. Intrinsic Awareness is like the mirror reflecting all this busy mental activity (*rtsal*), yet it is detached and unaffected by it, like an old man sitting in the park watching the children at play. But if we follow these thoughts, then we become like the philosopher Chandrakirti's father, who lay upon his bed beneath a large sack of rice suspended by a rope from the roof beam of his hut. As he speculated and daydreamed about what he would do with his newfound wealth, represented by this quantity of rice, the rope broke. The sack fell upon his head, and he was killed instantly.

If we know the methods of meditation, but do not know the methods of liberation, we will be like the gods or Devas dwelling on the various Dhyanas or mental planes. We will just be maintaining the state of calm with the practice of Shamatha. So it is necessary to break our Shamatha (*zhi-gnas 'jig-pa*) and enter into the practice of higher insight or Vipashyana (*lhag-mthong*). Some scholars say that just recognizing the calm state as against the movement of thoughts is sufficient. But this is a mistake, for we will find ourselves in danger of being overwhelmed by adverse circumstances, forgetting all we have learned. Within Vipashyana practice, we no longer strictly remain a detached witness, passively watching the playful activity of thoughts like the old man watching the children play, but our awareness reintegrates with activity, so that there is no difference between action and awareness. But a practitioner cannot do this until he or she first separates awareness from action, as one does, for example, in the Rushan exercises. The goal is not Kaivalya, the isolation of awareness from activity, as is the case with Jainism and the Samkhya philosophy, but their reintegration (Skt. *yuganaddha*). This is a perspective wherein Dzogchen differs from many other systems of meditation, which define the goal as the isolation (Skt. *kaivalya*) of a passive awareness or consciousness (called variously Skt. *puruṣa, jīva*, or *ātman*) from the play of energy which is the world and nature (Skt. *prakṛti*). In Dzogchen, Awareness is active just as Buddhahood is active in the world, although its essence transcends the world.

18. The Arising of Thoughts Becomes the Meditation

When we practice habitually in this way for a long time, the mere arising of thoughts becomes the meditation itself. It makes no difference whether thoughts arise or do not arise. The boundaries between the calm state and the movement of thoughts collapses completely. The movement of thoughts is now seen directly as indescribable light, the manifestation of the clear luminosity of the Base which is the Primordial State. These movements bring no harm or disturbance to the profound calm at the center. Rather than movement occurring as discursive thoughts that are inherently limited and restrictive, it occurs as a direct and immediate knowledge or gnosis (*ye-shes*) that is everywhere directly penetrating (*zang-thal*). Thoughts spontaneously manifest as this directly penetrating knowledge (*ye-shes zang-thal*) without any intervening process of transforming impure karmic vision into pure vision, as is the case with the Tantra system of practice. Nevertheless, to the outside observer, the mind of the Siddha may look deceptively like an ordinary mind because very mundane thoughts continue to arise; but all is not sweetness and light here. The Yogin continues to lust, hunger, and defecate as long as he is in a physical body, the product of past karma. Even though the morning sun strikes the glacier, the ice does not melt immediately; similarly, all the qualities of enlightenment do not immediately manifest, even though the mind has realized enlightenment. But whereas the ordinary individual is forever trying to create or suppress thoughts (*dgag sgrub*) and so continues to accumulate the energy of the samskaras (unconscious impulses), the Yogin realizes the liberation of these same thoughts precisely at the moment when they arise.

19. The Four Modes of Liberation

In Dzogchen, we speak of three or four modes of liberation (*grol lugs*):

1. *gcer-grol* (pronounced cher-drol), "liberation through bare attention,"
2. *shar-grol* (pronounced shar-drol), "liberation as soon as it arises,"
3. *rang grol* (pronounced rang-drol), "self-liberation," and
4. *ye-grol* (pronounced ye-drol), "primordial liberation."

In the text, certain metaphors are given to illustrate the meaning of the modes of liberation. *gCer-grol*, which is liberation by way of recognizing thoughts, is like meeting a person whom we have met before. *Shar-grol*, where thoughts liberate themselves after arising, is like a snake unknotting itself from its coils. But *rang-grol*, where thoughts arise into their immediate and spontaneous liberation, is like a thief entering an empty house and finding there nothing to steal. Thus, no harm or benefit comes to the state of contemplation from the arising and liberating of thoughts. The first three modes of liberation refer to the process of liberating thoughts, whereas primordial liberation refers to Rigpa itself, which has never been otherwise than totally liberated from the very beginning.

Within this method of *gcer-grol*, "liberation through bare attention," there exists a minimal mental activity; we turn our attention to the thought as soon as it arises and recognize it as a thought. This is like seeing the person on the crowded street as a stranger, and then suddenly recognizing him as an old acquaintance. Although this may have become a largely automatic process, there still exists a small time gap between the arising of the thought, the becoming aware of its presence, and the recognition of it as a thought, on the one hand, and its dissolving again, on the other hand. For the beginner this practice is appropriate, but later it will become a fault if it is not transcended.

At the next stage, the thought disintegrates as soon as it arises. Patrul Rinpoche illustrates this process with the example of drawing pictures on the surface of the water. The picture disintegrates as soon as it is drawn. The drawing and the dissolving are simultaneous. So here the arising (*shar-ba*) and the liberating (*grol-ba*) of the thought are simultaneous. There is no interval or discontinuity between the self-arising and the self-liberating of thoughts. Thus, this process differs from liberation through bare attention and is known as *shar-grol*, "liberation as soon as it arises." There still subsists some small distinction in terms of phases between the arising and the liberating. However, within this practice of *shar-grol*, there is no attempt whatsoever to suppress the arising of thoughts. No energy is invested in that effort, and so the process of liberation is spontaneous, automatic, and effortless (*rtsol med*). Whereas with the practice of *gcer-grol*, there still remained the minimum effort of bare attention, there is no such effort here. Whatever thoughts arise, they are immediately carried along by their own momentum into the natural state and liberated. Thus, thoughts which arise are purified (that is, liberated) by way of the very potentiality (*rtsal*) of the Dharmakaya. They come into liberation effortlessly (*rtsol med*) by means of the very energy and momentum of their arising. Thus, the text cites the image of the snake unknotting itself. When a thought arises bearing a strong change of energy, such as a thought of desire or a thought of anger, then the Awareness (*rig-pa*) present at that thought's liberation will be that much stronger and clearer. Thus, the passion (Skt. *kleśa*) becomes the friend and helper of Rigpa, instead of its enemy and opponent. In this way, all discursive thoughts arise as manifestations of the inherent energy of the directly penetrating nature of Rigpa itself (*rig-pa zang-thal gyi ngang las rang rtsal du 'char-ba*). We continue in that state without accepting or rejecting anything whatsoever (*blang dor med-par bskyangs-pa*). Yet we continue to hold to the recognition of the Dharmakaya on the side of liberation (*grol-cha'i chos-sku ngos bzung*), and so there persists some subtle duality here.

With the third stage, even the distinction between arising and liberating or dissolving is transcended. Thus, the image, cited by the author, of a thief entering into an empty house and finding nothing to steal. When thoughts arise, they are instantaneously liberated and do not in any way go beyond the state of the Dharmakaya. That is to say, their very arising is their liberating, and so there no longer exists any distinction between these two phases or moments. Liberation is completely automatic, spontaneous, effortless, and instantaneous, the process known as self-liberation. Thoughts liberate as they arise; their very arising is the process of their liberating. This is the method proper to Dzogchen, and all else is but preparation.

20. Samsara and Nirvana

Thus we need not remain fettered within Samsara by our negative emotions, remaining caught up within the cyclic process of thoughts and passions endlessly arising. In the Sutra system, Samsara (*'khor-ba*, cycle, cyclic existence) is conventionally defined as the cycle of activity, both mental and physical, whereas Nirvana (*myang 'das*, passing beyond sorrow) is defined as quiescence or ultimate peace. Therefore, we have the Tibetan synonyms, *srid-pa*, "becoming," for Samsara and *zhi-ba*, "peace, quiescence," for Nirvana. Samsara represents conditioned existence (Skt. *saṃskṛta-dharma*), the conditioned state of the mind or thought process where mental phenomena (Skt. *dharmas*) are brought into consciousness by antecedent causes, as part of a beginningless chain of causality or interdependent origination (Skt. *pratītyasamutpāda*). Samsara is, *par excellence*, the movement of thoughts, whereas the Nirvana of the Arhats, as the Shravakas, or Hinayana practitioners, conceive of it, is a state of ultimate quiescence in which the movement of the passions will arise no more. But the Mahayana did not take this Nirvana of the Arhat as the ultimate goal, or even as unconditioned existence (Skt. *asaṃskṛta-dharma*). According to the Mahayana teaching, the Arhat is still afflicted with very subtle intellectual obscurations, and so, after his or her Nirvanic state is exhausted, he or she must take up existence once more in the higher worlds of the Rupadhatu. And thereafter, in order to attain true liberation from Samsara, one must set about practicing the career of the Bodhisattva. Only then can one realize the ultimate goal of Buddhahood. Nevertheless, one need not be reborn again as a human being after attaining the status of an Arhat (*dgra-bcom-pa*), a perfect saint who has vanquished the passions.

However, Dzogchen understands matters in a different way. For Dzogchen liberation means liberation from both Samsara and Nirvana. The goal in Dzogchen is to become liberated, either in this present life, or immediately following physical death in the Bardo state, rather than there being something to be obtained in some future heaven-world. In the Tantra system, Samsara and Nirvana are conceived of as two parallel or alternative realities, that of the impure karmic vision of the six realms of rebirth belonging to ordinary deluded beings and that of the pure vision of the deities and the mandalas belonging to enlightened beings. The first is the result of the ignorance and the obscurations of ordinary sentient beings, whereas the other is the result of the knowledge or gnosis of enlightened beings. But in Dzogchen these two separate realities, Samsara and Nirvana, are simultaneously in phase with no resulting confusion. The external world is a mandala, and all living beings are deities, yet everything looks just as it did previously, there being no antecedent process of visualization or transformation to bring this shift in perception about. Mountains are mountains, but every mountain is Sumeru. Enlightenment is not an ascent to somewhere else, an escape from earth to some heavenly paradise above, this being a common metaphor for the spiritual path in mystical traditions found throughout the world. Rather, enlightenment is something that occurs here and now. In the light of Dzogchen, discursive thoughts transcend their inherent limitations and stand revealed as knowledge. This is the self-revelation of what had been concealed or hidden previously. What is found at the end is what existed at the beginning; the Alpha and the Omega are simultaneously present. This is the self-revealing of gnosis: there is unity (*mnyam nyid*), and yet diversity remains unimpaired. Both are encompassed within gnosis or primordial knowledge.

21. The Special Teaching of Dzogchen

This method, whereby thoughts are purified by self-liberation without leaving a trace behind, is the special teaching of the natural Great Perfection (*rang-bzhin rdzogs-pa chen-po'i khyad-chos*), and it is not found elsewhere in the Sutras and the Tantras. It is the essential point in question, whereby deluded thoughts (*'khrul rtog*) are purified so that they stand revealed as knowledge or pristine cognition, as primordial awareness (*ye-shes*). By means of this method, our passions or negative emotions (*nyon-mongs-pa*, Skt. *kleśa*) may be transformed from being fetters binding us to the wheel of Samsara into the very means to liberation, and the energies they release can be utilized for this purpose. Through the liberation of all thoughts, positive and negative, we are freed from the limitations of both Samsara and

Nirvana. We come to realize our inherent freedom, our primordial liberation, or *ye-grol*, which we possessed before we fell into the deviations and limitations of constricted Samsaric existence. This is a freedom we have never lost; it is only that we have forgotten it and are now unaware of it. We have forgotten our real nature, who we really are. But now we return to the original primeval fullness or wholeness out of our current condition of privation, this alien condition in which we found ourselves exiled and coerced to suffer time and conditioning. We now come into the stage where there is nothing left to do (*mi slob-pa'i lam*), having been freed from the necessity to strive to accomplish something, yet we are free to do everything.

If we have practiced well in this way, we will realize spontaneously all of the paths and stages (*sa lam*), that is, the five paths (*lam lnga*) and the ten stages (*sa bcu*) that, according to the Sutra system, demarcate the career of the Bodhisattva. But whereas, according to the Sutra system, it will take the practitioner countless lifetimes extending over three immeasurable kalpas to realize the goal of Buddhahood, the Dzogchen practitioner may accomplish this within a single lifetime through the realization of Rigpa. Thus, Dzogchen speaks of only a single stage (*sa gcig-pa*). The Dzogchen practitioner is like the great Garuda bird who is fully formed, even with its wings complete, inside the egg. When the shell is broken, the Garuda springs forth whole and fully developed; it can instantly fly anywhere in the universe. Or again, one is like a lion cub emerging from the womb of its mother; it roars and all of the animals of the forest are subdued.

If we do not possess this confidence in self-liberation, yet boast that our view is high and that our meditation is profound, we will not have the method to dissolve the negative emotions (Skt. *kleśa*) when they arise. We will be no more than braggarts and hypocrites, deluding both ourselves and others, like false Gurus do. There exists no shortage of such wrong guides (*log 'dren*) in our world. This is not the true path and can only lead the perpetrator into a self-created Vajra Hell. It is like being a snake in a hollow tube. The snake can only go upward to freedom or downward to perdition; there are no other options. This is the way it is for the Dzogchen practitioner.

But if we truly understand the essential point of the self-liberation of thoughts, having relied upon the instructions of the master, then we do not need to look elsewhere for a higher view. Possessing this essential point, we cannot do otherwise than liberate our stream of consciousness from all bondage to dualistic thinking (*rang rgyud gnyis 'dzin gyi 'ching-ba las grol-ba*). Having come to an island full of gold nuggets, we do not search about for ordinary rocks and stones. This is the significance of the third statement of Garab Dorje.

CONCLUSION

22. Upadesha Teaching

The author, Patrul Rinpoche, concludes by saying that these three unerring essential points alone are sufficient to carry the practitioner immediately into the state of directly penetrating Awareness (*rig-pa zang-thal gyi ngang du chig-chod du khyer-ba'i gnad ma nor-bu*) and that, in fact, this directly penetrating Awareness (*rig-pa zang-thal*) represents in itself the unification of the view, the meditation, the conduct, and the fruit of the natural Great Perfection (*rang-bzhin rdzogs-pa chen-po'i lta sgom spyod 'bras bzhi-ka*). This text not only pertains to the view of Dzogchen, but equally to the meditation and to the conduct or behavior of the practitioner of Dzogchen.

The text we have here is preeminently an Upadesha (*man-ngag*), "a secret instruction," that is to say, an instruction communicated in private and in confidence from a master to his disciple. An Upadesha is based more on the personal experience of the master in meditation practice than on philosophical analysis and scholastic tradition. The Sanskrit term *upadeśa* is translated in Tibetan as *man-ngag*, that is, not (*man*) to be spoken aloud (*ngag*) in public. Thus an Upadesha is not as such a philosophical treatise or an exegesis, which would be a Shastra (*bstan-bcos*), a text that constructs (*bcos-pa*) a doctrine (*bstan-pa*).

However, according to the general doctrinal expositions of those who follow the scriptural system (*gzhung-lugs-pa spyi'i chos skad*), that is to say, the scholastic and philosophical methods of the Sutra system followed by Lama scholars belonging to the different schools of Tibetan Buddhism, objects of intellectual knowledge are evaluated according to various criteria (*gtan-tshigs*) in terms of rational analysis and citations from authoritative scriptures (*shes-bya'i blo yul la lung rigs gtan-tshigs gzhal*). In a philosophical treatise (*bstan-bcos*) a scholar sets matters down in a very systematic fashion (*gtan la 'bebs-pa*). But this is not the case here because the author is not writing from the standpoint of a philosopher or a scholar of the Sutras and the Shastras, but from the standpoint of the transmission he or she has received from his or her masters and of an understanding born from direct personal experience of this naked manifest primal awareness (*mngon-sum rjen-pa'i ye-shes*). Just that naked primal awareness is the view itself, the way of seeing of *rig-pa'i ye-shes*, "a knowledge or cognition which is immediate intrinsic Awareness" (*rig-pa'i ye-shes kyi lta-ba*). For this reason, the view ultimately encompasses and includes the meditation and the conduct as well. This is important to understand. The view and the meditation practice are ultimately identical, having but a single taste (*lta sgom du ro-gcig yin-pa*).

23. Culmination of the Nine Vehicles

This view, which possesses within itself the three essential points (*gnad gsum ldan-pa'i lta-ba*), is called the culmination or summit of the nine successive vehicles to enlightenment (*theg-pa rim dgu'i rtse-mo*), and it represents the unerring or unmistaken essential point of the Path of Primordial Purity, which is the natural Great Perfection (*rang-bzhin rdzogs-pa chen-po'i ka-dag gi lam gnad ma nor-ba*), that is to say, the practice of Thekchod. This Upadesha here has dealt with this practice.

Although each of the yanas, or vehicles (*theg-pa*) to enlightenment, is perfectly correct and sufficient to carry the practitioner to liberation, each of them possesses its own definitive view and its own particular methods, as explained in the introduction above. However, Dzogchen Atiyoga represents their culmination in terms of its being the view of the Dharmakaya itself. And since Dzogchen is itself not curtailed or restricted by any limitations in terms of practice, a Dzogchenpa, or Dzogchen practitioner, is able to use any of the methods found in these other vehicles and practice them when found useful or necessary. But this is always done while maintaining the Dzogchen point of view. Once having ascended to the summit of the mountain peak of Dzogchen, we should not retrace our steps to any lesser view, for this would create an obstacle to our further development. In terms of the spiritual path to liberation and enlightenment, the higher level of teaching includes and enhances the lower levels of teaching, rather than excluding them. Thus all of the methods found in the Sutras and the Tantras lie open to the Dzogchenpa, but such a practitioner is not thereby limited by them.

The practice should be tailored to the individual, to his or her needs and capacities, and not coercing the individual to fit the mold of the practice. This is a profound point and should be understood well. Thus it says in the text that all of the methods found in the eight lower vehicles, that is, the Sutras and the Tantras, accompany the view of Dzogchen as its friends and helpers.

24. The Light of Self-Originated Discriminating Wisdom

At the time when we directly encounter the true face of the inner light, the lamp of self-originated discriminating wisdom, which is primordially pure Awareness (*ka-dag rig-pa shes-rab rang-byung gi sgron-me'i rang zhal mjal-ba'i tshe*), this discriminating wisdom born from the power of meditation blazes up (*sgom byung gi shes-rab tu 'bar*) effortlessly and spontaneously and becomes like a flood of luminosity, inundating the world. Here there appears to be a reference to Thodgal practice. The Tibetan word *sgron-me*, literally, "lamp," may also be translated as "light." The lamp of self-originated discriminating wisdom (*shes-rab rang-byung gi sgron-me*) is one of the six lamps of Thodgal (*sgron-me drug*). (See the Interlinear Commentary below.) The purpose of Thodgal is to develop one's contemplation through the practice of vision (*snang-ba*). The interior Clear Light of one's own enlightened nature, chiefly residing in the hollow of the heart, is projected and manifests spontaneously, via the Kati channel and the two eyes, in the external space in front of the practitioner as tiny rainbow spheres (*thig-le*), vajra chains (*rdo-rje lu-gu rgyud*), and other photic phenomena and pure visions. These are all manifestations of the pure creative energy of intrinsic Awareness (*rig-pa'i rtsal*), and the six lamps refer to different aspects of the process. The manifestation of our innate intelligence is like that; it illuminates everything in the world.

Furthermore, the technical terms Jnana (*ye-shes*) and Prajna (*shes-rab*) should not be confused, although both are often carelessly translated as "wisdom" in English translations of Buddhist texts. Their meaning and their function are quite distinct. Jnana is a knowledge, a gnosis, or a cognition which is a direct and immediate intuition of reality. Its function is to know (*shes-pa*, Skt. *jñā*), but this knowing is nondual in its nature. It is immediate and intuitive, transcending the dichotomy or duality of subject and object. It is primal or primordial

(*ye, ye-nas*) because it functions as a direct immediate intuitive knowing of the phenomena before the processes of the mind or the intellect which identify, label, and judge an object to be this or that come
into operation. In terms of Buddhist psychology it is a direct perception of raw sense data before that data has been structured by the
mind (Skt. *manas*), by way of the application of the categories of time
and space, into a recognizable object and the calling up of memories
of similar objects with which to identify it. In terms of Dzogchen,
this Jnana exists outside of time. Thus, it is *ye-nas*, since time or the
temporal sequence comes into existence only through the operations
of the mind (*yid*, Skt. *manas*). By the term *mind* is meant the process
of mental consciousness (*yid kyi rnam-shes*, Skt. *manovijñāna*): the raw
sense data or appearances (*snang-ba*) in the external world become
structured in time and space as discrete recognizable objects. In this
sense the world is created by the mind, which is not the same as
saying only mind exists. The categories of time and space are created by the mind, but Jnana is prior to the mind and in that sense is
beyond the mind. In terms of our individual existence, there is one
rig-pa, but many *ye-shes* or cognitions. *Rig-pa* is compared to the sun
in the sky, and *ye-shes* is compared to the rays of the sun which stream
forth from it and illuminate everything in the world.

The term Prajna (*shes-rab*) occupies a different status, located below that of Jnana or gnosis (*ye-shes*), but above mere intellectual
knowledge (*go-ba*). Prajna (*shes-rab*) means a higher (*rab tu*) knowledge or awareness (*shes-pa*). In general, it is what is meant in the
West by philosophy, or more precisely, by philosophical investigation and philosophical analysis, because, properly speaking, the term
refers to a process rather than a body of systematically organized
knowledge. This latter is Shasana (*bstan-pa*), "teaching, doctrine." In
the Sutra system, Prajna is defined as a higher intellectual faculty
that engages in a sophisticated philosophical analysis of the nature
of phenomena; that is to say, it penetrates into the nature of phenomena (dharmas) as they are in themselves. It uncovers the truth that
they lack any inherent existence (Skt. *asvabhāva*) and that they are
empty and insubstantial (Skt. *śūnya*). The methods of this philosophical investigation (Skt. *prajñā*) are outlined in the Abhidharma literature of the Hinayana schools, and further developed in the Shastras,
or philosophical treatises, composed by the masters of
the Madhyamika and Yogacharin schools. All of these methods of

investigation have been preserved in the philosophy colleges attached to the monasteries of Tibet. The function of Prajna is to discriminate, and unlike Jnana (*ye-shes*), it is still dualistic in its operation. Prajna discriminates wisely between what is good or bad, real or unreal, true or false, beautiful or ugly, worthwhile or worthless, and so on. We use Prajna when we investigate and discriminate between something genuine and something false. The wise man possesses Prajna; the fool lacks it. Rigpa is like the mirror that reflects everything: light or dark, good or bad, beautiful or ugly without discrimination; but the function of prajna is to discriminate, to judge, to evaluate. It makes distinctions. In English this is the function of "wisdom." It is what the wise man does; he knows what is real and what is false, what is worthwhile and what is worthless. So Jnana, or *ye-shes*, should not be translated as wisdom. Prajna, or *shes-rab*, is wisdom, or more precisely, a wisdom that discriminates.

In the Greek tradition, a suggestive similar distinction is made between gnosis and sophia. Jnana (*ye-shes*) corresponds to gnosis, which is a knowledge of divine things and also a knowledge that liberates (in the Gnostic tradition), whereas Prajna (*shes-rab*) corresponds to Sophia or Wisdom. In the Gnostic tradition, Sophia became exalted as Hagia Sophia, "the Holy Wisdom," the Great Goddess archetype who is the uncreated eternal consort of God. The same religious development occurred in India in the Buddhist context around the beginning of the Christian era. In the Mahayana Sutras, Prajna became exalted into the Prajnaparamita, "the Holy Perfection of Wisdom," who, as the Great Goddess archetype, is the Mother of all the Buddhas of the three times of past, present, and future. As the Sutra states, a Buddha can only become so by virtue of the Prajnaparamita, the Holy Perfection of Wisdom. It is further said that a monk must love passionately this Holy Perfection of Wisdom, just as a man would love a beautiful woman. Then, in the Tantra system, the Adiprajna, or Primordial Wisdom, becomes the eternal consort of the Primordial Buddha, or Adibuddha. Whether or not there are direct historical connections between Gnosticism and Buddhism, there exist clear parallels here.[8] Thus Jnana (*ye-shes*) should be translated as gnosis or knowledge, at times as cognition, and generally as primordial awareness or primal awareness; and Prajna (*shes-rab*) should be translated as wisdom or discriminating wisdom.

25. Wisdom and Compassion

Wisdom (Skt. *prajñā*) and compassion (Skt. *karuṇā*) are the two aspects, or two coefficients, of the enlightenment of a Buddha, whether this is spoken of in terms of Sutra or Tantra or Dzogchen. When the true significance of the state of emptiness (shunyata) is realized, when all barriers emotional and intellectual have been dissolved, then an overwhelming feeling of universal compassion arises automatically and spontaneously. This compassion is called a great or total compassion (*thugs-rje chen-po*, Skt. *mahākaruṇā*) because it is extended equally and impartially to all living beings, and not just to those few individuals we know and like. This great compassion is inherent in our innate Buddha-nature, and so its manifestation is natural and effortless. It does not have to be cultivated or created by the mind. Thus, the text says that from the innate disposition of emptiness (*stong-nyid kyi gshis*) arises compassion or a fervent love (*brtse-ba*) for all sentient beings.

26. The Conduct of the Bodhisattvas

The essential point of the path of the Bodhisattvas, in terms of practice, is the unification of discriminating wisdom (Skt. *prajñā*), entailing the understanding of the emptiness (shunyata) of all things, with a universal compassion (Skt. *mahākaruṇā*) for all sentient beings expressed through skillful means (*stong-nyid snying-rje zung du 'jugpa'i lam gnad mngon du gyur*, Skt. *upāya*). The first five perfections of generosity, morality, patience, vigor, and meditation express compassion and skillful means, whereas the perfection of wisdom, the sixth perfection, represents the understanding of emptiness. The Bodhisattvas, whether male or female, who practice this path are also known as the Sons of the Victorious One or Jinaputras (*rgyal sras*), and the all-pervasive compassionate activities of the Bodhisattva are called the Conduct of the Jinaputra (*rgyal sras kyi spyod-pa*). Furthermore, from the standpoint of Dzogchen, these compassionate activities represent the inherent potentiality or energy of the Primordial State, and may be compared to the rays of the sun. Thus, they are spontaneous and in no way contrived. By virtue of these spontaneous actions the accumulation of merit is perfected and completed. All of one's actions become totally selfless, because there exists no more attachment to a self-concept or idea of an ego, this having been dissolved by the perfection of wisdom. In this Bodhisattva activity, the view, the meditation, and the action are inseparably united.

27. The Highest Teaching

Even if all of the Jinas or Victorious Ones of the three times deliberated together (*dus gsum rgyal-ba'i zhal bsdur*), they would discover nothing beyond this fundamental Primordial State of all the Buddhas (*rgyal-ba kun gyi dgongs-pa'i mthil yings*). Thus, the Dzogchen view is called the victorious summit of all of the Yanas or ways to enlightenment (*theg-pa thams-cad kyi rtse rgyal*). It is also called the essential point of the path of the diamond-like heart that is the Essence of the Mind (*snying-thig rdo-rje snying-po'i lam gnad*). This is, therefore, the quintessence of the Fruit (which is Buddhahood), and there is nothing higher than this (*'bras-bu'i thus-ka 'di las lhag-po med*). It is the nectar of the Upadesha of the transmission lineages (*brgyud-pa'i man-ngag gi snying-khur*), that is to say, the meaning of this Upadesha is the very essence of the three lineages: the direct, the symbolic, and the oral.

28. The Origin of this Teaching

From where did the teachings contained in this text arise? The words found in this Upadesha arose from an immediate spontaneous inspiration, that is to say, from the creative potentiality of the intrinsic Awareness of the Primordial State of Samantabhadra (*kun bzang dgongs-pa*). This hidden treasure (*gter-ma*) is said to have been revealed by a Terton, or treasure revealer (*gter-ston*) who is none other than the Dharmakaya itself (*chos-sku'i gter-ston gyis*), and it has been brought forth from out of the vast expanse of wisdom (*shes-rab klong nas gter du blangs*) that was its place of concealment. Here the comparison is with a Terton discovering a Terma, or hidden treasure, in its place of concealment, and here *shes-rab* means wisdom as a higher intelligence. There are three kinds of wisdom: wisdom arising from hearing the teaching (*thos-pa'i shes-rab*), wisdom arising from reflecting upon the teaching (*bsam-pa'i shes-rab*), and wisdom arising in meditation (*bsgom-pa'i shes-rab*), where wisdom and meditation are inseparably linked together. This therefore is a higher and more exalted state of consciousness than ordinary intellectual activity. This means that the author did not just compose this text with his

intellect, as a scholar would write a well-reasoned philosophical treatise; but rather, it came to him from a higher source (the Dharmakaya,
"the wise and glorious king"). It therefore represents the creative
potentiality (*rig rtsal chos-sku*) of his innate Buddha-nature. In other
words, this text is a kind of *dgongs-gter*, or mind treasure.

There exist many kinds of hidden treasure texts, such as *sa-gter*,
"earth treasure," *chu gter*, "water treasure," *nam-mkha' gter*, "sky
treasure," *rmi-lam gter*, "dream treasure," and so on. But a treasure
text that arises spontaneously in the mind, deriving from some higher
spiritual source, usually Guru Padmasambhava in the Nyingmapa tradition, is known as a *dgongs-gter* or *thugs-gter*, "mind treasure." Patrul Rinpoche is speaking about such a higher state of
consciousness.

Then, speaking with due modesty, Patrul Rinpoche says that all
his doubts had been eliminated by the inerrant oral teachings of his
Guru (*bla-ma dam-pa'i zhal-lung nor-ba med-pa*), and he arranged these
instructions (*gdams-ngag*) in the commentary accordingly. However,
this text, both the root text and the commentary, is not any ordinary
treasure, such as might be obtained by extracting a precious ore from
the rocks of the earth (*sa rdo'i bcud*). Such treasures can buy worldly
things but not provide liberation. Even if we had a mound of gold as
big as the Meru mountain at the center of the world, still we could
only buy food, clothing, horses, and other goods and services. When
we die, we will not be able to take any of this wealth with us when
our consciousness (*rnam-shes*) leaves our physical body and we find
ourselves in the Bardo. But it is quite otherwise with this Upadesha.
It is a treasure we can take with us into the Bardo and into our future
lives until we attain enlightenment. It is like a panacea which can
cure all the ills of Samsara, or like the wish-granting gem of the gods,
and the philosophical stone of the alchemists.

This last testament (*zhal 'chems*) of Garab Dorje, or Prahevajra, was
revealed to his disciple Manjushrimitra at the time when the master
Garab Dorje, after dissolving his material body into space, reappeared
in the middle of a mass of light in the sky (*nam-mkha' 'od phung gi
dkyil nas*). At that time, a transmission simultaneously direct, symbolic, and oral occurred. This was the revelation of the Upadesha
where their two minds or states, that of the master and that of his
disciple, were inseparably united (*dgongs-pa dbyer-med du gyur-pa'i
man-ngag*).

29. The Author's Three Masters

Here again, at the conclusion, the view, the meditation, and the conduct are correlated with the three Lineage Gurus of the author, as they were in the prologue. The view encompasses all three essential points. The meditation is linked to wisdom (*mkhyen-pa*), meaning higher insight (*lhag-mthong*). Compassion or love (*brtse-ba*), which is established in the calm state (*zhi-gnas*), is linked to conduct, that is, to the general activities of all the Bodhisattvas or Jinaputras. The view is that of the omniscient Dharma king (*kun mkhyen chos kyi rgyal-po*) Longchen Rabjampa, who realized enlightenment fully with the realization of the fourth stage in the development of Thodgal vision, namely, the state in which all phenomena are exhausted or extinguished into the primordial purity of the ultimate Reality (*ka-dag chos zad kyi dgongs-pa mngon du gyur*). Here reference is made to the four stages of vision in Thodgal practice. (See the Interlinear Commentary below.) Longchenpa is said to have received in full the direct transmission of the Jinas (*rgyal-ba dgongs brgyud*).

Centuries later Longchenpa appeared to Jigmed Lingpa, otherwise known as Khyentse Odzer, in a Wisdom Body, or Jnanakaya (*ye-shes kyi sku*) and bestowed upon him in a pure vision (*dag snang*) his knowledge and blessings in the manner of a symbolic transmission of the Vidyadharas (*rig-'dzin brda brgyud kyi tshul du byin gyis brlabs*). He, in turn, bestowed the teachings upon Patrul Rinpoche's own Root Guru, Gyalwe Nyugu, by way of an oral transmission from mouth to ear (*zhal bas snyan du brgyud-pa*), and, as a result, he encountered the vision of visibly manifest Reality (*chos-nyid mngon sum du mjal*), the first stage of vision in Thodgal practice. Thus, this Upadesha is more precious than highly refined gold and represents the heart nectar of the three transmission lineages (*brgyud gsum thugs bcud*). It is the very essence of the mind (*snying thig*).

30. The Secrecy of the Teachings

The author, Patrul Rinpoche, is reluctant to reveal these teachings to those who do not practice, for they will not understand them. For this reason, the Dzogchen teachings are said to be "self-secret." Or, worse, they will totally misunderstand the teachings and take Dzogchen as a license for engaging in all kinds of selfish and heedless behavior. But, for those individuals who are sincerely interested, who would cherish these teachings, and who have the capacity to understand them, it would be wrong not to reveal them. "The sons of one's heart" (*snying gi bu*) mean a master's close disciples. What is written here represents the heartfelt advice (*snying gtam*) of the author. He urges that the essential point of the real meaning (*don gnad*), which is Rigpa, should not be allowed to disappear. But because it is something sacred and rare beyond price, it should not be profaned or spoken of openly in the marketplace, where people will not value it much and will mistake it for something commonplace.

It is the hope of the translator, Vajranatha, that the foregoing translation and the notes provided above, compiled from the oral instructions of his various Lama teachers, may contribute in some small way to the general understanding of the real meaning of Dzogchen.

SARVA MANGALAM

The Last Testament of Garab Dorje

The Last Testament of Garab Dorje: "The Three Statements That Strike the Essential Points"
from "The Posthumous Teachings of the Vidyadharas"

The Golden Letters:
Here is contained "The Four Posthumous Teachings of the Vidyadharas, together with an Addendum." §

(As for the first among these texts:)
Here is contained "The Three Statements That Strike the Essential Points," according to the master Prahevajra (Garab Dorje). §

NAMO GURUVE §
Homage to that confidence deriving from understanding one's own state of immediate intrinsic Awareness. §

PROLOGUE

This state of immediate intrinsic Awareness (called Rigpa) is uncreated and self-existing. Its mode of being represents the essence that is the Primordial Base. Everywhere the manner in which it arises in response to external appearances, which are themselves diverse, is uninterrupted and unobstructed. Moreover, everything, all the phenomena that appear and that exist, arise (spontaneously self-per-fected) within the field of the Dharmakaya. Whatever appearances may manifest therein are directly liberated after their arising due to the presence of one's own state of immediate Awareness (*rig-pa*). §

As to the real meaning of this: All of the enlightened states, which consist of nondual knowledge that is primordial awareness (*ye-shes*), present within the hearts of all the Sugatas (Buddhas) are, in fact, encompassed within this single unique state of immediate intrinsic Awareness (*rig-pa*) found within every individual sentient being.§

In order to inspire Manjushrimitra, who had fallen down sense-less upon the ground (when his master had dissolved his physical body into space at the end of his life), this Upadesha, or secret in-struction, consisting of "The Three Statements That Strike the Essen-tial Points," was revealed by the master Prahevajra (Garab Dorje). For the purpose of eliminating all concepts relating to both Samsara and Nirvana (in the mind of his disciple), that is to say, his believing that either of them are actually self-existent in their own terms, this exceedingly excellent and well-demonstrated last testament was re-vealed at the time of the master's death. It should be concealed and preserved within one's own innermost heart! §

A §

Indeed, this state of immediate intrinsic Awareness is beyond all conception (by the intellect), being something uncreated and uncon-ditioned. §

THE THREE STATEMENTS

ATI §

This Upadesha, which unhesitatingly reveals the state of immedi-ate intrinsic Awareness, which is the capacity of the Primordial Base or Dharmakaya, is as follows: §

"One is directly introduced to one's own real nature," that is to say, one is introduced directly and ultimately to one's own real face or nature that is intrinsic Awareness, the state of immediate pure presence (*rig-pa*). And, furthermore, its nature is revealed, in actual-ity, to be completely pure from the very beginning. It is just this state of immediate Awareness that is introduced here, in the same way, for example, that anger can be liberated by itself. §

"One directly decides upon this single unique state," that is to say, one discovers directly for oneself (in the midst of a multitude of diverse experiences) this single and unique state of intrinsic Awareness, wherein one is aware in every respect, without there being any sense of duality of subject and object remaining. ⁒

"One then directly continues with confidence in liberation," that is to say, one continues directly in the state of contemplation with full confidence in the automatic process of self-liberation (of whatever thoughts and appearances arise). And, because of that, one's own Awareness finds itself inherently liberated on its own (without any intervention by the discursive intellect or by anything outside of itself). ⁒

There exists no single sentient being who, in terms of the self-manifesting of this intrinsic Awareness, does not find him- or herself inherently liberated. One's own individual state of existence (or condition of interior awareness), on the one hand, and the states of other things in the outer world which are presented to one's consciousness as external appearances, on the other hand, come to encounter each other and become integrated. (This represents a direct immediate intuition without there being any duality of subject and object, a primordial awareness.) But, where this is not understood by the individual, then oneself and other things (the "I," which is one's own interior awareness, and the "others," which are external appearances) are perceived as arising in the dualistic fashion of interior subject and external object. ⁒

This single Upadesha, or secret instruction (given above) for self-liberation immediately and straightforwardly is unique (among all spiritual paths to enlightenment), and its contrary does not exist (in terms of efficacy). It alone is sufficient for liberation. ⁒

THE FIRST STATEMENT

ATI ⁒

Whatever may arise or appear to the individual as external phenomena is merely one's own state of existence that manifests externally as appearances. Apart from this organized and highly structured system of phenomena (which is conventionally called "reality"), nothing whatsoever exists and from it one cannot obtain anything (substantial or worthwhile). However, by virtue of the totality of its power or inherent potency (*rang rtsal*), since one's Awareness (*rig-pa*) is in harmony with the various different kinds of things that arise as phenomena, it allows these various different kinds of phenomena to liberate themselves. There exists no other antidote for them (these diverse phenomena) than this process of self-liberation. ⚬

In terms of this process, the phenomena that arise to consciousness immediately and directly come to encounter their own nature, as, for example, when people who have the same language meet together somewhere in a foreign country where a different language is spoken. Immediately they recognize and know each other; just as, in the same way, anger itself is liberated by being recognized as anger. ⚬

When searching for its Mother, which is its source or origin, the knowledge or cognition (*ye-shes*) of the vision or phenomena directly encounters its own Mother (emptiness) and self-liberates. That is to say, the vision is self-liberated by means of the vision, like melted butter dissolving into butter. And while searching for the Son, the Son itself, which is this cognition or knowledge, encounters itself directly. This Awareness itself is self-liberated by means of Awareness; just like water dissolving into water. When searching for the unique state (of Rigpa), one encounters only one's own unique state. That is to say, one's own nature (Rigpa) simply encounters itself. But its essence transcends all expression in words; like space dissolving into space, or like the three coils of a snake liberating themselves simultaneously. ⚬

This singular and unique state of intrinsic Awareness can only be found within oneself. If that is the case, then when one recognizes one's essence, everything is brought together in a single moment within which a cognition is present that does not go beyond the knowledge of that singular unique essence (which is Rigpa). This is like a man and a woman who are in love and who meet together secretly in solitude in order to make love. ⚬

This singular and unique state itself can only be found within oneself. Even though external appearances are diverse, there is still present a general knowledge or primal awareness in which these differences of diverse phenomena are self-liberated by means of encountering these very differences. This cognition or knowledge is like the case where, by cutting through the single principal knot made in a rope, one thereby cuts through all of the one hundred strands of rope. ⅜

This single liberation can only be found within oneself. Since this cognition or primal awareness (*ye-shes*) is self-manifested, it represents a primordial knowledge that cannot be obtained anywhere other than in oneself. Self-liberation is just that primal awareness itself. It is like entering into a single great city that lies at the end of one hundred or one thousand roads. (Here concludes the elaboration of the first essential point pertaining to the Base.) ⅜

THE SECOND STATEMENT

In this state of immediate intrinsic Awareness, one directly discovers for oneself that all of one's "final visions" are actually arising from out of oneself. (These final visions are the tiny spheres of rainbow light that arise in Thodgal practice.) In the same way, since one recognizes one's own nature by oneself, that is, one remains in the state of contemplation, then this intrinsic Awareness is without any duality with respect to ignorance (which is considered to be the absence of awareness). For example, even though a man may be called by many different names from different directions, nevertheless, he will still come when called. These many different names do not go beyond the single meaning which is the individual man himself. ⅜

In that unique state which is immediate intrinsic Awareness, one directly discovers that all of these visions of tiny spheres of rainbow light (*thig-le*), and so on, are, in actual fact, merely one's own self-manifestations. And in this state of liberation, one discovers no doubt. This state of contemplation is self-liberation in itself, for Awareness is liberated by means of Awareness. Similarly, through recognizing that this Awareness is merely one's own state of existence, then everything that one understands is liberated into its own natural condition. This is like meeting a person whom one has previously known after a long separation. (Here concludes the elaboration of the second statement pertaining to the Path that is the process of self-liberation.) ⅜

THE THIRD STATEMENT

One's confidence becomes like a treasure containing vast riches that represent one's own concrete personal experiences with respect to oneself, that is, in terms of one's own nature, which is intrinsic Awareness. All movements of thought become self-liberated into their own original condition. This is like possessing a great treasure containing whatever one could desire. §

Then, having concrete experiences with regard to other people and things that are external objects, one's confidence becomes like a king who is a Chakravartin, or a universal monarch. That is to say, the state of immediate present Awareness becomes manifestly visible (as tiny spheres of rainbow light, and so on). Since these photic phenomena are not created by anything other than oneself, one's intrinsic awareness is like a Chakravartin emperor who brings everyone in the four continents under his power. §

Furthermore, since one's awareness has the capacity to bring even the physical elements under its power, and since one becomes liberated by reason of this condition (that is, the realizing of the Body of Light), one is no longer dependent on any other faculty. And having such a concrete experience with respect to the state of liberation, one's confidence becomes like the experience of space dissolving into space. That is to say, one is totally self-confident because one finds that everything upon arising self-liberates effortlessly into its own original condition, that is, into the immaculate, primordially pure Dharmata (the nature of Reality). This situation is, indeed, like space dissolving into space, or like the clouds dissipating in the sky. §

Everything arising in one's own dimension is self-liberated directly into its own state. That is to say, everything self-liberates by itself without any effort or outside intervention. This is like cracking rocks with rocks, or like tempering iron with iron, or like purifying dirt with dirt. §

In this unique state of immediate Awareness, everything is liberated into this single understanding of the state of immediate intrinsic Awareness. This is like taking fire from fire, or like transferring water into water, or like adding melted butter to butter. Thus, the Mother (the Primordial State) and her Son (knowledge) become united. Because one's own Mother, as the origin or source, is just itself (and nothing else, existing in its own state of existence, and this being emptiness), one can say that emptiness itself is liberated by means of emptiness. Thus, one's individual presence or Awareness dissolves (at the time of the realization of the Body of Light) and becomes integrated into the vision itself. ⚬

Because one recognizes one's own native state to be intrinsic Awareness, one is directly introduced to the Base of all existence. That is to say, one recognizes the visions (in Thodgal practice) to be merely self-manifestations of one's own mind. This is like seeing one's own face reflected inside of a mirror. And because of that belief (or recognition), where one has already been directly introduced to the Base of existence, this situation is like the meeting of the mother and her son after a long separation. One recognizes this to be the unique state of liberation. Since the vision directly self-liberates into its own state by itself, the vision or phenomenon is discovered to be empty (lacking in any substantial reality), and its quality of clear luminosity is recognized to be nothing other than one's own state of immediate Awareness. ⚬

Because the vision or phenomenon is recognized to be self-liberated by itself, one discovers that it has, indeed, represented ignorance from the very beginning. That is to say, Samsara is known or recognized in itself (like holding up a mirror before another mirror, so it can see itself). And with respect to the transcending of Samsara, that condition which is known as the state of Nirvana, one recognizes that one has transcended Samsara, and so ignorance itself is self-liberated. And for that reason, an actual example would be the washing away of dirt with dirt. ⚬

Because of discovering for oneself the real meaning of one's own state of existence, which is intrinsic Awareness, discursive thoughts are spontaneously liberated by themselves. And in this way, one discovers that one is not dependent on any other antidote. Since the discursive thought is liberated into the Base itself, one continues in a state of immediate presence or contemplation, and does so with confidence. This is like pouring water into water, or like pouring melted butter into butter. ⚬

And because of continuing in the state of contemplation everywhere (in all of one's daily activities), this situation is like the coils of a snake being effortlessly liberated by the snake itself. But an intelligence or awareness that looks elsewhere than to itself (after failing to find what it seeks,) will fall again into despair. Because it is liberated directly by itself, this state of immediate Awareness is self-sustaining and self-abiding. For this reason, continuing directly in one's own state of intrinsic Awareness is the principal consideration. (Here concludes the third statement pertaining to the realization of the Fruit.) ⁑

CONCLUSION

At the time when Prahevajra (Garab Dorje) revealed the method for completely transcending the suffering of Samsara, Manjushrimitra fell down senseless, and, having fallen on the ground, he uttered a great lamentation, "O alas!" Thereupon Vetalakshema (Garab Dorje), from the middle of the light (a sphere of rainbow light suspended in the sky), manifested effulgently his symbolic form. For the sake of causing inspiration to arise in Manjushrimitra, who had fallen senseless to the ground previously, these three statements that strike the essential points, relating to the ultimate liberation of the individual, and contained in this secret last testament, were revealed by the master. This last testament descended from the sky into the palm of Manjushrimitra's right hand. The text was written in ink made from melted azure-colored vaidurya (lapis lazuli). The paper on which the text was written had been put inside a small vessel one full thumbnail in size, and this was placed within a casket of precious crystal. Upon receiving this, Manjushrimitra was liberated from his faint, and, comprehending the teaching, he became one who possessed the confidence of sure understanding. And for that reason, this Upadesha, or secret instruction, was concealed in the mandala of his heart and kept secret from others. Thus, the nectar of the transmission of these three statements, which were oral teachings received at the time of the death of the master, became in his heart effulgent and overflowing, and the real meaning of the view of Dzogchen was displayed in his heart like precious gold. ⁑

   This event occurred at the great cremation ground of Shitavana in India. Subsequently, this holy instruction, which was brought into visible manifestation at the source of the Dan-tig River, became the very path that brings relief from the suffering of Samsara for all sentient beings. This Upadesha, which brings about an instantaneous liberation into the pure field of Buddhahood, is here completed. ⸘

Translated by Vajranatha
Jamestown, Colorado
July 1987

Interlinear Commentary to "The Last Testament of Garab Dorje" by the Translator

TITLE OF THE COLLECTION

The Golden Letters:
Here is contained The Four Posthumous Teachings of the Vidyadharas, together with an Addendum. ༔

Here at the very beginning we are told that the text was originally written in golden letters (*gser yig-can*). According to Nyingthig tradition, the great Vidyadhara Vimalamitra compiled the essence of the Dzogchen Upadesha teachings into five series of texts: "The Golden Letters" (*gSer yig*), written in gold ink, "The Copper Letters" (*Zangs yig*), written in red ink, "The Variegated Letters" (*Khra yig*), written in inks of various colors, "The Conch Shell Letters" (*Dung yig*), written in white ink, and "The Turquoise Letters" (*gYu yig*), written in blue ink. Moreover, the text is punctuated throughout with the *gter-dzar*, ༔, indicating that it is a Terma (*gter-ma*), or rediscovered text.

The text we have here belongs to a collection of Terma texts known as the *'Das-rjes*, or "posthumous teachings," from *'das-pa*, "to pass away, to die," and *rjes*, "afterwards." The title of the collection reads in full *Rig-'dzin gyi 'das-rjes bzhi zhar-'byung dang bcas-pa*, "The Four Posthumous Teachings (*'das rjes*) of the Vidyadharas (*rig-'dzin*), together with an Addendum (*zhar-'byung*)." The four Vidyadharas in question are Prahevajra (Garab Dorje), Manjushrimitra, Shrisimha, and Jnanasutra, the earliest human masters of the Dzogchen lineage according to the Nyingmapas. The Sanskrit term *Vidyadhara* (*rig-'dzin*) in Tibetan, means one who possesses or has realized (*'dzin-pa*, Skt. *dhara*) the knowledge (*rig-pa*, Skt. *vidyā*) of the Primordial State. In the more general Indian context, both Hindu and Buddhist, the term means one who possesses esoteric knowledge. As we have said, the *'Das-rjes* is a Terma, or rediscovered treasure text, and it is now found in the *Bi-ma snying-thig* collection of Longchen Rabjampa (kLong-chen rab-'byams-pa, dri-med 'od-zer, 1308–1363), the great redactor and synthesizer of the earlier traditions of Dzogchen. These Dzogchen precepts found in the *Bi-ma snying-thig* are said to ultimately derive from the Dzogchen master and Mahapandita Vimalamitra (8th cen. CE). Longchenpa received them from his master Kumararaja (rig-'dzin Kumaradza, 1266–1343). Specifically, this text is contained within volume 6A: *rDo-rje 'chang gis gsungs-pa mchod 'os rang bzhin gyi tshig dus gnad nges-pa* (pp. 273–344). The *Bi-ma snying-thig* is one of four collections of old Dzogchen teachings found in Longchenpa's famous *sNying-thig ya-bzhi*, the others being the *mKha'-'gro'i snying-thig*, the *mKha'-'gro'i yang-thig*, and the *bLa-ma'i yang-thig*. Many of the Termas found here, especially the *mKha'-'gro'i snying-thig*, are associated with the name of Padma Letreltsal (Padma las-'brel rtsal, 1291–1315?). Longchenpa is considered to be his successor, or even his reincarnation.

With regard to the *'Das-rjes*, in each case the master in question attained the Body of Light at the time of his death, when he dissolved his gross physical body into the dimension of the space of the sky. And then, in response to the distress and lamentations of their respective chief disciples, each master remanifested himself in a sphere of rainbow light (*thig-le*) suspended in the sky, whereupon he delivered his last testament to his astonished disciple. Here in the *'Das-rjes* collection are found the posthumous teachings, delivered in the form of a last testament, of the following masters:

1. *Tshig gsum gnad du brdeg-pa*, "The Three Statements That Strike the Essential Points," of Prahevajra or Garab Dorje (dGa'-rab rdo-rje) (pp. 304–310);

2. *sGom nyams drug-pa*, "The Six Meditation Experiences," of Manjushrimitra ('Jam dpal bshes-gnyen) (pp. 310–318);

3. *gZer-bu bdun-pa*, "The Seven Important Points," of Shrisimha (dPal gyi seng-ge mgon-po) (pp. 318–325);
4. *bZhags-thabs bzhi*, "The Four Methods for Remaining in Contemplation," of Jnanasutra (Ye-shes mdo) (pp. 325–331).

The Addendum (*zhar-'byung*) (pp. 331–344) contains a text attributed to the master Vimalamitra (Dri-med bshes-gnyen), namely, the *mKhas-pa bimala'i zhal-'chems*, "The Last Testament of the Learned Master Vimalamitra." At the end of his life, however, this master did not dissolve into the sky, becoming a Body of Light, but it is said that after leaving Tibet he went to the holy five-peaked mountain of Wu-tai Shan in northern China, where he remained. It is claimed that he never died, but on the contrary, he realized the Rainbow Body of the Great Transfer (*'pho-ba chen-po'i 'ja'-lus*), that is, he became a Body of Light while still alive without the necessity of waiting for the moment of death. Thus, in the *'Das-rjes* we have all the early principal masters of Dzogchen from Uddiyana and India represented, save Guru Padmasambhava. According to the Nyingmapa tradition, this latter master, like Vimalamitra, also realized the Great Transfer. Here in this present book, we have presented the translation of the last testament of Garab Dorje; the other texts of the *'Das-rjes* have been translated elsewhere, and hopefully they also will be published in the future.

TITLE OF THE TEXT

Here is contained "The Three Statements That Strike the Essential Points," according to the master Prahevajra (Garab Dorje). ༔

The title of the first text in the *'Das-rjes* collection is the *Tshig gsum gnad du brdeg-pa*, "The Three Statements (*tshig gsum*) that Strike (*brdeg-pa*) the Essential Points (*gnad*)." The essential points here refer to the view, meditation, and conduct in relation to contemplation, as explained above by Patrul Rinpoche. The Sanskrit form of the master's name, Prahevajra (this form or possibly Prajnabhava Hevajra, is a likely possibility suggested by Tulku Thondup), is a reconstruction of the Tibetan translation *dGa' rab rdo-rje*, "the diamond of supreme bliss." The original Sanskrit form is nowhere attested so far in extant colophons.

INVOCATION

NAMO SHRI GURUVE ⁝

Homage to the confidence (deriving from) understanding one's own state of immediate intrinsic Awareness. ⁝

Namo shri guruve is Sanskrit for "Homage to the glorious master!" Then there follows an invocation or verse of offering (*mchod brjod*) that reads in Tibetan: *Rang rig rtogs-pa'i gdeng la phyag 'tshal-lo*, meaning "Homage (*phyag 'tshal*) to the confidence (*gdeng*) that derives from the understanding (*rtogs-pa*) of one's own (*rang*) state of immediate intrinsic Awareness (*rig-pa*)." Generally I translate *rig-pa* as Awareness or immediate intrinsic Awareness. *Rig-pa* is *vidyā* in Sanskrit, but in the Dzogchen context it has a very special meaning, as against that in the Sutra system, where it generally means "intelligence," as pointed out previously. I use a capital *A* to distinguish *rig-pa*, "Awareness," from *shes-pa*, "awareness, to be aware, to know something," and *shes-rig*, "an awareness that knows something, a knowing awareness." Confidence (*gdeng*) indicates the confidence that develops within the practitioner from having been introduced to Rigpa (*rig-pa ngo-sprod*), when, because of the repeated practice of contemplation, one no longer has any doubt with regard to it. See Patrul Rinpoche's commentary on the third statement above.

PROLOGUE

Line 1: **As for this state of immediate intrinsic Awareness, which is uncreated and which exists in itself [that is, its mode of being represents the essence that is the Base,] . . . ⁝**

This Rigpa, or immediate Awareness, is uncreated (*grub-pa med-pa*) and exists in itself (*yin-pa*); that is, according to the note (*mchan*), the manner of its being or existence (*gnas tshul*) represents the essence, which is the Base or Foundation (*gzhi yi ngo-bo*). The Base (*gzhi*) is the Primordial State (*kun bzang dgongs-pa*), which is the source and ground of both ordinary experience and of Buddha enlightenment. It is primordially pure because it is beyond time and conditioning; it has never been mixed up with or contaminated by Samsara. Rigpa, the state of immediate intrinsic Awareness, the state of pure presence, is the subject of this final teaching of the master Garab Dorje. It is the essential point.

In the translation of the text here, the words and phrases within brackets [ ] represent the translation of the notes, or *mchan*, found in the original Tibetan text. They are written in smaller Tibetan letters and were presumably added by the editor of the text. Without the addition of these notes, the text is exceedingly terse and obscure, like the notes taken by a student at a university lecture in order to refresh his or her memory. The material found within parentheses ( ) has been added by myself, the translator, in order to facilitate the understanding of the translation of the text, and this follows the oral commentary provided by Namkhai Norbu Rinpoche.

Line 2: **Everywhere the manner in which it arises [appearances being diverse] is uninterrupted (and unobstructed).** ‰

The way in which external appearances arise or manifest themselves (*snang 'char tshul*) to the consciousness of the individual is everywhere (*cir yang*) uninterrupted, unceasing, and unobstructed. Appearances (*snang-ba*), that is, whatever arises externally to our senses, are said to be diverse, whereas Rigpa is singular and unique. This is also indicated in the six vajra verses of the *Rig-pa'i khu-byug*. (See Part Three, "Historical Origins of Dzogchen.") Appearances represent the play of the creative energy or inexhaustible potentiality of Awareness (*rig-pa'i rtsal*). They are not "mind," as in the Chittamatrin view (*sems tsam*, "mind only"), but rather they are manifestations of mind (*sems kyi snang-ba*), something constructed by mind out of the raw material of sense data.

Line 3: **Moreover, everything [all the phenomena] that appear and that exist, arise (spontaneously self-perfected) within the field of the Dharmakaya.** ‰

The word "everything" (*kun, thams-cad*) refers to all phenomenal existence (*snang srid*), and when this second term is analyzed it stands for "whatever appears (*snang-ba*) and whatever exists (*srid-pa*)." "Everything" means all phenomena (*chos kun*), and all of these phenomena (Skt. *dharmas*) arise or present themselves within the space or the field of the Dharmakaya (*chos-sku'i zhing du shar*). The Dharmakaya, the dimension of all existence, is the context of all dharmas or phenomena. Thus, it may be compared to the infinite space of the sky, since it is all-pervading (*kun-khyab*) and without boundaries or limits (*mtha' bral*). The arising of interior thoughts and the arising of external appearances may be compared to the clouds visible in the sky. The space (*nam-mkha'*) or dimension (*dbyings*) or expanse (*klong*) of the Dharmakaya provides room for all possible manifestations of phenomena to arise without obstruction. Thus, the literal significance of Dharmakaya (*chos-sku*) is not "body," such as "Truth Body" or "Law Body," as some would translate it, but the dimension (*sku*, Skt. *kāya*) of all existence (*chos*, Skt. *dharma*). Dharma is what exists, that is, "reality"; and, therefore, it is also the teaching about what really exists. The term *kāya* (*sku*) means not only "body" in the ordinary physical sense, but the entire manifest dimension of the individual. The physical body is, of course, the central locus of that dimension, but this body does not just stop at the skin. It represents not so much a static form, like a statue, but a dynamic relationship between the individual and one's environment. In terms of the Trikaya, "the Three Bodies of the Buddha," the Nirmanakaya is more related to one's physical existence, the Sambhogakaya to the dimension of energy of the individual manifesting as light, and the Dharmakaya to the dimension of the nature of mind. Among these three, the Dharmakaya is the ground of all-existence, the dimension encompassing the arising and the dissolution of all phenomena, even of all universes. The word *arise* (*shar-ba*) means "to appear," "to manifest," or "to present itself."

Line 4: **That which arises (or manifests) therein is liberated directly due to one's own [state of immediate Awareness (*rig-pa*)].** ⸸

That which arises or manifests (*shar-ba de nyid*) within the dimension or context of the Dharmakaya is liberated directly (*thog tu grol*) and immediately by virtue of the practitioner's remaining in the state of contemplation, that is to say, by one's continuing in one's own (*rang gi*) state of intrinsic Awareness (*rig-pa nyid*). However, the thoughts that arise when the individual is in a state of ignorance or lack of awareness (*ma rig-pa*) do not liberate by themselves. Rather, one follows them and becomes attached and tangled up in them. But when Rigpa is wholly present and when there is no interference or intervention by the discursive thoughts or by the functional mind (*yid*), the phenomena that present themselves are immediately liberated into their own original condition, which is emptiness, leaving no traces behind, like clouds dissipating in the sky. This is the process of self-liberation, which represents the practice specific to Dzogchen.

Line 5: **As for the real meaning of this: [All of] the states [consisting of the nondual gnosis or knowledge (which is primordial awareness) present in the hearts] of all of the Sugatas are encompassed within this (single unique state of immediate intrinsic Awareness found within every individual sentient being).** §

Next the text addresses the real meaning (*don*) of what was said above. *Sugata* (*bde-bar gshegs-pa*), literally, "well gone" or "one into happiness," is a title of the Buddha. The text speaks of the Primordial States (*dgongs-pa*) present in the hearts (*thugs*) or "Minds" of all of the Buddhas of the three times of past, present, and future. This Primordial State manifests a nondual gnosis or knowledge (*gnyis su med-pa'i ye-shes*, Skt. *advaya-jñāna*) as primordial awareness. It is nondual because it is prior to and transcends the dichotomy of subject and object (*gzung 'dzin*) which besets all operations of mind. (For the discussion of translating *jñāna* or *ye-shes* as "gnosis," see my commentary on the Patrul Rinpoche text.) The potentiality for all possible varieties of knowledge is found within this single and unique state of Rigpa, just as a mirror possesses the potentiality to reflect all possible reflections. This mirror is the Dharmakaya residing within the hearts of all the enlightened Buddhas; and it resides within the hearts of all unenlightened sentient beings as well. It is present in both the enlightened and the unenlightened as the nature of mind (*sems-nyid*). However, a "mirror" is merely a metaphor, because a mirror is a two-dimensional surface, whereas the Dharmakaya possesses dimensions without limit, for it is the source and matrix of all possible manifestations. As a better example, one could speak of a crystalline holographic mirror possessing infinite reflective surfaces, like the fabulous Indrajala, or "net of Indra."

Line 6: **In order to inspire [Manjushimitra], who had fallen down senseless (upon the ground), this Upadesha (or secret instruction) consisting of "The Three Statements That Strike the Essential Points" (was revealed by the master known as Prahevajra or Garab Dorje).** §

With the vanishing of his beloved master, who had dissolved (*yal-ba*) his physical body into the empty space of the sky upon realizing the Body of Light (*'od lus*), Manjushrimitra fell into a faint (*brgyal-ba bslang*). When he regained consciousness, his master was again visible, but now in the guise of a young child sitting in the middle of a sphere of rainbow light (*thig-le*). At that moment, the master presented to his heart-son (*thugs-sras*), or chief disciple, his last testament in the form of an Upadesha (*man-ngag*), or secret instruction. (For the life of Garab Dorje, see Part Two).

Line 7: **For the purpose of eliminating all concepts relating to these two, Samsara and Nirvana [that is to say, believing either of them actually to be self-existing (in their own terms)] ...** ⁑

The text speaks of eliminating or cutting off all concepts relating to Samsara and Nirvana (*'khor 'das gnyis kyi rdos thag-bcad*), that is, all concepts regarding belief in the reality of these two as self-existing entities or objective realities (*gnyis-ka rang yin-par shes-pa*).

Line 8: **[This exceedingly excellent and well demonstrated] last testament, given out at the time of his death, should be well concealed (and preserved) in one's own innermost heart!** ⁑

This Upadesha should be concealed within one's innermost heart (*dkyil du sbos*); the exhortation is addressed to the listener or reader.

Line 9: *A* ⁑ **[Indeed, it (this state of immediate intrinsic Awareness) is beyond all conception (by the intellect), being something uncreated (and unconditioned)].** ⁑

The note in the text informs us that Rigpa is beyond concepts (*la bzla-ba*) and is something uncreated (*skye med*). It is not produced by the mind as thoughts are. This uncreated Primordial State is the significance of the syllable *A*. *A* is the source of all sound and communication since, according to Sanskrit phonology, this sound accompanies the articulation of every vowel and consonant. Fixation on the white Tibetan letter *A* is an important practice in Dzogchen. In the Tantra system, *A* is the symbol of the state of shunyata, the source of all phenomena and the matrix of all existence. It is the seed-syllable of the Great Goddess, Prajnaparamita. Now the prologue is completed, and we come to the Three Statements proper.

THE THREE STATEMENTS

Line 10: ATI ⁑ **As for this Upadesha, which unhesitatingly reveals the state of immediate intrinsic Awareness (and which represents the capacity of the Primordial State, it is as follows:)** ⁑

The Dzogchen teachings are also known as Atiyoga, where *ati* may be interpreted to mean "primordial" (*gdod-ma*, Skt. *ādi*). Often in Dzogchen texts, the term *ati*, left untranslated, is used as an abbreviation for Atiyoga. This Upadesha is unhesitatingly revealed (*spyi brtol du bstan-pa'i man-ngag*) to the disciple, and here once more it is indicated that the subject matter of the entire teaching is Rigpa.

Line 11: **One is directly introduced to one's own real nature, [to one's own real nature as being Awareness, which is revealed to be completely pure; and it is just this state of immediate presence (*rig-pa*) that is introduced here, in the same way that anger can be liberated by itself].** §

The first statement of Garab Dorje reads *ngo rang thog tu sprad-pa*, "one is directly (*thog tu*) introduced (*ngo-sprad-pa*) to one's own (*rang*) face or nature (*ngo*)," and one's own real nature (*rang ngo*) is precisely this state of immediate Awareness called Rigpa. (See the autocommentary by Patrul Rinpoche.) Here the introduction is accomplished in the same way that anger is self-liberated (*zhe-sdang nyid kyis grol-ba*). An intense passion like anger (*zhe-sdang*) will dissolve of its own accord into its own original condition of emptiness, if there is no interference from the mind.

Line 12: **One directly decides upon this single unique state [(that is to say, one discovers for oneself) this intrinsic Awareness (*rig-pa*) which is aware without there being in it any duality (of subject and object)].** §

This second statement of Garab Dorje reads *thag gcig thog tu bcad*, "one discovers (*thag-bcad*) directly (*thog tu*) this single (state) (*gcig*)." (On this statement, see Patrul Rinpoche's auto-commentary.)

Line 13: **One (then) directly continues with confidence in (self-)liberation [and because of that, one's own Awareness (finds itself) inherently liberated on its own.]** §

The third statement reads *gdeng grol thog-tu bca'*, "one directly continues (*thog tu bca'*) with confidence (*gdeng*) in liberation (*grol*)." (On this also, see Patrul Rinpoche's auto-commentary.)

Line 14: **One's own state of existence, [there being no single sentient being who, in the self-manifesting (of his or her intrinsic Awareness) does not find him- or herself (inherently) liberated],** and the states of other things (animate and inanimate, in the outer world), which present themselves as external appearances, encounter (each other) and become integrated. [But where this is not understood, oneself and others (the "I," which is interior awareness, and the "others," which are external appearances, are seen to) arise in a dualistic manner (as subject and object).] §

Here a further explanation is given. The individual's own state of existence (*rang ngo yin-pa*) means interior Awareness (*nang rig-pa*). Strictly speaking, this interior Awareness (*nang rig-pa*) exists prior to consciousness (*rnam-shes*) because the operation of consciousness, as defined in Buddhist psychology, is always dualistic, the dichotomy between internal subject and external object having come into play. This consciousness represents a discursive (*rnam-par*) awareness (*shes-pa*). But Rigpa is inherently liberated; thus there is no single sentient being who, in the self-manifesting of this awareness, does not find him- or herself liberated (*sems-can rang-snang du ma grol-ba gcig kyang med*). Self-manifestation (*rang-snang*) means that something appears or comes into manifestation without an antecedent cause. Its opposite is *gzhan-snang*, a manifestation or appearance due to something else. This state of self-manifested internal awareness is in contrast to the states of other things, both animate and inanimate, which present themselves to awareness as external appearances (*gzhan ngo snang tshul*) in the outer world.

The text here is speaking in the context of contemplation, rather than ordinary discursive consciousness (*rnam-shes*). In the state of contemplation, these two, internal awareness and external appearance, encounter each other, in one way or another, depending on the physical construction of the sense organs, and they become integrated (*gnyis 'dres-pa . . . 'phrad-pa*). But where this process is not understood, internal awareness and external appearances arise by way of the duality of subject and object (*ma rtogs-pa la rang gzhan gnyis su byung*).

Line 15: [This single Upadesha (or secret instruction) for directly self-liberating (thoughts and appearances) is unique, and the contrary does not exist; it alone is sufficient (for liberation).] §

THE FIRST STATEMENT

Line 16: ATI ⸽ Whatever may arise or appear (as external phenomena), is merely one's own state of existence (that manifests). [Apart from this organized and structured system of phenomena, which (in fact) does not exist (in reality), one can obtain nothing.] By virtue of the totality of its inherent (capacity or) power, [since it (Rigpa or Awareness) is in harmony with the various different kinds of things (that arise), it allows various different kinds (of phenomena) to liberate (of themselves), and, therefore, there exists no other antidote.] ⸽

Now the three statements are dealt with in a bit more detail, beginning with the first, direct introduction (*ngo-sprod-pa*). In the following elaboration of the three statements, the presentation involves the viewpoints of both Thekchod and Thodgal. These standpoints are integrated and treated together, rather than being treated separately, as is the case in the later Terma tradition. As an example of the latter, see Jigmed Lingpa's famous *Khrid-yig ye-shes bla-ma*, which I have translated elsewhere, where Rushans, Thekchod, Thodgal, and Bardo are treated separately.

Whatever may arise, appearing as external phenomena to the individual, is merely one's own internal state of existence manifesting externally (*cir snang rang yin*), that is to say, it is merely the potentiality or creative energy of Awareness (*rig-pa'i rtsal*) becoming visible to the individual. Apart from this organized system of phenomena, nothing exists in reality (*ma yin-pa'i chos lugs*). It is merely the projection of one's potentiality of Awareness (*rig-pa'i rtsal*), and one will find, after exhaustive investigation, nothing solid, substantial, or real in it. There are no noumena, things-in-themselves, that are real or exist inherently, lying somewhere behind the visible facade of phenomena. These phenomena spontaneously manifest in empty space like a cinema projection or a hologram. The manifestation of phenomena is a projection of the energy (*rtsal*) of the mind, a phantom show projected into space; but the vast expanse of space (*klong*) is, in itself, empty and unlimited. The manifestation of phenomena is like the sunlight being refracted through a clear crystal which then appears as rainbows on the walls of the room. Nevertheless, the mind (*yid*) does possess the inherent capacity to organize and structure these photic and sensory experiences, and so the text speaks of an organized system of phenomena (*chos lugs*); but this structure, although one erroneously mistakes it for an objective reality, in fact has no inherent existence. It is not something independent of mind, but on the other hand, neither is it just made up of mind in the sense of a solipsistic fantasy. Rather, there is a distinct process at work here involving secondary causes and conditions on the side of ignorance. Only on the side of enlightenment is intrinsic freedom realized.

The Clear Light of the Dharmakaya has abided in the heart of the individual from the very beginning. The heart (*tsit ta*) may be compared to a magic lantern, an early type of cinema projector. All possible images exist potentially in the primordial light of intrinsic Awareness. Then the light, as the energy of Awareness, is channeled through the Kati nerve to the eyes; the latter serve as the twin lenses of the projector, and the images are projected out into space as holograms or three-dimensional images. These images in their nature are ultimately empty and insubstantial, but they possess, at the relative level, a kind of apparitional, almost magical, reality (*rdzu-'phrul*), much in the same fashion as a mirage in the desert or a conjurer's trick in a stage show. The apparition looks and seems real, but it is not. We are not speaking of "mind only" (*sems-tsam*) here, the doctrine of Chittamatra, but of the activity and capacity of energy (*rtsal*). These images or appearances projected into space are not mind, but manifestations of mind (*sems kyi snang-ba*). Yet these manifestations are not independent of mind. If the mind and the senses have been purified, then the individual will perceive the world with pure vision (*dag snang*); one will perceive it as the pure dimension of the mandala. But if the mind, one's internal awareness, is still covered with layers of obscuration, these obscurations will distort one's vision and one will perceive the world with impure karmic vision (*ma dag las snang*); one will perceive the world as an ordinary ignorant sentient being does, a being who lives within the dimensions of the six destinies of rebirth. Thus, in Dzogchen, it is not a case of transforming one kind of vision into another, as the practitioner does in Tantra. Rather, one purifies oneself by entering into the state of contemplation, which lies beyond all karmic conditioning, and then vision manifests spontaneously. That is why one must thoroughly master Thekchod before practicing Thodgal. Otherwise, because of heavy karmic habits inherited from the immemorial past, a time without beginning, impure karmic visions will reappear and one will find oneself caught up once more in the cycles of Samsara.

By virtue of its own inherent capacity or power (*stobs rang gis*), Awareness, that is, one's own natural state of existence (*yin-lugs*), facilitates the arising of these various kinds of appearances that then liberate of themselves, because Awareness is in harmony with their nature and not in opposition to it. Appearances and Awareness come to exist in a state of happy integration, so that liberation is inherent and spontaneous. Therefore, no other antidote exists (*gnyen-po gzhan med-pa*) or is needed. This is in contrast to the meditation practices of the Sutra system, which frequently employ antidotes. Such antidotes represent the working of the mind. But in Dzogchen, the practitioner of meditation does not try to block thoughts or invoke antidotes against them. Dzogchen is like a homeopathic, rather than an allopathic, therapeutic process. The state of immediate present Awareness is the sole antidote, the universal panacea. In the state of contemplation, everything is integrated with this presence of Awareness, so the consideration is not that of the Two Truths, the Relative Truth and the Absolute Truth, as in the Sutra system. There is only the single truth, the Primordial State where appearances and emptiness are inseparable (*snang stong dbyer-med*).

Line 17: **(Rather a phenomenon) comes to encounter its own self (or face) directly [as, for example, when people who have the same (native) language meet (each other) somewhere in a (foreign) country where a different language is spoken, and (immediately they recognize and) know each other; just as, in the same way, anger (itself) is liberated by being recognized as anger].** $\frac{8}{8}$

Here again the text makes reference to the practice of Thodgal (see below, line 30). These visions (*snang-ba*), whether they represent pure vision (Nirvana) or impure karmic vision (Samsara), are visible manifestations of the energy of the state of Awareness (*rig-pa'i rtsal*). Thus, in the state of contemplation these visions or phenomena, just being themselves and nothing else, come to encounter themselves (*rang rang phrad-pa*), like seeing one's face in a mirror, or like two people from the same place meeting by chance in a foreign country. They immediately recognize each other (*rang du ngo-shes-pa*). This is the moment of self-recognition, and in that moment, they self-liberate. Rigpa is the mirror of awareness held up to all things, so that everywhere, under all circumstances, in each event that occurs, there exists this self-recognition. This is like the great net of Indra made of chains of linked mirrors, where every mirror reflects every other mirror. In Indian mythology, it is said that Indra, the king of the Devas, had the divine artisan Vishvakarman construct such a net of mirrors for his celestial palace of Vijayanti atop the central cosmic mountain of Sumeru. In this Indrajala, or net of Indra, every event that occurs in the universe reflects every other event. In Dzogchen, however, Rigpa is single, and cognitions (*ye-shes*) multiply without limit.

As this applies to the arising of external appearances (*phyi snang*), so it equally applies to the arising of internal thoughts (*nang rtog*), such as the passions. Thus, the passion of anger is itself liberated by being recognized as anger (*zhe-sdang dus shes-pas grol*). In the mirror of Awareness, anger recognizes itself as anger, and its energy immediately dissolves. Here the method is *gcer-grol*, liberation through bare attention or recognition. (See Patrul Rinpoche's auto-commentary.)

Line 18: **(When searching for its) Mother (which is its source or origin), the cognition (the knowledge of the vision or phenomena) directly encounters its own Mother, [(that is to say,) the vision itself is (self-)liberated by means of the vision; like melted butter dissolving into butter.]** ⚬

When searching for its Mother (*ma*), the light-source that has given birth to it, the cognition (*ye-shes*, knowledge) of the vision (or phenomena) directly encounters its own Mother (*ma thog tu ma rang phrad-pa*), which is the Primordial State of the Clear Light of the Base (*gzhi*). It is like a sunbeam meeting the sun, like light (*ye-shes*) merging into light (*'od gsal*). All visible phenomena liberate in this light of Awareness. So, the vision itself is self-liberated by means of the vision (*snang-ba nyid snang-bas grol*). It is only by first looking at one's own reflection in the mirror that one discovers the mirror.

Line 19: **(Searching for the Son,) the Son (which is this cognition or primal awareness) encounters itself directly.** ⚬

The Son (*bu*), which is the individual cognition or primary awareness (*ye-shes*) of some sense phenomena existing prior to the mind (*yid*) coming into operation, stands naked in the presence of contemplation, the state of Rigpa. It is like seeing oneself reflected in a mirror. This mirror is the Mother (*ma*), the Bodhichitta or Primordial State of enlightenment. The Son (*bu*) is a cognition, an individual moment of primary awareness or knowledge. For the individual, there exist many such cognitions, but all of them are the children of a single Mother. There are many cognitions and only one Rigpa, but their nature is the same.

Line 20: [**Awareness itself is (self-)liberated by means of Awareness, like water dissolving into water.**] $\frac{8}{8}$

Line 21: (**When searching for) this unique state, one encounters one's own unique state.** $\frac{8}{8}$

When searching for this unique state (*gcig*) which is Rigpa, one encounters the unique state directly (*gcig thog tu rang phrad-pa*). This is the case when one discovers the unique state of Awareness in a multitude of various different experiences.

Line 22: [**One's own nature (simply) encounters itself; but its essence transcends all expression (in words); it is like space dissolving into space or like the three coils of a snake liberating themselves spontaneously.**] $\frac{8}{8}$

One's own nature or face (*rang ngo*) encounters or meets itself (*rang ngo rang du phrad-pa*). When one comes face to face with oneself, it is like looking at oneself in a mirror and then discovering that one is the mirror itself. This is one's essence (*ngo-bo*), which is the state of emptiness, corresponding to the nature of the mirror, and this essence transcends all expression in words (*brjod las 'das-pa*). This experience of integration is like space dissolving into space (*nam-mkha' la nam-mkha' thim-pa lta-bu*). The internal space (*nang dbyings*) of interior Awareness (*nang rig-pa*) and external space (*phyi dbyings*), which is the dimension in which appearances or visions (*snang-ba*) manifest, integrate, and are realized to be identical. For example, when the clay pot is broken, there are no longer two spaces, the space inside the pot and the space outside the pot, but only one space or dimension (*dbyings*). Yet space has in no way been changed or modified. The clay pot represents the skandhas (*phung-po lnga*), the individual's embodied or limited existence due to personal karma. This process of self-liberation may be compared to the three coils of a snake freeing themselves simultaneously (*sbrul gyi mdud gsum dus gcig la grol-ba lta-bu*).

Line 23: **This singular and unique state of immediate Awareness can only be found within oneself.** ⁸⁄₈

The unique state of Rigpa (*rig-pa gcig-pu*) is only found within oneself, literally, "connected with oneself" (*rang dang 'brel-ba*).

Line 24: **If it is like that, then when one knows (or recognizes one's own essence), everything is brought together simultaneously in a single moment, wherein there is present a primary awareness (or cognition) which does not go beyond (this knowledge of) that singular unique essence. [This is like a man and a woman who are in love and who meet together (secretly) in solitude (in order to make love).]** ⁸⁄₈

The essence (*ngo-bo*) is shunyata, or emptiness, the condition of the nature of the mirror. If one knows or recognizes one's essence (*rang gi ngo-bo shes na*), that is to say, if one knows that one is the mirror, then everything comes together simultaneously at one single moment (*dus gcig la thams-cad 'dus*). In this condition, one transcends time, for time is something created by the mind and exists only in terms of the reflections, not in the condition of the mirror itself. This timeless condition is a fourth time beyond the three times of past, present, and future; it is the "great time" that is the context or dimension containing these three times simultaneously. In this condition of being the mirror and not the reflections, there is continuously present a cognition or primal awareness (*ye-shes*) that does not go beyond knowing just that unique and singular essence (*ngo-bo gcig las ma 'das-pa'i ye-shes*). By discovering just this one single experience of the state of immediate Awareness (*rig-pa*), one discovers the entire universe. By knowing just one single phenomenon, or dharma, where Rigpa is present, then one knows all dharmas. To know this one thing is to know all things. Although phenomena are infinitely diverse, this state of immediate Awareness is singular. It is a single mirror that reflects all events. There is no other unique cognition; it is *rig-pa'i ye-shes*, the knowledge of the state of immediate intrinsic Awareness. And this is like two lovers coming to meet together in secret.

Line 25: **This singular and unique state itself can only be found within oneself.** ⁸₈

This singular unique state (*rang gcig-pu*) means *rig-pa'i ye-shes*, the knowledge of the state of Awareness.

Line 26: **Even though appearances are diverse, there is still present a general knowledge, or primal awareness, wherein these differences themselves (the diverse phenomena) are (self-)liberated by means of these very differences. [(Such a cognition) is like cutting through the single principal knot (made in a rope), and thereby cutting through all one hundred strands in the rope.]** ⁸₈

External appearances are infinitely diverse (*sna-tshogs su snang yang*), but Rigpa is unique, a singularity. It is a general knowledge or primal awareness (*ye-shes spyi*) where these diverse phenomena are self-liberated by means of their very arising as different phenomena (*tha-dad nyid tha-dad nyid kyis grol-ba'i ye-shes spyi*). Rigpa is the sword that instantly cuts through the Gordian knot of appearances.

Line 27: **This single liberation can only be found within oneself.** ⁸₈

Line 28: **[Since (this cognition) is self-manifested, it is a knowledge or primal awareness which cannot be obtained elsewhere (other than within oneself). (Self-liberation) is just that primal awareness itself.]** ⁸₈

This single mode of liberation (*grol-ba gcig-pu*) is found only within oneself. This knowledge of the state of Awareness (*rig-pa'i ye-shes*) is self-manifested (*rang snang*); it is a primordial awareness that is not found elsewhere outside oneself (*gzhan du mi rnyed-pa'i ye-shes*).

Line 29: **[For example, it is like entering into a single great city which lies at the end of one hundred or one thousand roads.]** ⁸₈

All the different spiritual paths belonging to the different vehicles to enlightenment converge upon the same goal; all roads lead to this city of liberation (*grol-ba'i grong-khyer*) which is the Kingdom. Thus we are introduced to our own nature, which is intrinsic Awareness, and here concludes the first statement.

THE SECOND STATEMENT

Line 30: **(In the state of immediate Awareness) one directly discovers that all of one's final visions (that is to say, the tiny spheres of rainbow light one sees in practice) are actually arising from within oneself. ꛷**

The first statement is primarily concerned with the Base, this being the province of Thekchod, but in the second statement the emphasis is now on the Path, which is represented by the practice of Thodgal. One's "final visions," or "what appears finally" (*mthar snang*), are the tiny spheres of rainbow light (*thig-le*, Skt. *bindu*), often strung together in vajra chains (*rdo-rje lu-gu-rgyud*) and in other patterns, that appear to one's vision spontaneously during Thodgal practice. It is these visions of the *thig-le* that are developed in the four stages of vision (*snang-ba bzhi*) that represent the culmination of the path. Beyond the stages of vision is the attainment of the Rainbow Body of Light. For this reason they are called final (*mtha'*) visions (*snang*). The practice of contemplation is always integrated with these four stages of vision:

1. the vision of the direct perception of Reality (*chos nyid mngon-sum kyi snang-ba*),
2. the vision of the developing of experiences (*nyams gong 'phel gyi snang-ba*),
3. the vision of the increasing to the full measure of Awareness (*rig-pa tshad phebs kyi snang-ba*),
4. the vision of the consummation or exhausting of Reality (*chos nyid zad-pa'i snang-ba*).

In doing the Thodgal practice with sunlight, the *thig-le*, or tiny spheres of rainbow light, manifest in the first stage above. In one's own natural state (*rang thog tu*) as practitioners, that is, in the state of contemplation, one definitively determines (*thag-bcad*) that these final visions of the *thig-le*, and so on, actually originate within oneself, although they appear in external space as projections. They are manifestations of one's own potentiality or inner light.

Everything that arises as manifest phenomena, consisting of sounds, lights, and rays (*sgra 'od zer gsum*), whether as pure vision or as impure karmic vision, is part of one's own potentiality (*rang rtsal*), the manifesting of the energy of one's intrinsic Awareness (*rig-pa'i rtsal*) in external space (*phyi dbyings*). This energy, in the form of light, originates in the heart of the individual. That is to say, the inherent clear luminosity or self-radiance (*rang gsal*) of one's own Primordial State, although all-pervasive in the physical body, primarily resides in the physical heart (*tsit ta*). From the interior space or hollow within the heart, this inner light (*nang 'od*, Skt. *antarajyotih*) proceeds upward through a translucent channel called the Kati, or smooth white nerve (*dkar 'jam rtsa*), and then exits the body by way of the gateway of the physical eyes. This internal luminosity, projected outside the heart, manifests in external space as something apparently real and substantial, like a cinema show projected onto a great screen surrounding the individual on all sides. One then becomes lost in the fascinating display of that show, as if one were caught up in a dream where everything seems objective, solid, and real. However, the screen onto which this phantom show is projected is not some solid wall, but consists only of empty space, the dimension of all existence. Everything perceived within this open dimension is but the light show of Awareness, much like a holographic projection. The individual, ignorant of the true nature of what he or she sees as the outer world, wanders about in circles, becoming lost in this projection like finding oneself in a labyrinth that has no exit. Thus, one comes to live in one's projections and not in their source. This process of projection (*'phro-ba*) is described in terms of six lights or lamps (*sgron-ma drug*):

1. the lamp of the dimension of Awareness (*rig-pa dbyings kyi sgron-ma*),
2. the lamp of the flesh-like heart (*tsit ta sha'i sgron-ma*),
3. the lamp of the smooth white nerve (*dkar 'jam rtsa'i sgron-ma*),
4. the lamp of the water (globelike eye) that lassos everything at a distance (*rgyang zhags chu'i sgron-ma*),
5. the lamp of the empty tiny spheres of light (*thig-le stong-pa'i sgron-ma*), and
6. the lamp of self-originated wisdom (*shes-rab rang-byung gi sgron-ma*).

Thus, what seems to manifest outside of the individual in external space (*phyi dbyings*) is actually what exists within oneself in the internal space (*nang dbyings*) of the individual. In Thodgal practice, one discovers that the self-originated inner light of the dimension of Awareness resides in the hollow of the physical heart, much like a flaming lamp inside of a hollow vase. This light proceeds up the translucent channel and is projected through the eyes into external space. This light then manifests as tiny spheres of light (*thig-le*) or as vajra chains (*rdo-rje lu-gu-rgyud*), and so on. With continued practice, the spaces inside of these empty tiny spheres open up and develop spontaneously like fractals, and eventually one comes to see visions inside of them that eventually include visions of Buddhas and Buddha realms. Thus, one speaks of six lamps (*sgron-ma drug*). If one has purified one's obscurations and karmic propensities by way of the practice of contemplation, then the visions will be pure (*dag snang*) and one will behold the pure Buddha fields within these tiny rainbow spheres of light in external space. But if the mind is still obscured, then the visions will continue to be the impure karmic vision of the six destinies of rebirth. It must be understood that Thodgal is not a process of transformation (*sgyur-ba*), of transforming the impure into the pure by way of the visualization process employed in the tantric sadhana. Visualization is work done by the mind, whereas the practitioner of Thodgal finds him- or herself in contemplation, a state that is beyond the mind. The visions (*snang-ba*) arise spontaneously and effortlessly of their own accord, whether the Yogin practices with sunlight, or with the clear empty sky, or with the total darkness of the dark retreat. In this way the external space of the sky, where the *thig-le* and other photic phenomena appear, and the internal space of Awareness become integrated. In the end, the clay pot is shattered, and there is no difference between the inner space contained within and the outer space that surrounds it. But one must understand that these photic phenomena and visions that spontaneously manifest in the sky are only projections into external space of one's own primordial inner light. The purpose of this Thodgal practice is to integrate with this light, which, although it seemingly manifests externally to the individual, is really internal. This light represents the inherent translucent radiance (*rang gdangs*) of one's own Primordial State, the Clear Light of the Base, here manifesting as the Clear Light of the Path.

But before one can practice Thodgal, one must first purify the twofold obscurations and master the state of contemplation through Thekchod practice, a releasing or a cutting through of all one's tensions and rigidities. If one does not first perfect Thekchod as an absolutely necessary prerequisite, then the Thodgal practice will be little better than watching a cinema show. Although one practices Thodgal not in the state of ordinary consciousness but in the state of contemplation, there is nevertheless the ever-present danger that one will become attached to the visions that arise. In that case, the individual again falls into the dreamworld of Samsara and gets caught up once more in transmigration. Even though the ultimate goal of Thodgal is the realization of the Rainbow Body of Light ('ja'-lus), which takes the individual beyond Samsara, its practice is also an excellent preparation for the after-death experiences of the Bardo, where visions spontaneously manifest to one's disembodied consciousness. These visions are the results of past karmic traces (bag-chags). Becoming caught up once more in these labyrinthine visions, one goes on to a future rebirth in a new embodiment. But also here, there exists the possibility for liberation by way of recognizing the Clear Light of one's own Primordial State.

Line 31: **Similarly, since one recognizes one's own nature by oneself (that is, one remains in the state of contemplation), then it (this Awareness) is without any duality with regard to ignorance (which is considered to be the absence of Awareness). For example, even though a man may be called from different directions by many different names, nevertheless, he will still come (when called); and these (many different names) do not go beyond the single meaning (which is the individual himself).** ⁸₈

By remaining in the state of contemplation (*rig-pa*), one comes to recognize one's own nature (*rang gis nang ngo-shes-pas*), which is Awareness itself. And while practicing Thodgal, the visions of *thigle*, and so on, that arise are recognized to be manifestations or projections of one's own nature of mind (*sems kyi snang-ba*). It is like seeing the reflection of one's face in a mirror and recognizing it as such. Then Awareness (*rig-pa*) is experienced without any duality of subject and object, and this condition is conventionally distinguished from ignorance (*ma rig-pa*). Under the normal conditions of everyday life, ignorance is experienced as the impure karmic vision of

Samsara. However, when one is in the state of contemplation and recognizes one's real nature as being the Primordial State, there is no more distinction between impure vision (Samsara) and pure vision (Nirvana). The mirror reflects whatever is set before it, whether beautiful or ugly, and those reflections in no way affect or change the nature of the mirror. In the same way, whatever arises before the nature of mind, whether the pure vision of Nirvana or the impure karmic vision of Samsara, the original condition of the nature of mind remains unchanged. There is only this single Primordial Base, but there exist two Paths: the pure vision of Nirvana in the light of Rigpa and the impure vision of Samsara in the obscurity of ignorance. And these two Paths lead to two results or Fruits: the enlightenment of a Buddha and the delusion of an ordinary sentient being. But once one has realized the Base, one may survey both vistas impartially. Even if impure karmic visions arise, such as will be the case in the Sidpa Bardo, this event will in no way impede, limit, or defile one's immediate intrinsic Awareness. In this sense, one can say that Awareness and ignorance are without duality (*ma rig-pa dang gnyis su med-pa*).

In this state of true understanding, where one recognizes one's own original face or real nature (*rang ngo*), one is integrated, without accepting or rejecting anything, with these final visions that spontaneously manifest inside of the *thig-le*. In Dzogchen, unlike Tantra, one meditates with open eyes because there is no consideration of pure vision being good and impure vision being bad. These visions are both projections of mind. They have but a single flavor or taste (*ro gcig*) for the nature of mind (*sems kyi snang-ba*). And with respect to the practice of self-liberation, it does not matter what arises in vision, whether a vision is pure or impure. But if the mind has been purified, then the pure visions of Buddhahood will arise spontaneously, easily, and without effort, for they are what lie inherent, but at present dormant, in the hearts of all living beings. Such is one's heritage, which one has possessed since time without beginning. The individual need not look elsewhere for the visions of paradise. The truth may be called by many names, but these many names do not go beyond this single meaning (*don gcig las ma 'das-pa*).

Line 32: **In that single state (which is immediate intrinsic Awareness), one directly discovers that (all of these visions of tiny** spheres of rainbow light, and so on) are (in fact) just one's own self-manifestations. ⁸

In this single unique state of Rigpa, one discovers that all of these visions are self-manifestations (*rang-snang gi thag-bcad*). These visions arise spontaneously (*lhun*), and they are completely perfect (*rdzogs*) just as they are, needing no corrections or modifications (*ma bcos-pa*), because they are manifestations of the inherent radiance or energy of our Primordial State.

Line 33: **And in this state of (self-)liberation, one does not discover any doubt.** ⁸

Line 34: **(This state) is inherently liberated in itself, for Awareness is liberated by means of Awareness. [Similarly, through recognizing that (Awareness) is merely one's own state of existence, then everything that one understands is liberated into its own (natural) condition; and this is like meeting a person whom one has known previously.]** ⁸

Awareness is liberated by Awareness (*rig-pas rig-pa grol-ba*); it is inherently liberated in itself (*rang gi rang grol*). Because one understands and recognizes it as one's own state of being (*rang yin-par ngo-shes-pas*), everything that one understands is liberated into its own original condition (*rtogs-pa thams-cad rang sar grol-ba*). Previously, the text was speaking of external appearances (*phyi snang*), but here it is speaking of the individual's internal thoughts (*nang rtog*). They are similarly self-liberated as they arise. One recognizes them as soon as they arise, like meeting a person whom we have known previously (*sngar 'dris kyi mi phyis mthong-ba lta-bu*). (On *gcer-grol* and *shar-grol*, see Patrul Rinpoche's auto-commentary.) This concludes the consideration of the second statement, which gives instruction on the practice of the Path, Thodgal.

THE THIRD STATEMENT

Line 35: **One's confidence becomes like a treasury containing vast riches, which are (one's own) concrete personal experiences with regard to oneself (that is, with regard to one's own nature, which is intrinsic Awareness).** ⁸

Having considered the Base in terms of primordial purity and the Path in terms of spontaneous self-perfection, now the text speaks of the Fruit. Primordial purity and spontaneous perfection are considered here in terms of their inseparability (*dbyer-med*). Confidence is realized as the result of many concrete personal experiences (*byan-tshud-pa*) where one has a knowledge of contemplation.

Line 36: **[All movements of thought become (self-)liberated into their own condition; this is like a (great) treasury containing whatever one could desire.]** ⁹⁄₈

Line 37: **Then, having concrete experiences with regard to the others (which are external things and people), one's confidence becomes like a king who is a Chakravartin.** ⁹⁄₈

With respect to oneself (*rang la*), one develops a confidence (*gdeng*) born of concrete personal experiences (*byan-tshud-pa*), and so all internal movements of thought (*'gyu-ba thams-cad*) become liberated into their own original condition (*rang sar grol-ba*),which is emptiness. And with respect to others (*gzhan la*), that is, external appearances, one becomes like a Chakravartin, or universal monarch (*'khor-lo brgyur-pa'i rgyal-po lta-bu'i gdeng*). Such an emperor rules over four great continents and therefore has nothing to fear from anyone else or any force outside of himself. Having mastered contemplation we can integrate all of existence into that state. This is Dzogchen, the state of the "Great Perfection."

Line 38: **[(That is to say,) the state of immediate Awareness becomes visibly manifest (as visions of mandalas, and so on), and since these (visions) are not created by anything else, (one's intrinsic Awareness) is like (a Chakravartin) who brings everything in the four continents under his power.]** ⁹⁄₈

One's interior Awareness becomes visibly manifest (*rig-pa mngon-sum snang-ba*) in space, first as light phenomena and then as visions, and these are all self-manifestations (*rang snang*); they are not created by anything else (*gzhan gyis man grub-pas*) outside of themselves. With this realization, one approaches the final stage of vision.

Line 39: **Furthermore, (one's intrinsic Awareness) has the capacity to bring even the physical elements under its power; [and since** one becomes liberated by reason of this condition (of realizing the Body of Light), one is no longer dependent upon any other faculty.] $\frac{9}{8}$

Now the text makes reference to the Fruit, the Body of Light, which represents the culmination of the four stages of vision listed above. In terms of this process, Rigpa has the capacity to bring even the physical elements under its power (*'byung-ba la dbang-bsgyur nus-pa*), and since one is liberated by reason of this condition (*rkyen gyis grol-ba*), one is not dependent on any other faculty or power (*dbang-po gzhan la rug ma lus-pa*) for the realization of the Fruit, which is the Body of Light. Why this Body of Light? Because the enlightenment of a Buddha means not only the realization of total wisdom (Skt. *prajñā*) and of the ultimate reality of the state of emptiness (Skt. *śunyatā*), but equally it means the realization or manifestation of compassion (Skt. *karuṇā*) and skillful means (Skt. *upāya*). Therefore, Buddhahood is not merely quiescent and passive, rather it is ever-active with Buddha activities, the manifestations of infinite and universal compassion. On the side of emptiness, there is the Dharmakaya, but on the side of compassion, there is the Rupakaya. Both "bodies" or dimensions, the Dharmakaya and the Rupakaya, are co-emergent in Bodhi, the state of enlightenment. The Sutra system describes how the Rupakaya is realized over the course of some three immeasurable kalpas by way of the cultivation of the perfections of generosity, morality, patience, vigor, and meditation. The Tantra system describes how the Rupakaya is realized by way of the practices of the generation process (Skt. *utpattikrama*) and the perfection process (Skt. *sampanna-krama*), especially the purified Illusion Body (*sgyu-lus*). Dzogchen describes the process of attaining the Rupakaya by way of realizing the Rainbow Body of Light. This Body of Light as a Nirmanakaya manifests to deluded sentient beings still caught up in Samsara and needing instruction and guidance on the path to liberation. The culmination of Thekchod is the discovery of the Dharmakaya, but the conclusion of Thodgal is the realization of the Rupakaya as the Body of Light.

By means of the practice of Thodgal one gains control and power over the energies of the five elements, because one liberates secondary causes (*rkyen*) by means of secondary causes (*rkyen gyis rkyen grol-ba*). The process has been described above. It is like the reflections (or cognitions) recognizing themselves in the mirror. Here the cognitions of the elements recognize themselves as they arise and resolve themselves back into their original empty condition. This process is known as Reversal (*ru-log*). One's gross physical elements (which are actually modes of the manifestation of energy, although seemingly solid, liquid, gaseous, and so on) are progressively refined and dissolved back into the subtle essences of the elements which are clear colored lights. Having realized the Body of Light, the Siddha or Adept remains active in terms of compassion and may continue to manifest in the world of the senses to other sentient beings in order to teach them and lead them to liberation and enlightenment, but the Siddha no longer lives under the tyranny of Samsara. Although the Siddha may visibly manifest to others, he or she has transcended material existence in every respect, either at the time of death or even while still alive—in this sense one has "ascended," whereas, in spatial terms, one has really not gone anywhere at all, but remains at the rediscovered primordial center of existence.

Line 40: **And having a concrete experience with respect to the state of liberation, one's confidence becomes like space dissolving into space.** ⅜

When a Siddha, like the master Garab Dorje, attains the Body of Light, it appears as if the material body dissolves into the vast space of the sky, or else dissolves into pure radiant energy, the lights of the rainbow. Matter is transformed into energy, and this radiant energy remains the vehicle of Awareness. The rainbow is the symbol of the bridge linking heaven and earth. According to Tibetan legend, in ancient times the first kings, at the time of death, reascended to heaven (*dmu*) by way of dissolving their physical bodies into the rainbow cord (*dmu thag*) attached to the top of their heads. Thus, they left no physical body or trace behind on the earth. Only when this heavenly link was severed was it necessary to build tombs for the bodies of dead kings. The Siddha, however, does not really ascend in a physical sense to some extraterrestrial heaven world—but simply returns to the center of his or her being, the Primordial State. The Siddha lives in the condition of the mirror, rather than in the reflections, the world illusion.

Line 41: **[(That is to say) one liberates oneself into one's own original condition, into the immaculate primordially pure Dharmata (the** nature of the ultimate Reality), and that is indeed like space dissolving into space or like the clouds dissipating in the sky.] §

Having a concrete experience of the state of liberation (*grol sa*), one's confidence is like space dissolving into space (*mkha' la mkha' thim-pa lta-bu'i gdeng*). In the process of realizing the Body of Light, one liberates oneself into one's own original condition (*rang sar grol-ba*), which is the state of the immaculate primordially pure Dharmata (*chos nyid ka-dag dri-ma med-pa la*). One liberates one's own embodied existence into space just as, during the practice of the path, one allowed whatever thoughts or appearance arose to self-liberate. This is the culmination of Thodgal practice and is realized by transcending the fourth stage, known as the vision of the consummation of Reality (*chos nyid zad-pa'i snang-ba*). One liberates into this state of primordial purity, which is like space dissolving into space, or like the clouds dissipating in the sky (*nam-mkha' la nam-mkha' thim-pa' am nam-mkha' la sprin dengs-pa lta-bu*).

Line 42: (Everything, all of one's dimension,) is self-liberated directly into its own state. §

Line 43: [That is to say, everything) self-liberates by itself; and this is like cracking rocks with rocks, or like tempering iron with iron, or like purifying dirt with dirt.] §

Line 44: In this unique state (of immediate Awareness, everything) is liberated into this single (understanding of the state of immediate intrinsic Awareness). §

Line 45: [And this is like taking fire from (another) fire, or like transferring water into water, or like adding (melted) butter to butter.] §

Line 46: Thus, the Mother and the Son become reunited. §

Line 47: [Since (the origin that is) one's own Mother is just itself (and nothing else, existing in its own state of existence, and this being emptiness), emptiness itself is liberated by means of emptiness; and thus (individual presence or) Awareness dissolves (becoming integrated) into the vision itself.] §

All of one's dimension is self-liberated directly (*rang thog tu rang-grol*); it self-liberates by itself (*rang rang gis grol*). It is liberated into this single state (*gcig grol*) of Rigpa. Thus the Mother who is the Primordial State and the Son who is knowledge or gnosis (*ye-shes*) are inseparably united without any duality (*ma bu gnyis sbyor-ba*). Since the origin, which is the Mother (*ma*), simply exists in its own state of existence (*rang gi ma rang yin-pas*), this being the state of emptiness, emptiness itself is liberated by way of emptiness (*stong-pas stong-pa grol-bas*) and, thus, individual Awareness is dissolved, that is, it becomes integrated into the vision (*rig-pa snang-bu la thim-pa*). One's own sense of presence and reality dissolves and integrates into the vision visible inside the *thig-le,* or sphere of rainbow light, a vision of the Buddha and the mandala or dimension of Buddhahood. This is like looking at one's reflection in a mirror, and suddenly finding oneself not looking at a reflection in a mirror, but being in the mirror looking outward. One becomes the mirror. The Mother, the mirror, and the Son, the reflection, merge and become one. One becomes this pure vision of Buddhahood, which is actually one's own manifestation, and not something outside oneself. One is now at the center, no longer at the periphery. The Mother is just herself (*rang yin-pa*) and nothing else. The Primordial State is just the Primordial State, and never otherwise, since time without beginning. The Primordial State (the Mother) and one's individual sense of presence (the Son) are unified (*ma bu gnyis sbyor-ba*); they are realized as not being two. This is quite different from a mystical experience of light (*gsal-ba'i nyams*) or of the void and the loss of individuality (*mi rtog-pa'i nyams*), which represent only a temporary alteration of consciousness. Here one's individual sense of presence is integrated into the total dimension of one's primordial Buddhahood.

The holographic image, self-arisen and self-manifested (*rang shar rang snang*), of the Buddha and mandala appearing inside of the *thig-le* before one in external space is actually a projection of the radiance of the inner light of one's own Awareness residing in the heart. One's individual sense of presence integrates with that vision and finds itself totally in that vision, literally being the vision itself. One's material body, having lost its support, can no longer be sustained by the power of consciousness, and so it fades away, dissolving into space. Both the form of the Buddha and one's physical form are projections from the Primordial State. But whereas the latter is the product of past karmic traces (*bag-chags*) and impure karmic vision (*las snang*), the former is the spontaneous manifestation of one's unobstructed enlightened nature. One has become manifestly the pure vision of the dimension of Buddhahood, and one's limited physical reality, conditioned by past karma which is now exhausted, fades away. One finds oneself instead in a spontaneously perfected Body of Light, the Rupakaya, observing the dissolution of one's former physical abode.

Rigpa integrates into the pure vision before one in space and becomes that vision. One becomes a Rainbow Body, light without shadow. This, despite Jung's protestations to the contrary, occurs because the obscurations or shadow (*sgrib-pa*), inherited from an immemorial past, have become exhausted in the process of purification by way of practicing contemplation. The causes for obscuration have been eliminated, so no more obscurations need arise to limit and distort awareness. One finds oneself in a state of total global awareness—this is what "omniscience" means. The Body of Light represents a complete and total radical transformation of one's status of being, a rediscovery of what was primordially present, and this condition is permanent. It is Awareness itself (*rig-pa nyid*) and is dependent on nothing else. This may be compared to the various Christian notions of transfiguration, resurrection, and ascension; but in the case of Dzogchen, the methodology of how this is accomplished, namely, the realizing of the Body of Light, is presented in precise terms. There exist in history many examples of the successful completion of this process. Even in recent years there have been a number of Tibetan Lamas, both Buddhist and Bonpo, who attained realization of the Rainbow Body (*'ja'-lus-pa*) at the end of their lives, and some of these occurrences were witnessed by Chinese Communist officials.[1]

Generally, there are three different ways in which this process may occur:

1. The Rainbow Body (*'ja'-lus*) is attained at the time of death by means of Thekchod practice. One's physical body is dissolved into its subatomic constituents and becomes pure radiant energy, leaving behind only hair and nails. The process generally takes seven days, during which time the body progressively shrinks in size.
2. The Body of Light (*'od-lus*) is realized at the time of death by means of the practice of Thodgal, as was the case with Garab Dorje, described above.

3. The Great Transfer (*'pho-ba chen-po*) is accomplished also by way of Thodgal, but here there is no necessity of going through the process of dying. Padmasambhava, Vimalamitra, and the Bonpo master Tapihritsa are all examples, according to tradition, of individual masters who realized the Great Transfer.

Line 48: **Since one recognizes one's own native state (as intrinsic Awareness), one is (directly) introduced to the Base (of all existence).** ⚇

Line 49: **(That is to say) one knows (or recognizes) it (the vision in the sphere of rainbow light) to be a self-manifestation of oneself; [and this is like seeing one's own face (reflected) inside a mirror.]** ⚇

Recognizing one's own nature or face (*rang ngo shes-pa*), one is directly introduced to the Base (*gzhi dang ngo-phrod-pa*). The vision appearing inside the *thig-le* is recognized to be a self-manifestation of oneself (*rang gi rang snang du shes-pa*), like seeing one's face reflected in a mirror (*me-long nang du dzin mthong-ba lta-bu*).

Line 50: **And because of that [belief] (where one has been introduced directly to the Base of existence) this (situation) is like the meeting of the mother and her son; and one recognizes this to be the unique state of liberation.** ⚇

Line 51: **Since (the vision) is directly self-liberated by itself (into its own state), the vision (or phenomenon) is empty [and its (quality of luminous clarity) is recognized to be (nothing other than one's own) state of immediate Awareness.]** ⚇

There occurs the meeting of the Mother and the Son (*ma dang bu phrad-pa*), and one recognizes this to be the unique state of liberation (*grol sa gcig-po yin-par ngo-shes*). Directly liberated by itself into its own condition (*rang gi rang thog tu grol-bas*), the vision itself is empty (*snang-ba stong-pa*), that is, it is insubstantial, and its quality of clear luminosity is recognized to be Rigpa, or Awareness (*gsal-ba rig-par ngo-shes-pa*).

Line 52: **Since (the vision or phenomenon) is known (or recognized) to be self-liberated by itself, one discovers that it has represented ignorance from the very beginning.** ⸞

Line 53: **[(That is to say) Samsara is known (or recognized in itself, and with respect to the transcending of it, one knows (or recognizes) it to be transcended; and so ignorance (itself) is self-liberated.]** ⸞

Since the vision that arises is recognized as self-liberating by itself (*rang gis rang grol-bar shes-pas*), one discovers or decisively determines that this arising has represented a state of ignorance from the very beginning (*thog-ma ma rig-pa nyid la thag-bcad-pa*). Two types of ignorance (*ma rig-pa*) are distinguished:

1. spontaneously born ignorance (*lhan-skyes ma rig-pa*), which is existential or inherent in the very nature of existence; it represents the fundamental dichotomy of subject and object, and is "the primordial error," so to speak; and
2. ignorance that conceptualizes everything (*kun brtag ma rig-pa*), which is the delusory activity of the mind, creating conceptions about the nature of reality.

This second kind of ignorance is eliminated by the purification process of the path, but the first is much more radical in nature and therefore far more difficult to root out, being the habitual mode of our existence since the very beginning.

Samsara recognizes itself by itself (*'khor-ba rang gis shes-pa*), that is, it arises as awareness and self-liberates. This is like the mind recognizing itself as mind, or, while one is asleep, recognizing that one is dreaming. With respect to Nirvana or the transcending of Samsara, one recognizes that Samsara is transcended (*'khor-ba la 'das-par shes-pa*). Samsara and Nirvana are identical in their nature or essence; they are both empty and lacking in any inherent existence or substantial reality. The difference is that the state of Nirvana is aware, knowing the nature of reality, whereas the state of Samsara is ignorant and unaware, not knowing the nature of reality. But this knowledge or gnosis is not a conclusion arrived at through philosophical analysis or reason, nor is it knowledge by acquaintance; it is a state of being. To know is to be. To actually know Buddhahood is to be the

Buddha. Thus, gnosis is knowledge that liberates. A phenomenon that arises in terms of one's karmic vision is a manifestation of ignorance, a delusion or a false appearance (*'khrul snang*). But if this is recognized (*ngo-shes-pa*), then it is allowed to self-liberate without interference by the mind or thought process (Samsara), and so one says that Samsara recognizes itself and self-liberates. It is like the reflections recognizing that they are reflections. The phenomenon dissolves again into the state of emptiness, out of which it arose in the first place. In this way Samsara transcends itself, and ignorance self-liberates (*ma rig-pa rang grol yin*).

Line 54: **And because of that [the actual example is like] the washing away of dirt with dirt.** §

Line 55: **[And because of (discovering) the real meaning of one's own state of existence,] discursive thoughts are liberated by themselves (spontaneously) and one discovers that one is not dependent upon any other antidote.** §

Whereas previously the text has been speaking of external appearances' (*phyi snang*) or visions' being allowed to self-liberate, now it speaks of the interior thoughts (*nang rtog*) that arise to consciousness being allowed to do likewise. In terms of ascertaining the real meaning of one's own state of existence (*don rang yin-pa'i phyir*), which is Rigpa, discursive thoughts self-liberate as they arise, and so one discovers that one is not dependent on any other antidote (*gnyen-po gzhan la rag ma lus-par thag-bcad*).

Line 56: **Since (the discursive thought) is liberated into the Base itself, one continues (in a state of immediate present Awareness) everywhere with confidence.** §

Line 57: **[This is like pouring water into water or like pouring (melted) butter into butter.]** §

Line 58: **And because of that (continuing with confidence everywhere), this (situation) is like the coils of a snake being liberated (effortlessly) by the snake itself.** §

Here we find expressed the fundamental principle of the third statement. Since thoughts (*rnam-rtog*) are liberated into the state of the Base (*gzhi nyid las grol-bas*), one continues everywhere in life and experience with confidence (*gdeng gang yin tu bca'-ba*) in their liberation.

Line 59: **But an Awareness that looks elsewhere [since it is liberated directly by itself, this state of immediate presence being self-sustaining,] (after failing to find what it seeks,) it will fall into despair. ⸖**

Line 60: **And for this reason, continuing directly in the Base that is one's own state (of immediate intrinsic Awareness) is the principal consideration. ⸖**

Intrinsic Awareness looking elsewhere than to itself (*gzhan ltos gyi rig-pa*), that is, its following thoughts and becoming distracted, represents a deviation (*gol-sa*), a becoming unbalanced and moving off-center. Thus, one will fall into despair (*tshi-chad-pa*) and find no liberation from Samsara. But when everything is allowed to directly self-liberate by itself (*rang gis thog tu grol-bas*), then Rigpa is self-sustaining or self-abiding (*rig-pa rang gnas*), and there is no deviation or falling away from the center. This continuing directly in the Base, the state of contemplation, is the principal practice (*dngos-gzhi rang thog tu gzhi bca'-ba*). Here concludes the third statement, which concerns the Fruit, the realization of the Body of Light.

CONCLUSION

Line 61: **At the time when Garab Dorje (Prahevajra) revealed the method for completely transcending the suffering of Samsara, ⸖**

Line 62: **Manjushrimitra fell down senseless, and, having fallen to the ground, he uttered a great lamentation, "Oh, alas!" ⸖**

Line 63: **Thereupon Vetalakshema (Garab Dorje), from the middle of the light (the sphere of rainbow light suspended in the sky) manifested effulgently his symbolic form. ⸖**

Prahevajra or Garab Dorje (dGa'-rab rdo-rje) has a number of names, one of them being Vetalakshema (Ro-langs bde-ba), "the happy vampire." As for how he received these names, see the biographical account given in Part Two. Having dissolved his physical body into space, Garab Dorje reappears in the sky as a glorious Body of Light inside a sphere of rainbow light (*thig-le*). This is called his symbolic form (*phyag-rgya*, Skt. *mudrā*).

Line 64: **For the sake of causing inspiration to arise [in Manjushrimitra], who had fallen senseless previously, these three statements that strike the essential points [for the ultimate liberation of the individual] contained in this secret last testament (were revealed by the master).** ⣀

Line 65: **This (last testament) descended (from the sky) into the palm of (Manjushrimitra's) right hand; it was written in ink made of melted azure-colored vaidurya (lapis lazuli).** ⣀

Line 66: **And (the text) had been put inside a vessel one full thumbnail (in size), and placed within a casket of precious crystal;** ⣀

Line 67: **Whereupon Manjushrimitra was liberated from his faint.** ⣀

Line 68: **And he became one possessed of the confidence of sure understanding.** ⣀

Line 69: **Because of that, (this Upadesha) was concealed in the mandala of his heart [and kept secret there from others].** ⣀

Line 70: **And the nectar of the transmission of these three statements, which were the oral teachings received at the time of the death (of his master), became effulgent and overflowing (in his heart).** ⣀

The three statements were written on golden paper (*shog ser*) with ink made of azure-colored melted lapis lazuli (*mthing-kha zhun-mas*, Skt. *vaidūrya*). This paper was placed within a thumb-sized vessel and this, in turn, put inside a casket of precious crystal (*rin-po-che shel gyi za-ma-tog sen gang-ba cig snod du babs-pa*). The master then elaborated on the meaning of these three statements orally.

Line 71: **Wherein the real meaning of the view (of Dzogchen) was displayed like gold.** ⣀

Line 72: **This (event) occurred at the great cremation ground of Shitavana.** ⣀

The cremation ground of Shitavana (bSil-ba'i tshal), "the cool forest," is now identified by the Tibetans with Kolashri, near Vajrasana, modern Bodh Gaya.

Line 73: **This holy secret instruction, which was brought into visible manifestation at the source of the Dan-tig River,** ਃ

Line 74: **Is the very path that brings relief (from the suffering of Samsara) for all sentient beings.** ਃ

Line 75: **This Upadesha, which brings about an instantaneous liberation into the (pure) field of the Buddha, is here completed.** ਃ

Reference is again made to the culmination of Thodgal practice. Here concludes the literal translation of the text, "The Last Testament of Garab Dorje," known as "The Three Statements That Strike the Essential Points," as well as the interlinear commentary composed by the translator Vajranatha.

SARVA MANGALAM

PART TWO

The Life of Garab Dorje
and
Guru Sadhana

Translator's Introduction

Here is presented a translation of one of the oldest extant hagiographies of Garab Dorje. It is found in the *Lo-rgyus chen-mo,* (*The Great History*), by Zhangton Tashi Dorje (Zhang-ston bKra-shis rdo-rje, 1097–1167); a shorter version is found in the *rNying-ma'i chos-byung* (*History of the Nyingmapa School*), by Dudjom Rinpoche (bDud-'joms 'Jigs-bral ye-shes rdo-rje, 1904–1987).[1] Dudjom Rinpoche himself appears to have drawn most of his material from this same account. The full title of the text reads *rDzogs-pa chen-po snying-thig gi lo-rgyus chen-mo;* however, the name of the author is not specifically indicated in the colophon.[2] This text is contained in the collection known as the *Bi-ma snying-thig* made by Longchen Rabjampa (kLong-chen rab-byams-pa, Dri-med od-zer, 1308–1363).[3] The text was regarded as a Terma and bears the usual Terma punctuation. The *'Das-rjes,* a portion of which has been translated in Part One, is found in the same collection of *sNying-thig* or Upadesha texts (*man-ngag gi sde*) coming from the tradition that derives ultimately from Vimalamitra in the eighth century. Hence the name by which this collection is known: *Bi-ma snying-thig* (*The Essence of the Mind of Vimalamitra*). This *Das-rjes,* containing the last testaments of Garab Dorje, Manjushrimitra, Shrisimha, Jnanasutra, and Vimalamitra, constitutes the real heart or core of the *Bi-ma snying-thig.*[4] So, regarding the earthly career of Garab Dorje, we find a tradition coming from before the time of Longchenpa in the fourteenth century and going back at least to the tenth century.

The hagiographies in this *Lo-rgyus chen-mo* contain a great deal of imagery and symbolism more characteristic of the Mahayoga Tantras than of Dzogchen as such, that is to say, images of terrifying cremation grounds (*dur-khrod*) filled with decaying human corpses, wild animals, dangerous worldly gods such as Bhairava, and flesh-eating Dakinis. This is the lunar and chthonic symbolism of the night side of human consciousness, the collective unconscious psyche, and these visions are reminiscent of the European medieval fantasies of the Witches' Sabbat.[5] It is a world of magic and transformation; but it is an accurate reflection of the psychic world of the Higher or Anuttara Tantras, including the Mahayoga Tantra, out of which Dzogchen Atiyoga emerged as a separate movement in Tibet. The question of the historical origins of Dzogchen is considered below.

The Life of Garab Dorje

From the Lo-rgyus chen-mo

When there had passed some three hundred and sixty years from the Parinirvana of the Buddha,[1] in the region of Dhanakosha in the country of Uddiyana, which lies in the western direction from Vajrasana,[2] a region surrounded by sandalwood trees, there resided living creatures known as Koshana. Their bodies were human, but they had the faces of bears and their paws had iron claws. Also their entrails were filled with innumerable fine precious jewels.[3] This place was called the region of Dhanakosha because *dha* refers to areas of sandalwood trees. Then there also existed there a great temple called Mangala Shankarakuta (bKra-shis bde-byed brtsegs-pa), and this was completely surrounded in all directions by one thousand six hundred and eight smaller shrines, all of them linked together by ropes which were networks of tiny tinkling golden bells. The men, being very handsome and charming, had excellent forms and well-proportioned limbs. Their long hair was bound up in topknots on the crowns of their heads and adorned with gold, silver, emeralds, and so on. And they were attired in different kinds of robes of white and red cotton. The women had their long hair tied up in knots in front and back, and they adorned their bodies with various ornaments of conch and bone.

In that country there was a king named Uparaja (rGyal-po U-pa-ra-dza)[4] and his consort Abhasvaravati (sNang-ba gsal-ba'i 'od-ldan-ma), and to them there was born a daughter named Kudharma.[5]

When not a long time had passed after her taking Pravrajya vows, she took the Upasampada ordination and became a Bhikshuni.[6]

Then, to the west beyond one yojana (distance from the temple), there was a lake in which there was an island covered with golden sand. Here she erected a hut of thatched grass, and she lived there attended only by a serving girl, a Dakini named Sukhakarunavati (bDe-ba'i snying-rje ldan-ma). One night this princess, who resided there on the island, engaged herself in pious practices,[7] and afterwards she had a dream. In it a white man appeared to her, holding a long lance made of precious crystal, and on the crown of his head there was a vase made of precious crystal sealed with the letters *OM AH HUM SVAHA* as symbols indicating the empowerments of the Five Buddha Families.[8] Then he touched her three times on the crown of her head with the vase, and since rays of light emanated from this vase, she dreamed that she could see clearly everything in the three worlds simultaneously.

Then, in the morning, she was greatly astonished by the dream, and at midday she recounted it to her maidservant. The servant girl replied, "It is an omen that a Nirmanakaya will be born to the princess!" (She realized this because) this serving girl was in actuality a Dakini named Purnopashanti (Pu-rna nye-bar zhi-ba).

But the princess thought to herself, "How can this be?" and wondered about it greatly. Then the body of the princess began to feel uncomfortable and developed many pains. Finally, after nine months had elapsed and she was in her tenth month, a son without any father was born to this princess from a place on the right side of her ribs. The Bhikshuni was very ashamed at giving birth (to this illegitimate child), and thus she uttered many verses of lamentation:

> This fatherless son of mine comes not from worldly intercourse!
> Who possessed such a desire for me in all the three worlds
> Among the races of worldly Maras and Brahmas,
> Or among the Gyalpo, the Tsen, and the dMu?[9]
> If, indeed, this be an example of the birth
> Of the forms of various Devas and Asuras,
> It was not seen by anyone!
> Who in this kingdom devoid of Dharma could it possibly be?
> Oh, alas!
> I only desired to benefit beings through my exceedingly pure
>   morality,
> Yet I will be blamed for giving way to perversity and lust.
> It is a very great sin!

Having lamented in this way, she was suffering greatly.

Her serving girl replied, "He is a son of the Buddha."

But she did not hear this and shouted, "Put this thing into the ash pit and stir up the ashes in order to hide him!" However, when she threw him into the ash pit (outside the door of the hut), lights and sounds came forth from it.

Then, after three days had passed, she looked into the ash pit, and shedding tears, she saw that the child lay there without having been harmed in any way. Retrieving him, she placed the child on a clean white silken cloth and bathed him with milk and perfumed waters. She took him up in her arms and thought to herself, "He is surely a Nirmita,[10] or else this is the behavior of some man who cannot die."

Thereupon, from the atmosphere above, the Devas uttered verses of benediction:

> Our Protector and Teacher and exalted Lord!
> You, the protector of the world, manifest your own nature.
> We go to you for refuge and pray to you,
> O Vajra of the sky![11]

With this, the Dakinis assembled in the sky veritable clouds of offerings, and the Devas, the Nagas, and the Yakshas sent down a rainfall of sandalwood and saffron. And from all directions the Lokapalas, who protect the regions of the world[12] came beating the great drums of the Dharma and blew upon conch shells, as well as hoisting aloft victory banners and setting up ensigns and the rest. Even the great kings among the Rishis assembled like clouds immeasurable masses of medicines. Then, since this provided nourishment for the infant, he grew faster, sustained more by the nourishment of this food than he would have been by the nourishment provided by any other kind of food. He grew more quickly in one month than another child would have in one year and two months.

Then, after seven years had passed, the child addressed his mother, saying, "O my mother, I want to go to pay my respects to the learned Panditas.[13] Even though you will not be happy about my discussing the Dharma with them, please grant me your permission."

Since he had made this request, his mother replied, "O my son, you have not even lost your baby teeth from your mouth. How can you discuss the Dharma with them?"

The boy forcefully reiterated his request, saying, "Please grant me your permission!"

Thus his mother responded, "If you go beyond one yojana in the direction of the east from here, there in the illustrious region known as Dhanakosha you will find your own grandfather, King Uparaja. Since there are with him some five hundred Panditas who serve as his Purohitas,[14] you should request to go there. And having spoken in this way, his mother gave him her permission.

Then the young boy, becoming exceedingly delighted at this, set off for that country. When he met the king, he made prostrations before him and addressed him as follows, "O great king, I am your spiritual superior. Since there reside here with you some five hundred Panditas serving as your Purohitas, it is my desire to pay my respects to them. Even if you are not happy about the prospects of my discussing the Dharma with them, nevertheless, since I make this request, O great king, please grant it to me."

Since he had made this petition, the king looked him over with his eyes and exclaimed, "You are but a child who has not even lost the baby teeth in his mouth! How can you possibly discuss the Dharma with anyone? How can there exist any respects to be paid?"

"Please grant me your permission!" the boy insisted.

The king replied, "You are just a child! Nevertheless, since your body appears to be adorned with the many signs and marks of a Buddha,[15] it is indeed possible that you are a Nirmita. I shall arrange for you to meet with the Purohitas." And having said this, he withdrew inside.

Then, when the Purohitas had assembled together before midday, the king related to them his earlier conversation with the young boy. But some among these Purohitas protested, "Such crazy talk is not enjoyable. Do not allow him inside. What do the others say?"

However, the one who was the most learned among them advised, "We may send him away, but we cannot be certain that he is not someone similar to a Nirmita. In my dream last night, there occurred an excellent omen. Let him be sent in!"

Since he had spoken in this way, the young boy was brought inside. After having made his prostrations before them, the young boy proceeded to deliver to them a discourse on the Dharma. But try as they did, none of the learned Panditas were able to confound him with their questions relating to his teaching. Having failed to defeat him in debate, the Panditas made prostrations before him and accepted his foot on the crowns of their heads. They praised him excessively and thus they came to bestow upon him the name of Prajnabhava, meaning "he whose nature is wisdom," because his mind possessed a vast discriminating wisdom (prajna).

Thereupon the king, having been greatly delighted with him, gave him the name of the Acharya Prahevajra (sLob-dpon dGa'-rab rdo-rje), "the vajra of supreme delight." Then his mother, since she had concealed him in the ash pit, but found that he had not died, called him by the name of the great Acharya Vetalabhasmavarna (sLob-dpon chen-po Ro-langs thal-mdog), "the ash-colored vampire." And because, among all of the very handsome youths found among the people of that country, he was the most happy, he also became known by the name of the Acharya Vetalakshema (sLob-dpon Ro-langs bde-ba), "the happy vampire." So in this way he came to be known by these four names. Having previously listened to the expositions of the Lord Buddha while he inhabited the bodies of various sentient beings belonging to the four kinds of rebirth, he circulated in special realms of rebirth,[16] and thus, by virtue of the power of his merits, he accomplished countless deeds (to benefit others).

Then, on the mountain called Suryaprakashakara (Ri-bo Nyi-ma rab tu snang-ba byed-pa), among the masses of terrifying rocks, on top of a place where the fierce Pretas reside, he built a hut of thatched grass, and for thirty-two years, he demonstrated the method of remaining in equanimity with respect to samadhi.[17] Because of that, the earth shook seven times. Also innumerable different sounds came forth from the sky, and there were rainfalls of different kinds of flowers. On one occasion, a voice came forth from the sky, proclaiming, "The teachings of the Tirthikas will degenerate!"

In that region there was a king who followed the sinful ways of the Tirthikas.[18] One day the boys who tended his cattle in the mountains happened to see (the master meditating). They could not rouse him even by blowing a goat horn in his ear, nor could they rouse him by inserting a bamboo splinter into his flesh. They perceived that he was one who was not sensitive to anything.

They reported this matter to the king, and the king instructed them, saying, "This individual you have found has increased the power of the Teachings of the Buddha, whereas he has damaged and has brought low the teachings of the Tirthikas. You two executioners shall go and kill him!" And having provided these two with axes, he sent them away.

But when these executioners tried to kill him, whatever they did, they could not obtain an actual opportunity to do so. Then the Acharya arose (from his samadhi) and went off on a path between the clouds in the sky. And since he had departed in that manner, the Tirthika king, together with all of his retinue, were greatly astonished. And having eagerly made prostrations, they praised the master excessively, and in this way they entered into the Teachings of the Buddha.

Now, some thirty-two years having elapsed, all of the precious Pitakas, which had been expounded by the completely perfect Buddhas of the past, and in particular the sixty-four hundred thousand verses of the natural Great Perfection (*rang-bzhin rdzogs-pa chen-po*), came to be preserved in his heart. On the mountain peak of this extensive teaching activity, a mound of precious jewels located on the Malaya mountain, there resided a Dakini of the Vajradhatu known as Lokasukharasavati (rDo-rje dbyings kyi mkha'-'gro-ma, 'Jig-rten bde-ba'i ro dang ldan-ma). She had three faces and was attired in the skins of a tiger. Her four hands held parasols of peacock feathers, and she was actively mounted upon a tiger and a lion. And here also there resided the Dakini of limitless virtuous qualities called Pitashankara (bDe-byed ser-mo yon-tan mtha'-yas-pa'i mkha'-'gro-ma). She was mounted on a dragon and wore a bandolier of lightning bolts. She was exceedingly wrathful in appearance, but blissful in her mind.[19] For three years they compiled the indices (*dkar-chag*) of the letters and the words (of the Dzogchen Tantras). Together with all the Nirmanakaya letters, which were self-originated and self-occurring,[20] these were well arranged unerringly in letters (in many volumes of books). And having arranged them in that way, these two Dakinis became manifest (and visible to him) in a rock cave located there, and to those Dakinis, who possessed keen intelligence, he proposed, "Let us perform puja!" And having been given their consent, he prayed that they remain there with him (as custodians of the Teachings). Thereupon, by means of the actual arising of Nirmitas as visible manifestations, they caused the Teachings to become established. This shorter lineage of transmission,[21] which caused the Teachings to remain (in our world) for a long time, has been amply recounted here.

However, as for the special sources, that is to say, those special places where the Buddhas brought forth the Teachings for the sake of the benefit of everyone, I shall explain something with regard to this.[22]

Then, in the direction northeast from Vajrasana, when one passes beyond some five yojanas, there existed the great cremation ground of Shitavana (bSil-ba'i tshal), the cool forest, which is some two and a half yojanas in circumference. In the middle of the hilly country there, on an even surface like the palm of the hand, without any boundary or center, or any high or low, directly in front, there was a stupa which had descended from the glorious Deva realm above. It was made of copper and had such decorations as wheels anointed with gold, together with parasols, and there came forth the various sounds of little tinkling bells. In each of the four directions of the stupa there were images displayed, made from various kinds of precious jewels.

In the northeast direction of that cremation ground there was the image of a worldly deity called the wish-granting tree Bhisala. Hosts of scavenger birds descended onto it and dwelt there. Here also there was a worldly god called Anandakareshvara (dGa'-byed dbang-phyug), who was mounted on a black lion. In his hand he held a spearlike trident, and he was attired in flowing robes of red silk. He was uninhibited in taking the lives of living beings, and he resided there together with his multitudinous retinue.

Here also resided countless Dakinis. Some had the rays of the sun issuing from their eyes. Some roared with the sounds of thunder coming from their mouths and rode mounted on buffalos. Some held knives in their hands and had eyes shaped like grains. Some held piles of human skulls in their hands and rode mounted on tigers. Some held human corpses in their hands and rode mounted on lions. Some ate human entrails and rode mounted on Garuda birds. Some held human corpses impaled on the tips of their spears and rode mounted on jackals. Some swam in oceans of blood and had five or ten heads. Some held many different forms of sentient beings in their innumerable hands. Accordingly, some of them, having cut off their own heads, held them in their hands. Some others, having torn out their own hearts, grasped them in their hands. Yet some others, having disemboweled themselves, grasped their own intestines and ate them. Among them, some rode mounted on horses or on elephants or on bulls. And in the midst of this place where there dwelt these countless Dakinis, there was a lake which caused delight to them.

Moreover, there were countless living creatures who resided in that cremation ground. There were beings who could not move immediately, and there were also others living there who would actually try to take their lives and eat them. Having the intention of taming by his wisdom those beings who were engaged in these perversions, the Acharya Prahevajra decided to go there. Mounted upon a daughter of Vishnu, who was naked except for her loose flowing hair,[23] he departed (from the mountains in the north and flew southeastward) until he arrived there. The living creatures who had lived in that cremation ground were exceedingly terrified (by his arrival), and so they gathered up many miraculous bilva fruits and offered them to the Acharya and made prostrations to him. Then, having supported the back of his body against the stupa located in the midst of all this, he proceeded to teach the Dharma to countless Dakinis, such as Suryaprabha (Nyi-ma'i 'od-zer) and others.

During that time, in a town called Dvikrama (Rim-pa gnyis-pa), in the western direction from Vajrasana, there lived the son of the Brahman Bhagavan Shastri (Bram-ze Legs-ldan ston-pa) and his wife Abhasadipa (sNang-ba'i sgron-me). He was a lord who adhered to the Holy Teachings of the Buddha, and, since he was especially learned in the five sciences,[24] he was called by the name of Manjushrimitra ('Jam-dpal bshes-gnyen). Then one day, a prophecy of Manjushri Vajratikshna came from the sky, proclaiming the existence of an excellent great cremation ground in the words, "O noble son, if you desire to attain the fruit of Buddhahood in this present physical body within a single lifetime, you should go to the great cremation ground of Shitavana!" This was the prophecy.

Then, having arrived at this cremation ground of Shitavana, Manjushrimitra met Prahevajra face to face and presented his request. For seventy-five years he stayed there with the Nirmanakaya and listened to him expound the Dharma.

At the end of this period, having passed beyond suffering into Buddhahood, at the time when five hundred and forty-four years had elapsed (since the Parinirvana of the Buddha), at the headwaters of the Dan-tig River to the northeast of there (Shitavana), Prahevajra himself, having caused his physical body, together with its pollutants, (to dissolve and) disappear, demonstrated the method for the complete transcending of suffering. At that moment, the earth shook six times and there came forth innumerable masses of light and great sounds in the sky.

At that, Manjushrimitra fainted and fell supine upon the ground. Then, having awakened from his faint, he looked upward, and beholding his Guru sitting in the middle of a mass of light in the sky, Manjushrimitra uttered many lamentations, such as, "Oh alas, alas! When the light of the lamp who is our teacher has gone out, who exists who will remove the darkness of the world?" He repeated this three times.

Thereupon the Acharya extended downward his right arm to the elbow from the mandala of this mass of light in the sky, and there came forth (from his hand) a precious golden casket, about one full thumb joint in size, together with some terrifying sounds. This golden casket circumambulated Manjushrimitra three times and fell into the palm of his right hand. Having opened it and looked inside, he found therein the text of the *Tshig gsum gnad du brdeg-pa*, "The Three Statements That Strike the Essential Points," of Prahevajra, written on a surface made of five precious gems in letters of melted vaidurya (lapis lazuli), together with his own seal. By merely looking at this text, Manjushrimitra became like a vase filled to its full measure. Furthermore, the event where Prahevajra realized the consummation of reality and the event where Manjushrimitra realized the increasing of experiences occurred together (simultaneously).[25] This Nirmita (or apparition of Prahevajra), which was a self-manifestation of self-liberation, caused the Teaching to remain (in our world) for a long time. The Nirmita opened this state naturally.[26]

Homage to the Nirmanakaya who resembles a sphere of light!

Then, from among the hundreds of thousands of verses, Manjushrimitra divided the teachings of the natural Great Perfection into three series: the Chittavarga, or Mind Series (*sems-sde*), for those individuals who are established in the calm state, the Abhyantaravarga, or Space Series (*klong-sde*), for those individuals who are free of all worldly activity, and the Upadeshavarga, or Secret Instruction Series (*man-ngag gi sde*), for those individuals principally adhering to the essential point.[27]

From them also, he made a special condensation of the teachings. With regard to this *Thig-le rang gnad du phab-pa*, "The Essence Occurring as Its Own Essential Point,"[28] he divided it into two: the oral transmission (*snyan-rgyud*, Skt. *karṇatantra*) and the explanatory transmission (*bshad-rgyud*, Skt. *vyākhyātantra*). Although having made two copies of this *sNyan-rgyud*, as well as of the *bShad-rgyud snying gi ti-ka*, he did not find anyone upon whom he could bestow them, and so he concealed them beneath a vishvavajra-shaped boulder[29] which lay in a northeastern direction from Vajrasana. Sealing them with the seals of the Dakinis and of the Dharmapatis, he caused them to become invisible.[30]

Then, some distance to the west of Vajrasana there was the great cremation ground known as Sosaling (dur-khrod chen-po So-sa'i gling), which was one yojana in circumference. In the middle of that cremation ground was a single self-originated stupa, rising as high as possible, adorned with precious jewels and with silver, together with wheels and parasols and corals, and very beautifully decorated with latticeworks of little tinkling bells, as well as with ornaments of the sun and moon. At its sides there were self-originated images of the eight Matrika goddesses, such as Gauri and the rest.[31]

To the northeast of that stupa there was a lake called Kshuratamasa (sPu-gri mun), and within that lake resided various kinds of noxious creatures such as makaras.[32] At the borders of the lake, it was entirely surrounded by various kinds of rocks. To the southwest of that lake there resided marvelous worldly gods and demons. Here in one huge black nyagrodha tree there were found in its top branches the nests of scavenger birds, and around its trunk (and its lower branches) there were entwined poisonous black snakes, and among its roots were found the dens of grave-digging pigs. Here also there was located the image of the worldly god Anandakumara (that is, Bhairava).[33] He had the face of a lion and held in his hands a sword resembling a human arm, as well as a human head, a wooden spear, and a spearlike trident with a human corpse impaled on its tip. His body was everywhere adorned with garlands of human skulls, and he was attired in a cloak of black silk. He was surrounded by a retinue of some hundred thousand murderous Matrika goddesses who were mounted on elephants (and other wild creatures) and who were excessively desirous of flesh and blood.[34]

Here also there were innumerable hosts of Dakinis. Some were mounted on lions and had loose flowing hair, and they hoisted aloft victory banners having nine stacked skulls. Some were mounted on hosts of birds and held aloft victory banners of lions. Some had a single body but with eleven heads attached to it, and they were feeding upon human hearts, entrails, and so on. Some were black women who shook their long hair and caused wolves to come forth from their open mouths. Some chopped apart human corpses and caused rainfalls and thunderbolts of meteorite iron to descend from between the ends of the sky; and in their hands they held aloft victory banners of tigers. Some separated the upper and lower parts of their bodies and tore out their own lungs and hearts. Some others, having cut off their own limbs, scattered them about in all directions. In that way, there existed innumerable displays of various kinds of magical power.

In the vicinity, there were many scavenger birds, grave-digging pigs, poisonous snakes, many human-colored jackals, wolves, and so on, as well as multitudes of terrifying bees. All about were countless masses of human corpses, both old and new, piles of bones, lakes of blood, houses made of human heads, and huts made from piles of dried skulls. Some of these creatures scratched about (in the earth), some of them ate, some of them roamed about, some of them howled, some of them plucked out eyes (of corpses), some of them chewed on legs or gnawed on bones or devoured entrails, and so on.

In the midst of all this carnage resided the Yogeshvaras; many Yogins and Yoginis moved about, practicing various kinds of ascetic conduct of the Yogins.[35] Here the great Acharya Manjushrimitra sat in vajraparyanka position upon a throne of copulating lions, upon which also stood various kinds of victory banners, as well as parasols and canopies of peacock feathers, and so on. Here he resided in a multistoried house in the middle of this terrifying cremation ground, being completely surrounded by hosts of Dakinis. For one hundred and nine years he continued in samadhi and abided in a state of equanimity.[36]

Translated by Vajranatha
Baudhnath, Nepal
March 1978

Guru Sadhana for Garab Dorje

by Dzongsar Khyentse Rinpoche

I. VISUALIZATION

A ⁑

The world and all living things are pure from the very beginning.
From the state of the Great Primordial Emptiness,
My own body clearly manifests as the peaceful Vajrapani.
In the sky in front of me, within a great azure space,
Self-perfection manifests as a mass of visible light;
And in the middle of that, within a sphere which is a vast expanse
 of light,
On a bejewelled throne, upon a lotus, a solar disc, and a lunar disc,
Is the great chariot of the Teachings of the Supreme Vehicle:
Garab Dorje, dressed in the attire of the Sambhogakaya.
He is peaceful and smiling, of a clear white color, adorned with all
 the marks and characteristics.
With His right hand He makes before Him the gesture of granting
refuge;
And His left hand is supported on the seat at His hip.
He is beautifully attired in a silk garment and adorned with precious
 gems.
His two legs are held in the manner of the Bodhisattva position,
And His body is seated upright in a majestic posture.
His three secret places are marked with the three vajras.
Lights emanate from them and invoke the Wisdom Beings
(And these beings unite with Him) like water poured into water.

II. SEVENFOLD SERVICE

(1) We do homage with the view that our own pure intrinsic
    Awareness is the real Guru.
(2) We present as offerings all phenomenal existence, completely
    perfected from the very beginning.
(3) We confess all our sins and downfalls (by remaining) in the great
    unborn vast expanse.
(4) We rejoice at all virtues which (come about) without any
    deliberate action.
(5) May the Buddhas turn the Wheel of the Teachings of the
    spontaneous Self-Perfection,
(6) And remain in that state which is unborn and unceasing.
(7) We dedicate our merit (by remaining) in the spontaneously
    self-perfected youthful vaselike Body.
That we may we attain Enlightenment as the great Three Bodies.

III. PRAYER

OM AH HUM
To the heroic Garab Dorje who is Himself Vajrasattva
We pray with unfailing fierce and fervent devotion.
From the perfection of the great energy of the State which is the
    Clear Light,
May we obtain the Vajrakaya Rainbow Body of the Great Transfer!

IV. MANTRA RECITATION

OM AH GURU PRAJNABHAVA HEVAJRA SARVA SIDDHI HUM

V. EMPOWERMENT

From the three syllables in the three places of the Guru
Flow streams of nectar which are the light rays of the three syllables,
Together with forms and mantra garlands and syllables;
And they are absorbed into my own three places gradually and then
    altogether.
By means of this link I obtain the four initiations and purify my four
    obscurations.
Thus there is placed within me the seed for transcending all
    limitations
Through meditating upon the four paths and upon the four Visions.

VI. UNIFICATION

Finally, the Guru, who is greatly pleased with me,
Enters through the aperture at the crown of my head and takes up
His residence in the center of my heart.
In His own heart center, within a swirling vast expanse of the five
    colored lights,
Sits Samantabhadra Himself with His Consort;
And in the center of His heart, on top of a blue sphere
Is the white letter *A*, surrounded by the syllables which are the
    letters of the Six Vast Spaces.
All of the aggregates of my own six sense consciousnesses
Are dissolved into the vast expanse of purity.

VII. FINAL INSTRUCTIONS

[In the state of total Clear Light wherein Awareness and Emptiness
    are inseparably united,
Being without distractions, one should perform the vajra recitation,
Or recite the mantra aloud with one's voice, or recite it with the breath,
    as much as one can.
At the end of the session, one should dedicate the merit and carry on
    along the path (of everyday life).
Moreover, as for this shorter Sadhana of the Guru,
Being inspired by the symbols appearing in his experiences while he
    (Khyentse Rinpoche) was dreaming,
He wrote down whatever spontaneously occurred before the face of
    his own Awareness.
May one's own Awareness become liberated into the state of the
    Guru!]

COLOPHON

In the water-snake year (1893), on the fifteenth day of the tenth month,
this text was written down by Kunzang Odsal Nyingpo (Jamyang
Khyentse Chokyi Lodro).

*Translated at Merigar in the hills of Tuscany during the spring retreat of
1985 by Vajranatha.*

SARVA MANGALAM

NOTES TO THE GURU SADHANA

This Guru Sadhana (*bla sgrub*) has a number of parts:

I. Visualization: Having received the proper authorization (*lung*) to do the practice, one dissolves everything, one's own physical body and one's environment, into the state of the great Primordial Emptiness (*ye stong chen-po'i ngang*). Thereupon one reappears in space in the form of the peaceful Vajrapani (Phyag-rdor zhi-ba). He is blue in color, having one face and two arms, holding a vajra in his right hand, and is attired as a great Bodhisattva. Then in the sky in front of oneself appears the master Garab Dorje himself as described in the liturgy, sitting within a sphere of rainbow light (*thig-le*). His three secret places—the forehead, the throat, and the heart—are marked with the three vajras, that is, three luminous syllables: the white syllable *OM* at his forehead, the red syllable *AH* at his throat, and the azure blue syllable *HUM* at his heart. These are in the visible aspect of Tibetan letters. Rays of light emanate from these syllables and invoke the Jnanasattvas, or Knowledge Beings (*ye-shes-pa*), from out of the vast sky of the Enlightened Mind. And they descend like a rainfall of miniature images of the Guru and merge into and unite with the visualization of the Guru in front of oneself, which is known as the Samayasattva, or Symbolic Being (*dam-tshig-pa*). These two become one and inseparable (*dam ye dbyer-med*).

II. Sevenfold Service: This is a standard practice according to the Sutra system, but here it is cast in terms of the view of Dzogchen. There are seven parts: (1) doing homage, (2) making offerings, (3) confessing sins, (4) rejoicing at the merit of others, (5) requesting the Buddhas to turn the Wheel of the Dharma (i.e., teach), (6) entreating them to remain in this world in order to continue to teach, and (7) dedicating one's meritorious karma to the welfare and liberation of all other living beings.

III. Prayer: Here Garab Dorje is identified with Vajrasattva, the Sambhogakaya aspect of Buddhahood. One prays to realize ultimately, by way of one's practice of Dzogchen, the Vajrakaya, "the indestructible diamondlike body," that is to say, the Rainbow Body of the Great Transfer (*'pho chen 'ja' lus rdo-rje'i sku*).

IV. Mantra Recitation: The Mantra of the Guru is recited at least 108 times.

V. Empowerment: Rays of light stream forth from the three secret places of the Guru and enter into one's own corresponding three places. White light comes forth from the luminous white syllable *OM* at the forehead center of the Guru and enters one's own forehead center. This purifies all of one's obscurations of body and represents a cause for the realization of the Nirmanakaya. Red light comes forth from the red syllable *AH* and enters one's own throat center. This purifies all of one's obscurations of speech or energy and represents a cause for the realization of the Sambhogakaya. Blue light comes forth from the blue syllable *HUM* and enters one's own heart center. This purifies all of one's obscurations of mind and represents a cause for the realization of the Dharmakaya. Then these different colored lights come forth from all three secret places simultaneously and enter into oneself, so that one becomes purified of all obscurations, both gross and subtle. Thus, according to the method of Tantra or the path of transformation, one has received from the Guru all four initiations or empowerments (*dbang bzhi*) for Body, Speech, Mind, and their unification. One may then progress along the four Paths of the Bodhisattva career, namely, Accumulation, Application, Vision, and Meditation Development, and as the Fruit one comes to realize the four stages in the development of vision (*snang-ba bzhi*) in terms of the Thodgal practice.

VI. Unification: The Guru then dissolves into a mass of light, and this light enters the aperture at the top of one's head and descends through the central channel. Finally the Guru reappears in the center of one's own heart as described in the text of the liturgy. This moment of unification is the real Guru Yoga. Then in the heart center of the Guru residing in one's own heart sits the Primordial Buddha Samantabhadra in union with the Primordial Wisdom Samantabhadri. In the heart of this Buddha is the white syllable *A* (the Tibetan letter) within a blue sphere of light (*thig-le*), surrounded by the six syllables representing the Six Vast Spaces of Samantabhadra (*kun-bzang klong drug*), namely, *A A HA SHA SA MA* (in the form of Tibetan letters). These indicate the purified nature of the six realms or destinies of rebirth (*'gro-ba drug*). Now the six consciousness aggregates (*tshogs drug*), that is, mind plus the usual five sense consciousnesses, are dissolved into this vast expanse of Primordial Purity (*dag-pa'i klong*), the state of emptiness, and one finds oneself in the state of the Clear Light, where Awareness and Emptiness are inseparably united (*rig stong 'od gsal chen-po'i ngang*) in the state of contemplation.

VII. Final Instructions: Then without distraction or moving from that state, one practices Vajrajapa, or the vajra recitation (*rdo-rje bzlas-pa*). Here one recites aloud (*ngag bzlas*) the syllables *OM AH HUM*, or alternatively, one correlates them with one's breathing (*rlung bzlas*). While inhaling, one silently fixates on the sound of *OM*; while holding the breath, one silently fixates on the sound of *AH*; and while exhaling, one silently fixates on the sound of *HUM*.

Colophon: This practice was received as a pure vision (*dag snang*) in his dreams by Kunzang Odsal Nyingpo, otherwise known as Dzongsar Khyentse Rinpoche or Jamyang Khyentse Chokyi Lodro ('Jam-dbyangs mkhyen-rtse chos kyi blo-gros, 1896–1959).

PART THREE:

Historical Origins
of Dzogchen

The Problems of Historiography

The questions concerning the actual historical existence of Garab Dorje and the authenticity of the *Tshig gsum gnad du brdeg-pa* attributed to him are complex, and there is no space to deal with them fully here. Nevertheless, it is necessary to address the problem in brief.

In general, it has been the custom among Western scholars, following the conventions of nineteenth-century higher criticism, to doubt the actual historical existence of any legendary figure for whom there exists no near contemporary evidence, such as texts, inscriptions, and so on. It is only human nature to overlay the history or the biography of a charismatic figure—whether religious, military, or political—with myth, so that this figure comes to approximate a pre-existing archetype. Thus, in later times, what we find in tradition, both written and oral, is not biography in the modern sense but hagiography. This is the case with Garab Dorje and with the other early masters of Dzogchen in both India and Tibet. But this fact does not in itself disprove the real historical existence of these masters.

In the later Terma tradition found among the Nyingmapas, for example, Guru Padmasambhava is exalted into a culture-hero, solar savior, and second Buddha. But this mythological elaboration does not preclude the real existence in the eighth century of our era of a historical figure, a Buddhist tantric master coming from India to Tibet, behind all this. Quite the contrary. Similarly, in the West, Jesus of Nazareth is exalted in the Gospels as the Messiah and the Savior, even the Son of God. The Gospels ignore most of the biography of the human Jesus, which was no doubt known at that time in oral tradition. Only his miracles and his parables, revealed during his three-year public teaching career, were important to the authors of the Gospels, because these were presented as proofs of the theological claims of these writers and certain parties within the early Church. Neither the hagiography of Garab Dorje nor that of Jesus of Nazareth is history in the proper sense. However, this does not mean that these figures did not exist historically or that they did not do and say many of the things that they were reported to have done and said.

Again, the excess of solar imagery and symbolism and the solar epiphanies found in the Mahayana Sutras, such as those found in the famous *Lotus Sutra*, or *Saddharmapundarika Sutra*, do not prove that Buddha Shakyamuni was merely a sun god or a solar hero and that he therefore did not have any historical existence.[1] On the contrary, the very existence of Buddhism for some two thousand five hundred years as a workable and successful spiritual path to enlightenment and liberation testifies to the real historical existence of its founder, the Buddha. He is no more a mere fiction or myth than Jesus, Muhammad, or Zoroaster, no matter how much myth has been projected onto him by later generations. Nor does this mythology necessarily alter the original intent of the teachings of these masters.

In the same way, the very existence of Dzogchen as a viable and successful spiritual path points to the real existence of its early masters; for if not with them, with whom did Dzogchen originate? This indication, however, which is bestowed by tradition, is not at all the same thing as historical proof. Was Dzogchen merely a deliberate fabrication by certain writers in later centuries? It is possible, theoretically at least, that Tibetan masters living at a later time, say the tenth century of our era, composed the Dzogchen Tantras upon which this tradition was originally founded, and then attributed these texts to figures belonging to an earlier era in order to have these texts accepted by the Buddhist scholars and practitioners of their own day.[2]

This was a practice not unknown in the West. When the Jewish authorities closed the Hebrew canon, known to Christians as the Old Testament, around 150 BCE, the age of prophecy came to an end; no new prophets were recognized by the temple hierarchy in the capital of Jerusalem. No more books could be added to the official canon of scriptures maintained by the priesthood. Therefore, an apocryphal work such as the Book of Enoch (probably composed in the first century BCE, and which was well known to Jesus of Nazareth and even mentioned by name in the New Testament) was not admitted to the canon, even though it was attributed to the antediluvian patriarch Enoch. According to this book, Enoch was taken up into the heavens by the angels and, returning to earth, he delivered many prophecies to his sons concerning events which would occur far in the future. Or again, the well-known Book of Daniel, which was subsequently accepted into the Hebrew canon, unlike Enoch, was written, according to internal evidence, in the time of the Greco-Syrian King Antiochus Epiphanes (176–164 BCE), but was attributed to an otherwise unknown prophet named Daniel, who lived in Babylon in the time of King Nebuchadnezzar, centuries earlier.[3] Aside from the Book of Daniel, there exists no other real evidence for the historical existence of this prophet, although Daniel, like Job, is a name well known from ancient Canaanite tradition found in the literature of Ugarit on the north Syrian coast. Both the Daniel in the Bible and the Daniel in Ugaritic literature were famous for their wisdom and sagacity. So a continuity of oral tradition, at least, may be found here.[4]

Similarly, in the Nyingmapa tradition, there are found many texts purporting to be accounts of earlier times, especially the Golden Age of the eighth century, when Guru Padmasambhava was said to have established the tantric form of Buddhism known as Vajrayana in Tibet. However, these works are, in fact, Termas, or hidden treasure texts, discovered in later centuries. For example, this was the case with the famous *Padma bka'-thang*, recovered by Urgyan Lingpa (O-rgyan gling-pa, 1323–1360), which claimed to give a contemporary account of the career of Padmasambhava set down by his consort and anamnesis, the Tibetan princess Yeshe Tsogyal. Most modern critical scholarship does not accept such Termas as genuine historical sources. Some Lama scholars of the Newer Schools also reject them, especially among the Gelugpas. The latter tend to dismiss the Nyingmapa Termas out of hand, although they do accept some Termalike texts, such as the *Mani bka' 'bum* and the *rGyud bzhi*, when it suits their own doctrinal or political interests, or for some other practical reasons. What can be said is that this particular Terma text, the *Padma bka'-thang*, dates at least from the time of Urgyan Lingpa (fourteenth century CE); he either wrote it himself *in toto* or pieced it together from earlier materials. A critical examination of the text seems to support the latter view, for it does contain some very early material.

Another factor here is oral tradition. A tradition may exist for a long time, even for centuries, before it is written down. Priestly castes, such as the Brahmans in India and the Druids in Western Europe, had great disdain for written texts, quite unlike the Chinese scholars of the Confucian tradition and the Rabbis of the biblical tradition in the West. Among the Brahmans and the Druids, the holy scriptures were retained in memory in the form of verses, and these verses were passed down from generation to generation by way of oral transmission. Living nowadays in an abundantly literate urban civilization, it is difficult for us to realize how great a quantity of knowledge these ancient sages could retain in memory alone. The discourses of the Buddha were at first solely retained in the memory of his disciple and personal attendant Ananda. In turn, these discourses were memorized and recited from memory by others, and no attempt was made to write them down for almost a hundred years after the Parinirvana of the Buddha. The sacred Vedas of the Brahmans were similarly passed down orally through the generations, and the texts of the Rigveda were actually not written down in Devanagari script until the eighteenth century at the behest of British scholars of the Sanskrit language. Modern scholars, conditioned by our literate civilization and our text-dominated educational system, tend to overlook the importance of oral tradition.

An authentic text, found in the treasure trove of Tibetan texts preserved in the Tun Huang Library (ninth–tenth century CE), may prove that the ideas or doctrines found therein did indeed exist at that time. Thus the discovery of two Dzogchen texts among these Tun Huang documents proves the existence of Dzogchen teaching in Tibet in at least the tenth century, after which time the library was sealed up until its discovery in the twentieth century. But the finding of such datable texts does not disprove the existence of these same ideas or doctrines before that time in earlier oral tradition or in earlier texts no longer extant. It would seem obvious that the appearance of a text at a particular time in history does not prove that the ideas the text contains first came into existence when these were written down in that text. Quite the contrary.

In the Tibetan context, the presence of an oral tradition is very likely, since such oral traditions exist even today. Originally all Upadeshas were orally transmitted; only later were they written down. It is merely the bias of most modern scholars to think that something does not exist unless it is written down in some text. In the early days, the masters relied less on written texts than on memory. Often their texts were merely mnemonic devices. Only at a later time were these root texts, composed in a highly terse and elliptical language, written down and explicated by commentaries authored by monk-scholars resident in monasteries supported by royal patronage. Thus these monks had the leisure for engaging themselves in this sort of literary activity, which was not the case with the Mahasiddhas, who were the actual sources of these Upadeshas.[5]

Nowadays, in our urban industrial civilization, books are commonplace, but in ancient times, and in general before the advent of printing and a ready supply of paper, they were not. Often a text served, as we have said, as a mnemonic device, an aid to memory, rather than as an elaborate treatise. Moreover, large books, consisting of many pages, were heavy and therefore were difficult to carry about easily from place to place before modern means of transportation appeared. The lifestyle of the early Buddhist Mahasiddhas, like that of contemporary Hindu Sadhus, was itinerant and peripatetic. It would be impossible in those days for a master, wandering from place to place, to carry a large collection of books with him.

The Historical Existence of Garab Dorje

There exists an interesting parallel to the legend of Garab Dorje, as translated above, in the legend of Sophia in the life of Jesus Christ, that is to say, the immaculate conception, the virgin birth, the confounding of the elders in the temple with his precocious learning while yet a child, the performing of various miracles, the final resurrection and ascension to heaven, and so on. Jesus is called Christ and the Son of God; Garab Dorje is called the Nirmanakaya and the emanation (Skt. *nirmita*) of Vajrasattva. There exist many interesting parallels and historical connections between Gnosticism and Mahayana Buddhism, particularly Dzogchen, and I have dealt with these questions elsewhere.[1] But it is not necessary to postulate direct historical influences either way, for the historical figures Rabbi Jesus of Nazareth and Dzogchen master Garab Dorje of Uddiyana both participate in the same transhistorical archetype.

Moreover, just as there is more historical evidence for the existence of Paul of Tarsus than for that of Jesus of Nazareth, the historical existence of Manjushrimitra seems much more assured and firmly established than that of Garab Dorje, because there exists an extant text attributed to him, namely, the *rDo la gser zhun*, "Gold Refined from Ore," also known as the *Byang-chub sems bsgom-pa*, "Meditation on the Bodhichitta [i.e., the Primordial State]."[2] However, this text represents a rather scholastic presentation of Dzogchen and is quite different from the Upadesha found in the *'Das-rjes*. The name "Dzogchen" is not even found in the text. Since Manjushrimitra was said to have originally been a scholar belonging to the Yogacharin school, which adhered to this Chittamatra philosophy, it is likely that the text represents an effort to present Dzogchen, that is, the Primordial State, from a Yogacharin or Chittamatrin point of view, using the vocabulary of that philosophical school.[3]

But the matter is a bit more complex, since there appear to be two Manjushrimitras, an elder Manjushrimitra (*snga-ba*), who was a disciple of Garab Dorje, and a later Manjushrimitra (*phyi-ma*), who had a miraculous birth and was considered to be the reincarnation of the earlier Manjushrimitra. The younger Manjushrimitra was said to have instructed Padmasambhava in the outer and the inner Tantras (*sngags phyi dang nang*) and also to have taught the Mahasiddha Aryadeva. It was not an uncommon practice for Indian Mahasiddhas to adopt the names of earlier historical figures whom they considered to be their previous incarnations. The second Manjushrimitra is cited in the histories of Padma Karpo ('Brug-pa kun-mkhyen Padma dkar-po, 1527–1592) and of Pawo Tsuglag Trengwa (dPa'-bo gTsug-lag phreng-ba, 1503–1565).[4]

Oral tradition has passed down to later times much of the lore and the teaching of the early Mahasiddhas, and it would appear that this was the case with Garab Dorje, even though the *'Das-rjes*, as we find it in the *Bi-ma snying-thig*, is a Terma. It is quite possible that the contents of the text, though perhaps not the notes, do go back to Garab Dorje and Manjushrimitra.

The principal historical questions surrounding Garab Dorje center on his dates, his original name in the Sanskrit language, and his country of origin. The dates of Garab Dorje are uncertain, and the different Tibetan sources do not agree among themselves. Because the existence of Padmasambhava and that of Vimalamitra are attested in the mid-eighth century in Tibet, then if we count back generations, this would appear to put Garab Dorje in the late sixth century. The traditional Tibetan historical accounts would place him farther back in time. According to the *rNying-ma'i chos-'byung* of Dudjom Rinpoche, Garab Dorje is said to have been born some 166 years after the Parinirvana of the historical Buddha Shakyamuni. Tulku Thondup in his study follows Dudjom Rinpoche in this.[5] According to the *Phug-lugs*, the prevailing system of astrology and chronology in Tibet, the Parinirvana of the Buddha occurred in the year 881 BCE.[6] Western scholars, who reject the traditional Tibetan dates out of hand, also disagree among themselves, but generally they place the birth of the Buddha in the sixth century BCE, based on the chronicles found in the Pali tradition.[7] In one place Namkhai Norbu Rinpoche gives the birth of Garab Dorje as c. 55 CE; however, he does not explain how he has come to this date.[8] Tarthang Tulku gives another account of the career of Garab Dorje, without citing his sources, but he also gives the date c. 55 CE for the birth of the master.[9] Elsewhere, in the Dzogchen Upadesha tradition and also in many Terma texts, biographical details of Garab Dorje are given, and it is said that he was born some 360 years after the Parinirvana. Namkhai Norbu Rinpoche says that, according to the Dzogchen Upadesha Series, Garab Dorje was born 360 years after the Parinirvana of the Buddha; taking that to be the year 544 BCE (the date according to the Pali tradition), Rinpoche calculates the year 184 BCE for the birth of the master.[10]

According to yet another tradition, Garab Dorje was born miraculously of a virgin in the country of Uddiyana twenty-eight years after the Parinirvana of the Buddha. Similarly, Padmasambhava was said to have been born miraculously in the center of a lotus blossom in the middle of Dhanakosha Lake in Uddiyana some eight years afterward. There exists an important Dzogchen Semde text, the *rDo-rje sems-dpa' nam-mkha'-che'i rgyud*, together with a commentary by Vairochana, preserved in the *Bai-ro'i rgyud 'bum* (vol. 1). At the end of this commentary, the colophon states that the above text was transmitted by Garab Dorje some twenty-eight years after the Parinirvana. It also states that Garab Dorje was the son of a princess of Uddiyana, Praharini by name, the daughter of King Indrabhuti.[11] The calculation found here is based on the assumption that Garab Dorje expounded the *rDo-rje sems-dpa' nam-mkha'-che*, "The Great Sky of Vajrasattva," to the Dakinis shortly after his birth. Garab Dorje was considered to be not only a great adept, or Mahasiddha, but also the Nirmanakaya, or emanation, of Vajrasattva. Thus he was enlightened even before his birth in our world-system, and it followed that he taught the Dzogchen precepts to humans and nonhumans, principally the Dakinis, since earliest childhood, beginning with the exposition of the above Tantra when he was a three-day-old infant. At that time Garab Dorje explained that the true Vajrasattva, the diamondlike being, is the Primordial State of the individual, and this is the real meaning of Dzogchen. It is deathless, indestructible, and unchanging, like the diamond, or vajra. Vajrasattva is generally regarded as the transcendent source of Garab Dorje's teachings, as was explained previously.

A. W. Hanson-Barber would identify Garab Dorje with a Mahasiddha known from other sources who bears the name Anandavajra.[12] Several texts translated and preserved in the *Tangyur* collection are attributed to this master. The principal question here is how to Sanskritize the various Tibetan names given by tradition to Garab Dorje. In the various hagiographical accounts, his two principal names are given as dGa'-rab rdo-rje and Ro-langs bde-ba. In the Peking edition of the *Tangyur* published in Japan, the Sanskrit for Garab Dorje is given as Surativajra in one colophon, but this was a questionable restoration by D. T. Suzuki.[13] H. V. Guenther suggests the possibilities Praharshavajra, Surativajra, and Pramuditavajra, but gives no reasons for these Sanskritizations. [14] Consulting the Tibetan dictionary of Sarat Chandra Das, *A Tibetan-English Dictionary*,[15] it is found that seventeen different Sanskrit words are translated by the Tibetan word *dga-'ba* (pp. 263–65), and five different Sanskrit elements are translated by Tibetan *rab* (pp. 1167–68). If *rab* stands for *rab-tu*, "very much, exceedingly, supreme," it is the equivalent of the Sanskrit *pra-*. Generally Tibetan *dga'-ba* translates Sanskrit *nanda* or *ānanda* as "happiness, bliss." Hanson-Barber suggests relying on the *Mahavyutpatti* (ninth century CE) rather than the Das dictionary. This early vocabulary list, however, is notorious for excluding the Sanskrit terminology of the Tantras. Hanson-Barber would make *dga'-rab* stand for *ānanda*, but there is no corroborating evidence for this. The Sanskrit for Garab Dorje therefore remains uncertain. Moreover, a Mahasiddha Anandavajra was well known in the New Tantra tradition (*sngags gsar-ma*), and his name is translated in all sources as dGa'-ba'i rdo-rje and not as dGa'-rab rdo-rje. Tulku Thondup has suggested Prahevajra as the original; this form reflects the Sanskrit mantra found in the short sadhana translated above, which gives Prajnabhava Hevajra as the master's full name. In general, I have adopted Prahevajra, with reservations. As for the second name, according to the dictionaries, *ro-langs* is Sanskrit *vetāla*, and *bde-ba* is *kṣema* or *sukha*. It seems likely, therefore, that the latter Tibetan name translates Vetalakshema.[16]

It must be observed that Hanson-Barber bases his proposed identification of Garab Dorje with the Mahasiddha Anandavajra not only on an apparent similarity of names but also on a hypothetical date for Garab Dorje, supposedly derived from several Mahasiddha lineages. He would reject the traditional dates given above as too early.

In his method, Hanson-Barber would locate Garab Dorje in the Mahasiddha lineages and then count forward by generations to some known historical figure in order to derive a date for him. He assumes the identification of Anandavajra with Vetalakshema (Garab Dorje). According to the *'Dra 'bag chen-mo*, the traditional biography of Vairochana the translator, when Vairochana went to India, he met personally and studied under the Dzogchen master Shrisimha, who had also been the master of Vimalamitra, Jnanasutra, and Padmasambhava. Vairochana is known to have flourished in Tibet in the latter half of the eighth century of our era, and so, according to Hanson-Barber, by counting a standard generation as 35 years, this would give:

Vairochana and Vimalamitra II	760 CE
Shrisimha	725
Manjushrimitra II	690
Vimalamitra I	655
(an unknown master)	620
Manjushrimitra I	585
Garab Dorje	550

This reconstruction of the lineage by Hanson-Barber is based on the notion that there were two Manjushrimitras, both of whom taught Dzogchen.[17] And since Vimalamitra is said to have lived for two hundred years, Hanson-Barber assumes that there were two individuals of that name. No other teacher, other than Shrisimha, is mentioned for Vimalamitra, and so he postulates an unknown teacher for this supposed earlier Vimalamitra.[18] All of this seems a bit arbitrary and dubious.

Hanson-Barber also relies on the *Blue Annals* (*Deb-ther sngon-po*) of Go Lotsawa ('Gos lo-tswa-ba gZhon-nu dpal, 1392–1481),[19] where there is found a lineage for the Anuyoga Tantra, as follows:

Vajrapani	
King Dza	
Indrabodhi	485 CE
Kukuraja	520
Vetalakshema	555
Vajrahasa	590
Prabhahasti	625
Shakyasimha	660
Danarakshita and Che-btsan-skyes	695

Sthiramati	730
Sukhaprasanna	765
Dharmabodhi and Vasudhara of Nepal	800
gNubs-chen Sangs-rgyas ye-shes	ninth century

And again, by counting generations, he arrives at the above results. Here the name Vetalakshema (Ro-langs bde-ba) does occur and is linked with the names Indrabodhi and Kukuraja, both of Uddiyana and important figures in the lineages of transmission for the Mahayoga and the Anuyoga Tantras according to the Nyingmapa tradition. If this Vetalakshema is Garab Dorje, then he flourished in the mid- or late sixth century. However, a somewhat different lineage list for the Anuyoga Tantra is given by Dudjom Rinpoche in his *rNying-ma'i chos-'byung*.

Hanson-Barber introduces a third source, the lineage given for the *Jnanasiddhi*, a text attributed to King Indrabodhi,[20] and this lineage is laid out in the *Blue Annals*.[21] However, this text, the *Jnanasiddhi*, is associated with the Mahasiddha tradition, or at least this was the case after the eleventh century in Tibet. Hanson-Barber points out that Mahamudra and Dzogchen have a great deal in common, and he assumes that they had a historical connection, not only later, in the time of Kumararaja and the Third Karmapa (twelfth–thirteenth century CE), but also at the time of their birth.[22] Dombhi Heruka, who was a contemporary of Padmasambhava and a teacher of Vairochana in India, transmitting to the latter the teachings of Yantra Yoga,[23] occurs in this lineage. Hanson-Barber counts the generations backward from him as follows:

Dombhi Heruka	eighth century CE
Shri Lakshminkara, sister of King Indrabodhi	730
Chittavajra	695
Sarvajagannatha	660
Siddhivajra	625
Brahmavajra	590
Anandavajra, etc.	555

On this basis, Hanson-Barber believes he can make the equation Anandavajra = Vetalakshema = Garab Dorje and can therefore date Garab Dorje at 555 CE. But all of this is rather arbitrary and not at all conclusive. These Mahasiddha lineages vary from source to source; they do not agree among themselves, as is the case with Go Lotsawa

and Dudjom Rinpoche.[24] The Mahasiddhas in the lists are not necessarily successive; at times many of them were actually contemporary with each other. Moreover, Mahasiddhas transmitted their teachings not just to a single disciple, but to many different disciples. Thus
Shrisimha taught Jnanasutra, Vimalamitra, Padmasambhava, and
Vairochana. If we count them by generations, then the time span from
Shrisimha to Vairochana would represent some 140 years, although
all of these masters were in fact contemporaries. Also, one cannot
assume that a Mahasiddha lived and taught for precisely 35 years.
Counting by generations is only a rule of thumb; it cannot yield precise dates. But even if Anandavajra and Garab Dorje could be shown
to be contemporary, this does not prove that they are the same individual. Not all Johns living in London in 1990 are the same individual. To attempt to construct a precise history out of these lineages
and legends of the Mahasiddhas is a hazardous undertaking.

Nor is the location of Garab Dorje's homeland of Uddiyana (O-
rgyan) entirely certain. According to Nyingmapa tradition, it was
said to have lain somewhere to the northwest of India, that is to say,
northwest of Vajrasana, the diamond seat of the enlightenment of
the Buddha (the modern Bodh Gaya). This pilgrimage site was taken
to be the center of the Indian subcontinent, and all directions were
measured from that sacred site at the center of the world. Native-
born Indian scholars of the tantric tradition in the early part of this
century, such as Bhattacharyya, Shahi, and others, located Uddiyana
in eastern India in Bengal or in Orissa. Giuseppe Tucci proposed the
Swat Valley in Pakistan, as this location is indicated in the works of
two medieval Tibetan authors he translated.[25] At least one of those
Lamas, Urgyanpa, believed the Swat Valley was Uddiyana, but he
visited there at a time when Islam had eradicated most traces of Buddhism, as it had done earlier in Afghanistan and Central Asia. Ar-
chaeological research by Aurel Stein, Tucci, and others failed to un-
cover a flourishing tantric culture in Swat, the presence of which is
called for by the evidence found in the literary sources. Ruins of stupas
and monasteries are found in quantity in Swat, but nothing like the
abundance of tantric art which appears later in Bengal and Nepal.
Similarly, the archaeology of Central Asia has not yet yielded much
in the way of tantric art. But as an esoteric tradition, perhaps it took
some time before the Tantras were translated into the plastic arts.

For example, the famous tantric yab-yum, or images of copulating deities, so popular in Nepali and Tibetan Buddhism, have not been found in India. This does not prove that the concept of yuganaddha (yab-yum) did not exist in India; we know that it did from extant Buddhist Sanskrit texts, but perhaps the doctrine was as yet too esoteric, too unconventional and controversial, to be expressed in the public art of the Pala era. And with regard to Uddiyana itself, perhaps Uddiyana was actually the name of a much wider geographical area than the Swat Valley alone, one embracing parts of Pakistan, Afghanistan, and even western Tibet (Zhang-zhung). The best approach is to remain open-minded and not restrict the name only to the Swat Valley.

Although at the moment the real historical existence of Garab Dorje cannot be proved conclusively due to the lack of evidence in the form of texts and inscriptions actually discovered in the country of Uddiyana, there still exists no reason to disparage Nyingmapa tradition and assert with confidence that this master did not exist sometime in the past as the source of the Dzogchen teachings. Even if all of the events in his life that are recorded in Nyingmapa tradition prove to be myth and hagiography, it does not change the issue. There still exists a mysterious historical presence behind all of the surviving traditions. Tradition itself is always pointing toward a higher source and ultimate origin which lies beyond mere history. No Asian Buddhist really believes that Buddha Shakyamuni was only an ordinary human being who during the course of some eighty years said a few things and did a few things, and then died and was no more. Buddha Shakyamuni was an epiphany, an eruption of a higher spiritual reality into profane time and history. And for the Buddhist, history itself is but a phantom show without an ultimate goal or purpose. In the Buddhist perspective, there is no salvation to be found in history, because history represents conditioned existence, and conditioned existence is inevitably cyclical. Just as individuals are born and die and are reborn again, so it is with entire universes. This contrasts with the conventional view held in the West since the time of Saint Augustine that time is unilinear and that history is under the personal direction of God or of some rational historical process. This assumption regarding time and history is found in both Christianity and Marxism, for example. However, in the Buddhist view, the plan of salvation will not be disclosed by any exhaustive study of the events of the past, nor will history culminate in some utopian future where all human suffering is eliminated. Suffering is inherent in human existence. History is only conditioned existence; it is cyclical in nature; it is Samsara. The true spiritual goal lies beyond time and history, neither at the beginning nor at the end. And what is transcendent and beyond history is often best expressed as myth. Thus it is not of ultimate significance for the Dzogchen practitioner whether Garab Dorje, or Padmasambhava and Vimalamitra for that matter, actually existed historically, because the Dzogchen teachings are true, effective, and bring concrete results.

Possible Historical Scources of Dzogchen

Did the Dzogchen teachings originate with Garab Dorje in Uddiyana and spread subsequently to India and Tibet as the Nyingmapa tradition asserts, or did they originate later in Tibet in the tenth century under Hindu and Bonpo influences, as some of its Tibetan detractors claim and some modern scholars assert? As pointed out in the introduction, the Nyingmapa tradition consists of both *bka'-ma*, texts which originated in the early period and which have been transmitted down to the present day within a continuous and uninterrupted lineage of masters, and *gter-ma*, or treasure texts, which are also said to have originated in the early period, but which were concealed and then rediscovered in later centuries. Generally, many scholars belonging to the Sarmapa or Newer Schools in Tibet do not accept the authenticity of these Termas, and Western scholars also usually assume that the Terma text in question was actually written by the individual who discovered it. But up until the fourteenth century the history of the Nyingmapa school was generally characterized by an orderly transmission of both *bka'-ma* and *gter-ma*.[1] The first text recognized as a Terma appears to have been discovered in the tenth century by the Nyingmapa master Sangye Lama (Sangs-rgyas bla-ma), a contemporary of the famous translator Rinchen Zangpo (Rinchen bzang-po, 958–1051). The work of this latter scholar was largely responsible for the Later Translations (*phyi 'gyur*) of the Buddhist Tantras, which resulted in the movement known as the Later Spreading of the Dharma (*phyi dar*) and the formation of the Sarmapa schools (*gsar-ma-pa*), whose teachings and practices were based on these new translations. The first school to be organized as a recognizable dis-

crete entity was the Kadampa (*bka'-gdams-pa*), founded by the illustrious teacher Dromton ('Brom-ston, 1008–1064), the principal disciple of the famous Indian master Atisha, who came to Tibet in 1042.
But only as the result of the translation activities of Rinchen Zangpo
and followed by the organizing activities of the new monasteries by
the Kadampas, soon to be followed by the Sakyapas and the
Kagyudpas, did those masters who followed the older traditions
come to think of themselves as being distinct, as Nyingmapa (*rnying-
ma-pa*), or the Old Tantra school.

According to the received Nyingmapa tradition, it was Padmasambhava, Vimalamitra, and Vairochana the translator who originally transmitted the Dzogchen teachings to Tibet in the eighth century. And it was Vairochana, in particular, who first translated
Dzogchen texts into Tibetan, the earliest of these being the *Rig-pa'i
khu-byug*. His detractors among the later scholars of the Newer
Schools claimed that Vairochana was not the translator, but actually
the author of these early texts of the Semde Series, such as the *Kun-
byed rgyal-po Tantra*, and so on. As indicated in the introduction, it
was Vairochana and Vimalamitra who translated the Dzogchen
Semde teachings and Vairochana alone who translated the Dzogchen
Longde teachings. However, both of these masters had received the
Dzogchen precepts from the same master in India, namely, Shrisimha.
The Tantras belonging to these two series are now found in the *rNying-
ma'i rgyud 'bum* collection and represent *bka'-ma*, or a continuous
tradition.

The teachings belonging to the Upadesha Series (*rdzogs-chen man-
ngag gi sde*) are generally Terma, or rediscovered texts, and they principally descend through two separate lineages of transmission:

(1) *Pan-chen bi-ma'i bka'-srol:* the tradition of Mahapandita
    Vimalamitra, as represented, for example, by the *Bi-ma
    snying-thig* collection made by Longchenpa (fourteenth cen-
    tury). From Vimalamitra (eighth century CE) the Nyingthig
    precepts were transmitted to:

Myang ting-nge-'dzin bzang-po	ninth century
dBas blo-gros dbang-phyug	tenth century
Dang-ma lhun-rgyal	eleventh century
lCe-btsun seng-ge dbang-phyug	eleventh–twelfth century
Zhang-ston bkra-shis rdo-rje	1097–1167
mKhas-pa nyi-ma 'bum	1158–1213
Guru Ju-'ber	1196–1255

'Khrul-zhig seng-ge rgyal-po	13 century
sGrub-chen me-long rdo-rje	1243–1303
Rig-'dzin Kuma-radza (Kumararaja)	1266–1343
kLong-chen rab-'byams-pa	1308–1363[2]

This tradition of the Dzogchen Nyingthig teachings, therefore, came to be known as the *Bi-ma sying-thig*, "The Essence of the Mind of Vimalamitra."

(2) *sLob-dpon Padma'i bka'-srol*: the tradition of Acharya Padmasambhava. This tradition of the Nyingthig precepts is said to have been transmitted by Guru Padmasambhava to Lhacham Padma-sal (Lha-lcam padma-gsal), a daughter of the Tibetan king Tisong Detsan. She died at the age of eight, and then, like Jesus reviving Lazarus, Padmasambhava, with his miraculous powers, called her consciousness (*rnam-shes*) back into her body, and she was restored to life. He bestowed the Nyingthig precepts upon her, and then he and Yeshe Tsogyal concealed the texts. This royal princess was later reborn as the master Padma Letreltsal (Padma las-'brel-rtsal, 1291–1315). At the age of twenty-three, inspired by the Dakinis, he extracted these texts from their places of concealment in Dwagpo (Dwags-po) in southern Tibet. They were written on golden paper (*shog ser*). As Terma, this tradition represents a short lineage:

Padmasambhava	eighth century
Lha-lcam padma-gsal	eighth century
Padma las-'brel-rtsal	1291–1315
rGyal-sras legs-pa	1290–1366
kLong-chen rab-'byams-pa	1308–1363[3]

This tradition of Dzogchen Nyingthig teaching came to be known as the *mKha'-'gro snying-thig*, "The Essence of the Mind of the Dakini," because they were transmitted through the Dakini Padma-sal. In turn they were inherited by Longchenpa and included in his monumental collection of Nyingthig teachings, the *sNying-thig ya-bzhi*.

Indian Buddhism

According to conventional Nyingmapa tradition, it was Guru Padmasambhava, of course, who first introduced the Dzogchen teachings into Tibet. But this has recently been contested by Eva Dargyay.[4]

She asserts that while he was in Tibet, Padmasambhava taught only the tantric system of the Mahayoga, specifically the *sGrub-pa bka' brgyad*, the combined Sadhana System of the Eight Herukas. This is in line with past Gelugpa scholarly attacks on the authenticity of the Dzogchen teachings, most notably by Sumpa Khanpo (Sum-pa mkhan-po ye-shes dpal-'byor, 1704–1788) in his famous *chos-'byung*, or history of Buddhism, the *dPag-bsam ljon-bzang*, part 2. In this work Sumpa Khanpo asserts that Padmasambhava visited Tibet only for a short period of time, some eighteen months, as against the many years claimed in the traditional Nyingmapa account. And then, soon after his departure from Tibet, an unscrupulous Hindu sadhu, wearing identical hat and robes, appeared in Tibet claiming to be Guru Padma and taught to certain Tibetans the Hindu Vedanta doctrines (*mu-stegs rtag gi lta-ba*), that is to say, Dzogchen, falsely asserting that these teachings were Buddhist. These heretical doctrines subsequently became the basis of the Nyingmapa system. This, however, is not historical scholarship, as is the case with Dargyay, but merely sectarian polemic and propaganda. Dargyay asserts that while in Tibet, Padmasambhava did teach the *bKa' brgyad*, yet it cannot be proved that he taught Dzogchen. Rather, Dzogchen was introduced by Vairochana and Vimalamitra and attributed only in a later age (post-tenth century) to Padmasambhava when the Nyingmapas, in response to the growing prestige and power of the Sarmapa Schools, attempted to consolidate their own position by attributing, unhistorically and anachronistically, the introduction into Tibet of the entire Nyingmapa system, including Dzogchen, to Padmasambhava. With the accelerating development of the Terma tradition, during the twelfth through the fourteenth centuries, the role of Padmasambhava as cultural hero and founder grew in importance until he assumed the status of a second Buddha. All things came to be attributed to him, even the present-day physiognomy of Tibet. Some scholars, such as Helmut Hoffmann, even accused Padmasambhava of attempting to invent his own religion, which Hoffmann calls "Padmaism" in order to distinguish it from more traditional orthodox Buddhism.[5]

But despite the exaggerated claims of the later Nyingmapa tradition found in the Termas, there is something to be said for the direct connection of Padmasambhava with Dzogchen. Nyingmapa authorities like Dudjom Rinpoche agree that Padmasambhava principally taught the Mahayoga system in the form of the *sGrub-pa bka' brgyad* while he was in Tibet. In the Nyingmapa canon of the Old Transla-tion Tantras found in the *rNying-ma'i rgyud 'bum* collection, the texts of the Mahayoga are classified into two groups: (1) *rGyud-sde*, or the Tantra Section, consisting of eighteen Tantras, chief among them be-ing the *Guhyagarbha Tantra* (*gSang-ba snying-po*); and (2) *sGrub-sde*, or the Sadhana Section, consisting of the eight sadhanas for the eight Herukas.

These sadhana texts in the second group were revealed to eight Vidyadharas or Mahasiddhas, including Padmasambhava, at the great cremation ground of Shitavana (bSil-ba'i tshal) to the west of Bodh Gaya, where previously Garab Dorje had also resided and taught. The sadhana texts were brought forth from their concealment in a stupa located in the cremation ground by the Dakini Karmendrani (Las-kyi dbang-mo), and she presented them to the eight Maha-siddhas in turn, inside caskets made of different kinds of materials. These Yogins practiced the sadhanas in eight different caves in the vicinity, and all of them attained realization of siddhi, or success in practice. Thereafter Padmasambhava collected together these sadhanas, systematized them, and integrated them into a single system of tantric practice. It was into the combined mandala of these eight Herukas that Padmasambhava initiated his principal disciples at Chimphu Cave near Samye Monastery.[6]

Nevertheless, according to Nyingmapa authorities,[7] Padma-sambhava did subsequently teach the Dzogchen precepts to some of his disciples but in the context of the Mahayoga Tantras, and thus as a part of the path of transformation. In the system of Padmasambhava, the culmination or final stage in tantric transformation is not known as Mahamudra, as is the case with the Anuttara Tantra system of the New Translation Tantras, but as Dzogchen. This is the Great Perfec-tion or the Great Completion (*rdzogs-pa chen-po*) that lies beyond both the generation process (*bskyed-rim*) and the perfection process (*rdzogs-rim*). Moreover, Padmasambhava taught a nongradual method of transformation, one that is usually designated as Anuyoga, and so we may say that Padmasambhava was teaching Tantra, but Tantra in the Anuyoga style of practice. Usually the Mahayoga style of prac-tice requires a complicated gradual process of transformation, as is the case with the Anuttara Tantras of the Sarmapa schools. It is not clear whether, in the case of Padmasambhava, this Anuyoga was precisely distinguished from the Mahayoga, as was the case in later centuries. It would appear that, in the days of the activities of Padmasambhava and Vairochana, the principal text of the Anuyoga cycle had not yet been translated into Tibetan. This Tantra, also called a Sutra (*mdo*) and an Agama (*lung*), is known as the *dGongs 'dus*, and it was translated from the Drusha (*bru-sha*) language of Gilgit into Tibetan by Chetsunkye (Che-btsun-skyes), a native of Gilgit, in the late eighth or early ninth century. This master was a teacher of the famous Mahayoga Tantra adept Nubchen Sangye Yeshe (gNubs-chen sang-rgyas ye-shes, ninth century), a leading exponent not only of Mahayoga Tantra but also of Dzogchen.

Chan Buddhism

Giuseppe Tucci acknowledges that Dzogchen has its original source in the Mahasiddha tradition of India, the so-called Sahajayana, although this particular term was coined in modern times and is not found in traditional Sanskrit and Tibetan sources. But Tucci also felt that Dzogchen had been strongly influenced by the Chan Buddhism of China. Like Dzogchen, Chan has a nongradual approach to the path and speaks of a sudden or instantaneous enlightenment. This enlightenment experience is called *satori* in Japanese and expresses the Chinese term *wu*, which translates the Sanskrit verb *vibudhyati*, "to awaken." Tucci points to Nyingmapa traditions that Vairochana the translator actually studied under the Hwashang Mahayana, the leading Chinese exponent of Chan in eighth-century Tibet.[8] And indeed, the Nyingmapas, for example Longchenpa himself, are the only Tibetans who have a good word to say about the Hwashang. Otherwise, he has generally been vilified and has even been reduced to a figure of ridicule in the Tibetan Lama dances, playing the role of the clown who imitates the actions of Lamas, but who gets everything wrong. The name *hwa-shang* comes from the Chinese *ho-shang*, translating the Sanskrit *upadhyaya*, "abbot," and so *hwa-shang* came to mean "Chan master" in Tibetan.

Even scholars of wide and encyclopedic learning among the Tibetans, such as the famous Sakya Pandita (Sa-skya Pandita Kun-dga' rgyal-mtshan, 1181–1251), came to accuse Dzogchen of being a Chinese doctrine (*rgya nag gi chos*) deriving from Chan. As a dialectically engaged scholar defending what he regarded as the orthodox view of Buddhism, he resorted, on occasion, to a fierce polemic against the teachings of Gampopa concerning the doctrine of Mahamudra, the culmination of the tantric path of transformation. He rejected out of hand the notion of a sudden enlightenment and discussed all pertinent matters in a large work of doctrinal criticism, the *sDom gsum rab-dbye*. Gampopa (sGom-po-pa bsod-nams rin-chen, 1079–1153), originally a Kadampa monk, later became the principal disciple of the famous Yogin and mountain recluse Milarepa (Mi-la ras-pa, 1040–1123), from whom he received the teachings of the *Na-ro chos drug* and the *Phyag-rgya chen-po*, or Mahamudra. Both of these teachings pertain to *rDzogs-rim*, or the perfection process, the second stage in tantric transformation. Gampopa became the actual founder of the Kagyudpa tradition as a distinct school and monastic order by merging the Kadampa tradition of monastic piety with the tantric teachings he had received from Milarepa. In his *Lam-rim rdor bsdus*, he discusses the nature of instantaneous or sudden enlightenment. Here Gampopa asserts that such a sudden enlightenment is not yet the actual state of Buddhahood, but that this Buddhahood is present in the individual its full potentiality, although at the moment it is prevented from becoming manifest due to the presence of the physical body, which is the fruit of previous karma. However, the fully realized state of Buddhahood will actualize and become present immediately after the death of the individual upon the advent of the Bardo state. This text also mentions the *rnal-'byor bzhi*, the four stages in the practice of Mahamudra, in terms very similar to the four stages of the practice of the Dzogchen Semde Series of teachings.

Also in his *Dus-gsum mkhyen-pa'i zhus-lan*, where he replies to the questions of his disciple the First Karmapa Dusum Khyenpa (Dus-gsum mkhyen-pa, 1110–1193), Gampopa appears to portray Dzogchen as parallel to Mahamudra, both of them representing Upadeshas for the *rDzogs-rim*, or perfection process. In other places, he appears to identify Mahamudra with Dzogchen. In the *Tshogs bshad legs mdzes-ma*, he describes Mahamudra as *phyag-chen dri-med zang-thal*. This last word, *zang-thal*, "directly penetrating," is a characteristic Dzogchen term. Yet, when replying to Dusum Khyenpa in the text mentioned above, he tries to distance himself somewhat from the more extreme sudden enlightenment doctrines of Dzogchen. Gampopa distinguished two types of individual practitioners: the gradualists (*rim-gyis-pa*) and the nongradualists (*cig-car-ba*). He goes on to say that the method of the latter is exceedingly difficult, and he describes himself humbly as a gradualist. Gampopa is also best known, at least in the West, as the author of a work on the gradual path to enlightenment in the *Lam-rim* genre, namely, the *Thar-pa rin-po-che'i rgyan.*[9] It does appear that the Dzogchen Semde did influence Gampopa in his exposition of the Mahamudra Upadesha, but there exist no historical grounds for lumping together Dzogchen and the Mahamudra of Gampopa as teachings and methods derived from the Chan of China.[10]

In the minds of Tibetans, it is uncertain which represents the greater insult: asserting that Dzogchen is a heresy coming from Hindu Vedanta or a heresy coming from Chinese Chan. Since the eleventh century it has been the custom among Tibetan scholars to disparage Chan as a false teaching. The later medieval Tibetan historians all recorded how the Tibetan king Tisong Detsan proposed a debate between Kamalashila, the chief disciple of Shantirakshita, the first abbot of Samye Monastery, as the representative of the Indian side (the Madhyamika school), and the Hwashang Mahayana, the Chan master, as the representative of the Chinese side. This public debate would decide which doctrine, the Madhyamika or the Chan, was true and best. All of the Tibetan histories agree that the Hwashang was decisively defeated in the debate, and as a result the king expelled the Hwashang and his Chinese cohorts from the kingdom of Tibet. Nonetheless, the Chinese arranged to have the victor, Kamalashila, assassinated in order to avenge their defeat at his hands. All of this makes good melodrama, but is it history?

With the discovery of the Tun Huang library in this century, our view of this debate changed radically. At Tun Huang a number of Chinese and Tibetan texts turned up which presented the Chinese side of this famous debate. These texts have been translated and studied by Paul Demieville,[11] and it appears that many modern Western readers prefer the presentation by the Hwashang of his side of the debate to that represented by Kamalashila in his *Bhavanakrama.*[12] The doctrinal issues involved in this supposed debate between Indian Madhyamika and Chinese Chan have greatly interested Western scholars, but now it seems doubtful that a debate ever took place in the sense of a direct face-to-face confrontation between Kamalashila and the Hwashang. Rather, it appears that King Tisong Detsan, himself a rather literate and learned man, wrote to various authorities and solicited their views on the Dharma. To judge from the Tun Huang finds, the king seemed to have been quite satisfied with the Hwashang's replies. The exclusion of Chan from Tibet seemed to have more to do with politics than with doctrine, such as fear at the court of Chinese political influence or the defeat of some pro-Chinese party among the ministers of the king.

The attitudes of the Tibetan Lamas from the eleventh century until today toward Chan have been, by and large, exceedingly negative, except for certain Nyingmapas like Longchenpa and Urgyan Lingpa. The Tibetan Lamas are content with their Indian-derived traditions as representing the authentic corpus of the Buddha's teachings. They have had absolutely no interest in the post-eighth-century developments of Buddhism in China, including Chan, and have had little or no contact personally with the Chinese teachers of Chan and the Japanese teachers of Zen. This has been the case until recently. Chögyam Trungpa Rinpoche (the eleventh Trung-pa Rin-poche of Zur-mang Monastery, 1939–1987), when residing in the United States, was a notable exception, having developed a close personal relationship with a notable Zen master residing in California, the late Suzuki Roshi, who belonged to the Soto tradition. This Olympian disinterest, if not disdain, for non-Tibetan manifestations of Buddhism clearly represents a feeling on the part of Tibetans of their cultural superiority more than anything else. What accurate knowledge Tibetan Lama-scholars do have of Chan is largely drawn from Nubchen Sangye Yeshe's *bSan-gtan mig-sgrom* (ninth century CE), and this description reflects a type of Northern Chan prevalent in Central Asia only in the eighth and ninth centuries.

When I have asked various modern Tibetan Dzogchen masters what the difference is between Dzogchen and Chan or Zen, this was certainly the case.[13] Dudjom Rinpoche replied that one principal difference lies in the fact that, whereas Chan emphasizes the realization of emptiness through a nongradual method, Dzogchen and Mahamudra place an equal emphasis on emptiness (*stong-pa nyid*) and on luminous clarity (*gsal-ba*). In fact, in the state of contemplation, emptiness and clarity are inseparable (*gsal stong dbyer-med*). Chan does not speak of matters in this way, having arisen historically out of the context of the Sutra system, the culmination of which is the realization of shunyata, the state of emptiness. On the other hand, Dzogchen arises out of the context of the Tantra system, which deals not only with the side of pure potentiality or emptiness (*stong cha*), but equally deals with the side of manifestation or luminous clarity (*gsal cha*) in terms of the transformations of energy. Chan and Zen have little to do, in terms of practice, with visualizations, with transformations of energy, and with photic phenomena. But then my personal experience with Chan practice is limited, and, moreover, Chan and Zen developed further after the ninth century in China, Korea, and Japan.

Furthermore, in Japan the different schools of Buddhist teachings deriving originally from China have kept their own doctrines, practices, and lineages very separate from each other. To tour the temples in Nara and Kyoto belonging to the various schools of Hasso, Hwayen, Tendai, Shingon, Zen, Jodo, and so on, is like walking through a museum of the Buddhist movements of the past. In China, however, the situation was quite different. With the ending of the Tang Dynasty, at the instigation of the Taoists and some Confucianists, a government persecution was launched against the Buddhist monastic system. The Buddhist monasteries were closed by reason of their being refuges for indolent social parasites, the sole exception being the monasteries belonging to the Chan school, because the Chan monks worked in the fields and at various arts and crafts. Consequently, all of Chinese Buddhism is now Chan, although this Chan has absorbed much from the previous Buddhist movements and schools and therefore is eclectic and all-embracing, in contrast to Japanese Zen. In a Chan temple, one will find practitioners, monks, and laypeople alike engaged in mantra recitation and pure land devotions as much as or even more than Chan sitting meditation as such. Thus, real dialogue between the practitioners of Dzogchen and the practitioners of Chan, Tibetan and Chinese, is a development for the future, but one that would be very worthwhile.

From the *bSam-gtan mig sgron* of Nubchen Sangye Yeshe (gNubschen sangs-rgyas ye-shes), it is clear that at least as early as the ninth century, and probably before, Tibetan Lamas could clearly distinguish the respective viewpoints of Dzogchen and Chan. In this text Nubchen distinguishes among four kinds of Buddhist teaching:

1. Chapter 4: *Tsen-man rim-gyis 'jug-pa'i gzhung bstan-pa'i le'u* (pp. 65–118) deals with the gradualist path of the Mahayana Sutra system, specifically the Madhyamika-Yogachara synthesis of Shantirakshita. This system is outlined in the *Bhavanakrama* (*bsgom-rim*) of the latter's disciple Kamalashila and elsewhere.
2. Chapter 5: *sTon-mun cig-car 'jug-pa'i lugs bshad-pa'i le'u* (pp. 118–186) deals with the nongradual path of the Sutra system as expounded by the Hwashang Mahayana and others. These teachers are known as *bsam-gtan gyi mkhan-po*, or Chan masters.
3. Chapter 6: *rNal-'byor chen-po'i gzhung bshad-pa'i le'u* (pp. 186–290) deals with the Tantra system of the Mahayoga which later came to be identified with the Nyingmapa school.
4. Chapter 7: *rDzogs-pa chen-po'i gzhung rgyas-par bkod-pa'ile'u* (pp. 290–494) deals extensively with the system of Dzogchen.

The question of whether Dzogchen, in one way or another, originated from or was heavily influenced at its inception by Chan has been dealt with by such scholars as Samten G. Karmay, Per Kvaerne, David Ruegg, and others.[14] However, the assertions made by Tucci have often been repeated uncritically by other Western scholars. Although Tucci claims that Chan elements are to be found in Dzogchen (see his *Minor Buddhist Texts*, part 1), he nowhere demonstrates that this is actually the case or shows that similarities, such as a nongradual method in Dzogchen, must derive from Chan. We must look to the Indo-Tibetan context for the sources of Dzogchen and deal with Chan in eighth- and ninth-century Tibet as a separate and independent movement.

Bon

Dzogchen has also been accused by some native Tibetan scholars of being Bonpo in origin, rather than Buddhist, and that Dzogchen therefore represents a non-Buddhist system of teaching and practice. It is true that Dzogchen is also found in the Bon tradition, that the Nyingmapa and the Bonpo systems are very similar with respect to Dzogchen, and that they employ a largely identical terminology. At least one of these Bonpo Dzogchen systems represents *bka'-ma*, or a continuous tradition, the others being Termas from the tenth century or later.[15] This old tradition is known as the *Zhang-zhung snyan rgyud*, the oral transmission from Zhang-zhung. Zhang-zhung was the name of the ancient kingdom of Western Tibet, which was destroyed and absorbed into the Tibetan empire in the reign of King Tisong Detsan in the eighth century. The Bonpo master Gyerpung Nangzher Lodpo (Gyer-spungs snang-bzher lod-po) was a native of that country and a contemporary of this king. According to Bonpo tradition, he put into writing the oral tradition he had received from his own master Tapihritsa and transmitted the teachings to his Tibetan disciples. The Zhang-zhung dialect is somewhat related to Tibetan, but it is closer to the modern Kanauri language of the Western Himalayas. Some examples of the Zhang-zhung language survive in book titles and in one short cosmological text, the *Srid-pa'i mdzod phug*. There exists a Tibetan translation and a commentary to this text by Dranpa Namkha (Dran-pa nam-mkha'), a Bonpo master, but also a disciple of Padmasambhava. Gyerpungpa came into conflict with the Tibetan king Tisong Detsan, because the latter, at the urging of the Indian Buddhist abbot Shantirakshita, launched a persecution of Bon practitioners in Central Tibet. At the instigation of the former queen of Zhang-zhung, in retaliation Gyerpungpa dispatched a magical attack against the king, employing a *btso*, or magical missile. The king, having fallen ill because of this attack, relented and excluded the Zhang-zhung Dzogchen teachings from proscription. Thus the texts of the *Zhang-zhung snyan rgyud* survive until this day and have been republished in India.[16]

There is evidence that a kind of Central Asian Buddhism that included Dzogchen and Tantra was introduced into Western Tibet, that is, into the kingdom of Zhang-zhung, centuries before the introduction of Indian Buddhism into Central Tibet in the seventh and eighth centuries.[17] Like Hindu Sadhus and Yogins who make pilgrimages to Mount Kailas even today, it is likely that wandering Buddhist Yogins or Mahasiddhas came to this same mountain in Western Tibet before the historical advent of Buddhism in Central Tibet. This is a probability admitted even by the eminent Tibetologist David Snellgrove. He also points to Iranian and Central Asian influences on the syncretistic traditions of Bon.[18] Moreover, many scholars have pointed to the similarities existing between Dzogchen and the ideas expressed in the Dohas, or songs of practice, composed by various Mahasiddhas, which are said to represent the so-called Sahajayana.[19] However, it appears that many of these Dohas were composed after the period in question and that the Dohakosha collections made of them were not translated into Tibetan until the eleventh century, and even afterwards, in the New Translation period. It may also be observed that the teacher and master of Gyerpungpa, who bestowed the Dzogchen precepts upon him for both Thekchod and Thodgal, was named Tapihritsa or Tapiraja, which appears to be an Indian name or title. In the lineage of masters preceding Gyerpungpa (eighth century CE), there is found a master named Zhang-zhung dGa'-rab, who may be Garab Dorje. If so, this would place Garab Dorje in a much wider cultural and social context than indicated by the Nyingmapa sources alone. Thus, there exist two authentic lineages for the transmission of the Dzogchen teachings to Tibet: (1) the Nyingmapa lineage coming from India and ultimately from Uddiyana with Padmasambhava, Vimalamitra, and Vairochana; and (2) the Bonpo lineage coming from Zhang-zhung with Tapihritsa and Gyerpungpa. Both of these lineages could very well have sprung from the country of Uddiyana to the west of Tibet. We may postulate that in the early days, that is, before the seventh century, when the Tibetan kingdom was established in Central Tibet under the Yarlung Dynasty, there were close cultural connections between the independent kingdom of Zhang-zhung on the one hand, and Uddiyana and Iranian Central Asia (sTag-gzig) on the other, since these regions are contiguous.[20] So it is to this Indo-Tibetan and Indo-Iranian borderland that we must look for the historical origins of Dzogchen.

Four Early Texts Relating to Dzogchen

Some of the issues surrounding the origin of Dzogchen may be clarified somewhat further by an examination of four key texts:

1. the *Rig-pa'i khu-byug*,
2. the *Kun-byed rgyal-po*,
3. the *bSam-gtan mig sgron*, and
4. the *'Dra 'bag chen-mo*.

The *Rig-pa'i khu-byug* is one of the two Dzogchen texts found in the discoveries at the famous library in the caves at Tun Huang (tenth century CE) in Central Asia. Since, according to Nyingmapa tradition, it was the first Dzogchen text translated by Vairochana when he returned to Tibet from India, it may possibly be cited as the earliest extant Dzogchen text from Tibet. The *Kulayaraja Tantra*, or *Kun-byed rgyal-po*, was not listed in later times among the eighteen earliest Dzogchen Semde texts; nevertheless, its translation was still attributed to Vairochana, and it is often regarded as the principal Tantra of the Dzogchen Semde Series. The *bSam-gtan mig sgron*, attributed to Nubchen Sangye Yeshe (ninth century), is one of the earliest systematic philosophical expositions of Dzogchen and one written by a native Tibetan scholar. This text compares the views of Dzogchen with those of Sutra and Tantra, and thus aims to distinguish clearly Dzogchen from Chan Buddhism. The *'Dra 'bag chen-mo* purports to be a biography of the Tibetan translator Vairochana and speaks of the masters he met in India and of the teachings he received from them. Although this text is late (thirteenth century CE), it contains earlier material.

RIG-PA'I KHU-BYUG: THE EARLIEST DZOGCHEN TEXT

The well-known modern Dzogchen master Namkhai Norbu Rinpoche has written,

> Some people, wanting to dispute the authenticity of Dzogchen, have stated that the term *rdzogs-chen* was not found in the early period of Tibetan Buddhism, and that the many texts (of the Nyingmapas) that contain this term were fabrications by later scholars. However, the term is clearly found in many early texts, such as the *bSam-gtan mig-sgron* of gNubs-chen sangs-rgyas ye-shes, a direct disciple of Padmasambhava, as well as in the *Kun-byed rgyal-po*, which is the root Tantra of the *Sems-sde* tradition of Dzogchen. Not only that, but at the British Museum in London among the Tun Huang documents from the early period, I have found a text by the great Dzogchen yogi of the period, Sangs-rgyas sbas-pa (Buddhagupta): the *sBas-pa'i rgum chung.* I found there, as well, the *Sems-sde* text, the *Rig-pa'i khu-byug,* together with a commentary. This latter work is also found in the *Kun-byed rgyal-po* and is known as the Six Vajra Verses (*rDo-rje tshig drug*). The terms Atiyoga, i.e., primordial yoga (*gdod-ma'i rnal-'byor*) and *rdzogs-chen* are clearly found in these texts.[1]

Samten G. Karmay, however, asserts that Dzogchen only developed among the Nyingmapas and the Bonpos in the tenth century, although he admits that some ideas, such as *ka-dag*, the state of primordial purity, may have existed earlier in the context of Mahayoga Tantra. Of the four texts cited above by Namkhai Norbu Rinpoche as proofs that Dzogchen existed in the early period, that is, the eighth and ninth centuries, Karmay would assign the *bSam-gtan mig-sgron* of Nubchen to the tenth century. But it is equally possible that Nubchen and his text do belong to the ninth century. Karmay does concede that the two texts found in the Tun Huang library may belong to the ninth century: the *sBas-pa'i rgum chung* (IOL 595, two folia) and the *Rig-pa'i khu-byug* (IOL 647, five folia). To the first of these texts, Namkhai Norbu Rinpoche has devoted a detailed study.[2] Karmay has also studied the text.[3] It is uncertain when Buddhagupta lived, but it was at least before the sealing of the Tun Huang library in the tenth century, unless, as Go Lotsawa in his *Blue Annals* indicates, he is identical with the Indian master of the Yoga Tantras Buddhaguhya (Sangs-rgyas gsang-ba), who resided at Mount Kailas in the eighth century. According to the Tibetan histories, he had been invited to visit Central Tibet but never came.

The second text cited above, the *Rig-pa'i khu-byug*, is found in three places: (1) IOL/Stein 647 in the Tun Huang collection, (2) in vol. KA of the *rNying-ma'i rgyud 'bum*, and (3) as chapter 31 in the *Bodhichitta-kulayaraja Tantra*, or *Kun-byed rgyal-po*.[4]

In the third source cited above, the text is called the *rDo-rje tshig drug*, the Six Vajra Verses. This root text is exceedingly brief, consisting of only six lines (*tshig*). The Tun Huang version is accompanied by a commentary. Here the title of the text is given as the *Rig-pa'i khu-byug*, "The Cuckoo (*khu-byug*) of Awareness (*rig-pa*)," which would be *vidyākokila* in Sanskrit. The version in the *rNying-ma'i rgyud 'bum*, however, has *Santi darpa* as its supposed Sanskrit title, and this is translated into Tibetan as *rDzogs-pa chen-po sa gcig-pa*, "The Single Stage of the Great Perfection." Here *santi* would stand for *mahāsanti/ santimahā*, or *mahāsandhi*, which translates *rdzogs-chen*. According to Namkhai Norbu Rinpoche, *santi* is not just incorrect Sanskrit, but rather it is the form in the Uddiyana dialect corresponding to the Sanskrit *sandhi*, "union, perfection." In the context of Mahayoga Tantra, the union is that of the generation process and the perfection process, that is, *bskyed rdzogs zung-'jug*, and this state of the Great Perfection transcends both processes or stages. *Sa gcig-pa*, the single stage, refers to a single (*gcig*) bhumi (*sa*), that is, a state which is not to be attained by any intermediate stages or levels. The Sutra system speaks of the dasha-bhumi, or ten stages (*sa bcu*), of the career of the Bodhisattva that ultimately culminate in the enlightenment of a Buddha. Various Tantras speak of sixteen bhumis. But Dzogchen knows only one bhumi, the state of contemplation (*rig-pa*). The bhumis pertain to the gradual path, whereas Dzogchen represents a nongradual path, one characterized by sudden enlightenment. Karmay suggests that *darpa* is corrupt Sanskrit for *dhara*, earth, which is the same meaning as *bhūmi* found, for example, in the term *bhūmipati* (*sa-bdag*), "lord of the earth." In the commentary, it is explained that the metaphor (*dpe*) is "the Cuckoo of Awareness" (*rig-pa'i khu-byug ni dpe*) but that the real meaning (*don*) is "the ornaments which are manifestations created by Awareness" (*rig byed snang-ba'i rgyan ni don*), while the enumeration (*grangs*) is the Six Vajra Verses (*rdo-rje tshig drug ni grangs*). Internally occurring thoughts, as well as external appearances, represent the play of the creative energy of Awareness (*rig-pa'i rtsal*), and in the Semde Series especially, these manifestations of mind are known as ornaments (*rgyan*) of the Primordial State. Thus, we have the explanation of the title of the text.

But why the cuckoo? The cuckoo is an important symbol in the aboriginal Bon tradition of Tibet. It is the sacred bird of Tonpa Shenrab Miwo (sTon-pa gShen-rab mi-bo), who is the source and the founder of the Bonpo tradition. On certain occasions, he even manifested himself in the guise of a cuckoo, the sage Barnang Khujug (Bar-snang khu-byug). The blue color of the cuckoo is also a symbol of the Bon teachings, which are said to have come from the sky. Thus, for the Bonpo, the cuckoo is the bird of revelation and knowledge—the Cuckoo of Awareness. More mundanely, in the native Tibetan folk tradition, the cuckoo is the king of birds, that is, the most important bird among all birds. It comes to Tibet in the interval between winter and summer, and its singing heralds the summer season. Its song quickens the growth of all trees and plants upon which humans and animals depend for their very sustenance. In the same way, the Dzogchen teachings awaken the dormant Rigpa in all sentient beings.

The Tibetan text of the *Rig-pa'i khu-byug* from the *rNying-ma'i rgyud 'bum* is as follows:

> rgya-gar skad du / san-ti dar-pa / bod skad du / rdzogs-pa chen-po sa
> gcig-pa / SVASTI / dpal gyi dpal / bcom-ldan-'das kun tu bzang-po sku
> gsung thugs rdo-rje bde-ba chen-po lhun gyis rdzogs-pa la phyag 'tshal-
> lo //
> (1) sna-tshogs rang-bzhin mi gnyis kyang /
> (2) cha-shas nyid du spros dang bral /
> (3) ji-bzhin-pa zhes mi rtog kyang /
> (4) rnam-par snang mdzad kun tu bzang /
> (5) zin-pas rtsol-ba'i nad spangs te /
> (6) lhun gyis gnas-pa bzhag-pa yin //
> byang-chub kyi sems rig-pa'i khu-byug rdzogs-so //

The manuscript version of the text from Tun Huang (IOL 647) omits the title before *SVASTI* (Skt. *su-asti* 'well-being') and the colophon at the end. It also has the archaic spelling *myi* for *mi* 'not,' as in *myi gnyis* / *mi gnyis* 'not two'; otherwise the Six Vajra Verses are the same. Following the oral commentary on the Six Vajra Verses by Namkhai Norbu Rinpoche, I have translated them as follows:

> In the language of India: *Santi darpa*.
> In the language of Tibet: *rDzogs-pa chen-po sa gcig-pa* (the single
> stage which is the Great Perfection).

SVASTI

Homage to the spontaneously perfected Great Bliss of the indestructible vajras of the Body, Speech, and Mind of Shri Bhagavan
Samantabhadra, the glory of glories!

(1) Even though (*kyang*) the nature of the diversity (of all phenomena) (*sna-tshogs rang-bzhin*) is without any duality (*mi
gnyis*),

(2) In terms of the individuality of the things themselves (*cha-
shas nyid du*), they are free of any conceptual elaborations
(made by mind) (*spros dang bral*).

(3) Even though (*kyang*) there exists no thought or conception
(*mi rtog*) of what is called (*zhes*) the state of being just as it is
(*ji-bzhin-pa*),

(4) These various appearances which are created (*rnam-par snang
mdzad*) are but manifestations of Samantabhadra (the Primordial State) (*kun tu bzang*).

(5) Since everything is complete in itself (*zin-pas*), one comes to
abandon the illness of (or obsession with) efforts (*rtsol-ba'i nad
spangs te*),

(6) And thus one continues (*bzhag-pa yin*) spontaneously (*lhun
gyis*) in the calm state of contemplation (*gnas-pa*).

The Cuckoo of Awareness which is the Bodhichitta is completed.

In the above Six Vajra Verses, *sna-tshogs* indicates the diversity of
all phenomena as a whole, whereas *cha-shas* refers to individual
things. The term *mi gnyis*, "not two," is explained as *tha-mi-dad*, "not
different, not distinct," whereas *gnyis-med* is more properly
"nondual." *Spros-pa* (Skt. *prapañca*) is an elaboration made by the mind
or intellect, and *spros-bral* or *spros dang bral-ba* means being free of
such elaborations. The word *ji-bzhin-pa* is a contraction of *ji lta-ba
bzhin*, meaning "just as it is" and is synonymous with *de bzhin nyid*
(Skt. *tathatā*, "thusness, suchness"), a state of being just as it is. In this
context *rnam-par snang mdzad* does not refer to Vairochana, one of
the five Dhyani Buddhas, but to various (*rnam-par*) kinds of appearances or manifestations (*snang-ba*) which are caused (*mdzad*) to come
into existence. *Kun tu bzang (-po)* (Skt. *samantabhadra*) is a designation for the Primordial State which is the Base. All diverse phenomena are only manifestations (*snang-ba*) or "ornaments" (*rgyan*) of this
Primordial State, like reflections appearing in a mirror. The word
zin-pa means "finished, completed, accomplished, done," and when
linked with *ye nas*, "primordial, from the very beginning," it signifies something completed or perfected from the very beginning. The

term *gnas-pa*, of course, here refers to the state of contemplation. When one relaxes and gives up all effort and striving (*rtsol-ba spang*) on the part of the intellect and the thought process, one then settles into (*bzhag-pa*) the state of contemplation effortlessly and spontaneously (*lhun gyis*).[5]

The above text is speaking not about our ordinary thought processes, which represent the activities of delusion ('*khrul-pa*), but of what lies beyond the mind, that is to say, the state of contemplation or Rigpa, which represents liberation. In his oral commentary on the *Rig-pa'i khu-byug*, Namkhai Norbu Rinpoche relates the first two vajra verses to the Semde Series of Dzogchen teachings and to the first statement of Garab Dorje, the second two vajra verses to the Longde teachings and to the second statement, and the third two vajra verses to the Upadesha teachings and to the third statement. He goes on to state that the text gives a brief explanation of the Primordial State of the individual, and he asserts that in these Six Vajra Verses are found the principles of the Base, the Path, and the Fruit (*gzhi lam 'bras-bu*), together with the view, the meditation, and the action or conduct of Dzogchen (*lta sgom spyod*). These correspond as follows:

First two verses:	First Statement	Semde	Base	View
Second two verses:	Second Statement	Longde	Path	Meditation
Third two verses:	Third Statement	Upadesha	Fruit	Action

Karmay, on the other hand, maintains that this analysis of the Dzogchen teaching in terms of Base, Path, and Fruit was first applied to Dzogchen by Longchenpa in the fourteenth century.[6] But according to Namkhai Norbu Rinpoche, the *lta-ba*, the view or the way of seeing, is inseparable from real knowledge, which is a direct intuition of the nature of reality or the Base. The Path or the meditation practice develops this knowledge by way of various methods. And the Fruit is the uniting of one's actions or conduct with this knowledge of Rigpa, so that one takes contemplation into everyday life. All activities become totally integrated with Rigpa. Thus the understanding of Dzogchen in terms of the Base, the Path, and the Fruit must have been present in these teachings from the very beginning and do not represent something merely introduced by later scholars by way of interpretation. Through understanding these Six Vajra Verses, one gains direct access to the essence of Dzogchen.[7]

The Tun Huang library has proved a veritable treasure trove for Western scholars. Early in this century two scholar-explorers, Aurel Stein of England and Paul Pelliot of France, made many important discoveries in Chinese Turkestan, but most significant were the finds in the Buddhist cave temples at the ancient city of Tun Huang at the eastern end of the Takla-makan Desert.[8] Thousands of manuscripts in various languages, but mostly in Chinese and Tibetan, were discovered and brought back to London and Paris. Among these texts were the Annals and the Chronicles of the early Tibetan monarchy, and these proved of inestimable historical value. Tun Huang in those centuries (seventh–tenth century CE) was an important trade city on the famous Silk Route from China to the West and an important Buddhist center. During the reign of King Tisong Detsan, the military initiative passed to the Tibetan armies, and the Chinese garrisons were forced to withdraw from Central Asia. They did not return until the thirteenth century, with the Mongol conquest of China and the rise of the Yuan Dynasty. Tun Huang fell to the Tibetans about 787 and thereafter became a Tibetan administrative center.[9] Since it was a leading monastic enclave in Central Asia, King Tisong Detsan drew upon it in his efforts to establish Buddhism as the state religion of Tibet. Among the Tibetan texts found at Tun Huang there are three basic types: administrative, Buddhist, and pre-Buddhist (Bonpo rituals). The Buddhist material gives us a pretty good idea of the nature of Tibetan Buddhism at that time, that is, from the mid-eighth century until the tenth century, when the library was sealed. What is striking is that the bulk of the Tibetan Buddhist material belongs to the Sutra system, and as we have seen, only two short Dzogchen texts were found.

The existence of these two texts, the *sBas-pa'i sgum chung* and the *Rig-pa'i khu-byug*, in this library at least demonstrates the existence of Dzogchen texts in the tenth century, but it does not prove that they were written only then or that other Dzogchen texts did not circulate elsewhere. The Indian author of the first text, Buddhagupta, inspired Nyan Palyang (gNyan dpal-dbyangs, ninth century) to compose three short texts: (1) *rDo-rje sems-dpa'i zhus-lan*, (2) *lTa-ba rgum chung*, and (3) *Man-ngag rgum chung*. All of these texts are found in the Tibetan Tangyur collection and are attributed to Nyan Palyang their colophons. The *rGum chung* quoted in the *bSam-gtan mig sgron* of Nubchen Sangye Yeshe is the above text and not the one by Buddhagupta. It also appears that this Khanpo, Nyan Palyang, was one of the teachers of Nubchen.

Karmay doubts that the *Rig-pa'i khu-byug* ever existed in a Sanskrit original; it appears to him that the text was composed in Tibetan no earlier than the tenth century.[10] He also cites certain parallels with Bonpo texts. Moreover, Karmay argues that since Vairochana is not mentioned in a colophon to this Tun Huang text, he therefore did not translate it. Vairochana is specified as the translator, however, in the colophon attached to this text in the version found in the *rNying-ma'i rgyud 'bum*, as well as in the colophon to the *Kun-byed rgyal-po*, where this text is also found.

KUN-BYED RGYAL-PO: THE PRINCIPAL DZOGCHEN TANTRA

The next text mentioned is the *Kun-byed rgyal-po*, or more fully in Tibetan, *Chos thams-cad rdzogs-pa chen-po byang-chub kyi sems kun-byed rgyal-po'i rgyud* (Skt. *Sarva-dharma mahāsanti bodhicitta-kulayarāja tantra*). Although it contains the *Rig-pa'i khu-byug* text as its chapter 31, this Tantra was not found at Tun Huang. The chapter in question begins, "Then the Enlightened Mind, the king who creates everything (*byang-chub kyi sems kun-byed rgyal-po*), expounded (upon his own) nature which is the state of universal creativity (*kun-byed nyid kyi rang-bzhin*), spontaneously self-perfected and complete in itself without (any recourse to) any activity (of mind) (*bya-med rdzogs-pa lhun gyis grub-pa*). 'O Mahasattva, listen!' . . ." Then the text continues with the Six Vajra Verses of the *Rig-pa'i khu-byug*.

According to the Nyingmapa tradition, the *Kun-byed rgyal-po* is said to be the principal Tantra of the *Sems-phyogs* or Semde Series of Dzogchen teachings, just as the *kLong-chen rab-'byams rgyal-po* is the principal Tantra of the Longde Series and the *sGra-thal-gyur* is the principal Tantra of the Upadesha Series. In the collection of the Old Tantras, the *rNying-ma'i rgyud 'bum*, where the *Kun-byed rgyal-po* is found, there exists no commentary to the Tantra. There does exist, however, an introduction to this Tantra, together with some instructions on how to practice a Guru Yoga in relation to it, by Longchenpa (1308–1363) himself. This text is entitled the *Byang-chub sems kun-byed rgyal-po'i don khrid rin-chen gru-bo*. It represents an explanation of the essential meaning (*don khrid*), enabling the practitioner to grasp the essential point of Dzogchen. This text has been translated by Kennard Lipman as "The Jewel Ship."[11]

In Tibet, the authenticity of the *Kun-byed rgyal-po* as a Tantra and as a Buddhist teaching has often been doubted,[12] and more recently its authenticity has been called into question by Eva Dargyay.[13] However, Dargyay's speculations about the supposed theism of this text are not very convincing. In her brief study of the Tantra,[14] she would find in the *Kun-byed rgyal-po* an example of a heterodox Buddhist theism, presumably influenced by Shaivism. She goes on to say,

> The central figure of the Tantra is *Kun-byed rgyal-po*, "the All-Cre-ating King"; he is the One who is at the beginning and at the end of the universe. He is immanent in all existent phenomena, but at the same time transcending all phenomena. He exists prior to all Buddhas and all impermanent phenomena. His entourage are reflections of his own nature and constitute the entire created world. . . . (p. 291)

> So far most scholars agree that those traditions (Mahayana and Vajrayana) never developed a philosophical concept of God nor adopted theistic jargon in their canonical texts. The *Kun-byed rgyal-po*, however, makes it very clear that, at least at a certain point, the Vajrayana tradition formulated a philosophically defined concept of the Absolute in theistic language, which portrayed the Absolute as a person. Examining the *Kun-byed rgyal-po* will also show that this image of the Absolute is in accord with the funda-mental thought of Yogachara, where the mind is the hub of the entire universe. The *Kun-byed rgyal-po* identifies this Mind with the Absolute and addresses it as 'king'. . . . (pp. 292–93)

Here we have an echo of Evans-Wentz's "The One Mind" in the interpretation of the Dzogchen teachings.[15] However, the term *kun-byed rgyal-po*, as understood in the Nyingmapa tradition, does not mean "God." According to the Nyingmapa Lamas,[16] the real mean-ing of *kun-byed rgyal-po* is the Primordial State of the individual. This is *sems-nyid*, or "the nature of mind." In the Semde Series of teach-ings, this Primordial State is usually known as *byang-chub kyi sems*, or Bodhichitta, this being a state of pure and total Awareness (*rig-pa*), and the term is synonymous with *rdzogs-pa chen-po*, the Great Perfection. Thus in the context of this Tantra, *Bodhicitta-kulayarāja* refers not to a theistic formulation of the Absolute but to the nature of mind (*sems-nyid*, Skt. *cittatā*), and the Tibetan phrase *byang-chub kyi sems kun-byed rgyal-po* would translate as "the enlightened nature of mind which is the king that creates everything." It is like a clear mirror that can reflect (that is, know) everything in the universe. Yet it is simultaneously the universe itself because all the diversity found in the universe, like the reflections seen in the mirror, are manifestations of the creative energy (*rtsal*) of this source. Of course, the mirror is not a perfect example or metaphor (*dpe*) for the nature of mind, any more than the sky is one. Neither the mirror nor the sky is aware. Nor does a mirror possess its own inherent inner luminosity (*nang gsal*) which is then projected out into space as lights and rays ('*od zer*), only to be reflected again in the mirror—the mirror actually being the source of what it reflects. For this reason, the crystal is also used as a metaphor for the nature of mind, where colorless sunlight passing through the body of the crystal is refracted into all the colors of the rainbow on the far wall. But neither the mirror nor the crystal possesses its own internal inherent luminosity (*nang gsal*); both must depend on some outside source of light, such as sunlight, in order to produce their respective effects. In this regard, we might propose the hologram as a modern but suggestive metaphor.[17] In this Tantra the term *rgyal-po*, "king," is an example or metaphor (*dpe*): it means the chief of any class of things. In terms of our human existence as body, speech, and mind, the mind is supreme; it is the king. But this does not mean that the mind is literally a king sitting on a throne. Here the Tantra is speaking of the nature of mind, the Primordial State of the individual, not "The One Mind" of Evans-Wentz and not "God the Creator" of biblical tradition.[18] From the earliest days until the present, the Tibetan Lamas have been quite familiar with the notion of a personalized Absolute as found in Hindu theistic systems, both Shaiva and Vaishnava, and this theological concept was translated as *dbang-phyug* for the Sanskrit *iśvara*, "lord," and as *byed-pa-po* for the Sanskrit *kartṛ*, "creator." Moreover, this concept was usually refuted by means of the sophisticated Madhyamika dialectic.[19]

Like the Sutras, the Tantras are cast in the literary format of a dialogue between the Buddha and one or more of his disciples. In the Sutras and the Lower Tantras, the Teacher is the historical Buddha, Shakyamuni. Generally speaking, he teaches at some known geographical location in India, such as Sarnath in the *Dharmachakra-pravartana Sutra* and the Vulture Peak of Gridhrakuta in the

Prajnaparamita Sutras. Sometimes this is also the case with the Tantras, as, for example, Dhanyakataka in South India in the *Kalachakra Tantra.* But at other times he teaches in some celestial realm like Trayatrimsha-devaloka, the paradise of the Thirty-Three Gods atop the cosmic mountain Meru in the center of the world. In some Anuttara Tantras, like the *Hevajra Tantra,* he may be teaching in some unspecified celestial dimension that signifies a transmundane or transcendental state of consciousness.[20] All of these expositions of the Dharma through the mouth of the Buddha have the literary form of a dialogue. This is true of the Dzogchen Tantras as well, where the Primordial Buddha Samantabhadra (Kun tu bzang-po) expounds the teaching to His disciple Vajrasattva (rDo-rje sems-dpa').

In the *Kun-byed rgyal-po,* Bodhichitta-kulayaraja, who is the Teacher (*ston-pa*), represents the Dharmakaya which is itself beyond time and conditioning, that is to say, beyond Samsara. The Dharmakaya is characterized by a twofold purity (*dag-pa gnyis-ldan*): it is inherently pure (*rang-bzhin rnam-dag*) and free of all adventitious or accidental impurities (*glo-bur dri-med*), that is, its nature has never been altered or modified (*ma bcos*) by the presence of the two obscurations (*sgrib-pa gnyis*), the emotional and the intellectual. This may be compared to the nature of the mirror, which is in no way altered or modified by what it reflects. Thus, it is primordially pure (*ka-dag*). It is free of all thought constructions and all conceptual elaborations (*spros-bral*), being like the clear luminous sky without clouds. Yet it possesses its own energy or capacity (*thugs-rje*); it freely and spontaneously acts for the benefit of beings still caught up in the delusion of Samsara, spontaneously manifesting as the Rupakaya. This is the aspect of its spontaneous self-perfection (*lhun-grub*). The Dharmakaya emanates or projects out of itself, as its audience (*'khor*), the manifestation known as Sattvavajra (Sems-dpa' rdo-rje). This figure is identical with Vajrasattva, although, in terms of iconography, he is envisioned as being blue in color, but with all the usual attributes and ornaments of the Sambhogakaya. Thus, the Teacher and His audience are in essence ultimately identical. Dudjom Rinpoche has explained that these dialogues between Samantabhadra, the Dharmakaya, and Vajrasattva, the Sambhogakaya, which are found in the Dzogchen Tantras, actually take place primordially, that is to say, in eternity outside of time and history.[21] The Teacher, Samantabhadra, and the audience, Vajrasattva, are really one. This dialogue is only an emanation or phantom show which is manifested for the benefit and instruction of sentient beings; it does not represent some division or schism within Buddhahood itself. It is only the mind dialoguing with itself. The dialogue between these two numinous figures is communicated within the richness and effulgence of the dimension of the Sambhogakaya. But this dialogue is only a convention, a literary device; it is not something to be taken literally as some historical event, like Moses dialoguing with his God on Mount Sinai. It does not mean that the Absolute is a person who actually speaks to this or that other person, imparting some teaching or promulgating some divine ordinance. Personhood belongs to the realm of multiplicity, to the domain of the activities of the skandhas. In each of one's lifetimes, the individual remanifests as a new personality or complex of skandhas; it is not that this personality, a conditioned structure that disintegrates following physical death, transmigrates from life to life. The person is something conditioned and impermanent. Rather, the nature of mind, the Primordial State of the individual, has been there from the very beginning, and this does not transmigrate at all. However, out of its inexhaustible effulgence and infinite potentiality, it projects a beginningless series of lifetimes on countless worlds. Although these lives may appear sequential, in a linear temporal sequence, from our limited one-dimensional view of time, all of these lives actually occur simultaneously from the standpoint of the nature of mind. This Primordial State is prior to and transcends personhood. The latter condition represents a contraction or limitation, whether self-imposed or involuntary, of a transcendent state that is originally and inherently unlimited and unconditioned. This is a view shared with Advaita Vedanta, Kashmiri Shaivism, and certain other varieties of mystical philosophy. But it is easy for us Westerners, conditioned as we are by biblical tradition and mythology, to seize exclusively upon the lexical meaning in this Tantra without reference to the real meaning, and thus to misconstrue the entire teaching. This is the case with Evans-Wentz, and I have dealt with his misunderstanding elsewhere.[22]

Dzogchen, like Buddhist teaching in general, addresses *sems*, or mind, as its central theme and problem, in terms of both theory and practice. Mind creates the world of illusion or delusory appearances (*'khrul snang*), and, due to its activities, our primordial nature has been obscured from time without beginning. Therefore, it is called *kun-byed rgyal-po*, the king who creates everything. But at the same time, the mind represents the sole path to liberation, and so it is also known as *rang shes rig gi rgyal-po*, the king that is the awareness which is self-knowing. There is no way to get at the state of the mirror except by way of the reflections. This same mind, or rather nature of mind (*sems-nyid*), is both the basis of delusion (*'khrul gzhi*) and the basis of liberation (*grol gzhi*). There is one Base but two Paths. We are enslaved by mind, and we are liberated by mind. We have forgotten who we are primordially, because we have turned away from our true face; but it is possible to turn back again, to look within and discover ourselves, rather than to look outside to some external authority which will inevitably be a false god.

Moreover, what we find here in the Tantra is the Dzogchen view and not the Chittamatra-Yogachara philosophy, as Dargyay would have it. Confusion can easily arise because Dzogchen has adopted some of the Chittamatra philosophical vocabulary, but these terms are not necessarily understood in the same way in the two systems. As pointed out previously, Dzogchen is more ontological in its outlook and Yogachara more epistemological. The Tantra speaks of mind as the king and as a creator (*byed-pa-po*) because from its inherent energy (*rang rtsal*) emanates all of the diversity of the perceived phenomenal universe. The nature of this diversity (*sna-tshogs rang-bzhin*), that is, the nature of mind (*sems-nyid*), is without duality (*mi gnyis*), whereas diversity itself, all thoughts and appearances, is the manifestations of mind (*sems snang*), that is, manifestations of the creative potentiality of Awareness (*rig-pa'i rtsal*). They are like the colored lights or rainbows projected on the wall when sunlight strikes a crystal. Our conventional dualistic consciousness lives in these projections, a holographic structure, beleiving them to be objective realities instead of self-creations. This is what is meant here by "the creator" (*byed-pa-po*) and not some transcendent God (or Supreme Person) who creates the universe. One must be very careful in how one translates the phrase *kun-byed rgyal-po*.

The title of the Tantra, the Sanskrit original for *Byang-chub kyi sems kun-byed rgyal-po*, is given as *Bodhicitta-kulayarāja*. Bodhichitta, as we have repeatedly said, in the context of Dzogchen means the Primordial State, and this is the usual designation found in all of the *rDzogs-chen Sems-sde Tantras*. But the term *kulayarāja* is otherwise unknown in Sanskrit. Dargyay would link it to the form *kularāja* found in certain texts of the Kashmiri Shaiva tradition. *Kula* has a wide range of meaning in this system, including reference to the manifestations of the Absolute. The term is also found in another related system particularly connected with Kali worship. The latter is known as Kaula and its practice as Kaulachara. The Kaulas of Bengal have a ninefold system of classification of their levels of teaching that is reminiscent of the nine vehicles (*theg-pa dgu*) of the Nyingmapas and the Bonpos. It is possible that *kulaya* was adopted from a Shaivite context, but this is not a sufficient reason to assume that the term has the same meaning in the Buddhist system that it does in a theistic Shaiva text. The appellation *Bhagavān* is applied to both the Buddha in the Buddhist system and to Krishna and Vishnu in the Vaishnava system, but this does not mean that its meaning is understood in precisely the same way in Buddhism and in Vaishnavism. The *Bhagavad Gita* was once translated into Tibetan, and from this we learn that *Bhagavān*, as a title of Krishna, is translated as *Legs-ldan*, whereas when it is applied to the Buddha, it is translated as *bCom-ldan-'das*.[23] It is said that when the famous translator Rinchen Zangpo (Rin-chen bzang-po, 958–1055) found this Tibetan translation of the *Bhagavad Gita* in Western Tibet and read its opening chapters, he was so horrified that he threw the entire text into the river. So now, except for a few sample verses which have been preserved, the rest of the translation has been lost.[24] Such was the new puritanism of the eleventh century! In the canonical *Tangyur* will be found translations of other Shaiva texts relating to dreams, omens, and so forth, and a large Shaiva text dealing with astrology, the *Svarodaya Tantra* (*dByangs 'char*), but these are considered to be texts dealing with the secular sciences (*rig-gnas*), rather than the innermost science of spiritual liberation.[25] Whether the Tantra we have here can be shown to have any relationship to Kashmiri Shaivism other than this mysterious term *kulaya* must await a comprehensive study of the entire text.[26]

Shaivism is indeed an ancient religious movement in India. Of unknown, but of undoubtedly pre-Indo-European origin, the god Shiva came in later times to be identified with the Vedic deity Rudra. One of the principal early Upanishads, the *Shvetopanishad*, with its notion of Ishvara or the Lord, appears to have links with Shaiva tradition. The oldest sectarian Shaiva texts, known as the Shaivagamas, deal with the cult practices of the god Shiva. The earliest systematic philosophical statement of the Shaiva system is represented by the

Pashupata Sutras, associated with the name of the sage Lagulisha.[27] The most popular and widespread system of Shaiva philosophy, the Shaiva Siddhanta, came to South India in the sixth or seventh century CE, where it became the major rival of the earlier Buddhism and Jainism. North Indian texts summarizing the more unsystematic Agamas were translated into the Tamil language, like the famous *Tirumandiram* of Tirumular (ninth century CE). All of these forms of Shaiva philosophy were pluralistic, postulating the ultimate reality of three principles: *pati, paśu,* and *paśa,* that is, God, individual souls, and bondage to the cycle of death and rebirth.[28]

Whereas these earlier forms of Agamic Shaivism, like Pashupata and Shaiva Siddhanta, are distinctly dualistic and theistic in character, Kashmiri Shaivism has a thoroughgoing monistic or advaita view. This monistic standpoint is shared with the Advaita Vedanta of Shankaracharya (eighth century CE) and with the Shakta system of Bengal.[29] However, a key difference does exist here. The view adhered to by the Advaita Vedanta is known as Mayavada, that is to say, the appearance of diversity in the world is merely an illusion (maya). It is like a man seeing a rope lying across his path and in the darkness mistaking it for a snake. This illusion has no ontological status. Rather, it represents an epistemological problem. In the Vedantic system the ultimate reality is known as Brahman, and nothing else exists. The view associated with Kashmiri Shaivism and with Shaktism is known as Shaktivada, wherein Maya, or the world illusion, in all its diversity is granted a certain ontological status. This diversity is an illusion in the sense that it lacks any inherent or independent reality, but it does possess a kind of relative reality in that it represents the energy, or shakti, of Chit, or primordial awareness (Skt. *citśakti*). Maya is thus not just a mistake in perception, mistaking the rope for a snake; it is not something merely passive but something active and dynamic, a creative energy, or Mayashakti, which brings diversity into manifestation. Here there are some philosophical parallels with Dzogchen. Although the Tibetan term *rtsal*, "energy, potency, potentiality," is never glossed as *shakti* in the Dzogchen texts, the conceptions embodied in these two terms are quite similar. The Dzogchen term *rig-pa'i rtsal*, "the potency or energy of awareness," could almost be translated as *Vidyashakti*, which is a technical term found in the Shaiva and Shakta systems. It refers to the energy inherent within primordial nondual Awareness which gives rise to the diversity of manifestations. Also, the term for "manifestation" or "appearance" (*snang-ba*, Skt. *ābhāsa*), is found in a similar context in both systems.[30]

Kashmiri Shaivism, as a distinct movement separate from the earlier forms of dualistic Shaivism based on the *Shaivagamas*, certainly arose with the *Shiva Sutras* of Vasugupta in ninth-century Kashmir, if not before. Have we a synchronicity here? This is precisely the era when Dzogchen was developing and spreading in Tibet among both Buddhists and Bonpos. According to Nyingmapa tradition, the historical advent of Dzogchen occurred earlier than the ninth century with the activities of Garab Dorje in Uddiyana and India and so on; however, the ninth century may have been the time of the composing of part or all of the *Kun-byed rgyal-po*.

But could there have been influence the other way, from Tibet into Kashmir? Mount Kailas in Western Tibet is equally a sacred region for the followers of Shiva and for the Bonpo tradition of the *Zhang-zhung snyan rgyud*. Why must we always assume that the Tibetans must have borrowed everything from India? Are there no contributions made the other way? Perhaps Tibetan speculations in Buddhist and Bonpo circles influenced the Shaivism of Kashmir. It is known that Abhinavagupta, the foremost scholar and polymath of this Kashmiri tradition, had among his teachers a Buddhist master.[31]

Elsewhere there is at least one clear instance of Tibetan influence on a Hindu tantric cult. In Bengal there exists a system of Kali worship known as Chinachara, a tradition said to have been brought to Bengal by the sage Vashishtha from the country of Mahachina. This name literally means "great China," but in this context, it clearly indicates Tibet. According to the *Tara Tantra*, Vashishtha prayed beside the river to the goddess Kali to reveal to him the highest form of her worship. Kali appeared to him in a vision and told him that if he desired to learn this highest form of her worship, he must go to Mahachina and ask this of the Buddha. Here, of course, the Buddha is regarded as an avatara or manifestation of the god Vishnu. Journeying to Mahachina, or Tibet, the sage discovers the Buddha residing in a temple, drinking wine, eating meat, and engaged in erotic play with his Yogini consorts. Vashishtha is astonished, for such conduct is exactly the opposite of that incumbent on a good Brahman priest. But nonetheless, he receives the transmission from the Buddha, consisting of initiation and instruction, and he returns with this to Bengal. This method of sadhana practice is known as Chinachara, "the practice from Mahachina," and here Kali is worshipped as Tara, considered to be one of the ten Mahavidyas, or aspects of the goddess. Chinachara is classified as Vamachara, "a left-hand path," in contrast to Dakshinachara, "a right-hand path," because of the use made in its rituals of the five substances known as Pancha-makara: meat (Skt. *māṃsa*), wine (Skt. *madana*), fish (Skt. *mātsya*), parched grain (Skt. *mudrā*), and sexual intercourse (Skt. *maithuna*). This procedure is very similar to the Ganachakrapuja and other practices found in Mahayoga Tantra and Anuttara Tantra generally.[32]

Some Tibetan scholars have asserted that the *Kun-byed rgyal-po* is not truly a Tantra because it lacks the ten definitive qualities which a Tantra must possess, namely, view, meditation, conduct, initiation, mandala, compassionate activity, samaya, capacities, puja, and mantra. If a text deals with these ten essential topics, it may then rightly be called a Mula-tantra, or "Root Tantra." If a text only expands upon and clarifies these above topics, it may then be classified as a Vyakhya-tantra, or "Explanatory Tantra." A text that focuses on a particular essential point is called an Anga-tantra, or "Branch Tantra," and a text which presents the core or quintessential meaning of a Mula-tantra is known as an Uttama-tantra, or "Appended Tantra."[33]

In reply to this criticism, Namkhai Norbu Rinpoche asserts that when a practitioner of superior capacity (*rab*) practices the Higher Tantras, whether Yoga Tantra or Anuttara Tantra, he or she must cultivate the two stages (*rim gnyis*) of the generation process and the perfection process and realize their unification (*bskyed rdzogs zung-'jug*). To actualize the state of Vajradhara, which is the fruit of the tantric path of transformation, the practitioner must first engage these two stages, and the above ten topics must be present on the path as well. However, if one is a practitioner of exceedingly superior capacity (*yang rab*), then one has no need for these two stages and these ten essential topics. To assert that one cannot reach the unitary state of Vajradhara-yuganaddha is to remain conditioned by the tantric view. This indicates that one does not understand the difference between the Base, the Path, and the Fruit of Tantra, which is the path of transformation, and the Base, the Path, and the Fruit of Dzogchen, which is the path of self-liberation. The path of renunciation (*spong lam*) taught in the Sutras relates more to the level of body, the path of transformation (*sgyur lam*) taught in the Tantras relates more to the level of speech or energy, and the path of self-liberation (*grol lam*) taught in the Upadeshas of Dzogchen relates more to the level of mind. So each teaching and method has its own proper level and context. The *Kun-byed rgyal-po*, properly speaking, is a text of Dzogchen, not an Anuttara Tantra. Instead of expounding upon the ten topics listed above, it teaches the *med-pa bcu*, the ten nonexistences of view, meditation, conduct, samaya, activity, mandala, initiation, generation process, perfection process, purification of obscurations, and realization of Buddhahood. The requirements of the tantric path are not necessarily those of Dzogchen.[34]

Nevertheless, from the very beginning of the revival of monastic Buddhism in the eleventh century in Western Tibet, the authenticity of the *Kun-byed rgyal-po* as a Buddhist text was called into question. The edict (*bka'-shog*) of Prince Zhiwa-od (Pho-brang Zhi-ba 'od), the nephew of Lhalama Yeshe-od (Lha bla-ma Ye-shes-'od), the king of Guge who inaugurated this revival, asserted that the text having the name *Kun-byed rgyal-po* was a heretical work composed by an individual named Drang-nga Shag-tsul (Drang-nga shag-tshul). In the words of this edict, it is said that "The eighteen Tantras of the *Sems-sde* written by Drang-nga Shag-tsul at the Copper Glacier in Upper Nyang, such as the *Kun-byed rgyal-po*, the ten esoteric Sutras (*mdo bcu*), the *Ye-shes gsang-ba*, commentaries, outlines, initiations, and meditation instructions on psychic phenomena, the *Srid-pa'i rgyud*, as well as all the teachings on the *Ma-mo*, such as the *Ma-mo Tantras*, and finally the Five Kingly Teachings: the innumerable Tantras, commentaries, instructions, and practical handbooks (associated with them, are prohibited)!"[35] This edict has been quoted by the Nyingma-pa scholar and historian Sog-dog-pa (Sog-zlog-pa blo-gros rgyal-mtshan, 1552–1624).[36] According to Sog-dog-pa, Zhiwa-od, who was both a prince belonging to the royal family of the kingdom of Guge in Western Tibet and a Buddhist monk affiliated with the Kadampa school, considered that Dzogchen resembled the eternalist view of the Hindus (*mu-stegs rtag lta-ba*). The name Drang-nga Shag-tsul is otherwise unknown, although the name appears to be Bonpo rather than Shaivite or Indian. Obviously he is connected in some way with the Dzogchen Tantras, but whether he is an author of some of them or merely their propagator in Western Tibet remains to be seen.[37]

In response to Zhiwa-od's edict, Sog-dog-pa replied,

> With regard to the statement that Drang-nga Shag-tshul wrote the eighteen *Sems-sde* texts, including the *Kun-byed rgyal-po,* the ten esoteric Sutras, and the *Ye-shes gsang-ba,* this does not refer to the (actual) eighteen *Sems-sde* texts: the five early translations of Vairochana and the thirteen later translations of Vimalamitra. The five early translations of Vairochana are the *Nam-mkha'-che, rTsal-chen yang-dag drug-pa, Rig-pa'i khu-byug, sKu la 'jug-pa,* and *rDzogs-pa spyi gcod.* Some people replace the last two with the *Khyung-chen lding-ba* and the *sGom don drug-pa.* The *Kun-byed rgyal-po,* the ten Sutras (*mdo bcu*), and the *Ye-shes gsang-ba* do not belong to these eighteen *Sems-sde* texts. Because Drigung Paldzin (a scholar who doubted the authenticity of these texts) did not make this distinction, he cannot see the target at which his arrow is aimed. There is no agreement among those who make such critical statements. Go Lhatse says that the thirteen later texts such as the *rMad byung* were (actually) written by Nubchen Sangye Yeshe, but this is refuted by saying that they are translations by Vimalamitra. As to Drang-nga Shag-tshul writing the *Kun-byed rgyal-po,* others say it was written by Vairochana; while others say it was the *gSang-ba'i snying-po* which Vairochana wrote. These assertions are without foundation.[38]

In the colophon of the text of the *Kun-byed rgyal-po* found in the *rNying-ma'i rgyud 'bum* collection[39] and also in the colophon of the version of the text found in the Kangyur of the Peking edition,[40] it is said that the Tantra was translated by Bhikshu Vairochana in consultation with the Indian Acharya Shrisimhanatha (dPal gyi seng-ge mgon-po). The main body of the *Kun-byed rgyal-po* is represented by chapters 1–57, after which, in the *rNying-ma'i rgyud 'bum* and the *Kangyur,* is found the Appended Tantra, consisting of chapters 58–84. Each chapter is called a Sutragama (*mdo lung*), but here Sutra (*mdo*) means not a text belonging to the Sutra system, but a summary of what is most essential, that is to say, the meaning of the essential point (*gnad gyi don*) or a condensing into one of the essential meanings that are intended (*gdongs don gyi snying-po rnams gcig to dril-ba*).

The colophon to chapter 57 of the Tantra in the Peking edition says that the preceding text was translated by the Indian Acharya Shrisimhaprabha and the Tibetan translator Pa-gor Vairochana, but this is not the case with the version of the Tantra in the *rNying-ma'i rgyud 'bum* (mTshams-brag edition). At the end of chapter 69 in both the Peking and the mTshams-brag versions, the colophon reads, "The twelve Sutragamas called the Appended Tantra are here completed." According to Kah-thog Gyurmed Tsewang (Kah-thog 'Gyur-med tshe-dbang mchog-grub, eighteenth century), it is said that Vairochana, with the aid of Shrisimha, translated the first fifty-seven chapters, and another Indian, Shrisimhanatha, translated chapters 58–84. And it is true that chapter 58 represents the beginning of a new text; it is an introductory chapter, or Nidana (*gleng-gzhi le'u*). It is uncertain whether these two Shrisimhas are the same individual or not.

There is no colophon to the *Kun-byed rgyal-po* text found in the *Bairo'i rgyud 'bum;* here only chapters 58–84 are found. But since these chapters are included in this collection, their translation is certainly attributed to Vairochana by tradition. According to Namkhai Norbu Rinpoche, these chapters provide the quintessential meaning of the entire Tantra. And according to Nyingmapa tradition generally, the Tantra descended from Garab Dorje to Shrisimha, who instructed Vairochana in it while he was residing in India; the latter subsequently introduced the Tantra into Tibet. In any event, in later centuries Vairochana himself was accused of being the actual author of this text.[41]

BSAM-GTAN MIG SGRON: **A PHILOSOPHICAL EXPOSITION OF DZOGCHEN**

The *bSam-gtan mig sgron*, attributed to Nubchen Sangye Yeshe (gNubs-chen sangs-rgyas ye-shes, nine century CE), contains an exposition of the four kinds of Buddhist teaching prevalent in Tibet in the eighth and ninth centuries. As we have seen, even in early times, Lama scholars clearly distinguished the view of Chan Buddhism from that of Dzogchen. These four kinds of Buddhist teaching are the gradualist path of the Mahayana Sutras, the nongradualist path of Chan, the path of the Mahayoga Tantra, and the path of Dzogchen.

In chapter 7, Nubchen provides a detailed exposition of Dzogchen and clearly indicates the close connections of Dzogchen with Mahayoga Tantra. The emphasis in the presentation of Dzogchen here is placed on the viewpoint of the Primordial Base (*ye-nas gzhi, gdod-ma'i gzhi*), which is primordially pure (*ka-nas dag-pa, ka-dag*). By way of exposition, Nubchen cites nine different views (*lta-ba dgu*) regarding Dzogchen held by leading Indian and Tibetan masters of the tradition:

1. The View Which Is Free of All Conceptions (*gza' gtad dang bral-ba'i lta-ba*) was the view held by the Maharaja of Uddiyana and by Vimalamitra;
2. The View of the Total State of Spontaneous Self-Perfection (*lhun-grub-pa'i ngang chen-po'i lta-ba*) was the view held by Garab Dorje;
3. The View of the Total State (*bdag-nyid chen-po'i lta-ba*) was the view held by Vairochana the translator;
4. The View of the Self-Originated Knowledge (*rang byung gi ye-shes kyi lta-ba*) was the view held by the Bhikshuni Ananda (*dge-slong-ma kun-dga'-mo*);
5. The View Which Is Free of All Action and Seeking (*bya btsal dang bral-ba'i lta-ba*) was the view held by Buddhagupta (Sangs-rgyas sbas-pa);
6. The View of the Great Bliss (*bde-ba chen-po'i lta-ba*) was the view held by Kukuraja and Shrisimha;
7. The View of Nonduality in accordance with the higher Mahayoga (*lhag-pa'i rnal-'byor chen-po nas gnyis su med-pa'i lta-ba*) was the view held by Manjushrimitra;
8. The View of the Single Total Sphere (*thig-le chen-po gcig gi lta-ba*) was the view held by Rajahasti (Thu-bo Radza-has-ti); and
9. The View of the Natural Base of All Phenomena, Which Exists Just as It Is (*chos thams-cad gzhi ji-bzhin-pa'i lta-ba*) was the view held by Garab Dorje, by King Dahenatalo of Uddiyana (rGyal-po 'Da-'he-na-ta-lo), and by our author Nubchen Sangye Yeshe.

Garab Dorje's views are cited in two places above. The first (number 2) is defined as follows: "As for the view with respect to the total state which is spontaneously self-perfected (*lhun gyis grub-pa'i ngang chen-po'i lta-ba ni*), (everything within) the natural range of the activities of the senses (*spyod-yul*) of both Buddhas and ordinary sentient beings is enlightened without remainder (*lhag-ma med-par sangs-rgyas-so*) in the nature of the total state of spontaneously self-perfected Reality (Dharmata) (*lhun gyis grub-pa'i chos-nyid ngang chen-po'i rang-bzhin du*) from the very beginning and without end (*ye gdod-ma med-pa nas tha-ma med-par*)."[42] The second view attributed to Garab Dorje (number 9) is described as "The view regarding the Natural Base of all phenomena, which exists just as it is (*chos thams-cad gzhi ji-bzhin-pa'i lta-ba*), is said to be the especially unmistaken view. And why is that? Because the suchness (Skt. *tathatā*) of all things (*dngos-po rnams kyi de kho-na nyid*) is inexpressible in speech and unadulterated (by anything else) (*kha na ma ma bcos bslad-pa nyid*); it is Atiyoga, the Great Perfection."[43]

In his study of early Dzogchen, Karmay asserts that the *bSam-gtan mig sgron* represents a product of the tenth century, and he also questions its authorship by Nubchen.[44] However, Nyingmapa tradition generally places Nubchen in the ninth century, making him a contemporary of the anti-Buddhist Tibetan king Lang Darma, who ascended to the throne upon the assassination of his brother Ralpachan c. 836 CE. Some later sources also place him in the eighth century and make him a direct disciple of Guru Padmasambhava. In his *mGur 'bum*,[45] Milarepa says that he learned the art of magic spells or mantras from Lharje Nubchung (Lha-rje gnubs chung). According to Nyingmapa tradition, this was actually Lharje Hum chung (Lha-rje hum-chung), the great-grandson of Nubchen, but this would not in itself conclusively place Nubchen in the tenth century, as Karmay claims, for Nubchen was said to have lived an exceedingly long life.

The author of *bSam-gtan mig sgron* identifies himself as Nuban (gNubs-ban), and this is most likely Nubchen Sangye Yeshe. He goes on to state that he had studied under various Indian and Nepali masters, and in particular with the Gilgit (*bru-sha*) translator Chetsunkye (lo-tswa-ba Che-btsun-skyes), who was responsible for translating the Anuyoga Tantras into Tibetan. These texts, under the designation *rNal-'byor grub-pa'i lung*, are much quoted in Nubchen's work. Some critics, like Prince Zhiwa-od (Pho-brang Zhi-ba 'od, tenth century CE), accuse Nubchen of actually composing Nyingmapa texts himself and then presenting them as translations of Indian originals. But the contents of the *bSam-gtan mig sgron* show its author to be a scholar and a thinker aware of subtle philosophical distinctions. Later Nyingmapa tradition portrays Nubchen as a black-hat magician, a Tantrika (*sngags-pa*) indulging in the performance of black magic rites (*drag sngags*, "fierce mantras"), and it is said that he was able to terrify and intimidate King Lang Darma by means of his sorceries. However, there is no contradiction in his being both a scholar of philosophical bent and a magician; such was the case with several well-known figures of the Renaissance period in Europe.

According to Nyingmapa tradition, Nubchen was born into the clan of Nub (gNubs) in the Drag Valley. At the age of seven, he became a master of the Tantras and received from Guru Padmasambhava the initiations for the *sGrub-pa bka'-brgyad*. When he tossed the flower into the Mandala of the Eight Herukas, it fell into the region of the mandala which is the residence of Yamantaka (*gshin-rje gshed*), the wrathful aspect of Manjushri, the great Bodhisattva of wisdom. After practicing the sadhana of Yamantaka for twenty-one days, he received a vision of the face of the meditation deity. Yamantaka thus became his *yi-dam*, or personal meditation deity, and Manjushri himself bestowed upon him a supreme intelligence. By means of his magical powers, he destroyed thirty-seven hostile villages in the Drag district and burned their armed men with magically conjured fire. He was the consummate master of the Fierce Mantras (*drag sngags*) or Black Magic. In the cave of Drag-yang-dzang, his *phurpa*, or three-bladed magic dagger, pierced the solid rock of the cliff as if it were butter. It is said that Nubchen then visited India, Nepal, and Gilgit, where he directly received teachings from Shrisimha, Vimalamitra, Shantigarbha, Dhanashila, Vasudhara, and Chetsunkye; and in Tibet he received teachings from Nyag Jnanakumara, Sogpo Palgyi Yeshe, and Zhang Gyalwe Yontan. Thus, all the lineages of transmission for Mahayoga, Anuyoga, and Dzogchen Semde converged in him.

When King Lang Darma set about to suppress the Buddhist teachings and to close the Buddhist monasteries, he summoned the tantric master Nubchen and his disciples before him, although the latter were not monks but Tantrikas (*sngags-pa*). The king challenged Nubchen, inquiring, "And what power do you have?" "Just observe the power I manifest merely from reciting mantras," Nubchen replied and raised his right hand above his head in a threatening gesture. Instantly, in the sky above the tantric sorcerer, the king saw nine scorpions appear, each the size of a yak. The king was terrified. He promptly promised not to harm the Buddhist Tantrikas and to refrain from disrobing and exiling them as he had done with the Buddhist monks. Then Nubchen pointed again with a threatening gesture, and lightning flashed, shattering into pieces a nearby boulder. Doubly terrified, the king vowed, "I will not in any way harm you or your white-robed followers!" and he ordered his prisoners released. Because of the magical powers of Nubchen, this anti-Buddhist king did not destroy the tantric teachings and their white-robed practitioners, the Ngagpas (*sngags-pa*, "one who uses mantras"). Consequently, they have flourished until this day.[46]

But it must be said in all fairness to Lang Darma, universally depicted in later medieval histories as being totally evil and depraved, that the so-called persecution of Buddhists he inaugurated came from political and economic motives rather than religious conviction, so far as historical scholarship can ascertain. His campaign was directed not so much against Buddhist teaching as such as against the monastic institutions the Buddhists had established in Tibet. This was also the case in China after the Tang Dynasty. There was a tendency in India, China, and Tibet for large monastic establishments to develop that would house hundreds, even thousands, of monks at public expense; that is, they were supported from the taxes collected by the king's government. In view of the presence of these large populations of indolent monks, it was not unnatural for resentment to develop in the hearts of those nobles and peasants who were somewhat less than piously devout. From the time of Tisong Detsan in the eighth century to Ralpachan in the ninth century, Buddhist monasteries such as Samye grew in size, wealth, and influence. Under Ralpachan in particular (reigning 815–836 CE), monks were taken into the government as important ministers in competition with the lay nobility, although both were derived from the same land-owning class and great families. During the reign of Ralpachan, resentment of ecclesiastical interference with the affairs of state was much in evidence, as well as of the diversion of the government's limited resources to support the growing population of Buddhist monks at Samye and Lhasa. This public subsidy became a great burden on the state at a time when fresh resources were needed in terms of money and men to prosecute foreign wars in order to preserve what territories remained to the diminishing Tibetan empire. This resentment culminated in a palace coup where the king was assassinated. The anticlerical faction among the ministers installed Lang Darma as king, in the place of his dead brother. The persecution was then launched, aimed at dismantling the monastic system, hence the enforced disrobing of monks and the closing of monasteries, both of which were viewed as drains on the state treasury. But since this was not a suppressing of the Buddhist teaching as such, the tantric tradition of teaching and practice of Ngagpas like Nubchen continued to flourish uninterrupted in Central Tibet during this period when the Buddhist monasteries were no longer state-supported. In fact, this so-called Dark Age was a creative and vital period for the later Nyingmapas and Bonpos. With the weakening and final collapse of the central administration, the government was no longer in a position to prevent or restrict the translating of the Tantras, as it had done previously. Moreover, tantric teaching and practice became even more widespread and popular than was the case previously, since practitioners were no longer dependent on government-sanctioned official translations and government-supported monasteries, but on transmission through lineages of married Lamas, like Nubchen and his sons.

In 842 King Lang Darma was assassinated by a Buddhist monk named Lhalung Palgyi Dorje (Lha-lung dpal gyi rdo-rje), said to have been the ninth abbot of Samye Monastery. Then followed the Dark Age of approximately one hundred years (842–950), of which very little is now known because of the collapse of all central authority and the lack of government involvement in religious affairs. Whereas monastic discipline was completely disrupted in Central Tibet, in contrast the tantric traditions of Mahayoga and Anuyoga continued to develop without interruption. This was also true of Dzogchen.

'DRA 'BAG CHEN-MO: THE BIOGRAPHY OF VAIROCHANA

Most scholars, Western as well as native Tibetan, agree that Vairochana the translator was instrumental in introducing Dzogchen itself, or at least the ideas that gave rise to Dzogchen, into Tibet. It is also known that Vairochana had strong Bonpo connections, and indeed he is still highly regarded among the Bonpos, according to Lopon Tenzin Namdak, the leading native-born scholar of the Bon tradition.[47] Most authorities agree that Dzogchen was introduced into Central Tibet in the eighth century, subsequent to the visit of Guru Padmasambhava, by Vairochana upon returning from his studies in India. In particular he introduced into Tibet the Semde and the Longde Series of teachings. Upon this all traditional sources agree. However, the Dzogchen teachings of Padmasambhava and of Vimalamitra represent Upadeshas, or *man-ngag gi sde*, as explained

above, and the *Zhang-zhung snyan rgyud* of Tapihritsa and
Gyerpungpa is also an Upadesha. So we must look to Vairochana as
the source of the Dzogchen Semde and the Dzogchen Longde teachings, which, according to tradition, he received from the master
Shrisimha in India.

Born into the Pagor (*pa-gor* or *ba-gor*) clan, which had strong Bonpo
connections, Vairochana was among the first seven native-born Tibetans (*sad-mi mi bdun*) to receive ordination as Buddhist monks at
the hands of the Indian master Shantirakshita, the first abbot of Samye
Monastery. As a boy, Vairochana mastered the Sanskrit language and
prepared for a career as a translator. It is also said in some sources
that he learned Chinese. Among his translations were the *rGyud bzhi*,
The Four Tantras, the classic Buddhist medicine text, and a number of
works on Chinese astrology. It is further said that he was personally
initiated by Guru Padmasambhava himself and was thus numbered
among the twenty-five disciples (*rje 'bangs nyer lnga*) of that master.
The account of his journey to India is found in some detail in his
biography, the *'Dra 'bag chen-mo*.[48] According to this account,
Vairochana was sent by King Tisong Detsan to India with a fellow
student in order to procure texts of advanced Buddhist teachings. It
is said that the king knew of the Dzogchen teachings, although they
were more or less unknown in Tibet at the time, because in a previous life he had been a monk in India who had practiced these teachings.

During his time in India, Vairochana is said to have met some
twenty-four masters, and in particular he met the Dzogchen master
Shrisimha, from whom he received the precepts for the Semde and
the Longde. Among other texts that he brought back with him to
Tibet, there were five texts belonging to the Dzogchen Semde that he
immediately translated into Tibetan. These are known as the five early
translations of Dzogchen (*rdzogs-chen snga 'gyur lnga*) and are as follows:

1. *Byang-chub sems rig-pa'i khu-byug,*
2. *Byang-chub sems bsgom-pa (rDo la gser zhun),*
3. *Byang-chub sems khyung-chen lding-ba,*
4. *Byang-chub sems rtsal-chen sprugs-pa,* and
5. *Byang-chub sems mi nub-pa'i rgyal-mtshan (rDo-rje sems-dpa'
   nam-mkha'-che).*

These texts are found in the *Bai-ro'i rgyud 'bum*.[49] According to Longchenpa in his *Chos-dbyings rin-po-che'i mdzod*,[50] to these early translations were added thirteen later translations (*rdzogs-chen phyi 'gyur bcu-gsum*), and together they comprise the eighteen basic texts of the Dzogchen Semde Series:

6. *rTse-mo byung-rgyal,*
7. *Nam-mkha' rgyal-po,*
8. *Byang-sems bde-ba 'phra bkod,*
9. *rDzogs-pa spyi chings,*
10. *bDe-ba rab-'byams,*
11. *Byang-chub sems tig,*
12. *Srog gi 'khor-lo,*
13. *Thig-le drug-pa,*
14. *Byang-chub sems rdzogs-pa spyi gcod,*
15. *Yid-bzhin nor-bu,*
16. *Kun 'dus rig-pa,*
17. *rJe-btsun dam-pa,* and
18. *bsGom-pa don grub.*

Also according to Longchenpa, to this list may be added:

19. *Byang-chub sems kun-byed rgyal-po,*
20. *rMad-byung rgyal-po,* and
21. *mDo bcu.*

This list of seventeen or eighteen Semde texts (*sems-sde bco-brgyad*) is old and is found in the history (*chos 'byung*) written by Nyima Odzer (Myang-ral nyi-ma 'od-zer, 1124–1192) entitled *Me-tog snying-po sbrang-rtsi'i bcud*.[51]

Vairochana did not have the opportunity to teach very much of what he had learned in India because of the opposition at court, although he was able to meet secretly at night with the king and instruct him in the Dzogchen precepts. At the instigation of Queen Tsepongza (Tshe-spong bza'; her personal name was dMar-rgyal ldong-ska), he was falsely accused, expelled from court, and exiled to Tsewarong in Eastern Tibet. Here Prince Yudra Nyingpo (gYu-sgra snying-po) became his principal disciple. Later, at the urging of Vimalamitra, he was recalled and allowed to return to Central Tibet, where he resided at Samye Monastery and completed many translations.[52]

The text we have here, the *'Dra 'bag chen-mo,* purports to be a history of the diffusion of the Dzogchen teachings. Chapter 4 (21a–24b) presents a history of Dzogchen, beginning with the legend of Garab Dorje. According to this account, in the country of Uddiyana there lived a king named Dhahenatalo (var. Dahenatalo) who had a son called Thuwo Rajahasti (Thu-bo ra-dza-ha-ti) and a daughter named Bharani. One day, the great Bodhisattva Vajrapani transformed himself into the guise of a golden water bird. When the princess, who had now become a nun, was walking along the lakeshore, she picked up this bird, which thereupon pecked at her breast. Nine months later she gave birth to a miraculous child who began immediately to recite the *rDo-rje sems-dpa' nam-mkha'-che Tantra.* This child was none other than Garab Dorje. Then the story is told of this master meeting with the scholar Manjushrimitra.

Manjushrimitra was born in Western India of Brahman parents, and while still a boy, inspired by the blessings of his tutelary deity Manjushri, he became a great scholar, mastering all sciences, both sacred and secular. He became widely famed as a Pandita, or Sanskrit scholar, and came to reside at the great monastic university of Nalanda at the time when Garab Dorje, still in the guise of a young boy, was residing and teaching the Dakinis in the cremation ground of Shitavana (according to the *Lo-rgyus chen-mo*). The account found in the *'Dra 'bag chen-mo* would locate Garab Dorje as still in Uddiyana at this time. Nevertheless, Garab Dorje very much represents the archetype of the *puer aeternus* and the wise child. All accounts mention a prophecy coming from Manjushri advising Manjushrimitra to seek out Garab Dorje, for this master would teach him a method whereby he could realize liberation within a single lifetime. This was something he would not discover in his books despite all his learning and all his erudition. Rumors had come to the university of a mysterious young boy who was teaching the doctrine of the Primordial State, which lies beyond cause and effect. This outraged the scholars because such a doctrine appeared to contradict the conventional Buddhist teaching on karma and causality as understood from the perspective of the Sutra system or Hetuyana, the causal vehicle. The assembly of Buddhist scholars declared such a teaching as false, heretical, and dangerous. So they decided to send a delegation consisting of Manjushrimitra and six other colleagues to confront this upstart, arrogant young boy who had challenged Buddhist orthodox scholastic tradition and to defeat him in debate.

According to the *'Dra 'bag chen-mo* (pp. 439–40),

> The promulgation and continuation of the extraordinary teaching of the self-originated effortlessly realized state of the Great Perfection (*rdzogs-chen*) is as follows: At that time (when Garab Dorje was teaching), an emanation (*sprul-pa*, Skt. *nirmita*) of Arya Manjushri was born as an exceedingly intelligent child, the son of the Brahman Shrisukhapala (dPal-ldan bde-skyong) and the Brahmani Mokutana. They called their child Sarasiddhi (sNying-po grub-pa) and Shamvaragarbha (bDe-mchog snying-po). He became learned in all aspects of the Hetuyana (the Sutra system) and the Phalayana (the Tantra system), as well as in the secular sciences. He became a Bhikshu and was supreme among the five hundred panditas (of his monastery).
>
> At that time, these Panditas heard that the Nirmanakaya Prahevajra (Garab Dorje) was expounding the doctrine of the effortless state (*rtsol med*) of the Great Perfection, the teaching of a state which lies beyond cause and effect, this being the quintessence of the marvelous Dharma of the Buddha, superior to all other teachings of cause and effect. At that time also, this Brahman youth Sarasiddhi received the prophecy of Arya Manjushri, which said, "To the northwest, in the land of Uddiyana, on the shore of Dhanakosha Lake, in the valley of Ha-chen bdal-ba, in the Vajradvipa Cave (rDo-rje gling) belonging to the great cremation ground of Suvarnadvipa (gSer gling), dwells the miraculous emanation of Vajrasattva, who is known as the Nirmanakaya Prahevajra. He has received the initiation (from Vajrasattva) for the effortless lamp of all the Buddhas (that is, the Thodgal teaching). Through him enlightenment may be effortlessly realized (*rtsol med*) in an instant by virtue of the precepts of Atiyoga, the quintessence of all Dharma teachings. You must go to obtain from him these teachings and make a collection of the precepts of that Nirmanakaya." The other scholars went there to debate (this boy) in order to refute his claim that there exists a Dharma superior to the teaching of cause and effect. . . .

Manjushrimitra and his colleague Panditas journeyed far to meet Garab Dorje, and upon encountering him face to face, Manjushrimitra was ashamed of his intention to debate with the master and threatened to cut out his own tongue. Garab Dorje dissuaded him, telling him that actions (meritorious deeds) alone will not purify his obscurations, but that the teaching of the master would. Manjushrimitra was very intelligent, and so with only an exchange of a few words, the whole conceptual structure he had erected by means of his learning and scholarship crumbled and he understood immediately. In order to perfect his understanding, Garab Dorje gave him the empowerment for complete realization and bestowed upon him all the Tantras and Upadeshas, such as the nine spaces (*klong dgu*) and the twenty thousand sections of the teaching. The master then gave him the name of Manjushrimitra ('Jam-dpal bshes-gnyen), "the friend of Manjushri."

Thereupon Garab Dorje expressed the essence of his teachings in a pure vajra song, and Manjushrimitra replied, "I am Manjushrimitra, who has attained the siddhi of Yamantaka (the wrathful buffalo-headed form of Manjushri). Having understood that Samsara and Nirvana are identical (in essence), a knowledge that thoroughly comprehends all things arises in me." Garab Dorje told him that, since he was a great scholar, he should write a book, and thereafter he composed the *rDo la gser zhun*, "Gold Refined from Ore."[53] At this time Manjushrimitra was new to Dzogchen, having previously been a scholar belonging to the Yogacharin school, which adhered to the Chittamatra, or Mind-Only doctrine. Thus, while Manjushrimitra speaks about this Primordial State beyond cause and effect called the Bodhichitta, he largely does so from the Yogacharin standpoint, and without the familiar Dzogchen terminology.[54]

It is also said that Manjushrimitra divided the sixty-four myriad verses of Dzogchen into three series of teachings (*rdzogs-chen sde gsum*) as follows:

1. the Mind Series (*sems-sde*), concerned with the realization of the calm state of mind (*sems gnas rnams la sems sde*)
2. the Space Series (*klong-sde*), concerned with the realization of a state free of activities (*bya-bral rnams la klongsde*)
3. the Secret Instruction Series (*man-ngag gi sde*), concerned with the principal essential point (*gnad gtso-bo la man-ngag sde*) of continuing in contemplation

These three series of teachings are related to the three statements of Garab Dorje as explained previously. The Upadesha Series was then subdivided as follows:

A. the oral transmission (*snyan brgyud*)
   1. the orally transmitted Tantras (*rnar rgyud*)
   2. the Explanatory Tantras (*bshad rgyud*)
B. the transmission of the explanations (i.e., the Explanatory Tantras apart from those cited above, *bshad rgyud*)

It is said that when Shrisimha went to Vajrasana (Bodh Gaya), he discovered the texts of the Upadesha Series which Manjushrimitra had concealed there. This final series of teachings, also known as *sNying-thig* (Skt. *citta-tilaka*), he divided into four parts:

1. the outer cycle (*phyi skor*)
2. the inner cycle (*nang skor*)
3. the secret cycle (*gsang skor*)
4. the unsurpassably secret cycle (*gsang-ba bla-na med-pa'i skor*)

In the following chapter (24b–43a), we are presented with the lineage of transmission of the Dzogchen teachings from Garab Dorje down to Vimalamitra:

1. Prahevajra (dGa'-rab rdo-rje)
2. the elder Manjushrimitra ('Jam-dpal bshes-gnyen snga-ba)
3. King Dhahenatalo (rGyal-po 'Dha-'he-na-ta-lo)
4. Rajahasti (Thu-bo Ra-dza-ha-ti)
5. the Bhikshuni Bharani (dGe-slong-ma Ba-ra-na)
6. Nagaraja (kLu'i rgyal-po)
7. the Yakshini Bodhi (gNod-sbyin-ma Byang-chub-ma)
8. the prostitute Bharani (sMad-'tshong-ma Ba-ra-na)
9. the Upadhyaya Prabhasa of Kashmir (mKhan-po Rab-snang)
10. the Upadhyaya Maharaja of Uddiyana (mKhan-po rGyal-po chen-po)
11. his daughter Gomadevi (Sras-mo Go-ma-de-vi)
12. Achintyaloka (A-tsan-tra a-lo-ke)
13. the elder Kukuraja (Ku-ku-ra-dza snga-ba)
14. the Rishi Bhashita (Drang-srong Bha-shi-ta)
15. the prostitute Atma (sMad-'tshong-ma bDag-nyid-ma)
16. Nagarjuna (Na-ga-dzu-na)
17. the younger Kukuraja (Ku-ku-ra-dza phyi-ma)
18. the younger Manjushrimitra ('Jam-dpal bshes-gnyen phyi-ma)
19. Devaraja (De-wa-ra-dza)
20. Buddhagupta (Bhu-ta-kug-ta)
21. Shrisimhaprabha (Shri sing-ba pra-pa-ta)
22. the Bhikshuni Ananda (dGe-slong-ma Kun-dga'-ma)
23. Vimalamitra

Note the presence of a number of women masters in this lineage list for the Dzogchen teachings. A prostitute (*smad-'tshong-ma*) in this context probably does not mean a woman who sells her body on the street, but more likely a wealthy courtesan, literate and educated, that is to say, an independent woman in a patriarchal society, like the famous Greek *hetairai*, or courtesans, Lais and Thais. In a traditional patriarchal society, an unmarried woman of independent means who relates to men on a level of equality is often designated in literary sources as a prostitute or courtesan. A Rishi (*drang-srong*) is a Brahman sage, a Bhikshuni (*dge-slong-ma*) is a fully ordained nun, and an Upadhyaya (*mkhan-po*) is a Buddhist professor or an abbot. Three figures in this lineage may be nonhuman: the Nagaraja (kLu'i rgyal-po), or the Naga king, the Devaraja (Lha'i rgyal-po), or the Deva king, and the Yakshini (*gnod-sbyin-ma*), or female earth spirit. On the other hand, they may be proper names or nicknames, and it was not unusual in ancient India to identify aboriginal tribal peoples as Nagas, Yakshas, and Rakshasas, and so forth. The Princess Gomadevi of Uddiyana is also known from the lineage of the Mahayoga teachings. The members of this lineage vary in different sources. Obviously the function of such a lineage is to establish the authenticity of the Dzogchen teachings, like the famous lineage extending from Buddha Shakyamuni down to Bodhidharma which serves to authenticate the Chan teachings. But since here there is no attempt made to trace the Dzogchen teachings directly to Shakyamuni, but only to an otherwise mysterious and unknown figure, Garab Dorje, this would testify to his being the real source of the Dzogchen teachings. Nor should the above lineage list be rejected out of hand as totally unhistorical.

Karmay, in his study of this text,[55] regards the *'Dra 'bag chen-mo* as a hagiography of Vairochana and not as a history of Dzogchen. A hagiography is neither history nor biography, but is written to support a certain theological perspective. This is also the case with the four Gospels found in the New Testament. The same account of the journey of Vairochana to India and his meeting with various masters there is found in the *Me-tog snying-po sbrang-rtsi'i bcud*, written by Nyang-ral Nyima Odzer (Myang-ral nyi-ma 'od-zer, 1136–1209). Therefore Karmay considers the *'Dra 'bag chen-mo* to be an elaboration of this hagiographic account and dates the latter text as thirteenth century. According to the colophon of the text (Dehra Dun edition, no date), the text was edited by Khams-smyong Dharma seng-ge, Dharmasimha, the madman from Kham (nineteenth century). The Leh edition is taken from the *Bai-ro'i rgyud 'bum* collection. According to Dharmasimha's colophon, originally there were two versions of the *'Dra 'bag chen-mo* put into concealment. One was rediscovered by Jomo Manmo (Jo-mo sman-mo, 1248–1283), a famous woman Terton and the wife of another famous Terton, Guru Chowang (Guru Chos-dbang, 1212–1270). This first version was a Terma, but there also existed a *bka'-ma* version revised and elaborated by Droban Tashi Jyungne ('Bro-ban bkra-shis 'byung-gnas). So it seems probable that much material in the *'Dra 'bag chen-mo* is older than the thirteenth century. Karmay also concludes that Vairochana had a definite historical existence and that he flourished in the second half of the eighth century.

Is Dzogchen an Authentic Buddhist Teaching?

Criticism of this type, as represented by the edict of Prince Zhiwa-od, called into question the authenticity of the Dzogchen teachings, first with respect to the genuineness of its source texts and second with respect to the validity of its doctrines as being orthodox Buddhist teaching. In subsequent centuries during the medieval period, certain scholars belonging to the New Tantra schools (gSar-ma-pa) wrote disparagingly of Dzogchen and claimed that its fundamental texts, such as the *Kun-byed rgyal-po*, had no Indian originals in Sanskrit but were fabrications written by native Tibetan scholars. For example, Drigung Paldzin ('Bri-gung dpal-'dzin nyi-'od bzang-po, fourteenth century), in his *Chos dang chos ma yin-pa rnam-par dbye-ba rab tu byed-pa*, asserts that no Dzogchen texts existed before the persecution of Buddhists by King Lang Darma (c. 836 CE) and goes on to claim that Nyangton (Myang-ston smra-ba'i seng-ge) actually wrote the eighteen Tantras of the Semde Series. He rejects the Sanskrit rendering *mahāsanti/mahāsandhi*, which is translated into Tibetan as *rdzogs-pa chen-po*, and says that this term is nowhere to be found in the Buddhist Tantras of Indian origin translated in the later period. The word *rdzogs-chen*, he says, is merely a Tibetan creation.

Nyingmapa scholars therefore felt compelled to refute these accusations hurled against Dzogchen. The first such was Rongzom Pandita (Rong-zom chos kyi bzang-po, eleventh century) in his *Theg-pa chen-po'i tshul la 'jug-pa*. In the fourteenth century this was done in a comprehensive fashion by Longchenpa (kLong-chen rab-

'byams-pa dri-med 'od-zer, 1308–1363) in his monumental *mDzod bdun, The Seven Treasures*. Then again, with respect to Drigung Paldzin, in the seventeenth century Sog-dog-pa (Sog-zlog-pa bLo-gros rgyal-mtshan, 1552–1627), in his *Nges-don 'brug sgra*, replies to all of these points of criticism. In terms of doctrine, he compares Dzogchen to Mahamudra, quoting in support of this contention the *Mahamudra Upadesha* of Tilopa and the *Dohas* of Virupa.[1] The famous sixteenth-century Kagyudpa historian Pawo Tsuglag (dPa'-bo gtsug-lag phreng-ba, 1504–1566), in his history of Buddhism, the *mKhas-pa'i dga'-ston*, defended the authenticity of the Dzogchen Tantras. And in our own time two scholars of Dzogchen have done likewise, Dudjom Rinpoche (bDud-'joms 'jigs-bral ye-shes rdo-rje, 1904–1987) in his *rNying-ma'i chos-'byung* and elsewhere, and Chögyal Namkhai Norbu (Chos-rgyal nam-mkha'i nor-bu) in his *The Small Collection of Hidden Precepts* and elsewhere.[2]

It is true that the term *rdzogs-pa chen-po*, the Great Perfection, is not found in the *Mahavyutpatti*, the famous Sanskrit-Tibetan dictionary of Buddhist technical terms compiled and given official sanction in the time of King Sanaleg (Sad-na-legs, Khri-lde srong-brtsan, c. 800–815), the father of King Ralpachan.[3] This dictionary represents an attempt by the Tibetan government to standardize the translation of Buddhist technical terms into Tibetan. The accompanying *Madhyavyutpatti* explains why the Sanskrit terms are translated in the way they are and provides Sanskrit citations and etymologies in support of this. Here also is found the royal proclamation that henceforward this will be the official procedure for translations. Thus, some scholars assert that since the term *rdzogs-pa chen-po* is not found in this early dictionary, as well as nowhere attested in the translations of the New Tantras, it does not represent the translation of any Sanskrit original, but is a purely Tibetan invention. While it is true that the form *mahāsanti* appears in the supposed Sanskrit titles provided at the beginning of Tibetan translations of the Dzogchen Tantras, *mahāsanti/santimahā* does not appear to be proper Sanskrit. Namkhai Norbu Rinpoche, on the other hand, suggests that, in view of the tradition that the majority of the Dzogchen Tantras were translated not from Sanskrit directly but from the Uddiyana language, the form *mahāsanti* is not incorrect Sanskrit, but represents the Uddiyana dialect. This would also account for the variant *santimahā*, where the adjective succeeds the noun instead of preceding it as in Sanskrit.[4] It is known that the oldest verse portions of many Sanskrit Mahayana Sutras were originally composed in Prakrit dialects and that the later *Dakarnava Tantra* is partly written in Apabramsha, an eastern Middle Indic dialect, so this argument should not be dismissed out of hand. Rongzom Pandita (eleventh century) asserts that *mahāsandhi* is the proper Sanskrit form and that it means "the great union."[5] The union alluded to here is likely that of the generation process and the perfection process and therefore represents a state transcending them both.

Moreover, the term *rdzogs-chen* is found in an early text, the *Man-ngag lta-ba'i phreng-ba*, a work traditionally attributed to Padmasambhava himself.[6] Here it occurs in relation to the term *rdzogs-rim* in the phrase *bskyed rdzogs rnam-pa gsum gyi tshul*, the methods of the three: the generation process, the perfection process, (and the Great Perfection). Here Dzogchen is not mentioned as a distinct term, but its presence is to be inferred. It also occurs in the commentary to this text by Rongzom Pandita.[7] Furthermore, the phrase *bskyed rdzogs gsum*, again referring to the three: *bskyed-rim*, *rdzogs-rim*, and *rdzogs-chen*, is found in many other texts. There it occurs in the context of Mahayoga Tantra, where the term *rdzogs-chen* designates the culminating stage in the process of transformation known as *rdzogs-rim*, or the perfection process. In the *sGyu-'phrul dbang gi gal-po'i don 'grel* of Buddhaguhya (eighth century), the process of *rdzogs-rim* is explained as being divided into three levels or phases of samadhi (*ting-nge-'dzin*, "contemplation"). The last of these is called *rdzogs-pa'i rdzogs-pa*, the completing of perfection, and this is explained as follows, "This is called the Great Perfection because from that point one does not need to make any effort to obtain all the qualities of a Buddha."[8] But scholars like Drigung Paldzin claim that this term is never found in the newer translations of the Tantras, even though the master Buddhaguhya and his commentaries are well known to these scholars. In the newer translations of the Anuttara Tantras, the culminating stage of the process of transformation known as *rdzogs-rim* is generally called *phyag-rgya chen-po*, or Mahamudra. All of the evidence suggests that the Dzogchen teachings of Garab Dorje originally pertained to the state which lay beyond tantric transformation, beyond *bskyed-rim* and *rdzogs-rim*, and that Garab Dorje transmitted these teachings as Upadesha (*man-ngag*), or secret oral instructions, only to his close disciples, and not publicly. This is not at all unusual in the context of Tantra. Generally Upadesha is very private and intimate instruction given by a master to a disciple, offering advice on practice drawn from his or her own personal experience. Other teachings relating to *rdzogs-rim* were transmitted in an identical manner, as for example, the famous *Na-ro chos drug*, or Six Teachings of Naropa, bestowed by that master upon his Tibetan disciple Marpa. In both cases, original transmission consisted of brief Upadeshas, and this was subsequently expanded and elaborated into larger texts and commentaries by scholars belonging to later generations.[9]

As we have seen, Padmasambhava largely taught Dzogchen in the context of Mahayoga Tantra as the culmination of the process of transformation. But this does not preclude the possibility that the Dzogchen precepts also existed autonomously in their own terms as Upadesha coming originally from Garab Dorje and being transmitted orally or in the form of short texts. However, this does not mean that Dzogchen in the time of Padmasambhava was considered to be a separate vehicle to enlightenment, as it certainly was later in Nyingmapa tradition. With regard to this, in the Tangyur there is found the text mentioned above, the *Man-ngag lta-ba'i phreng-ba*, which is attributed by its colophon to Padmasambhava himself. It is the only text by Padmasambhava that is *bka'-ma*; all other texts attributed to this master are *gter-ma*. Even such harsh and uncompromising critics of Dzogchen as Drigung Paldzin hold that this text is authentic and belongs to the *snga-dar*, the early spreading of the Buddhist teachings.[10]

In the title of this text, which is called an Upadesha (*man-ngag*), *lta-ba'i phreng-ba* means "The Rosary of Views." These views are arranged as follows:

    I. Wrong and perverted views

        A. *Phyal-ba*—the so-called common sense view of ordinary people. The views of beings belonging to the six destinies of rebirth mostly belong to this category. Here their minds are obscured by their impure karmic vision.

        B. *Gyang 'phen-pa*—the view of the materialists (Skt. *lokāyata*), who assert that only matter exists, and of nihilists (Skt. *ucchedavādin*), who deny the law of karma, that is, the causes and consequences of karma and the existence of a future life. This view is more philosophical and is not just the naive realism of the above.

C. *Mur-thug-pa*—the view of those nihilists who assert that all events are merely accidental. Both this view and the preceding represent nihilism, or Ucchedavada (*chad lta-ba*).

D. *Mu-stegs-pa*—the view of those Tirthikas or Hindus who assert the real existence of a permanent abiding unchanging entity called the self (*bdag*, Skt. *ātman*). This view is current among the Vedantins and the Shaivas and represents an eternalist view, or Shashvatavada (*rtag lta-ba*).

II. Views associated with the Path which leads to liberation from Samsara

A. The Lakshanayana (*mtshan-nyid kyi theg-pa*), or Sutra system, which relies upon definitions and intellectual analysis

   1. Shravakayana (*nyan-thos kyi theg-pa*)
   2. Pratyekabuddhayana (*rang sangs-rgyas kyi theg-pa*)
   3. Bodhisattvayana (*byang-chub sems-dpa'i theg-pa*)

B. The Vajrayana (*rdo-rje'i theg-pa*), or Tantra system

   1. Kriya Tantra (*bya-ba'i rgyud kyi theg-pa*),
   2. Ubhaya Tantra (*gnyis-ka'i rgyud kyi theg-pa*)
   3. Yoga Tantra (*rnal-'byor rgyud kyi theg-pa*)

     a. The Vehicle of the Outer Tantras (*rnal-'byor phyi-pa thub-pa'i rgyud kyi theg-pa*)
     b. The Vehicle of the Inner Tantras (*rnal-'byor nang-pa thabs rgyud kyi theg-pa*)

       1. The method of the generation process (*bskyed-pa'i tshul*)
       2. The method of the perfection process (*rdzogs-pa'i tshul*)
       3. The method of the Great Perfection (*rdzogs-pa chen-po'i tshul*)

This text definitely proposes a framework of various approaches to enlightenment, which can be counted as nine in number, although the term *theg-pa dgu*, the nine vehicles, is not used. In later Nyingmapa tradition, each Yana, or *theg-pa,* is an autonomous and independent means to enlightenment, sufficient in itself, although each successive vehicle is more efficacious and more comprehensive than the preceding one, and hence the texts speak of *theg-pa rim dgu,* nine successive vehicles. Each vehicle possesses its own view, meditation, and conduct appropriate to the levels of intelligence and capacities of respective practitioners. In the Nyingmapa tradition, Dzogchen is regarded as the highest and ultimate vehicle to enlightenment, an assertion that has incurred much criticism from the Newer Schools, who hold the Buddhist teachings to consist only of the Triyana, the three vehicles to enlightenment. Recently, some practitioners of Zen have taken offense at this classification.[11] Nevertheless, this text suggests that in the time of Padmasambhava, the eighth century, Dzogchen still rested within the bosom of Mahayoga (*rnal-'byor nang-pa thabs rgyud kyi theg-pa*), and was not yet regarded as an autonomous, separate, and independent Yana, as was the case later. However, in the *bSam-gtan mig sgron,* Nubchen Sangye Yeshe clearly differentiates between Mahayoga and Dzogchen.

Although two Dzogchen texts have been found in the library at Tun Huang, no Dzogchen texts are listed in the *lDan dkar-ma* catalogue of translated Buddhist texts in the early period (eighth century CE). According to Buton (Bu-ston rin-chen grub, 1290–1364) in his *chos-'byung,* or history, in the autumn of the dragon year (788), when the Tibetan king Tisong Detsan was residing at the Dankarma (lDan-dkar-ma) palace, Lotsawa Paltseg (Lo-tsa-ba dPal-brtsegs), Khon Luiwangpo ('Khon klu'i dbang-po), and others compiled a catalogue of all the translations made to date under government sponsorship, giving the numbers of chapters and verses found in each. These were translations that had official government approval. Again according to Buton, the *mChims-phu-ma* and the *Phang-thang-ma* catalogues were compiled sometime after this. Since the *sDe-dge bstan-'gyur* catalogue states that the *Phang-thang-ma* catalogue was compiled in the reign of King Sanaleg (Sad-na-legs, c. 800–815), this would appear to be the case. And since it includes reference to the *Bhavanakrama* (*bsGom-rim*) of Kamalashila, this *lDan dkar-ma* catalogue must have been compiled after the Samye debate.[12]

Although the overwhelming number of texts in this catalogue belong to the Sutra system, a certain number of tantric texts are also listed here, such as the *Aparamitayurjnana Dharani,* but these all belong to the Lower Tantras. The copies of Lower Tantra texts found at Tun Huang are all written in elaborate script, which suggests that they were translations that had official government sponsorship. But at Tun Huang, tantric texts not listed in the above catalogue were also found, texts generally written in rough handwriting, which suggests that they were private copies. Most of these texts belong to the Mahayoga class of Tantra. The catalogue of the Stein Collection[13] records a number of liturgical texts belonging to the Tantra system, either whole texts or parts thereof, as being recovered from Tun Huang. These include fragments of the *Sarvatathagata Tattvasamgraha Tantra* and the *Durgati-parishodhana Tantra*.[14] These two are both Yoga Tantras, but they are not listed in the *lDan dkar-ma* catalogue. However, there were also found tantric texts belonging to the Mahayoga cycle: the *Guhyasamaja Tantra* and fragments of texts parallel to this Tantra, a Phurpa manuscript belonging to the *sGrub-pa bka' brgyad* cycle, many liturgical texts for the *zhi-khro* (the Peaceful and Wrathful Deities) of the *Mayajala Tantra* cycle, and a sadhana for Mahashri Heruka. The Phurpa text here speaks directly of Padmasambhava.[15] Thus it appears that these Mahayoga Tantras largely circulated underground and unofficially among tantric practitioners and therefore survived the collapse of the central monarchy. This underground Mahayoga Tantra tradition is closely linked to the Nyingmapas; indeed, it is the source of what is characteristically Nyingmapa. However, Nyingmapa as a distinct self-conscious movement did not come into existence until the inauguration of the New Translations and the onset of sectarian propaganda by the Newer Schools in the eleventh century.

In the later period of the Tibetan monarchy (eighth–ninth century), during the reigns of Tisong Detsan, his son Sanaleg, and his grandson Ralpachan, the three unquestionable Buddhist kings of this period, what the Tibetan government promoted was not the Buddhism of the Tantras and of Dzogchen, but the Buddhism of the Sutra system as embodied in the social institution of monks and monasteries. This official Buddhist establishment, supported at government expense, was based on the current monastic practice of India, with its large monastic universities, like Nalanda, Vikramashila, and Odantapuri. In fact, Samye Monastery itself was laid out according to the same ground plan as Odantapuri. The abbot Shantirakshita ordained the first native-born Tibetan monks, and the Vinaya (*'dul-ba*) of the Mulasarvastivadin school of India was adopted as the official system of monastic discipline. This Vinaya remains in force even today among all schools of Tibetan Buddhism. In the context of this monastic system, the study of the Sutras and the Shastras was predominant and in particular the syncretistic Yogachara-Madhyamika philosophical system of Shantirakshita. When in the eleventh century the works of the master Chandrakirti came to be translated into Tibetan, then his version of the Madhyamaka philosophy, the Prasangika, became the philosophical basis of all of the Newer Schools of Tibetan Buddhism, replacing the old Madhyamaka eclectic system of Shantirakshita. Prasangika-Madhyamika is now the official philosophical system, not only of all the newer Sarmapa schools, but also of the older Nyingmapa and Bonpo schools.[16]

With regard to practice, the monks residing in the newly erected Buddhist monasteries in Tibet could practice the Lower Tantras, either as individuals or in the form of congregational worship (Skt. *pūjā*). But it was quite otherwise in the early period for the Higher Tantras, or Mahayoga. The translation and practice of these Tantras was not approved or sanctioned by the government. The wall paintings that survive from the early period in Central Tibet, and those that survive from the Western Tibetan kingdom of Guge (tenth–eleventh century), largely depict deities and mandalas belonging to the Lower Tantras, mainly the Yoga Tantras.[17] Only in later centuries did the Anuttara Tantras became the most popular form of tantric practice among all the Tibetan schools. Nonetheless, translations of the Mahayoga Tantras had been made and without government approval or sponsorship. This was also the case with the Dzogchen Tantras. According to the *'Dra 'bag chen-mo*, Vairochana was not permitted to teach Dzogchen openly to the king or to anyone else. So he met secretly with the king at night in order to bestow upon him the Dzogchen precepts. Thus we should not expect to find Mahayoga and Dzogchen texts listed in the official catalogues of the translations made at that time, any more than we would expect to find Gnostic texts, regarded as heretical by the Christian Church, included in the canon of the New Testament. Although translations of Mahayoga and Dzogchen texts are not listed in these catalogues, this fact does not prove that they did not exist and discreetly circulate among practitioners—both monastic and nonmonastic—in those days.

In India, the Higher Tantras, or Anuttara Tantras, and this includes the classification Mahayoga, were not something openly practiced by monks in monasteries, because their practice involved the breaking, or at least the temporary suspension of, certain monastic vows, in particular, celibacy and avoidance of intoxicants. Rather, these Tantras were practiced among Mahasiddhas or wandering Yogins who lived as recluses in the wilderness or among the common people in the villages of the countryside. Coming from diverse social backgrounds, from the aristocracy to the outcast tribes, these Mahasiddhas often supported themselves by means of crafts and other humble occupations.[18] In their lifestyle, the Mahasiddhas were not bound by the strict ordinances of the monks. It was among these Mahasiddhas that the Anuttara Tantras arose in the first place by way of visions and revelations. In some cases the names of particular Mahasiddhas are associated with the revelation or the discovery of specific Tantras, such as Saraha with the *Buddhakapala Tantra.* And so it was with Garab Dorje and the Dzogchen Tantras.

These Anuttara Tantras are filled with a bizarre symbolism involving open sexuality, even promiscuity, and a cult of wrathful deities, which in its aspect is sanguine to the utmost. Although not involving actual blood sacrifice, as in the related Hindu cults of Bhairava and Kali, the practices were otherwise similar. However, the bali, which in Hindu tantric practice is an offering of blood sacrifice, in the context of Buddhist Tantra becomes a dough figure or sacrificial cake (*gtor-ma,* Skt. *bali*) serving as a substitute for an actual animal or human being to be sacrificed. Such blood offerings, chiefly goats and buffalos, are still made in Eastern India and in Nepal to the goddess Kali even today, especially during the great festival of Durga Puja in October. The practices of the cult of Kali are delineated in the *Shakta Tantras,* which are so called because the goddess is the embodiment of Shakti, or divine energy.[19] Again, in the same way as the Shaktas, or followers of Kali, the Buddhist Mahasiddhas often sought out low-caste or outcast girls as their tantric partners. Moreover, originally the Ganachakrapuja, or tantric feast, required, in addition to the eating of meat and the drinking of wine, the engaging in actual sexual intercourse between partners in the same way as does the related Shakta rite of Chakrapuja. In every way the practice and symbolism of Anuttara Tantra, and deliberately so for its shock value, violated the social conventions of the establishment, whether of the Buddhist monastery or of Brahmanical priestly piety. It takes the practitioner beyond socially conditioned limitations. The Anuttara Tantra, with its chthonic symbolism of the nocturnal Witches' Sabbat, corresponds, as an archetype, to the Satanism of medieval Europe, which, although it never existed as a historical reality, is a fantasy that obsessed the minds of medieval churchmen and obsesses the minds of Christian Fundamentalists even to this day. Here we are dealing not with the historical influences of underground cults on each other, but with the emergence in different places of the same antiestablishment archetype—an archetype that derives ultimately from ancient pagan fertility cults. Thus, first in India, and then later in Tibet, Anuttara Tantra was something practiced in secret in order to avoid social censure and government persecution. It is no wonder that Buddhist yab-yum images, depicting deities engaged in sexual intercourse, have not been found in India. It took centuries before Anuttara Tantra became socially acceptable in India, Nepal, and Tibet.[20]

And it is no wonder that in the early days in Tibet, the texts of Mahayoga Tantra did not have wide currency. To allow the uninitiated to see and read them was not only a violation of one's tantric vows (Skt. *samaya*), but dangerous and possibly life-threatening for the adept. It is the same today in the West when neopagan witches go public with their rites; they are in danger of attack by Fundamentalist Christians, who regard them as Satanists, although they are nothing of the sort. Rather, they are devoted to the religious revival of the pagan cult of the Great Goddess, which has been suppressed for so long by the Bible-based patriarchal religious culture of the West.[21] Anuttara Tantra does not represent some sort of degeneration of higher Buddhism, a view held by an older generation of Western scholars. Its philosophy is completely consonant with Madhyamaka teaching. But the uninitiated, perceiving only the surface, would easily misunderstand the symbolism, for here the practitioner is creatively working with the repressed archaic contents of the collective unconscious psyche of humanity. This is the basis of higher magic. The eleventh-century reformers in Tibet accused the Nyingmapas of fornicating in the temple, but these Yogins were not doing something that could better be accomplished with greater comfort in a brothel.[22] Anuttara Tantra is a highly sophisticated yoga practice involving two partners, male and female. These methods, known as *thabs-lam*, are part of *rdzogs-rim*, the perfection process. In Anuttara Tantra, sex is a sacred matter. Sex is one of the most potent sources of energy known to humanity, and Tantra deals with energy and its transformation. But the puritanical reformers in Tibet were shocked and appalled by these Tantras.

By the end of the tenth century, the teachings and practices of Mahayoga Tantra had become widespread, which incited a general criticism of tantric practice by the royal monk Lhalama Yeshe-od (La bla-ma Ye-shes-'od) in the Western Tibetan kingdom of Guge. After the collapse of the Tibetan monarchy in Central Tibet, certain members of the royal family of the Yarlung Dynasty emigrated to Western Tibet, and in less than a century they had established an independent Tibetan kingdom in this region, including the famous sites of Tholing and Tsaparang. Eventually Yeshe-od abdicated as king and became a monk himself in pursuit of his efforts to reestablish the Buddhist monastic system in his country. This king did not regard the tantric practices of Mahayoga as being genuine Buddhism, especially the *sbyor sgrol* rites associated with the *Guhyagarbha Tantra*. *sByor*, union, refers to tantric sexual practices with a consort partner, and *sgrol*, deliverance, refers to the killing of evil-doers by means of magical rites without incurring any negative karma for the practitioner. *sByor sgrol* is the subject matter of chapter 11 of the *Guhyagarbha Tantra* (*gSang-ba snying-po*), the principal Mahayoga scripture. Such practices belonged to the Tantra system and had no connection with Dzogchen. Nevertheless, the edict promulgated by this king condemned Dzogchen, saying, "That which is called by the name Dzogchen spread in Tibet as a wrong teaching (*rdzogs-chen ming btags chos log bod du dar*)." This edict, however, criticized Dzogchen not as a heretical doctrine (that was to come later), but only as an illicit practice.

When in the eleventh century the Anuttara Tantra became the most popular religious practice in Tibet, as it was already in contemporary India, Anuttara Tantra was taken into the newly reestablished monasteries. Its prestige was too high in India and Nepal to do otherwise, and too high to continue to insist that it was not genuine Buddhism. But in order for the Anuttara Tantra to be accepted, its style of practice had to be altered to make it suitable for monks so that they might still keep their vows intact. Thus, Anuttara Tantra came to be practiced in the style of the lower Yoga Tantra. Yoginis, or female practitioners, were not allowed to attend the rites of the Ganachakrapuja held in the monasteries; their presence was only visualized by the monks. Meat and wine were consumed, but only in very small amounts, and their nature was considered to have been transubstantiated during the course of the ritual, so that the monk was not partaking of ordinary meat and wine, but of amrita. Moreover, there was a growing tendency, especially among the Sakyapas and the Gelugpas, to explicate and comment upon the Tantras in accordance with the definitions and categories of thought proper to the Sutra system. This process ultimately made the Anuttara Tantras respectable. All of the racy and bloody imagery remained, but it came to be interpreted symbolically and figuratively. What were originally nocturnal orgiastic rites under the moon in riverside cremation grounds became a sedate high church congregational practice for celibate monks. And this has largely been the case until the present day.

However, as mentioned before, in the eleventh century, the prince-monk Phodrang Zhiwa-od (Pho-brang Zhi-ba-'od), who was the grand-nephew of the above Yeshe-od, issued his own edict in which he categorically condemned Dzogchen as contaminated (*sres*) with false doctrines. He was supported in this condemnation by his brother, the king of Guge, Jyangchub-od (Byang-chub 'od), who was also striving to reestablish the Buddhist monastic system in West Tibet. According to the Nyingmapa apologist Sog-dog-pa (Sog-zlog-pa blo-gros rgyal-mtshan, 1552–1624), Prince Zhiwa-od believed that Dzogchen resembled the Vedanta doctrine of the Hindus, calling it *Mu-stegs rtag lta-ba*, "The Eternalist View of the Tirthikas." Thus, at least by the eleventh century, Dzogchen came to be criticized in terms of the genuineness of its source texts and in terms of the validity of its doctrine as orthodox Buddhist teaching. This official polemic against Mahayoga Tantra and against Dzogchen culminated in the inviting of the illustrious Indian master and scholar Dipankara-shrijnana Atisha to Guge in 1042. It was hoped that he would combat these Nyingmapa practices and reestablish a purified form of the Dharma.[23] His chief Tibetan disciple, Dromton ('Brom-ston, 1005–1064), established the Kadampa (bKa'-gdams-pa) school and its first monastery at Reting (Rwa-sgreng, 1056). The Kadampas were the first distinct sect of Tibetan Buddhism to come into existence. So opposed was Dromton to Nyingmapa practices that he did not permit his master to teach the Anuttara Tantras in Tibet, claiming that the Tibetans were as yet too immature and that they might pervert and abuse these teachings. The Kadampa tradition established by this puritanical reformer was later absorbed into the Gelugpa sect, and so the Kadampas no longer exist as an independent entity. With the triumph of this Buddhist revival in the eleventh century, both the Nyingmapas and the Bonpos came to be regarded as unorthodox by the Newer Schools.

In the twelfth century, the Sakyapa master Jetsun Dragpa Gyaltsan (rJe-btsun grags-pa rgyal-mtshan, 1147–1216) compiled a Kangyur written in gold ink. Another Kangyur was commissioned by Chögyal Phagpa (Chos-rgyal 'phags-pa, 1235–1280), the hierarch of the Sakyapa sect who was recognized by the Mongol emperor Kublai Khan as the ruler of Tibet. Then in the late thirteenth century, Chomdan Rig-ral (bCom-ldan rig-ral), Upa Losal Jyangchub Yeshe (dBus-pa blo-gsal byang-chub ye-shes), Lotsawa Sonam Odzer (Lo-tsa-ba bSod-nams 'od-zer), and Gyang-ro Jyangchub-bum (rGyang-ro byang-chub 'bum) collected many translated texts from various regions of Tibet. Having edited and revised them, they compiled a catalogue for both the *Kangyur* (bKa'-'gyur), the scriptures containing the actual words of the Buddha in Sutras and Tantras, and for the *Tangyur* (bsTan-'gyur), the philosophical treatises written by various Indian masters of the Buddhist tradition. Chim Jampalyang ('Chims 'jam-dpal-dbyangs), a disciple of Rig-ral and a personal chaplain to the Mongol princes, made a complete copy of the Kangyur and Tangyur of Rig-ral, which was written out at Narthang Monastery in 1334. (This was not the eighteenth-century sNar-thang block print edition.) This work was supervised by the famous scholar and polymath Buton in a newly rearranged order.

At this time, Buton Rinpoche (Bu-ston rin-chen grub, 1290–1364), who became the editor of the Tibetan Buddhist canon of the Kangyur and the Tangyur in its final form, excluded most of the Old Tantras from the Kangyur as not being the authentic word of the Buddha. In his history of Buddhism in India and Tibet, the *Chos-'byung chen-mo*, he says, "As for the Old Tantras coming from the period of the Early Translations: the great translator Rin-chen bzang-po, as well as Lha bla-ma Ye-shes 'od, Pho-brang Zhi-ba 'od, 'Gos khug-pa lhas-btsas, and others said that these Tantras are not authentic. Yet according to the statements of my own two masters, sMra-ba Nyi-ma'i mtshan-can and Rig-ral, the Sanskrit originals do exist at bSam-yas Monastery, whereas the original of the *Vajrakilaya Tantra* was discovered in Nepal.[24] Therefore, these texts are probably authentic Tantras. However, being not only apparently ignorant, but also actually so, I have come to have doubts about them as Dharma. And for this reason, I prefer to remain neutral and cause no harm (and so I have excluded them from the canon)."[25] However, even Buton felt compelled to place the *Kun-byed rgyal-po* in the Kangyur as a canonical text. It is found in both the Derge edition and the Peking edition.

With regard to the Old Tantras, Nyingmapa scholars felt the need to make their own collection of the texts rejected by Buton. Drogon Namkhapal ('Gro-mgon nam-mkha' dpal, 1170–1236), the son of the famous Nyingmapa master, and discoverer of Terma texts Nyang-ral Nyima Odzer (mNga'-bdag Myang-ral nyi-ma 'od-zer, 1124–1192), made a collection of old Tantras, *rGyud 'bum*, which he had written out in gold ink. From this, his disciples compiled a *rNying-ma'i rgyud 'bum* in thirty volumes. Independently of these efforts, Zur-ug-pa made a rather unsystematic collection. Ratna Lingpa (Ratna gling-pa, 1403–1478) continued the task of locating and collecting the rejected old Tantras. Later, a much-enlarged *rNying-ma'i rgyud 'bum* was compiled by Minling Terchen (sMin-gling gter-chen, 'Gyur-med rdo-rje, 1646–1714) in a new edition (1686). An edition was also compiled by Chug Chopal Zangpo (gCug Chos-dpal bzang-po, 1654–1717). In the next century, the illustrious Kunkhyen Jigmed Lingpa (Kun-mkhyen 'Jigs-med gling-pa, mKhyen-brtse'i 'od-zer, 1729–1798) made the above Minling edition the basis of his own work, compiling a new edition with twenty-five additional volumes. And for this edition he wrote a *dkar-chag*, or table of contents. Based on his work, the Derge (sDe-dge) xylograph edition was printed. In Bhutan, in the sixteenth century, Kah-thog-pa Sonam Gyaltsan (Kah-thog-pa bSod-nams rgyal-mtshan) also made a collection, and in the seventeenth century Tsamdrag (mTshams-brag) Monastery compiled an edition in forty-six volumes.[26] Nyingmapa tradition regards all of these Old Translation Tantras, including the *Kun-byed rgyal-po*, as being Buddha-vachana, or the authentic word of the Buddha, and as thoroughly orthodox in doctrine.

THE PRIMORDIAL STATE OF THE GREAT PERFECTION

But it was not just a matter of supposedly spurious texts. Many Tibetan scholars of the Newer Schools from the eleventh century until the present day did not regard Dzogchen as an authentic teaching of the Buddha. They asserted that it was derived from or was contaminated by Chan, Hindu, or Bonpo elements. As we have seen, Sakya Pandita called Dzogchen a Chinese system (*rgya nag lugs kyi rdzogs-chen*), together with the Mahamudra of Gampopa. Drigung Paldzin accused Nubchen of contaminating the contents of the *Man-ngag lta-ba'i phreng-ba* with the teachings of the Hwashang. But what is this doctrine so frequently attacked and condemned? It is the teaching that there is a Primordial State which lies beyond cause and effect, what Garab Dorje taught in his Upadesha at the very beginning.

This Primordial State is given many names in the early Dzogchen literature:

> *byang-chub kyi sems*—the Enlightened Mind or Bodhichitta
> *sems-nyid*—the nature of mind
> *rdzogs-pa chen-po*—the Great Perfection
> *gzhi*—the Base
> *ye gzhi*—the Primordial Base
> *gdod-ma'i gzhi*—the Primordial Base
> *spyi gzhi*—the Universal Base
> *kun-gzhi*—the basis of everything
> *gzhi ji-bzhin-pa*—the Base just as it is
> *kun tu bzang-po*—the Ultimate Good (Samantabhadra)
> *kun-byed rgyal-po*—the King who creates everything
> *spyi mes chen-po*—the great universal Ancestor
> *ye phyi-mo*—the Primordial Grandmother
> *bdag-nyid chen-po*—the Total State
> *rang shes rig gi rgyal-po*—the King who is self-knowing
>   Awareness

This Primordial State is at the core of every single sentient being throughout the universe as awareness itself. But at the same time, it is transcendent because it has never been caught up in the delusions of Samsara. The mirror is not the reflections. Never having been modified or adulterated (*bcos med bslad med*) by Samsara or cyclical existence, it is characterized as being primordially pure (*ka-dag*). This aspect is the Dharmakaya, the dimension of all existence, and yet without contradiction, it is individualized as sentient beings found in the six destinies of rebirth. For example, there exists one universal space containing all individual things in our experience, yet this same space may be contained without modifying or adulterating its nature within a series of empty clay pots. Break any of these pots and what remains? The clay pot is a metaphor for the skandhas of the individual. The state of innate Buddhahood is thus simultaneously immanent and transcendent, relative and absolute, individual and universal. When one speaks in terms of the Base, there exists only this one nondual Base. It is the same Dharmakaya that is found in ignorant, deluded sentient beings and in Buddhas, or enlightened beings. But there exist two Paths, the path of delusion (*'khrul lam*) and the path of liberation (*grol lam*), and, correspondingly, there exist two Fruits, ordinary sentient beings, who are deluded and ignorant, and Buddhas, or enlightened beings.

Is this Dzogchen doctrine of the Base (*gzhi*) radically different than the shunyata of the Madhyamaka, the so-called orthodoxy of Tibetan Buddhism? Is Dzogchen the one Buddhist doctrine that steps out of the mainstream of Buddhist teaching—its central doctrine of the Primordial State postulating the existence of a positive entity? This would make Dzogchen and Madhyamaka diametrically opposed, for if Dzogchen asserts the real existence of some positive entity, then the Madhyamaka dialectic would negate the arguments invoked for the existence of any such entity.

The thrust of Indian Buddhist philosophy, both Madhyamaka and Chittamatra, is epistemological, concerned with the problem of valid knowledge, whereas Tibetan thought is more ontological, concerned with the problem of being.[27] Therefore, in Tibetan thought, and particularly in Dzogchen thought, a rather different philosophical vocabulary developed than that found in the translations of the Buddhist Shastras of Indian origin. In the Sutra system, shunyata is treated as an object of knowledge (*yul*). And here there is a specific method involved. By means of an exhaustive philosophical analysis, an empirical object is resolved into its ultimate constituents, which are defined as clusters of momentary events or "dharmas" occurring in empty space. The process of ordinary perception is dependent upon the anatomy and physiology of the sense organs and the nervous system, as well as the processing of sensory information correlated with memory by the Manas (*yid*) or the bio-computer in the brain. Out of this raw sense data, a recognizable object is constructed by the Manas, like a color picture on a television screen or like a hologram. However, these bits of data, these dharmas or momentary events, are contingent and lack any inherent nature, and so, by way of a process of exhaustive analysis, the higher critical intellect (Skt. *prajñā*) discovers that they are empty. They lack any abiding self; they lack any substance whatsoever. They are as ephemeral as electrical impulses, and they are not the same as consciousness (Skt. *citta*). Rather, they represent the contents of consciousness (Skt. *caitta*). Yet these dharmas are all the mind knows of the external world. Indeed, out of these ephemeral dharmas or momentary event phenomena, the mind creates the perceived world. And through the discipline of repeated exhaustive analysis, the process known as Prajna, the practitioner discovers that all things, external and internal, are empty and lacking any substantial reality. All that remains after the completion of this exhaustive analysis is shunyata. Thus, this shunyata is an object of intellectual knowledge.[28] But this is not how Dzogchen speaks of shunyata.

Some scholars assert that Dzogchen appears to speak of the Base (*gzhi*) as a subject or an existence which cognizes something (*yul-can*). Therefore they say that Dzogchen is like the *gzhan-stong* theory entertained by the Jonangpa school of Tibet. A lively controversy has continued for several centuries between the proponents of this *gzhan-stong* theory and the orthodox proponents of the *rang-stong* position.[29] This Jonangpa school was suppressed and abolished by the Fifth Dalai Lama (Ngag-dbang blo-bzang rgya-mtsho, 1617–1682), not for doctrinal reasons but because, like the Karma Kagyudpas, the Jonangpas supported the kings of Tsang, who were the political enemies of the Gelugpas.[30] Generally, throughout the history of Tibet, religious persecutions had more connection with political struggles than they did with any attempt to suppress heresy. If it was merely a matter of orthodoxy struggling against heresy, the Nyingmapas and the Bonpos, who were far more radical in their doctrines than were the Jonangpas, would have been suppressed.

Moreover, the Fifth Dalai Lama had strong Nyingmapa sympathies and was himself a practitioner of Dzogchen and a discoverer of Termas.

The Nyingmapa presentation of Dzogchen is not an eternalist view (*rtag lta-ba*), as some scholars assert. Rather, according to their own account, Dzogchen represents a middle way between the extremes of eternalism (*rtag*) and nihilism (*chad*). One should not be led astray by the ontological rather than epistemological language employed in Dzogchen texts. According to Dzogchen, those who rigidly follow the Prasangika Madhyamika of Chandrakirti perpetually find themselves in danger of falling into the extreme of nihilism and asserting that nothing exists. They overly stress the negative side of shunyata. But the balance is redressed in Tantra and in Dzogchen, where shunyata has its positive side, which is luminous clarity (*gsal-ba*). This should not be perceived as an abandoning of the middle way by the Tantra system, and it must be remembered that there exists more than one interpretation of Madhyamaka.

In the early period of Tibet, the syncretistic Madhyamaka system of Shantirakshita was the prevalent form of Madhyamaka philosophy. This system of Shantirakshita was able to use the vocabulary of the Chittamatra philosophy, but this did not mean that it uncritically adopted the philosophical standpoint of Chittamatra, "mind only." The Tantra system likewise did this. But whereas the Sutra system, by means of philosophical analysis, culminates in the realization of a universal shunyata as its conclusion, the Tantra system begins with the state of shunyata as a given, in terms of the three samadhis or contemplations,[31] and it is out of this state of emptiness (*stong-nyid ngang nas*) that the transformation arises. This state of emptiness, the Tathata-samadhi, "the contemplation of reality," is the primal phase with which any sadhana or process of transformation begins. But this state is not just empty; it is simultaneously clear luminosity (*gsal-ba*), and this aspect is the second samadhi, the Samantabhasa-samadhi, "the contemplation of what manifests everywhere." It is light or luminosity, whereas the first samadhi refers to the depths of open empty space. The inseparable unity of these two bring into being the third samadhi, the Hetu-samadhi, or "causal contemplation," the seed or germ out of which manifest forms are generated or created (*bskyed-pa*), like a tree growing from a seed. Commencing the sadhana practice in this purified primordial state of emptiness, which is like the clear open sky, the method of the Tantra proceeds to invoke and develop the energy that is concealed, enfolded, and inherent in the state of emptiness—that is to say, visible forms are regenerated or remanifested out of the pristine state of shunyata, just as they were at the time of the beginning, symbolically the time of the first creation.[32] Shunyata, the state of emptiness itself, is the source of this primordial energy that brings all possible forms, even the universe itself, into manifestation. The vast and infinite empty space of the state of shunyata is pregnant with all possibilities; it has within itself the potentiality or creative energy for manifesting all possible manifestations, whether pure vision or impure vision, whether Nirvana or Samsara. In this way, during the course of sadhana practice, one's obscurations of knowledge and one's impure karmic vision are progressively purified.

Thus, the Base, the Primordial State, is not just emptiness in the negative sense of void or nothingness, a mere absence of something. Rather, the state of shunyata, this vast empty space where emptiness and luminosity are inseparable (*gsal stong dbyer-med*), represents the state of pure potentiality. It is the space or dimension or matrix of all existence out of which all possible forms or manifestations (*snang-ba*) arise, like clouds appearing spontaneously in the empty open sky. It is not just that forms lack an inherent nature (*rang-bzhin med-pa*) or substance, but equally inherent in shunyata is the potentiality for the arising of forms; this is the meaning of luminosity (*gsal-ba*). Thus Dzogchen speaks of *stong-cha* and *gsal-cha*, "the side of emptiness" and "the side of clarity," which are the two aspects or sides of the Primordial Base. These two aspects are also known as *ka-dag*, "primordial purity," and *lhun-grub*, "spontaneous self-perfection." This fact transcends conventional logic, because it is not a matter of the Base being either A or not-A, of being either emptiness or manifestation. If shunyata were a mere nothing, then nothing would arise at all. But this pure nonexistence or nothingness contradicts our experience. Thoughts and appearances are arising all the time, arising continuously, and this is only natural. But equally, if forms were not empty, then there would exist no possibility for change because all things would be locked up in a static unchanging state of their own self-identical essence or inherent nature (*rang-bzhin*, Skt. *svabhāva*).

But that is not our experience. We experience that things continuously change. They are in a state of becoming.

When Dzogchen speaks of the Base, it speaks of its qualities (*gzhi'i yon-tan*) in terms of Essence, Nature, and Energy. Its Essence (*ngo-bo*) is shunyata (*stong-pa nyid*), and its Nature (*rang-bzhin*) is luminous clarity (*gsal-ba*), whereas their unity or inseparability is Energy (*thugs-rje*).[33] Both of the Tibetan terms *ngo-bo* and *rang-bzhin* translate the single Sanskrit word *svabhāva*. Perhaps this is indicative that this particular line of philosophical thought developed in Tibet rather than India. But making these statements about the Base is not the same thing as asserting that it is a substance or an entity. The Base is empty. Dzogchen does not lapse or deviate from the central Buddhist teaching of Anatman into some kind of Shashvatavada, or eternalist view.

Dzogchen begins with shunyata because shunyata is the Base as its Essence (*ngo-bo*), but an entity called shunyata will not be found anywhere. If one looks into the mind to see where a thought arises, where it abides, and where it goes, one will not find any place from where it arises (*byung sa med*), nor any place where it abides (*gnas sa med*), nor any place where it goes to (*'gro sa med*). Where is this shunyata then? Thoughts arise and dissolve, but they do not arise from anywhere and do not go anywhere. This is their aspect of emptiness (*stong-cha*). Yet thoughts continue to arise incessantly; this is their aspect of inexhaustible luminosity (*gsal-cha*). And these two aspects are inseparable in the Base (*gsal stong dbyer-med*). This empty aspect of mind is its primordial purity (*ka-dag*), but this purity is not some substance or entity, not some mind-stuff out of which thoughts are made, like ocean waves made up of the water contained in the ocean. It is only the quality of the nature of mind, and this nature of mind remains primordially uncontaminated, unchanged, and unadulterated by whatever thoughts arise in the mind. Since this nature of mind, or *sems-nyid*, transcends the thought process (that is to say, Samsara) from the very beginning, being itself outside the temporal process and the causal sequence, it is said to be primordially pure (*ka-dag*). But simultaneously it is mind, or *sems*. Mind has the power or capacity to bring all thoughts and phenomena into manifestation in consciousness through its latent energy. Forms continuously arise as manifestations of mind (*sems kyi snang-ba*), and this is called spontaneous self-perfection (*lhun-grub*). Here there is no contradiction with the doctrine of Anatman (*bdag-med*).

Does this teaching of a Primordial State beyond cause and effect contradict the kerygma, the original core message of the Buddha? It is said in an ancient verse that "All conditioned things are impermanent, are without a self, and are suffering—this is the teaching of the Buddha." But the Primordial State is not a thing or a substance. It is unconditioned (Skt. *asaṃskṛta-dharma*), but ultimately it cannot be defined by the intellect or expressed in words. It is the Noble Silence that the Buddha maintained after he first attained enlightenment. And yet, because of his unstinting universal compassion for all sentient beings, he spoke of that which cannot be expressed in words. It is like trying to explain the taste of sugar to a man who has never tasted anything sweet. But all speech and language, as useful and as necessary as they may be, represent limitation. Language cannot perfectly mirror reality; direct immediate experience transcends expression in words and arrangement in syllogisms. Just as the way to the mirror is through the reflections, so the Buddha spoke of conditioned things (Skt. *saṃskṛta-dharma*); but he also spoke of the unconditioned (Skt. *asaṃskṛta-dharma*), usually by way of negative statements, employing a kind of *via negativa*. Hence he spoke of Anatman and shunyata.

The core message of the Buddha is often expressed as a *via negativa*, but was this always so? The Pali canon of the Theravadin school was edited in its final form circa 500 CE in Sri Lanka by scholars belonging to the Mahaviharika subsect of that school. The Mahaviharikas go to extremes in their interpretation of the Anatman doctrine. They assert that only momentary atomic events (psychic and physical) called dharmas occurring in the stream of consciousness of a sentient being are real. There exists no Pudgala or person present there as an integrating structure for the mental events continuously manifesting in that stream of consciousness, despite our ordinary everyday experience to the contrary. This so-called person or ego is only an idea-complex comprised of a large number of impersonal momentary mental events. It is not real; it is not a thing or a substance. Thus they assert Pudgala-nairatma or Pudgala-shunya, the absence of a self in individual sentient beings, and in this way they faithfully carry on the Abhidharmika tradition inherited from Shariputra. This master was a leading disciple of the Buddha and was famous for his discriminating wisdom or powers of philosophical analysis (prajna).

But among the Mahasanghikas, there were preserved other traditions of the Buddha's teachings. About one hundred and forty years after the Parinirvana of the Buddha, probably at the Council of Pataliputra, the Sthaviras or Elders—the ancestors of the Theravadins and related sects—separated from the Mahasanghikas, those of the greater assembly, who may have been in the majority at that council. These Mahasanghikas, whose traditions go back to the time of the Buddha as well, represent a kind of proto-Mahayana or matrix which gave birth to the Mahayana. Many of the principal ideas of the Mahayana circulated among the Mahasanghikas centuries before the emergence of the Mahayana as a distinct movement. For example, the Mahasanghikas preserved a tradition coming from the master Subhuti, who, like Shariputra, was a senior disciple of the Buddha. According to later Mahayana tradition, Subhuti had a more profound understanding of the real meaning of the teaching of the Buddha than did Shariputra, whose views gave rise to the Abhidharmika philosophy of the later Hinayana schools. This tradition of Subhuti is found in the *Prajnaparamita Sutras*. It was originally set down in Prakrit and later translated into Sanskrit and much elaborated in larger Sutras.[34] The view we find here is Dharma-nairatma or Dharma-shunya, the insubstantiality or emptiness of all things. These momentary events called dharmas are also not real. This Second Turning of the Wheel of the Dharma, the promulgation of the *Prajnaparamita Sutras*, which expound the doctrine of Shunyavada, is regarded as the ultimate teaching of the Buddha by the Tibetan Lamas. But this teaching can be carried to extremes by way of destructive dialectics and, so, unfortunately can lead to nihilism. This trend was counterbalanced by the Third Turning of the Wheel of the Dharma in such Sutras as the *Sandhinirmochana Sutra* and the *Lankavatara Sutra*, and also by the Yogachara school's emphasis on the importance of meditation practice, as against an overemphasis on philosophical analysis. In these Sutras we find reference to the doctrine of the luminous quality of mind. Although the Second Turning in a sense is the ultimate teaching of the Buddha, the Third Turning was not just a sop thrown to those disciples who feared shunyata or who possessed a lesser intellectual capacity. Rather it served as a corrective to a wrong or purely negative understanding of the doctrine of shunyata. Chan, for example, when it first came to China was very much linked to the *Lankavatara Sutra,* which belongs to this Third Turning.[35] Yet no one can accuse Chan of harboring a substantialist view or wrongly understanding shunyata. Like Tantra and Dzogchen, Chan approaches shunyata in terms of direct immediate experience rather than by way of philosophical analysis, as is the case with the Madhyamika school.[36]

Again, this doctrine of the luminous quality of mind is not something extraneous to the kerygma of the Buddha or a later Hinduizing development. As has been pointed out by Edward Conze,

> The Canon of the Sthaviras [i.e., the Pali canon of the Theravada school] contains occasionally ideas which conflict with their own orthodoxy. Some Polish scholars [Stanislaus Schayer, etc.] have argued that they belong to a very old, "pre-Canonical" tradition, which was too venerable to be discarded by the compilers of the Canon. How otherwise could one account for the numerous references to a "person" [Skt. *pudgala*]? Then there is the special role assigned to "consciousness." The *Saddhatusutra* assumes an eternal consciousness [or awareness], and the Absolute, or Nirvana, is identified with an "invisible infinite consciousness, which shines everywhere." Side by side with the oft-repeated negation of an *ātman,* there are traces of a belief in consciousness [awareness] as the nonimpermanent center of the personality which constitutes an absolute element in this contingent world. The idea of an absolute thought which is perfectly pure and translucent (prabhasvara-chitta) in its own nature, its own being, its own substance, and which remains so forever, does not fit in very well with the dharma-theory of the Sthaviras. They accordingly did not quite know what to do with it, whereas the Mahasanghikas and the Mahayana gave it a central place in their scheme of things. Though Nirvana is generally kept transcendentally remote and defined only by negations, there are distinct vestiges of a more positive concept, and of an unorthodox ontology, which regards Nirvana as a place (pada) or an entity (and not merely a state), identical with the eternal and absolute reality (dharma) and with the translucent thought or consciousness. Deliverance is then conceived as the gradual purification of this consciousness which finally attains the summit of the "Realm of Dharma" (Dharmadhatu), from which it will no longer fall back (acyuta). . . . For the theme of this book it does not matter whether these "aberrant"

doctrines represented a "pre-Canonical" stratum of Buddhism, or whether they were concessions to popular demand, just as the lower goal of rebirth in heaven (svarga) came to be admitted side by side with Nirvana. Whatever the date of their introduction, there were these "aberrant" doctrines, the Sthaviras mentioned them in passing; the Mahasanghikas both emphasized and probably developed them. [Brackets are mine.][37]

But these so-called aberrant or unorthodox views (and orthodoxy came into existence much later with the rise of the Adhidharmika schools) may have actually formed part of the kerygma, or original core teachings of the Buddha, and suspect teachings, like Dzogchen and Mahamudra, only continue this ancient tradition.

Dzogchen is an Upadesha of the masters concerning the state that lies beyond Tantra, the process of transformation. I submit that there exists here no contradiction to or deviation from the original teaching of the Buddha. It is true that the methods of meditation, Shamatha and Vipashyana, expounded in the Sutras found in the Pali canon do not much deal with visualization and transformation, but these elements are not totally absent either, as, for example, with the meditation practices of the Kasinas and Buddha-anussati.[38] Moreover, in the oldest Sutra texts there is a consistent emphasis on the key importance of smriti (Pali *sati*), mindfulness or self-remembering. It is even said that mindfulness is absolutely essential.[39] This is in perfect harmony with the essential point of Dzogchen. At times in Dzogchen texts, *dran-pa* (Skt. *smṛti*, "mindfulness") is used as a synonym for *rig-pa*. The essence of mindfulness is awareness (*rig-pa*), and the opposite is a lack of awareness (*ma rig-pa*). Thus we discover that, despite many historical and cultural differences, a fundamental unity of approach with regard to this basic Theravadin meditation exists in Chan and Dzogchen. Mere reference to texts cannot establish this, however, because fundamentally the question belongs to the realm of experience, and that can only be explored in dialogue among practitioners of these different Buddhist traditions.

Note on the Translation of Dzogchen Technical Terms

A few words must be said in general about the method of translation employed here and in particular about the translations of a number of technical terms used in Dzogchen texts. Anyone who has read through translations of Buddhist texts made from Sanskrit and other Asian languages will have immediately observed that Western scholars in the field of Buddhist studies do not agree in their translations of the key technical terms involved and often in their interpretations of Buddhist doctrines. This is especially the case with translations of Tibetan Buddhist texts.

In the cases of Sanskrit and Chinese, two of the principal classical Buddhist languages of Asia, these languages and their respective literatures have been studied for over two hundred years by Western scholars and some excellent dictionaries have been compiled. However, this is not the case with Tibetan, and until recently Tibetan was not treated as a field of study in its own right as a language and as a literature, but only as auxiliary to the study of Buddhist Sanskrit texts. This situation has now begun to change. Since 1959 many native Tibetan Lama-scholars have fled their occupied homeland as refugees, and subsequently, in India and Nepal, as well as in the West, they have come into direct personal contact with Western scholars and with students of Buddhism. Moreover, the conversion to Buddhism as a philosophy of life and the active participation in one or another form of Tibetan Buddhism by a large number of people in Europe and America, and now elsewhere, since the 1970s, has greatly stimulated the demand for translations of Tibetan Buddhist texts.

However, the Tibetan-English dictionaries in existence are sadly lacking in breadth and accuracy in terms of Buddhist terminology for their role in response to the above need. The Tibetan-English dictionary (London, 1881) compiled by H. A. Jaeschke, a Moravian Christian missionary, during his years of residence in Lahoul in the latter half of the nineteenth century, is adequate for some purposes, but totally misses the point in its translations of Dharma words, that is, the technical vocabulary of Tibetan Buddhism. Reverend Jaeschke saw his dictionary primarily as a tool for the translating of the Christian Bible into the Tibetan language, and his primary aim was to facilitate the conversion of Buddhist Tibetans to Protestant Christianity.[1] The much larger Tibetan-English dictionary edited by Sarat Chandra Das and published in 1902 by the West Bengal Government, and reprinted by other publishers subsequently, was an improvement over Jaeschke, although just about all of Jaeschke's dictionary was uncritically incorporated into this newer dictionary (with the exception of the material listed under the letter "g"). As it says in the Revisor's Preface to the dictionary, "The vast amount of original matter had been throughout greatly interlarded with lengthy extracts from Jaeschke's dictionary, not always separable from the new information, and this imparted a second-hand appearance to large portions of the work, which was, in reality, by no means deserved. Moreover, in this way, no attempt had been made to improve upon Jaeschke's definitions of many of the commoner Buddhist philosophical terms or to incorporate the later results of European scholarship in these instances."[2] Thus Jaeschke's theological misstatements about Buddhism are perpetuated without change. One only has to look up the listing for the Tibetan word *dkon-mchog* (pp. 53–54) to verify this. The revisors of this dictionary, Sandberg and Heyde, were also Christian missionaries.

Moreover, Sarat Chandra Das, a Bengali Hindu who became a scholar of Buddhism after he had served the British India Government as a spy and undercover agent inside Tibet, employed a trio of native informants, all Gelugpa Lamas attached to Ghoom Monastery in Darjeeling district, to do the bulk of the work of gathering material for him, and so fortunately these native speakers were able to draw on a much wider spectrum of Tibetan literature than was available to Jaeschke years before. Most translators of Tibetan texts into English rely on this Das dictionary as their guide for making a lexical translation of the text. Nevertheless, this dictionary is almost no help when it comes to translating Buddhist technical terms for reasons mentioned above. Furthermore, the Gelugpa Lamas who worked under Das used no Nyingmapa texts, save the *Bar-do thos-grol*; and so the meanings listed in the Das dictionary are no guide when it comes to the special usages of Buddhist terms in a Dzogchen text. Nor would these Gelugpa Lamas necessarily know these special usages, due to their own specialized education and to the endemic sectarianism existing among many Tibetans in those days. I have dealt with this problem in relation to the Dzogchen translations associated with the name of W. Y. Evans-Wentz in the Appendix of my *Self-Liberation through Seeing with Naked Awareness*.[3]

However, since the time of Das, a number of useful dictionaries have been published in China (Tibetan-Tibetan-Chinese). In the USSR George Roerich has published his own *Tibetan-Russian-English Dictionary with Sanskrit Parallels*,[4] and in Munich, Germany, a monumental Tibetan-German-English dictionary is being compiled in consultation with a number of native-born Lama-scholars. So gradually the situation with regard to Tibetan-English dictionaries is improving.

But since the situation in general with respect to translating Buddhist technical terms is still so nebulous, it is imperative that each translation from Tibetan include the Tibetan originals for the key technical terms involved, either in a glossary at the back of the book, or in the footnotes, or in parentheses after at least the first use of the term or, ideally, all three. It is gratifying to see that the new generation of Buddhist scholars in the West is consistently doing this with their Tibetan translations, and I follow the same procedure here with my translations. Speaking for myself at least, I can pick up a recent publication of a translation from Tibetan and not know what the text is talking about until I learn what are the Sanskrit and Tibetan originals of the key terms. I suspect that I am not alone in this problem.

Sanskrit is the recognized international language of Mahayana Buddhism, being generally the original language of the Sutras, the Tantras, and the Shastras, and so the Sanskrit term is something Buddhist scholars of diverse backgrounds—Indian, Chinese, Japanese,

290 The Golden Letters

Tibetan, and Western—can all agree upon. Moreover, Sanskrit is a language of particularly refined intellectual subtlety and one of great phonetic beauty. It is also said to be the language of the Devas, or gods. And so we may expect that more Sanskrit words will be adopted by English, at least the English used in Western Buddhist circles. Of course, English translations of Buddhist texts should avoid the extreme sometimes seen in India today, where in the translation of some Hindu text it seems that almost every other word is Sanskrit.

Although most of the borrowings of Buddhist terms into English come from Sanskrit, at times Tibetan words are also adopted, as for example, *Lama* (Skt. *guru*), *Bardo* (Skt. *antarābhava*), and *phurpa* (Skt. *kīlaya*). We also have the name for the tradition of teaching here, *Dzogchen* (Skt. *mahāsandhi*). The word *Bardo* has already entered into general currency due to the widespread popularity of the *Tibetan Book of the Dead*. Although there do exist Sanskrit equivalents for many of these words, but because they first became known and popularized in the Tibetan context and have specifically Tibetan associations, translators use the Tibetan term rather than the Sanskrit one. Furthermore, in the case of certain Dzogchen technical terms, there are no known Sanskrit forms available, such as, for example, *khregs-chod* and *ru-shan*, and so these are converted into English words, spelled according to their approximate English pronunciation, *Thekchod* and *Rushan*, respectively.

However, for most readers who are nonscholars and non-Tibetologists, the incorporation into the translated text of many Sanskrit and Tibetan words, in parentheses or otherwise, is found to be very distracting and rather a hindrance. For this reason I endeavor to keep the Tibetan terms appearing in the translation of the text at a minimum; however, I pepper Tibetan words and phrases in parentheses rather frequently throughout the notes and the commentaries to the translation. I also realize that readers who are nonscholars tend not to read the footnotes, and so rather than trying to explicate the entire text by means of a massive volume of notes found at the back of the book, I follow the text of the translation with a translator's commentary, where needed, which serves not only to explicate the text, but also to provide all of the relevant Tibetan terms. Moreover, I have found that it is better to put this sort of material in a commentary coming after the translation, rather than putting it all into an introduction, which would then grow into monumental proportions and prevent easy access to the translation in question by the reader. Also, including within the book the full original Tibetan text, whether in photocopy or in transliteration, is useful to those readers with a knowledge of Tibetan, but this is not always possible or practical.

In the early days of translation work in Tibet, from the eighth to the twelfth centuries, translations were generally made from Sanskrit into Tibetan by way of the collaboration of a Pandita, a Sanskrit scholar from India, and a Lotsawa, a native Tibetan translator. This collaboration ensured the accuracy of the translation in question, and afterwards other scholars, both Indian and Tibetan, would check the translation for accuracy. All of this may readily be discovered by inspecting the colophons to the translations found in the monumental Kangyur and Tangyur collections in the Tibetan Buddhist canon. As much as possible I have tried to follow this procedure, consulting with learned Tibetan Lamas regarding each translation I make. This is because my aim in making the translation of a Tibetan text is to present the meaning of the text as clearly and as accurately as possible to the modern Western reader as the Lamas themselves, the leading representatives of these spiritual traditions, understand the text. I believe that the oral traditions preserved by these Lamas are more true to the original meaning of the text than speculations by Western scholars about the supposed original meaning of the text.

This is not to deny the worth and validity of historical scholarship. Dzogchen as a system of thought and teaching has developed and evolved in time like every other human activity. The way in which Dzogchen is presented has not just survived unchanged from the eighth century, like a fossil exhibited in a museum showcase. It is a living philosophy, a way of life and a way of looking at the world, which has grown and developed in response to changing circumstances over time. The presentation of Dzogchen by Nubchen Sangye Yeshe (ninth century) is not the same as that found in Longchenpa (fourteenth century) or in Jigmed Lingpa (eighteenth century) or in Namkhai Norbu (twentieth century). Nevertheless, throughout time and history the fundamental principle of Dzogchen has remained the same, because, in essence, it is something outside of time. What I have received of this oral tradition of Dzogchen I have tried to embody in the commentaries appended to the translations I make.

I see the translations I have done in this book and elsewhere as being principally directed at those readers who have more than a passing casual interest in Dzogchen and Tibetan Buddhism. Specifically, they are aimed at practitioners, that is to say, individuals who find that Dzogchen, its teachings and its methods, has some use for them in present-day Western urban industrial civilization at the threshold of the twenty-first century. So my commentaries are not filled with the usual scholarly apparatus, nor with references to various modern-day Western books. That I save for the appendices. The explication of the meaning of the text is what is uppermost in my mind. For this I draw primarily on the Tibetan oral traditions as I have received them and secondarily on my own meditation experiences in the context of my training under a number of Tibetan Lamas in India and the West.

It is too early in the history of Buddhism in the West to expect realistically all translators to adopt a single consistent and standardized system for the translation of Buddhist technical terms. That is one reason why it is important to keep citing the Sanskrit and Tibetan originals for these Buddhist terms. The historical and cultural situation in the English-speaking world at the end of the twentieth century is not the same as that of Tibet in the eighth and ninth centuries, when the translations from Sanskrit were first made into Tibetan. When Buddhism came to Tibet, the people of Central Tibet had no written language, although possibly it may have been otherwise with the people of the Zhang-zhung kingdom of Western Tibet. Thus, when it came to translating these Sanskrit Buddhist texts in Central Tibet, a literary translation language was created almost *de novo*. This newly created literary language for the purpose of translating Sanskrit texts differed in many ways, of course, from the contemporary spoken dialects of the Yarlung Valley and of other regions in Tibet. In this new language, each element in a Sanskrit word or phrase, including prefixes and so on, had a corresponding Tibetan element. Thus, a Sanskrit word like *vikalpa*, meaning "a discursive thought," was translated into Tibetan as *rnam-par rtog-pa*, or more briefly as *rnam-rtog*, where *rnam-par* corresponds to *vi-* and *rtog-pa* to *kalpa*. Most Buddhist technical terms were translated into Tibetan in this way, rather than by adopting the Sanskrit word directly into the vocabulary of the Tibetan language, as was done in the case of the Newari language of Nepal, for example.

Over the course of several centuries, this process in Tibet resulted in one of the most extensive translation projects ever undertaken in human history. At a later time these translations of the Sutras and the Tantras, as well as the Indian commentaries and philosophical treatises belonging to these two systems of Sutra and Tantra, were collected and edited by Buton (1290–1364) and other scholars into two large collections, the Kangyur and the Tangyur. A number of early translations were omitted by Buton in his collections because the Sanskrit originals were no longer extant, and so some Tibetan scholars doubted their authenticity. These rejected texts were later collected together by Ratna Lingpa (1403–1479) and others in the *Nyingmai Gyud-bum* (*rNying-ma'i rgyud 'bum*).

About a hundred years after all this translation activity had begun, the king of Tibet convened a conference of Indian Sanskrit scholars and native Tibetan translators. The traditional Tibetan histories attribute this action to Ralpachan (reigned 815–836), but historical evidence makes it more likely that it was his father, Sanaleg (reigned 800–815). The work of the committee thereby set up resulted in the compiling of a Sanskrit-Tibetan dictionary known as the *Mahavyutpatti*. This dictionary established the official Tibetan translations for a large number of Buddhist Sanskrit terms belonging to the Sutra system. A second volume, the *Madhyavyutpatti*, elucidated the reasons why many of these Sanskrit terms were translated the way they were, and the book included a royal proclamation that henceforward these words were to be translated only in this way and no other. On the basis of this proclamation, a number of earlier translations were revised.

Nowadays, however, there exists no Dharma king to issue such proclamations. So it will only be after the translation of many more Tibetan texts and much further research into Buddhist texts and commentaries, and much scholarly discussion and debate, that a consensus may evolve with regard to the translation into English of these crucial terms. Our situation in the West is more analogous to that which existed in China than to what existed in Tibet. When Buddhism came to China, China already possessed nearly a thousand years of literary and philosophical tradition. When translations of Sanskrit texts were first made into Chinese, frequently the translator rendered the Buddhist Sanskrit terms with supposed Taoist equivalents, and this led to endless confusion because these were not really equivalents. Although Buddhism and Taoism may both be described as mystical paths, the view, the meditation, and the conduct of Buddhism and the view, the meditation, and the conduct of Taoism are quite different. At first the philosophical distinctions between Buddhism and Taoism and other types of Chinese mystical philosophy were not always clear to Chinese authors. In the early years of the Han Dynasty, Buddhism was often written about and interpreted as a species of Taoism, and Buddha Shakyamuni was even said to have been a disciple of the Taoist sage Lao Tzu, who, at the end of his earthly career, disappeared into the West riding on the back of a buffalo. It took several hundred years to sort out all of this terminological confusion. In fact, it was not until the time of Kumarajiva in the fifth century of our era. A Buddhist monk from the Central Asian city of Kucha, he was brought to the Chinese capital of Ch'ang-an in 402 CE, where he introduced the Madhyamaka philosophy into China and produced an enormous number of Chinese translations of Buddhist texts with the help of a large team of scholars.

Similarly, the West has some three thousand years of religious, philosophical, and literary tradition, going back to the ancient Greeks and Hebrews, who represent the two pillars of the Western spiritual tradition. In Europe and the Americas many centuries of intellectual and cultural domination imposed by the Christian Churches— Catholic, Protestant, and Orthodox—have informed our assumptions about the world. Thus, when translating a Buddhist text from an Asian language, it is necessary to be aware of the Western intellectual traditions and cultural assumptions underlying our everyday use of language, because otherwise we can be led into many misunderstandings.

This lack of knowledge of the Western intellectual heritage is what makes it difficult for Tibetan Lamas, who otherwise may be quite conversant with the English language and who are certainly learned in their own tradition, to translate many texts of a religious and philosophical nature on their own. What is needed here is collaboration between Tibetan Lamas and educated Western translators. Increasingly this is the procedure adopted by Western translators, and this is very laudable, especially in view of the fact of the inadequacy of the existing Tibetan-English dictionaries.

This is not the place to embark on a lengthy discussion of how particular Buddhist technical terms should be translated, a project that will require the collaboration of many Lamas, scholars, and translators, researching into the usages of specific terms in many different texts belonging to many different historical periods. This is more than any one individual can handle in view of the vast volume of extant Tibetan literature, for the greater part untranslated. Here I can only speak briefly of my own approach.

I began my formal linguistic and semantic studies of Buddhist texts when I read Buddhist Sanskrit with Professor Edward Conze at the University of Washington in Seattle and participated in his seminar on Buddhist technical terminology in the late sixties. For this seminar we used texts in Sanskrit, Pali, and Tibetan. Professor Conze also emphasized the importance of doing some Buddhist meditation practices in order to gain a bit of firsthand experience of what these texts were actually talking about. He had followed this course himself. With respect to his translations of the *Prajnaparamita Sutras*, Professor Conze indicated to me that he followed two principles: (1) accuracy of translation and (2) eloquence of language. I have adopted these two principles in my own translation work. I have not hesitated to revise my translation of a text or of a specific technical term when I have discovered in my reading elsewhere more accurate and more precise language.

This brings us to the question of certain specific Tibetan terms and their translations into English. I provide below a glossary of many of these terms, especially those peculiar to Dzogchen and which occur in the text of Patrul Rinpoche. A number of others are also included. In general, in my translations I have kept to the translations of Buddhist terms used by Professor Conze,[5] but he dealt almost exclusively with the Sutra system in general and with the *Prajnaparamita Sutras* in particular. An individual Sanskrit or Tibetan word may not have precisely the same meaning in the context of the Tantra system or in the context of the Upadesha of Dzogchen. For example, as I have pointed out, both *bodhicitta* (*byang-chub kyi sems*) and *vidyā* (*rig-pa*) have quite different meanings in the Dzogchen context than they do in the Sutras. Some of these Dzogchen terms require quite a bit of discussion, and so, in the commentaries to my translations appearing in this book and elsewhere, I speak a little more about the reasons why I translate them the way I do. In every case the translator must be aware of the context in which the term is used and also of the level of teaching to which it belongs. It is my hope as a translator that my discussions of the meanings of the various Dzogchen terms found in this book and elsewhere may prove useful to the interested reader.

Appendix:
Brief Biography of Patrul Rinpoche

Both the root text of the *mKhas-pa shri rgyal-pa'i khyad-chos* and its commentary were written by Patrul Rinpoche. An erudite scholar who had a vast and profound knowledge of the teachings of Dzogchen, he was one of the most important spiritual leaders of both the Nyingmapa school and of the Rimed Movement (*ris-med*, "non-sectarian")[1] in nineteenth-century Eastern Tibet (Khams). rDza dPal-sprul O-rgyan 'jigs-med chos kyi dbang-po (1808–1887) is better known among Tibetans as dPal-sprul Rin-po-che or A-bu Rin-po-che, or rDza dPal-dge. He often signed his writings with the nickname A-bu hral-po, "the old ragged one." As a child, Patrul Rinpoche was recognized to be the reincarnation or Tulku of Palge Tulku Sonam Chinpa (dPal-dge sprul-sku bSod-nams sbyin-pa). However, he was a difficult young Tulku, and because of his excesses in behavior the monks summarily expelled him from the monastery. As a result, his incarnation line came to an end. There exist many accounts of Patrul Rinpoche's renunciation of the high lifestyle of a Tulku and of his adoption of the career of a wandering ascetic.[2]

Patrul Rinpoche was sometimes regarded as a reincarnation of Shantideva, the famous Indian master of the eighth century who was the author of the *Bodhicharyavatara* (*sPyod 'jug*), "the entering into the career of the Bodhisattva," which is an essential Buddhist text relating to the practices pursued by the Bodhisattva according to the

Mahayana Sutra system. This text had received much attention from scholars belonging to the Nyingmapa school. Patrul Rinpoche specialized in the exposition of this text, as he wandered from place to place as an itinerant teacher and scholar in Eastern Tibet, elucidating the text upon request at different monasteries. He was famous for his unpretentious humble ways and for his all-embracing compassion. It is said that when he sat in meditation, he would not even swat at the flies that came to bite him.

In general, it can be said that the eighteenth century represented a golden age for the Nyingmapa school,[3] despite the persecution of the Nyingmapas by the Dzungar Mongols early in that century (1717–1720), when in Central Tibet the great Nyingmapa monasteries of Mindoling (sMin-grol gling) and Dorjedrak (rDo-rje brag) were looted and destroyed.[4] Gradually the devastated monasteries were rebuilt and a distinct religious tolerance developed, in contrast to the preceding period. The illustrious Jigmed Lingpa ('Jigs-med gling-pa, Rang-byung rdo-rje mkhyen-brtse'i 'od-zer, 1730–1798), the leading Dzogchen master of his time, dominated Nyingmapa thought in that century, as he continues to do today; he stands second only to Longchen Rabjampa in the development of Dzogchen as a philosophical system. Longchenpa himself appeared to Jigmed Lingpa some three times in pure visions and directly inspired him to set down in writing the teachings of the *kLong-chen snying-thig* cycle. This completed a cycle of teaching begun previously by Longchenpa himself in the fourteenth century. Jigmed Lingpa also had close ties with Kagyudpa traditions, and he was the source of inspiration for the Rimed Movement, which developed in the next century. This movement was centered in Derge (sDe-dge), the intellectual and artistic center of Kham, or Eastern Tibet. Both Jigmed Lingpa and his disciple Dodrubchen Rinpoche had close relations with the royal family of Derge, serving as spiritual advisors. In the nineteenth century the Rimed Movement was led by the Sakyapa master Jamyang Khyentse Wangpo ('Jam-dbyang mkhyen-brtse'i dbang-po, 1820–1892), the Kagyudpa master Jamgon Kongtrul ('Jam-mgon kong-sprul, 1813–1899), and the Nyingmapa master Chogyur Lingpa (mChog-gyur gling-pa, 1829–1870). In general, they and other Lamas belonging to this movement sought to reorient religious life toward a mutual understanding of all of the spiritual paths of teaching

and practice found within the Dharma, regardless of sectarian affiliations, and toward a return to the original texts or Shastras upon
which the Mahayana tradition is based, rather than exclusively relying on the biased and sectarian manuals (*yig-cha*) of one's own school.[5]

The two principal disciples of Jigmed Lingpa were Dodrupchen
(rDo-ba Grub-chen, 'Jigs-med phrin-las 'od-zer, 1745–1821) and
Jigmed Gyalwe Nyugu ('Jigs-med rgyal-ba'i myu-gu, eighteenth-
nineteenth century). The former was the first Dodrupchen Rinpoche
and established his seat at Dodrub Monastery (rDo-grub chos-sgar)
in Amdo. This new system of Jigmed Lingpa spread widely among
the Golog ('Go-log) tribes living in the Amnye Machen mountain
range between Amdo and Kham. Jigmed Gyalwe Nyugu founded
his own monastery at Trawa (Phra-ba) in Dzachukha (rDza-chu-kha),
the district lying along the Nyagchu River in northern Kham. Based
at his monastery of Trawa Gonpa (Phra-ba dgon, also known as rGyal-
dgon), he propagated the Dzogchen precepts of the *kLong-chen snying-
thig* among the nomads inhabiting the Dzachukha region.[6]

From his Root Guru, Jigmed Gyalwe Nyugu, Patrul Rinpoche received the oral explanation lineage for the *kLong-chen snying-thig*, the
most important cycle of teaching of the master Kunkhyen Jigmed
Lingpa, and he himself became recognized as one of the Tulkus or
reincarnations of Jigmed Lingpa. There were three reincarnations of
this master, embodying his different aspects:

1. his Mind Incarnation (*thugs kyi sprul-sku*) was Jamyang
   Khyentse Wangpo ('Jam-dbyangs mkhyen-brtse'i dbang-
   po, Kun-dga' bstan-pa'i rgyal-mtshan, 1820–1892);
2. his Speech Incarnation (*gsung gi sprul-sku*) was Dza Patrul
   Rinpoche (rDza dPal-sprul Rin-po-che, O-rgyan 'jigs-med
   chos kyi dbang-po, 1808–1887);
3. and his Body Incarnation (*sku yi sprul-sku*) was Do Khyentse
   (mDo mKhyen-brtse Ye-shes rdo-rje, 1800–?).

Thus Jigmed Lingpa was the source of the famous Khyentse line
of incarnations, which, after the passing of Jamyang Khyentse
Wangpo, proliferated into a number of Tulkus among the Nyingmapas, the Sakyapas, and the Kagyudpas.[7]

Patrul Rinpoche was also a prolific writer, and besides the above
text, he was famous for writing the *Kun-bzang bla-ma'i zhal-lung*, containing the oral instructions of his own Root Guru concerning the

preliminary practices (*sngon-'gro*) of the *kLong-chen snying-thig*. In this text he presented these profound teachings in a form comprehensible even to uneducated people, writing it in the Khampa nomad dialect and filling his text with references to popular sayings and folk tales. Among the Nyingmapas and Kagyudpas of Eastern Tibet nowadays, this work is generally regarded as a classic. Patrul Rinpoche also wrote two other texts for a lay audience, the *Drang-srong gdol-ba'i gtam* and the *gTam padma tshal gyi zlos-gar*. The latter is a poetical work on the topic of the impermanence of happiness, and was written to console a Derge nobleman whose wife had recently died.

Stories of Patrul Rinpoche's wit and compassion are widely told even today by the Khampas of eastern Tibet. One of these, the story of Patrul Rinpoche's encounter with two monk dialecticians, was retold by Gene Smith.[8] Once when Patrul Rinpoche was in a retreat, several scholar-monks opposed to his nonsectarian views came to the entrance of his cave with the intention of publicly refuting his views in a debate. They were accompanied by a large crowd of monks and curious village people. Patrul Rinpoche received these guests with his usual courtesy and humility. Then one of the scholar-monks asked him what his religious affiliation was, thinking that he would reply, "Nyingmapa." However, Patrul Rinpoche replied that he was merely a follower of the Buddha. Again trying to establish his Nyingmapa connections, the monk asked the name of his refuge Lama and of his Root Guru, expecting Patrul Rinpoche to reply that it was Gyalwe Nyugu. But Patrul Rinpoche replied that his Root Guru, with whom he had taken refuge, was the Triratna. These answers left his opponents no ground on which to debate him.

Then in frustration, the chief scholar-monk and debate master asked Patrul Rinpoche what secret name (*gsang mtshan*) was given him at the time of his initiation by his Root Guru, for this would surely indicate his Nyingmapa affiliation without any question. Patrul Rinpoche pulled up his robes and displayed his penis, indicating that this was his "secret name." In honorific Tibetan speech, the penis is called *gsang mtshan*, or "secret sign." The crowd of villagers howled with laughter. Abandoning their effort to engage him in debate, the arrogant scholar-monks left, suitably humiliated.

A RECENTLY PUBLISHED BIOGRAPHY

A brief biography of Patrul Rinpoche by Thubten Nyima was recently published in China.[9] A translation of this work follows.

rDza dPal-dge sprul-sku or rDzogs-chen dPal-sprul Rin-po-che was born in the earth-dragon year (1808) into the family rGyal-thog in the region of dGe-rtse rDza-chu-kha in the northern wilderness of Kham.[10] By rDo Grub-chen 'Jigs-med phrin-las 'od-zer (1745–1821), the disciple of 'Jigs-med gLing-pa, he was recognized as the reincarnation (*sprul-sku*) of dPal-dge bSam-gtan phun-tshogs, and this master bestowed upon the child the name of O-rgyan 'jigs-med chos kyi dbang-po. Even while he was still a young boy, he mastered letters, writing, and reading without difficulty. He received the novice monk ordination from mKhan-po Shes-rab bzang-po. Thereafter, on various occasions in the presence of rDo-bla 'Jigs-med bskal-bzang, of 'Jigs-med ngo-mtshar, and of rGyal-sras gZhan-phan mtha'-yas (b. 1740), he heard many scriptures belonging to the Sutra system and the Tantra system, such as the *Bodhicharyavatara* of Shantideva, the *Ngal-gso skor gsum* of Longchenpa, the *Guhyagarbha Mula-Tantra*, and so on, and in addition he studied the secular sciences (*rig-gnas*). From Zhe-chen dBon-sprul 'Gyur med mthu-stobs rnam-rgyal he received the scriptural authorization (*lung*) for the bKa'-'gyur, and also studied the science of grammar (*sgra rig*) with this master. On many occasions he listened to excellent expositions of the Dharma composed by eminent scholars belonging to both the old and the new traditions, such as the omniscient father and son of the Nyingmapas (i.e., Longchenpa and Jigmed Lingpa), Sakya Pandita, Je Tsongkhapa, and others. He reflected upon these teachings impartially without regard to sect, and since he strove always to understand them by way of concrete examples, he became especially learned in the practice of the Paramitas.

From his root master 'Jigs-med rgyal-ba'i myu-gu he listened without out exhaustion some twenty-five times to the oral explanations for the practice (*lam khrid*) of the *sngon-'gro* for the *kLong-chen snying-thig*, and he pursued as much as he was able the purification practices explained (*khrid sbyong*) therein. Elsewhere, on other occasions, he listened to the expositions of many Dharma cycles belonging to the early translation tradition (*snga-'gyur bka'-ma*) and to explanations (*khrid*) of Dzogchen and of *rtsa-rlung*.[11] From mDo mKhyen-brtse ye-shes rdo-rje, by way of the practice of ascetic conduct (*brtul zhugs spyod-pa*), he was introduced to the method of Rig-pa bcar phog. For a long time he continued to pursue the purification teachings (*khrid sbyong*) of the *rtsa-rlung* from the *kLong-chen snying-thig*. Then, from rDzogs-chen Rin-po-che Mi-'gyur nam-mkha'i rdo-rje and others, he received the nectar of the Dharma while staying for a long time at Dzogchen Monastery. Here also, while residing in various caves, he practiced meditation, and, since he persevered and remained steadfast in this practice, he realized an understanding equal to the sky.

Then from the age of thirty, he went to various regions, such as Serthar (gSer-thar), Yarlung, Pemakod (Padma bkod) and elsewhere, where he gave extensive oral explanations of the teachings. At Serthar and also to assemblies of people gathered in Upper and Lower Do (rDo), he bestowed innumerable gifts of the Dharma, such as the *Bodhicharyavatara*, the *Mani bka'-'bum*, the *bDe-ba-can smon-lam*, and so on. He put an end to the activities of thieves and robbers and suppressed the custom of blood sacrifice (*dmar ston*). Then he went to Dzam-thang, where he listened to the exposition of the *sByor drug* (of the Kalachakra system) from gTsang-pa Ngag-dbang chos 'byor. Thereafter he went to the country of Mi-nyag, where he had many discussions regarding the cycle of Paramita teachings with dGe-bshes Tshul-khrims rnam-rgyal. And since he practiced renunciation and asceticism at many different places, Patrul Rinpoche continued to benefit beings impartially without regard to sect. At the college of rDzogs-chen shri seng chos grwa[12] and at Padma'i thang and elsewhere, he turned the Wheel of the Dharma without interruption, expounding such texts as the *Byams chos*, the *Madhyamaka*, the *Abhidharmakosha*, the *Guhyagarbha Tantra*, the *Yon-tan mdzod* of Jigmed Lingpa, the *sDom gsum rnam nges* of mNa' ris Pan-chen Padma dbang-rgyal (1487–1542), and so on.[13] Furthermore, since he repeatedly gave oral explanations for the *Bodhicharyavatara* wherever he went, he became famed as the sunflower of this text in the vicinity of rDzogs-chen shri seng college.

On the occasion of discovering the Termas (*gter-kha*) of Chakra-shamvara and Buddha-samayoga, the Terton mChog-gyur bde-chen gling-pa (1829–1870) appointed him the custodian (*chos-bdag*) of those

Dharma cycles, including the Rigs-gsum snying-thig, etc., and bestowed upon him, as secret teachings, the complete initiations,
authorizations, and explanations (*dbang lung khrid*) for them. Then
he went to Kah-thog rdo-rje gdan Monastery,[14] where he gave extensive explanations and guidance (*bshad khrid*) with respect to the
Bodhicharyavatara to the entire assembly of monks in accordance with
the request of Si-tu mChog-sprul chos kyi blo-gros. Having come to
many great monasteries, such as Ri-bo dge-ldan, Ser-sbul dgon, Lab
khri 'du dgon, Chu hor dgon, and so on, he extensively explained
the *Bodhicharyavatara* to all the monks. In a clear voice he elucidated
the text orally and condensed the meaning into a few words. In addition, having expounded the essential points of the practice he found
that many Geshe Lharampas submitted to him with devotion and
scattered about the flowers of his praises.

He made his seat for the exposition of his cycle of teaching (*chos
skor*) among the monks at rDza rgyal dgon monastery. There he re-
paired the rDo 'bum chen-mo temple, which had been built in the
previous generation by dPal-dge bSam-gtan phun-tshogs, and for
this purpose he used the best-quality materials. Thus he also became
famous as dPal-sprul rdo 'bum.

During the course of his entire life, this master practiced the lis-
tening to, reflecting on, and meditating upon the teachings (*thos bsam
sgom gsum*) for his own benefit, and he explained, debated, and wrote
about the teachings (*'chad rtsod rtsom gsum*) for the benefit of others.
In upper, lower, and middle Kham, he explained extensively (and
widely disseminated) the *Bodhicharyavatara*, the *Byams-chos*, the *sDom
gsum*, the *Yon-tan mdzod*, and so on, and thus these teachings became
widely disseminated like stones spread out on the earth.

Furthermore, when the current of explanation (*bshad rgyun*) for
the *Guhyagarbha Tantra* and the current of teaching (*chos rgyun*) for
the *rtsa-rlung* and the *khrid* (oral explanations) for the *kLong-chen
snying-thig* were in danger of becoming like a butter lamp exhausting its fuel, afterwards they both became very widespread because
of the kindness of his labors. Many persons who were learned scholars and accomplished practitioners (*mkhas grub*) among the
Nyingmapas became the disciples of this master, and they adhered
to, protected, and increased our own system of the teachings of the
adamantine essence of the Clear Light (*'od gsal rdo-rje snying-po'i bstan-
pa'i ring lugs*), that is to say, Dzogchen. Chief among them were

Kah-thog Si-tu mchog-sprul Chos kyi blo-gros, Thub-bstan chos rdor, the fifth Dzogchen successor, rGya-rong rnam-sprul kun-bzang theg-mchog rdo-rje, 'Jigs-med phun-tshogs 'byung-gnas, the second Dodrubchen successor, 'Jigs-med bstan-pa'i nyi-ma, the third Dodrubchen successor (1865–1926), bDe-chen rig-pa'i ral-gri, who was the son of mDo mkhyen-brtse, mChog-sprul gZhan-phan chos kyi snang-ba (mKhan-po gZhan-dga', 1871–1927), A-'dzom 'Brug-sprul 'Gro-'dul rdo-rje (1842–1924), gTer-ston Las-rab gling-pa (b. 1856), 'Ju Mi-pham rnam-rgyal (1846–1912), mKhan-chen Padma rdo-rje Dam-chos 'od-zer, sMyo-shul Lung-rtogs, A-lags mDo-sngags rgya-mtsho, and others. dBon-po bstan-li, also known as O-rgyan bstan-'dzin nor-bu, was a grandnephew of the famous gZhan-phan mtha'-yas, and he also passed the tradition onto mKhan-po gZhan-dga' (gZhan-phan chos kyi snang-ba, 1871–1927). sMyo-shul lung-rtogs passed the teachings onto mKhan-po Ngag-dga' (Ngag-dbang dpal-bzang, 1879–1941), Abbot of Kah-thog Monastery and Root Guru of the renowned contemporary Dzogchen master Bya-bral Sangs-rgyas rdo-rje.[15]

Elsewhere, among the Sakyapas, the Gelugpas, and the Kagyudpas, there were many illustrious persons adhering to the teachings who became his disciples, such as Sher-shul Lha-rams-pa Thub-bstan, dPal-spungs bla-ma bKra-shis 'od-zer, 'Ju bla-ma Grags-pa rgyal-mtshan, and so on, all of whom had seized the victory banner of fame in scholarship. Finally, in the fire-pig year (1887) on the eighteenth day of the month of Saga, the manifestation of his form body (*gzugs sku'i bkod-pa*) displayed the method for being gathered up into the Dharmadhatu (and he died).

During his lifetime, this master produced in the presence of his disciples an abundance of oral and written explanations. These precious teachings were arranged in print, and nowadays these volumes, adorned with the six perfections, have become nectar for the eyes. Among this multitude of writings are found indices and commentaries to the *Byams-chos*, the *Bodhicharyavatara*, the *Yon-tan mdzod*, and so on, as well as a cycle of explanations on the Upadeshas for the essential points of the profound instructions (*gdam zab gnad kyi man-ngag gi nyams khrid skor*) such as the *Kun-bzang bla-ma'i zhal-lung*, which is a manual for the preliminary practices. There also exist oral instructions (*zhal-gdams*) and collections of advice (*gtam tshogs*), such as the *gTam padma'i tshal gyi zlos-gar*. He wrote in various literary genres, such as collections of hymns (*bstod tshogs*). Moreover, without composing it in an elaborate manner in order to satisfy the scholars, but rather expounding it in accordance with the capacities of the mind-streams of disciples, he has bequeathed to us one unsurpassed extraordinary special teaching (*thun-min khyad-chos bla-na med-pa*), known as the *mKhas-pa shri rgyal-po'i khyad-chos*.[16]

As it says in the biography of this master, the *dPal-sprul rnam-thar*, composed by rDo grub-chen 'Jigs-med bstan-pa'i nyi-ma (the third Dodrubchen Rinpoche), regarding this text: "If it is examined by the wise, it will be found to be of excellent benefit, but even if it is heard by the foolish, it will also be easy to understand. Having condensed the essential points, he has made their practice easy. At the right moment it will produce a connection (by way of direct introduction) and to the ear it produces a pleasurable experience. Even if it is explained in any manner whatsoever, whether rough or smooth, since it originates in harmony with all (other Dzogchen) instructions, being of a single taste with them, it may easily be appropriated by the minds of all beings, whether they are wise or confused, or find themselves somewhere in between."[17]

Glossary of Dzogchen Terms

[Note: Listings according to the Tibetan alphabet]

KA

ka-ti a crystalline translucent nerve or channel connecting the heart with the eyes

ka-dag primordial purity, primordially pure

ka-dag chen-po the Great Primordial Purity, a state of total primordial purity

ka-dag gi lam the path of primordial purity

ka-dag rig-pa shes-rab rang-byung gi sgron-ma the lamp of self-originated discriminating wisdom which is primordially pure awareness

ka nas dag-pa primordial purity, pure from the very beginning

kun-khyab all-pervading

kun-mkhyen omniscient, all-knowing

kun tu snang-ba'i ting-nge-'dzin the samadhi or state of contemplation which illuminates everything

kun tu bzang-po Samantabhadra (name of the Primordial Buddha)

kun tu bzang-mo Samantabhadri (name of the Primordial Wisdom)

kun brtag ma rig-pa the ignorance which conceptualizes everything

kun-byed rgyal-po the king who creates everything

kun-rdzob relative

kun-rdzob bden-pa Relative Truth

kun-gzhi the basis of everything, *ālaya*

kun-gzhi rnam-shes the store consciousness, *ālaya-vijñāna*

kun-bzang dgongs-pa the Primordial State of Samantabhadra

klong vast expanse, vast expanse of space

klong-chen the great vast expanse

klong-sde Longde, the Space Series (a series of texts and teachings of Dzogchen)

dkar 'jam rtsa'i sgron-ma the lamp of the smooth white nerve

dkar-po chig-thub 1. panacea, the white panacea; 2. the Mahamudra teaching

bka' precept, word, command, *vacana*

bka'-ma tradition, continuous tradition (an oral tradition whose transmission has not been interrupted and is continuous)

rkyen secondary cause, secondary condition, *pratyaya*

sku Body, *kāya*

sku gsum Trikaya, the Three Bodies of the Buddha

sku gsung thugs Body, Speech, and Mind

skye 'gags med-pa uncreated and unceasing

skye med uncreated, not produced, unborn

bskyed rdzogs the generation process and the perfection process

bskyed rdzogs zung-'jug unification of the generation process and the perfection process

bskyed-rim generation process, steps of production, development stage, visualization process, *utpattikrama*

KHA

khyad-chos special teaching

khrid explanation, guiding explanation

khrid-yig explanatory text (a manual which gives an explanation of the meditation practice)

khregs-chod Thekchod, releasing tensions, cutting through rigidity (a special teaching of the Dzogchen Upadesha Series)

mkha' sky, space

mkha'-'gro-ma Dakini (a manifestation of energy in female form)

mkhas-pa wise, learned

mkhyen-pa wisdom, knowledge; to know

'khor 'das Samsara and Nirvana

'khor 'das ru-shan phye-ba distinguishing between Samsara and Nirvana 'khor-ba Samsara, cyclical existence

'khor-lo 1. wheel, circle, cycle; 2. chakra, psychic center (a center of psychic energy in the body)

'khor-lo bsgyur-pa'i rgyal-po Universal Monarch, Chakravartin, a wheel-turning universal emperor, *cakravartī-rāja*

'khrul rtog delusory thoughts, deluded thoughts

'khrul rtog gi rba-rlabs 'tshub-pa turbulent waves of deluded thoughts

'khrul snang delusory appearances

'khrul-pa delusion, deluded, delusory, *bhrānti*

'khrul-pa'i las rgyun mi chod-pa not interrupt the current of the delusory activities of the mind

'khrul 'byams ordinary profusion of deluded thoughts

'khrul 'byams tha-mal du shor-ba fall into the ordinary profusion of deluded thoughts

'khrul med without delusion

'khrul gzhi the basis of delusion

'khrul lam the path of delusion

GA

gang-zag person, *pudgala*

gang-zag gi bdag-med the absence of a self in persons, *pudgalanairātmya*

gang-zag snyan brgyud the oral transmission to various persons

go-ba mere intellectual knowledge; to know only intellectually

gol sgrib deviation and obscuration

gol-sa deviation (a deviation from the state of contemplation due to distractions)

grub-brgyud the Siddha Lineage, *siddhaparamparā*

grub-thob Siddha, adept

grub-mtha' a system of philosophy, philosophical tenets, *siddhānta*

grub med uncreated, not realized

grol-cha on the side of liberation

grol-cha'i chos-sku ngos bzung recognize the Dharmakaya on the side of liberation

grol-ba liberation; to liberate

grol-ba gcig-pu unique liberation, a single mode of liberation

grol-ba'i grong-khyer the city of liberation

grol gzhi the basis of liberation

grol gzhi'i ye-shes ngos 'dzin recognizing the knowledge (or gnosis) which is the basis of liberation

grol lam the path of liberation

grol lugs modes of liberation

grol lugs bzhi the four modes of liberation

grol sa the state of liberation

grol sa gcig-pu unique state of liberation

grol sa gcig-po yin-par ngo-shes recognize to be the unique state of liberation

glo-bur adventitious, accidental

glo-bur ma dag-pa adventitious impurities

dgag sgrub med-pa neither stopping nor creating (thoughts)

dgongs brgyud direct transmission, Mind Lineage

dgongs gter Mind Treasure

dgongs-pa 1. Primordial State, Mind; 2. intention

dgra-bcom-pa Arhat, perfect saint

'gags-med unobstructed, without obstruction

'gyu-ba movement of thought; to move

'grel-pa commentary

'gro sa med (thoughts) do not go anywhere

rgod-pa agitation, agitated

rgyang zhags chu'i sgron-ma the lamp of the water (globelike) eye which lassos everything at a distance

rgyan ornament (i.e., thoughts and appearances are the ornaments of the mind)

rgyal-po king

rgyal-ba Jina, the Victorious One (syn. Buddha)

rgyal-ba dgongs brgyud the direct mind-to-mind transmission of the Jinas

rgyal-ba rigs lnga the five Dhyani Buddhas

rgyal-sras Jinaputra, son of the Victorious One (syn. Bodhisattva)

rgyal-sras kyi spyod-pa Bodhisattva conduct, conduct or behavior of a Jinaputra

rgyu cause, primary cause, *hetu*

rgyu'i ting-nge-'dzin causal samadhi, causal contemplation, *hetu-samādhi*

rgyu'i theg-pa Hetuyana, the Causal Vehicle

rgyud 1.Tantra; 2. mind-stream

rgyud-sde the Tantra Section (the 18 Tantras of the Mahayoga)

rgyud smin ripen the stream of consciousness

sgom-pa, bsgom-pa meditation; to meditate, *bhāvanā*

sgom-pa nyams su len-pa tshul method of practicing meditation

sgom-pa'i shes-rab discriminating wisdom arising in meditation

sgom byung gi shes-rab wisdom which comes forth in meditation

sgom lam path of meditation development, *bhāvanā-mārga*

sgyu-ma illusion, *māyā*

sgyu-lus, sgyu-ma'i lus illusion body, *māyādeha*

sgyur-ba transformation; to transform

sgyur lam the path of transformation

sgra 'od zer sounds, lights, and rays

sgrib-pa obscuration

sgrib-pa gnyis the two obscurations (emotional and intellectual)

sgrub brgyud Lineage of the Siddhas

sgrub-thabs sadhana, process of realization

sgrub-sde the Sadhana Section (of Mahayoga)

sgrub-pa bka' brgyad the sadhana practices of the eight Herukas

sgrub-pa-po sadhaka, practitioner of sadhana

sgro-'dogs doubts

sgron-ma drug the six lamps (aspects of light in Thodgal)

sgrol-ba 1. to liberate, to deliver; 2. rites of deliverance, magical rituals employed to slay other beings

brgyud-pa transmission, lineage, *paramparā*

brgyud-pa'i bla-ma Lineage Gurus, masters of the lineage of transmission

bsgom-pa chen-po the great meditation, state of total meditation

bsgom-med nonmeditation, without meditating

NGA

ngang state, condition

ngang bskyangs continuing in the state

ngang chen-po the great state, total state

ngang dwangs lucid state, luminous state

ngang bzhag chu-bo'i rgyun gyi sgom-pa remain in a state where meditation is like the continuous flow of a river

ngang la bzhag-pa remain in the state

ngan sngags evil mantras

ngan-song evil destinies of rebirth, *durgati*

nges-don real meaning, ultimate meaning, definitive meaning, *nītārtha*

ngo-sprad-pa directly introduced

ngo-sprod-pa introduction, direct introduction; to introduce

ngo-'phrad-pa to be introduced to

ngo-bo essence, *svabhāva*

ngo-bo gcig unique essence

ngo-bo nyid kyi sku Svabhavakaya, Svabhavikakaya

ngo-shes-pa recognition; to recognize

ngos 'dzin-pa to recognize

ngos bzung recognize

dngos-grub siddhi, attainments

dngos-po entity, a concrete thing

dngos-gzhi principal practice, principal section

mngon-'gyur become manifest

mngon-shes clairvoyance, clairvoyant power, *abhijñā*

mngon-shes drug the six clairvoyant powers

mngon-sum 1. manifest, evident to the senses; perception, *pratyakṣa*

mngon-sum rjen-pa'i ye-shes naked manifest primal awareness

snga-'gyur Early Translation

snga-'gyur lnga the five earliest translations (of Dzogchen)

snga dar the earlier spreading of the Dharma in Tibet

sngags mantra, incantation, magic spell

sngags rnying-ma the Old Tantras

sngags nang-pa the Inner Tantras, the Higher Tantras

sngags-pa Tantrika, Ngagpa, a practitioner of the Mantras

sngags-lugs the Tantra system, *mantranaya*

sngags gsar-ma the New Tantras

sngar 'dris kyi ye-shes a knowledge met with previously

sngon-'gro preliminaries, preliminary practice, preliminary section

CA

cig-car, cig-char instantaneous, immediate

cig-car 'jug-pa entering instantaneously

cig-car-ba nongradualist

cir snang rang yin one's own state of existence manifesting everywhere

cog-bzhag bzhi the four modes of just being there

gcig one, single, unique, single state, singularity, *eka*

gcig grol liberated into a single state

gcig thag-bcad-pa discover one single state

gcig-pu, gcig-po single, unique

gcig shes kun grol knowing one thing, everything is liberated

gcer grol liberation through bare attention

gcer mthong seeing nakedly

bca'-ba to continue

bcom-ldan-'das Bhagavan, Lord

bcos med unfabricated, unmodified, uncorrected

bcos slad med-pa not modified or adulterated

CHA

chad lta-ba the view of nihilism, *ucchedavāda*

chen-po great, total

chos 1. Dharma, reality; 2. dharmas, phenomena; 3. Dharma, the teaching of the Buddha

chos kun all dharmas, all phenomena

chos kyi bdag-med the insubstantiality of phenomena

chos-sku Dharmakaya

chos-sku rgyal-po'i rtsal the creative potentiality of the king who is the Dharmakaya (syn. **rig-pa'i rtsal**)

chos-sku gcig-po'i yo-langs bskyang continuing in the unique state of the Dharmakaya

chos-sku'i klong du dag-pa purified into the vast expanse of the Dharmakaya

chos-sku'i lta-ba the view of the Dharmakaya

chos-sku'i yo-langs the state (or nature) of the Dharmakaya

chos-nyid Dharmata, Reality

chos-nyid kyi rang ngo skyong-ba continuing in the inherent state of Reality

chos-nyid mngon-sum kyi snang-ba the vision of the direct perception of Reality

chos-nyid bar-do the Bardo of Reality

chos-nyid zad-pa'i snang-ba the vision of the consummation of Reality

chos rnams dharmas, phenomena

chos-dbyings Dharmadhatu, the dimension of all existence

chos lugs an organized system of phenomena, religion

chos log wrong teaching, perverted teaching

mchan note

mchod-brjod verse of offering

'char tshul manner of arising, how it arises

'char lugs mode of arising

'chi-kha'i bar-do the Bardo of Dying

JA

ji snyed-pa mkhyen-pa'i ye-shes the Knowledge of Quantity, the knowledge which knows the quantity of all phenomena

ji lta-ba bzhin the state of being just as it is

ji lta-ba gzigs-pa'i ye-shes the Knowledge of Quality, the knowledge which sees the state just as it is

ji bzhin nyid the state of being just as it is

ji bzhin-pa the state of being just as it is

ji bzhin-par bzhugs-pa remaining in the state of being just as it is

'ja'-lus the Rainbow Body

'ja'-lus 'pho-ba chen-po the Rainbow Body of the Great Transfer

'jur dran coarse memories

rjes concluding section

rjes thob subsequent realization, postmeditation experience, *pṛṣṭhalabdha*

rjes med without leaving a trace behind

rjes med rang dag self-purified without leaving a trace

rjes su rnal-'byor Anuyoga

rjes su rnal-'byor gyi theg-pa Anuyogayana, the Vehicle of the Anuyoga Tantra

brjod-med inexpressible (in words)

brjod med kyi rig-pa zang-thal an indescribable directly penetrating awareness

NYA

nyan-thos-pa Shravaka, a Hinayana disciple, a listener

nyan-thos-kyi theg-pa Shravakayana, the Vehicle of the Hinayana Disciples

nyams experience, meditation experience, mystical experience

nyams gong 'phel kyi snang-ba the vision of the development of experiences (in vision)

nyams-myong experience; to experience

nyams zhen attachment to experiences

nyams-len practice; to practice

nyams su len-pa to practice

nyams gsum the three meditation experiences (of bliss, clarity, and no thought)

nyon-mongs-pa passion, negative emotion, *kleśa*

nyon-mongs-pa'i sgrib-pa obscuration due to the passions

nyon-mongs-pa'i rlung *kleśa-vāyu*, passion winds, winds (or psychic energies) defiled by the passions

gnyis-med nondual, without duality, *advaya*

gnyis-'dzin grasping at duality

gnyis-'dzin kyi 'ching-ba las 'grol-ba liberated from bondage to dualistic thinking

gnyen-po antidote, *pratipakṣa*

gnyug-ma natural, innate, *nija*

gnyug-ma'i rnal-'byor natural yoga, natural practice

mnyam rjes contemplation and subsequent realization

mnyam rjes kyi nyams-len the practice of contemplation and subsequent realization

mnyam-nyid, mnyam-pa nyid the state of identity, sameness, *samatā*

mnyam-bzhag the state of even contemplation, *samāhita*

rnying-ma-pa Nyingmapa, the Old Tantra school

snyan brgyud oral transmission, oral lineage, oral tradition

snying gi bu heart-son, chief disciple

snying-gtam heartfelt advice

snying-thig Nyingthig, the Essence of the Mind (syn. the Dzogchen Upadesha teachings)

snying-thig rdo-rje snying-po'i lam the path of the adamantine heart of the Essence of the Mind (syn. the Dzogchen Upadesha teachings)

snying-thig-pa a practitioner of the Nyingthig teachings

snying-po 1. heart, *hṛdaya;* 2. embryo, *garbha;* 3. essence, *sāra;* 4. mind, *citta*

TA

ting-nge-'dzin contemplation, the state of contemplation, *samādhi*

ting-nge-'dzin chen-po a state of total contemplation, the great contemplation, *mahāsamādhi*

gtad-pa fixation; to fixate the mind on

gtad-so concept, conception

gtad-so dang bral-ba free of conceptions

gtad-tshigs conclusion, criteria, reasoning

gtan la 'bebs-pa to systematize, to set down systematically

gter-ston Terton, Treasure Master, a discoverer of hidden treasure texts

gter-ma Terma, hidden treasure text

btag-grol liberation through wearing

rtag lta-ba the view of eternalism, Shashvatavada

rtags sign, indication

rtog-pa thought, discursive thought; to think

rtogs-pa understanding; to understand

lta sgom du ro-gcig a single taste as to view and meditation

lta sgom spyod view, meditation, and conduct

lta sgom spyod 'bras-bu view, meditation, conduct, and fruit

lta-ba view, way of seeing, *dṛṣṭi;* to see

stong-cha on the side of emptiness

stong-nyid kyi gshis the innate disposition which is emptiness

stong-nyid snying-rje zung-'jug the unification of emptiness and compassion

stong-pa empty, *śūnya*

stong-pa nyid emptiness, *śūnyatā*

brtag-pa examination, *vitarka;* to examine, to investigate

brtan-pa thob attain stability

bstan-bcos philosophical treatise, treatise, *śāstra*

bstan-pa teaching, doctrine, *śāsana*; taught, reveal

THA

tha-dad med-pa no difference, no distinction

thag-bcad-pa to decide definitively, to determine decisively, to decide

thabs Means, Skillful Means, method, *upāya*

thig-le sphere, tiny sphere, essence, *bindu*

thig-le chen-po the Great Sphere, total sphere, *mahābindu*

thig-le nyag-gcig the Unique Sphere, unique essence

thig-le stong-pa'i sgron-ma the lamp of the empty spheres

thugs Mind, Heart, *citta*

thugs-rje 1. Energy; 2. compassion, *karuṇā*

thugs sras heart-son, principal disciple

thun session, meditation session

thun dang thun-mtshams sessions and between sessions

the-tshom med without doubts, not remaining in doubt

theg-pa vehicle, way, *yāna*

theg-pa dgu the nine vehicles

theg-pa chen-po Mahayana, the Greater Vehicle

theg-pa thams-cad kyi rtse rgyal the victorious mountain peak of all the vehicles (to enlightenment) (i.e., Dzogchen)

theg-pa dman-pa Hinayana, the Lesser Vehicle

theg-pa rim dgu the nine successive vehicles to enlightenment

theg-pa rim dgu'i rtse-bo the pinnacle of the nine successive vehicles

theg-pa'i yang rtse highest peak of all vehicles

thog-ma'i sangs-rgyas the Primordial Buddha

thod-rgal Thodgal, passing over the summit (the development of vision practice in the Dzogchen Upadesha)

thol byung blo rdeg suddenly strike a thought

thos-pa'i shes-rab discriminating wisdom arising from hearing (the teachings)

mtha' limit, limitation, extreme, end, *anta*

mtha' grol liberated from all limitations

mtha' med unlimited, without limitation

mtha' las 'das-pa transcending limitations

mthar snang final visions

mthong lam the path of vision, *darśanamārga*

DA

dag snang pure vision

dang-po-pa beginner

dad-pa faith

dwangs luster, brightness; clear, pure

dam-bca' author's promise, the author's statement of purpose to his readers

dam-tshig sems-dpa' symbolic being, *samayasattva*

dur-khrod cremation ground

de kho na nyid Tathata, Reality, the state of being just as it is, suchness

de kho na nyid ting-nge-'dzin the contemplation of Reality, *tathatā-samādhi*

de bzhin nyid Tathata, Reality, the state of being just as it is

de bzhin gshegs-pa Tathagata (syn. Buddha)

de bzhin gshegs-pa'i snying-po Tathagatagarbha, inherent Buddha-nature

don meaning, real meaning, benefit, purpose, *artha*

don gyi lta-ba real view

don gyi ye-shes real knowledge

don gcig las ma 'das-pa not go beyond the single meaning

drag sngags fierce mantras

drang don conventional meaning, *neyārtha*

dri-med immaculate

gdangs translucency, translucent

gdams-ngag instruction

gdeng, gdengs confidence

gdod nas dag-pa primordially pure

gdod-ma primordial

gdod-ma'i mgon-po Adinatha (syn. the Primordial Buddha)

gdod-ma'i rnal-'byor the Primordial Yoga (syn. Dzogchen)

gdod-ma'i gzhi the Primordial Base

bdag-nyid chen-po the Great State, the great self (syn. Dzogchen, the Primordial State)

bdag-med without a self, insubstantial, Anatman

bdag-'dzin grasping at a self, grasping at the reality of, *ātmagraha*

bde-ba pleasurable sensation, happiness, bliss, *sukha*

bde-ba chen-po Mahasukha, the Great Bliss

bde-ba'i nyams experience of pleasurable sensation

bde-bar gshegs-pa Sugata (syn. Tathagata, Buddha)

bden-pa gnyis the Two Truths (absolute and relative)

bden-pa mthong-ba seeing the truth

bdud Mara, demon

mdangs luster, brightness, bright complexion

mdo Sutra, a discourse of the Buddha

mdo-sde spyod-pa'i dbu-ma Sautrantika-Madhyamika

mdo-lugs Sutra system

'das -rjes posthumous teachings

'du-byed samskaras, impulses, karmic formations

'du-byed kyi las activities of the samskaras

'dul-ba Vinaya, monastic discipline, monastic ordinances

'dren-pa'i bla-ma Guru who gives guidance

rdo-rje vajra, diamond; adamantine, diamondlike

rdo-rje theg-pa Vajrayana

rdo-rje zam-pa the Vajra Bridge teachings (of Dzogchen Longde)

rdo-rje lu-gu-rgyud vajra chains

rdo-rje slob-dpon Vajracharya

rdo-rje sems-dpa' Vajrasattva

rdo-rje gdan Vajrasana (modern Bodh Gaya), the diamond throne of enlightenment

brda sign, symbol

brda brgyud symbolic transmission, the Lineage of the Mystic Signs (of the Vidyadharas)

brda bzhi the Four Signs (in Dzogchen Longde practice)

NA

nang internal, inner, inner aspect

nang gi bla-ma the internal Guru

nang rgyud Inner Tantras

nang rtog internal thoughts

nang dbyings inner space, internal space, the internal dimension

nang 'od inner light, internal light

nang gsal inner luminosity, internal luminosity

nam-mkha' sky, space, the space element, *ākāśa*

gnad essential point

gnad gcig-po single essential point

gnad du brdeg-pa strike the essential point

gnad don the real meaning of the essential point

gnad ma nor-ba unmistaken essential point

gnad gsum ldan-pa'i lta-ba the view which possesses the three essential points

gnas-pa calm state; to abide, to be established

gnas 'phro still or diffusing

gnas-tshul mode of being

gnas-lugs Natural State, natural condition

gnas-lugs ji lta-ba gzigs-pa'i ye-shes the Knowledge of Quality, the knowledge which sees the Natural State just as it is

gnas sa med (thoughts) do not remain anywhere

rna brgyud oral transmission

rnam-rtog thought, discursive thought, *vikalpa*

rnam-rtog grol liberate discursive thoughts

rnam-rtog ngo shes-pa recognize discursive thoughts

rnam-rtog med-pa without discursive thoughts

rnam-par rtog-pa discursive thought, *vikalpa*

rnam-par mi rtog-pa without discursive thoughts, *nirvikalpa*

rnam-par shes-pa consciousness, *vijñāna*

rnam-shes consciousness, *vijñāna*

rnal-'byor yoga, union

rnal-'byor gyi rgyud Yoga Tantra

rnal-'byor gyi rgyud gyi theg-pa Yogatantrayana

rnal-'byor chen-po Mahayoga

rnal-'byor chen-po'i rgyud kyi theg-pa Mahayogatantrayana

rnal-'byor-pa Yogin, practitioner

rnal-'byor spyod-pa Yogachara, Yogacharin

rnal-'byor spyod-pa'i dbu-ma Yogachara-Madhyamika

rnal-'byor-ma Yogini

rnal-'byor bzhi the Four Yogas (stages in Dzogchen Semde practice)

rnal-'byor lam the Path of the Yogins, the Path of the Yogins

rnal bzhag chen-po totally settled into the natural state, the great self-settled natural state

sna-tshogs diversity, different kinds

sna-tshogs rdo-rje a double vajra, viśvavajra

snang 'char tshul the way in which appearances arise

snang stong dbyer-med the inseparability of appearance and emptiness

snang-ba appearance, manifestation, vision; to appear, to manifest, to be visible

snang-ba bzhi the Four Visions (in Thodgal practice)

snang-srid all phenomenal existence, all that appears and that exists

PA

dpal glorious, abundant, *śrī*

dpe example, metaphor

dpe'i ye-shes knowledge indicated by example

dpyad-pa analyzed, reason

dpyod-pa analysis; to analyze, to investigate, *vicāra*

spang blang med-pa without attachment or aversion

spong lam the path of renunciation

spyan lnga the five eyes

spyi 'byams irregular habits

spyi 'byams gshis shor falling away from one's innate disposition due to irregular habits

spyi mes chen-po the great universal Ancestor

spyi gzhi the universal Base

spyod-pa conduct, behavior, action, *caryā*

spyod-pa'i rgyud Charya Tantra

spyod-pa'i rgyud kyi theg-pa Charyatantrayana

spyod-yul sphere of action, the range of the activities of the senses

sprul-sku Nirmanakaya

sprul-pa Nirmita, emanation

spros-pa elaboration, multifarious activity, *prapañca*

spros-med without (conceptual) elaborations, *aprapañca*

spros bral free of conceptual elaborations

PHA

pha-rol tu phyin-pa perfection, *pāramita*

pha-rol tu phyin-pa drug the six perfections, the six paramitas

phun-sum tshogs-pa supreme, abundant

phyag-rgya mudra, symbol, symbolic form, gesture, consort

phyag-rgya chen-po Mahamudra, the Great Symbol

phyag-chen Mahamudra, the Great Symbol

phyag-na rdo-rje Vajrapani

phyam gnas even-minded

phyam gnas lhod-de even-minded and relaxed

phyam lhod equanimity and relaxation

phyal-ba omnipresent, common

phyi external, outer, outer aspect

phyi rgyud Outer Tantras

phyi dar the later spreading of the Dharma

phyi snang external appearances

phyi dbyings external space, the external dimension

phyi'i bla-ma the external Guru

'phags yul Aryadesha, India

'pho-ba the transference of consciousness; to transfer

'pho-ba chen-po the Great Transfer

'phrul-ba to emanate

'phro-ba to emanate, to project, to diffuse, to proliferate

BA

bag-chags karmic traces, karmic residues, unconscious propensities, *vāsanā*

bar-do Bardo, the intermediate state between death and rebirth, *antarābhava*

bu'i 'od gsal the Son Clear Light

bya-ba'i rgyud Kriya Tantra

bya-ba'i rgyud kyi theg-pa Kriyatantrayana

bya bral free of any deliberate action

byang-chub enlightenment, Bodhi

byang-chub kyi sems Bodhichitta, enlightened mind, the Thought of Enlightenment

byang-chub sems-dpa' Bodhisattva

byang-chub sems-dpa'i theg-pa Bodhisattvayana

byan tshud-pa concrete personal experience

bying-ba drowsiness

byin-rlabs blessing, *adhiṣṭhāna*

byung sa med (thoughts) do not arise from anywhere

byed-pa-po creator, actor, agent, *kartṛ*

bla-sgrub Guru Sadhana

bla-na med-pa unsurpassed, highest, *anuttara*

bla-na med-pa'i rgyud Anuttara Tantra

bla-ma Guru, master

bla-ma'i rnal-'byor Guru Yoga, Unification with the Guru

blang dor med-pa without accepting or rejecting

blang dor med-par bskyang-ba continue without accepting or rejecting anything

blo mind, thought, attitude

blo-gros intellect, *mati*

blo 'das brjod bral transcending conception by the intellect and beyond expression in words

blo ldog rnam bzhi the four meditations which change one's attitude (toward life)

blo byas bcos-ma'i lta sgom view and meditation fabricated by the mind

blo byas 'jur dran tangled memories made by mind

dbang initiation, empowerment, *abhiṣeka*

dbang-bskur to confer initiation

dbang-po sense faculty, intellectual capacity, *indriya*

dbang-po gzhan la rag ma lus-pa not depend on any other power

dbang-po rab 'bring tha-ma superior, intermediate, and inferior capacities

dbang-phyug Lord, God, *iśvara*

dbang-phyug-pa Shaiva, Shaivite, a follower of the god Shiva

dbang bzhi the four initiations (in Anuttara Tantra)

dbang lung khrid initiation, authorization, and explanation

dbu-ma 1. middle, center; 2. Madhyamaka

dbu-ma-pa Madhyamika

dbu-ma'i rtsa Avadhuti, the central channel

dbyings space, dimension, *dhātu*

dbyer-med inseparability; inseparable

sbyin-pa generosity

'bras-bu Fruit, result, consequence, goal, *phala*

'bras-bu'i theg-pa Phalayana, the Fruitional Vehicle

'bras-bu'i rdo-rje theg-pa the fruitional Vajrayana

sbyong lam the path of purification

sbyor sgrol sexual rituals and slaying rituals

sbyor lam the path of application, *prayoga-mārga*

MA

ma skye uncreated, unproduced, not born

ma 'gags-pa unobstructed, unceasing, *anirodha*

ma bcos-pa unfabricated, unmodified, uncontrived, uncorrected

ma bcos lhan-cig skyes-pa unfabricated and spontaneous

ma dag las snang impure karmic vision

ma bu 'phrad-pa encounter of the Mother and the Son (Clear Light)

ma bu sbyor-ba uniting of the Mother and the Son (Clear Light)

ma'i 'od gsal the Mother Clear Light

ma yin-pa'i chos lugs the organized system of phenomena which does not exist in reality

ma g.yeng-ba undistracted, without distraction

ma rig-pa ignorance, lack of awareness, *avidyā*

man-ngag upadesha, secret oral instruction

man-ngag gi sde Upadesha Series (a group of texts and series of Dzogchen teachings)

mi gnyis not two

mi rnyed unfindability, not find, not obtain

mi rtog-pa no thought, nondiscursive, without thoughts

mi rtog-pa'i nyams experience of no thought

mi bsdu not concentrating (thoughts)

mi spro not projecting, not diffusing, not proliferating (thoughts)

mi slob lam the path beyond training, *aśaikṣa-mārga*

mu-stegs rtag lta-ba the eternalist view of the Tirthikas (Hindus)

mu-stegs-pa Tirthika (i.e., a Hindu)

mya-ngan 'das-pa Nirvana, passing beyond suffering

dmigs-bcas fixation with an object

dmigs-pa visualization, conception, imagination

dmigs-med fixation without an object

TSA

tsit ta the physical heart

tsit ta sha'i sgron-ma the lamp of the fleshly heart

btson-sgrus vigor, diligence

rtsa a psychic channel, nerve, *nāḍi*

rtsa-ba root, source, root text, *mūla*

rtsa-ba'i bla-ma Root Guru

rtsa rlung the yoga of channels and energies, *nāḍivāyu yoga*

rtsa rlung thig-le'i rnal-'byor the yoga of Nadis, Vayus, and Bindus

rtsal energy, creative energy, potentiality

rtsal sbyong forceful purification

rtse-gcig one-pointed, one-pointedness of mind

rtsol sgrub searching for realization

rtsol-med the effortless state; effortless, without effort

rtsol-med kyi bstan-pa the doctrine of the effortless state

brtsis-med without calculating

brtse-ba love; to love

TSHA

tshad-med immeasurable, unlimited, *aprameya*

tshad-med bzhi the four unlimited states

tshi chad-pa fall into despair

tshig dbang word initiation

tshul method, manner, mode

tshul-khrims morality, moral precepts, *śila*

tshogs gnyis the two accumulations (of merit and wisdom)

tshogs drug the six aggregates of consciousness

tshogs lam the path of accumulation, *saṃbhāra-mārga*

mtshan name, title

mtshan-bcas fixation with an object

mtshan-nyid definitive characteristic, definition, *lakṣaṇa*

mtshan-nyid theg-pa Lakshanayana (syn. the Sutra system)

mtshan-ma mark, distinguishing mark, *nimitta*

mtshan-med 1. without a distinguishing mark; 2. fixation without an object

DZA

'dzin-pa subject, that which apprehends, *grāhaka*

rdzu-'phrul magical power, magical display, telekinesis, psychokinesis, *ṛddhi*

rdzogs-chen Dzogchen, the Great Perfection

rdzogs-chen sde gsum the three series of Dzogchen teachings

rdzogs-chen-pa a practitioner of Dzogchen

rdzogs-pa perfect, complete

rdzogs-pa chen-po Dzogchen, the Great Perfection, *mahāsandhi*

rdzogs-rim the perfection process, Sampannakrama

ZHA

zhar-byung addendum

zhal-'chems last testament

zhal-sgom oral teaching and meditation practice

zhal-gdams oral teaching, advice

zhal-lung oral teaching

zhi-khro Peaceful and Wrathful Deities

zhi-ba 1. peace, peaceful, pacification, *śānti;* 2. Ultimate Peace, Nirvana

zhi-gnas Shamatha, calming the mind, the state of peaceful calm, attaining peaceful calm

zhi lhag dbyer-med the inseparability of Shamatha and Vipashyana

zhe-sdang anger, hatred

zhen-pa attachment; to become attached

gzhan ngo snang tshul how they present themselves as external appearances

gzhan du mi rnyed-pa'i ye-shes a knowledge not found elsewhere outside of oneself

gzhan rig awareness of the other (i.e., external objects)

gzhi Base, Foundation, ground, basis

gzhi ji bzhin-pa the Base just as it is

gzhi nyid la grol-ba liberated into the state of the Base

gzhi dang ngo 'phrad-pa introduced to the Base

gzhi gnas ma'i 'od gsal the Mother Clear Light that abides as the Base

gzhi-ma the Base

gzhi med rtsa bral without any base and without any source

gzhi'i 'od gsal the Clear Light of the Base

gzhi yi ngo-bo the essence which is the Base

gzhi lam gyi 'od gsal gnyis bdyer-med the inseparability of the Clear Lights of the Base and of the Path

gzhi lam 'bras-bu the Base, the Path, and the Fruit

gzhir gnas remain as the Base, abide as the Base

gzhir gnas kyi rig-pa Awareness which abides as the Base

gzhir gnas kyi 'od gsal the Clear Light which abides as the Base

gzhung-lugs-pa a follower of the scriptural system

gzhon-nu bum sku the youthful vaselike Body

ZA

zag-pa med-pa'i dbyings unpolluted dimension, the pollutionless dimension (of the mind)

zang-thal direct penetration, directly penetrating

zang-thal rjen-pa'i rig-pa a directly penetrating naked Awareness

zang-thal-le directly penetrating

zang ma thal 'byung impeded

zin-pa completed, finished, accomplished, done

zung-'jug unification, unified, united, *yuganaddha*

gza' gtad concepts, conceptions

gza' gtad dang bral-ba free of all conceptions

gzugs-sku Rupakaya, Form Body
gzung-ba object, that which is apprehended, *grāhya*
gzung 'dzin subject and object
bzod-pa patience

'A

'og 'gyu undercurrent
'og 'gyu 'khrul 'byams undercurrent of proliferating delusions
'og 'gyu'i rnam-rtog undercurrent of discursive thoughts
'og-min Akanishtha, the highest plane of existence
'od lus the Body of Light
'od gsal the Clear Light
'od gsal rgyun-chad med-pa'i klong du in the vast expanse of unceasing Clear Light
'od gsal rdo-rje snying-po'i bstan-pa the doctrine of the adamantine essence of the Clear Light (syn. Dzogchen)
'od gsal-ba'i ye-shes the knowledge of the Clear Light, a primal awareness of Clear Light

YA

yang rtse the pinnacle, the highest peak
yang rab an individual of exceedingly superior capacity
yangs-pa vast expanse
yi-dam Yidam, a meditation deity, *devatā*
yid Manas, mind, functional mind
yid kyi rnam-rtog Manovijnana, mind-consciousness
yid-ches-pa belief
yid-dpyad mental analysis
yid la byed-pa attention, mind-work, mental activity, *manasikāra*
yid la mi byed-pa inattention, without mental activity
yin-lugs natural state of existence
yul object
yul-can subject
ye grol primordial liberation
ye ji bzhin-pa the primordial state of being just as it is

ye nas primordial, from the very beginning

ye nas dag-pa pure from the very beginning

ye nas shes-pa knowledge, gnosis, cognition, primal awareness, Primordial Awareness, *jñāna*

ye nas sangs-rgyas-pa enlightened from the very beginning, attained Buddhahood from the very beginning

ye nas lhun-grub spontaneously perfected from the very beginning

ye phyi-mo the Primordial Grandmother

ye med nonexistent from the very beginning

ye rdzogs primordially perfected

ye yod existing from the very beginning

ye gzhi the Primordial Base

ye gzhi snying-po byang-chub kyi sems the Bodhichitta which is the essence of the Primordial Base

ye-shes knowledge, gnosis, cognition, wisdom, primal awareness, Primordial Awareness, *jñāna*

ye-shes kyi sku Jnanakaya

ye-shes kyi tshogs accumulation of wisdom, *jñāna-saṃbhāra*

ye-shes kyi rang rtsal du bskyong-ba continue in the inherent potentiality of primal awareness

ye-shes kyi rlung wisdom winds, wisdom airs, *jñāna-vāyu*

ye-shes brjod bral an inexpressible primal awareness

ye-shes spyi a general or universal primal awareness

ye-shes zang-thal directly penetrating primal awareness

yo-langs the unobstructed and continuous state (of the Dharmakaya)

yongs su grub-pa fully realized, fully accomplished, *pariniṣpanna*

yongs su rdzogs-pa fully perfected, completed, *paripūrṇa*

yod med existence and nonexistence

g.yeng-ba distraction, distracted; to be distracted

RA

rag-pa'i rnam-rtog coarse thoughts

rang self, itself, one's own, inherent

rang gi ngo-bo one's own essence

rang gi rig-pa one's own immediate awareness

rang gis rang grol self-liberated by itself

rang gis rang rig-pa self-aware by itself

rang grol self-liberation, self-liberated

rang rgyud one's own mind-stream

rang rgyud gnyis 'dzin gyi 'ching-ba las grol-ba one's own mind-stream liberated from all bondage to dualistic thinking

rang ngo one's own real nature, one's own face

rang ngo rang du phrad-pa one's own face encountering itself, meeting oneself face to face

rang ngo-shes-pa self-recognition; recognizing one's own nature (face)

rang gcig-pa singular unique state

rang gcig-pu singular unique state

rang dang 'brel-ba found within oneself, connected with oneself

rang gdangs inherent translucent radiance

rang gnas self-sustaining, self-abiding, self-existent

rang gnas kyi ye-shes rjen-pa a naked self-sustaining primal awareness

rang-snang self-manifestation, self-manifesting

rang babs self-occurring

rang babs gnyug-ma'i dran-pa a natural self-occurring mindfulness

rang-byung self-originated

rang-byung ye-shes self-originated knowledge, self-originated primal awareness

rang zhal mjal-ba meeting one's own face (nature)

rang gzhan gnyis su byung originate as oneself and as another

rang-bzhag self-settled, remain as itself

rang-bzhin nature, nature, inherent nature, *svabhāva*

rang-bzhin rnam-dag naturally pure

rang-bzhin med-pa without any inherent nature

rang-bzhin rdzogs-pa chen-po the natural Great Perfection

rang-rtsal inherent energy, inherent potentiality

rang yin-pa one's own state of existence

rang yin-par ngo-shes-pa recognizing it as one's own state of being

rang rig self-awareness; aware of oneself

rang rig-pa one's own intrinsic Awareness

rang la byan tshud-pa concrete personal experiences with regard to one-self

rang-shar self-arising

rang shes rig-pa'i rgyal-po the King who is self-knowing Awareness

rang sar grol liberated into its own condition

rang sar zin remaining in its own (original) condition

rang sangs-rgyas pratyekabuddha

rang sangs-rgyas kyi theg-pa pratyekabuddhayana

rang sems one's own mind

rang sor zin remaining in its own (original) condition

rang gsal inherent clarity, inherent luminosity

rab-'byams-pa infinite

rab 'bring tha-ma superior, intermediate, and inferior capacities

rig-cha on the side of awareness

rig stong rjen-pa naked empty Awareness

rig stong dbyer-med the inseparability of awareness and emptiness

rig-pa 1. Awareness, immediate Awareness, intrinsic Awareness, the state of contemplation, *vidyā*; 2. intelligence

rig-pa ngo-sprod direct introduction to intrinsic Awareness

rig-pa gcer-bu naked Awareness

rig-pa gcer mthong seeing with naked Awareness

rig-pa rjen-pa naked Awareness

rig-pa dbyings kyi sgron-ma the lamp of the dimension of Awareness

rig-pa tshad pheb kyi snang-ba the vision of the increasing to the full measure of Awareness

rig-pa 'dzin-pa vidyadhara, knowledge-holder

rig-pa'i khu-byug the cockoo of Awareness

rig-pa'i rtsal the potentiality of Awareness, the creative energy of Awareness

rig-pa'i rtsal lhung-ba fall into the potentiality of Awareness

rig-pa'i ye-shes the knowledge which is immediate Awareness

rig-pa'i zang-thal directly penetrating Awareness

rig-pa zang-thal gyi ngang the state of directly penetrating Awareness

rig-pa rang gnas self-sustaining immediate Awareness

rig-ma a consort, a female partner for tantric practice

rig-'dzin Vidyadhara

rig-'dzin brda brgyud the symbolic transmission of the Vidyadharas

rig shes a knowing awareness

rig gsal clear awareness, awareness and clarity

rig gsal dbyer-med the inseparability of awareness and clarity

ring-lugs our own system, our own tradition

rim-gyis 'jug-pa entering gradually

rim-gyis-pa a gradualist

ris-med nonsectarian

ris-med-pa one who is nonsectarian, a follower of the Rimed or nonsectarian movement

ru-log reversal, the process of reversing solid matter into radiant energy

ru-shan distinction, the Rushan exercises (in Dzogchen)

ro-gcig single taste, single flavor, the state of being a single taste, *ekarasa*

ro-snyoms same taste, the process of making everything into the same taste, *samarasa*

ro-langs a vampire, *vetāla*

rol-pa manifestation; to manifest

rlung psychic energy, wind, air, *vāyu*

LA

la bzla-ba to transcend, to go beyond conceptions

lam the Path, path, way, road, *mārga*

lam-khyer carry on along the path, daily practice

lam gyi 'od gsal the Clear Light of the Path

las snang karmic vision

lung 1. Agama; 2. scriptural authorization, authorization

lung-ma-bstan a dull blank state of mind, neutral state

lung rig scriptural citations and reasoning

lus ngag yid body, speech, and mind

longs-sku Sambhogakaya

longs-spyod rdzogs-pa'i sku Sambhogakaya

SHA

shar grol liberation as soon as it arises

shar-ba to arise

shin tu rnal-'byor Atiyoga (syn. Dzogchen)

shin tu rnal-'byor gyi theg-pa Atiyogayana

shes rgyud stream of consciousness, *vijñānasantāna*

shes-pa awareness; to know, to be aware

shes-bya ji snyed-pa mkhyen-pa'i ye-shes the Knowledge of Quantity, the knowledge which knows the full quantity of what is known (i.e., conventional knowledge of phenomena)

shes-bya'i sgrib-pa obscurations due to (erroneous) intellectual knowledge

shes-rab wisdom, discriminating wisdom, *prajñā*

shes-rab rang-byung gi sgron-ma the lamp of self-originated wisdom

shes rig an awareness which knows

shog ser golden paper

gshis innate disposition

gshis shor gyi gol-sa deviation where one falls away from one's innate disposition

SA

sa stage, state, *bhūmi*

sa gcig-pa single stage

sa bcu the ten stages, the ten bhumis

sa-gter earth-treasure

sangs-rgyas Buddha, an enlightened being

sangs-rgyas-pa Buddhahood, attaining Buddhahood

sems mind, thoughts, thought process, *citta*

sems kyi ngo-bo the essence of mind

sems kyi snang-ba manifestation of mind

sems kyi yal-ba the dissolving of mental activities

sems bskyed 1. bodhichitta, producing the bodhichitta, *bodhicittotpāda*; 2. producing a thought

sems grol liberate the mind

sems rgyud mind-stream

sems-can sentient being, *sattva*

sems-nyid the Nature of Mind, *cittatā*

sems-nyid kyi rang zhal bsgribs obscuring the true face of the Nature of Mind

sems-sde Mind Series (a group of texts and series of Dzogchen teachings)

sems-phyogs teachings pertaining to the Dzogchen Semde

sems 'byung contents of mind, what arises in the mind, *caitta*

sems-tsam Chittamatra, the doctrine of Mind-Only

sems-tsam-pa Chittamatrin, a follower of the Mind-Only doctrine (syn. Yogacharin)

sems-'dzin fixation of mind, Semdzin (a series of meditation exercises in Dzogchen)

sems rang bzhag gnyug-ma'i ngang bskyangs the mind continues in a natural self-settled state

sems las 'das-pa transcending the mind

sems las 'das-pa'i ye-shes a primal awareness which transcends the mind

so-sa'i gling Sosaling (name of a cremation ground in India)

srid-pa existence (syn. *saṃsāra*)

srid-pa'i bar-do the Bardo of Existence

gsang sngags the Secret Mantras (syn. Vajrayana)

gsang sngags rdo-rje theg-pa the Secret Mantra Vajrayana

gsang spyod secret conduct (the sexual practices of yoga)

gsang-ba secret, secret aspect

gsang-ba'i bdag-po Guhyapati, the Master of Secrets (i.e., Vajrapani)

gsang-ba'i bla-ma the secret Guru

gsang mtshan secret name (obtained during initiation)

gsar-ma-pa Sarmapa, the New Tantra schools, the Newer Schools

gsal-cha on the side of luminous clarity

gsal stong dbyer-med the inseparability of clarity and emptiness

gsal-ba clarity, luminosity, luminous clarity, clear

gsal-ba'i nyams experience of clarity

bsam-gtan concentration, meditation, level of concentration, *dhyāna*

bsam-gtan gyi mkhan-po a teacher of Chan, a Chan master

bsam-gtan gyi rgyu tshogs accumulate the causes of concentration

bsam-pa'i shes-rab discriminating wisdom arising from reflection

bsil-ba'i tshal Shitavana, the cool forest (cremation ground near Bodh Gaya)

bsod-nams merit, meritorious karma, *puṇya*

bsod-nam kyi tshogs accumulation of merit, *puṇya-saṃbhāra*

HA

had-de-ba startled awareness, a state of shock

lha god, deity, Deva

lhag-mthong vipaśyanā, higher insight (Pali: *vipassana*)

lhag-pa'i rnal-'byor Atiyoga (syn. Dzogchen)

lhan-skyes spontaneously born

lhan-cig skyes-pa spontaneously born, *sahaja*

lhan-cig skyes-pa'i ma rig-pa spontaneously born ignorance

lhan-cig skyes-pa'i ye-shes spontaneously born knowledge, spontaneously born primal awareness

lha'i nga-rgyal divine pride

lhug-pa alert relaxation, alertly relaxed

lhun gyis spontaneously, effortlessly, naturally

lhun gyis grub-pa spontaneously self-perfected, effortlessly realized, *anābhoga*

lhun gyis 'jug-pa entering spontaneously

lhun gyis gnas-pa abiding spontaneously, remaining effortlessly

lhun gyis rdzogs-pa perfected spontaneously

lhun-grub spontaneously self-perfected

lhun-rdzogs spontaneously perfected

lhod-de relaxed

lhod-pa relaxation, relaxed; to relax

lhod-pa chen-po the Great Relaxation, totally relaxed, a state of total relaxation (syn. Dzogchen)

A

a-ti Atiyoga (syn. Dzogchen)

a-ti-yo-ga Atiyoga (syn. Dzogchen)

a-la-la how delightful!

e-ma-ho how wonderful!

o-rgyan Uddiyana

Notes

FOREWORD

1. This foreword was written by Namkhai Norbu Rinpoche in Tibetan and thereafter translated into English. Notes are by the translator. Any spiritual path may be analyzed into its Base, or Foundation (*gzhi*), its Path, or methods of spiritual practice and development (*lam*), and its Fruit, or Goal (*'bras-bu*). The Three Series of Dzogchen teachings (*rdzogs-chen sde gsum*) consist of the Semde (*sems-sde*), or "Mind Series," the Longde (*klong-sde*), or "Space Series," and the Upadesha (*man-ngag sde*), or "Secret Instruction Series." These three series correpond to the Base, the Path, and the Fruit of Dzogchen, respectively.

2. dGa'-rab rdo-rje, "the supremely blissful vajra." The original Sanskrit form of the name of this master is uncertain.

3. 'Jam-dpal gshes-gnyen.

4. *'Od lus*, "the Body of Light." This Body of Light represents the culmination of the Thodgal (*thod-rgal*) practice within Dzogchen.

5. *rDo-rje tshig gsum*, "the Three Vajra Verses." These three verses or statements (*tshig gsum*) comprise the Last Testament (*zhal-'chems*) of the Master Garab Dorje and bear the title of "The Three Statements That Strike the Essential Points" (*tshig gsum gnad brdeg*). The three essential points (*gnad gsum*) refer to the Base, the Path, and the Fruit, or alternatively, to the view (*lta-ba*), the meditation (*sgom-pa*), and the conduct or action (*spyod-pa*) of Dzogchen.

6. *Zhal-'chems*.

7. *Tshig gsum*.

8. *Sems-sde, klong-sde, man-ngag sde*.

9. *lTa grub* = *lta-ba dang grub-mtha'*, "views and tenets."

10. *lTa tshul.*

11. *Grub-mtha'*, "tenet, philosophical system."

12. *dGongs-pa rnal-ma*, "the natural Primordial State."

13. *Grub-mtha'.*

14. One's philosophical position or tenet (*grub-mtha'*) is established by way of the threefold logical process of the refutation of the opponent's view (*dgag*), the demonstration or logical establishment of one's own view (*bzhag*), and the rebuttal of the opponent's arguments against one's own view (*spang*).

15. *rDzogs-chen gyi dgongs-pa ngo-sprad-pa*, "the direct introduction (*ngo-sprad-pa*) to the Primordial State (*dgongs-pa*) of Dzogchen."

16. *Ati'i dgongs-pa.*

17. *gSal dag rnyogs-bral gyi gshis.*

18. *dPe.*

19. *rGyud lung man-ngag gsum.* Among these three types of texts, Tantra (*rgyud*) gives an extensive exposition of the teaching, Agama (*lung*) focuses on a particular aspect or point in the teaching, and Upadesha (*man-ngag*) distills the essence of the teaching in a few words.

20. The *sGra thal-'gyur gyi rgyud* is the chief Tantra in the Dzogchen Upadesha Series. This and other Dzogchen Tantras speak of worlds other than ours where the Dzogchen teachings are extant.

21. *rTsa rgyud.*

22. *bShad rgyud.*

23. *Man-ngag rgyud.*

24. *Thal-ba'i zhing chen-po.*

25. *kLong chen-po'i zhing.*

26. *rGyud kyi dngos-po bcu.*

27. *Rang grol lam.*

28. *lTa-stangs.*

29. 'Bri-gung dpal bzang. A critic of Dzogchen, he was a scholar belonging to the Drigung Kagyudpa school.

30. Kun-mkhyen kLong-chen Rab-'byams-pa, 1308–1363.

31. Sog-zlog-pa bLo-gros rgyal-mtshan, 1552—?.

32. *Rig-pa'i khu-byug*, "the Cuckoo of Awareness." According to Nyingmapa tradition, this was the first Dzogchen text to be translated into Tibetan by Vairochana the translator. It is listed among the eighteen root texts of the Dzogchen Semde Series. Vairochana, a native Tibetan despite his Sanskrit name, was a contemporary and a disciple of Guru Padmasambhava in the eighth century.

33. Sangs-rgyas sbas-pa, eighth-ninth century CE.

34. *Ati'i dgongs-pa.*

35. *dPal rdo-rje phur-pa'i rdzogs-rim.* The methods of the Tantra system consist of the two stages (*rim gnyis*): the Utpattikrama, or generation process (*bskyed-rim*) and the Sampannakrama, or perfection process (*rdzogs-rim*). In the system of the Old Tantras (*rgyud rnying-ma'i lugs*) practiced by the Nyingmapas, the final stage or culmination of the perfection process is known as Dzogchen, the Great Perfection (*rdzogs-pa chen-po*). In the colophon, this text is attributed to Guru Padmasambhava himself. Vajrakilaya (rDo-rje phur-pa) is the principal Yidam (*yi-dam*), or meditation deity, practiced in the Nyingmapa school.

36. Prior to the eighth century of our era, when Zhang-zhung, or Western Tibet centering around Mount Kailas, was conquered by the Yarlung Dynasty of Central Tibet, the country was ruled as an independent kingdom by two successive dynasties, the Jyaruchan (Bya-ru-can) and the Ligmincha (Lig-mi-rgya). The Zhang-zhung king Triwer Sergyi Jyaruchan (Khri-wer gser gyi bya-ru-can) belonged to this first dynasty. Oral communication from Lopon Tenzin Namdak.

37. The dates for the Zhang-zhung king Triwer Sergyi Jyaruchan are uncertain, but according to Bonpo tradition, he was a contemporary of the Central Asian Buddha who established the Bon teachings, Tonpa Shenrab Miwoche (sTon-pa gShen-rab mi-bo-che). Namkhai Norbu Rinpoche does not indicate how he arrives at his date for Tonpa Shenrab and this king. An eighteenth-century Bonpo source, the *bsTan rtsis*, gives a date for Tonpa Shenrab, and, therefore, also for the era of this king, but a purely fabulous one of some 18,000 years ago.

38. *Yang-dag-pa'i sems bon*, "the Doctrine of the Perfect Mind." In Bonpo texts, the Tibetan word *bon* generally has the same functions as the word *chos* in Buddhist texts; they both translate the Sanskrit technical term *dharma*, "teaching, doctrine, reality," etc. The Hungarian scholar Uray suggested that the word *bon* derived from an old Tibetan verb, *'bond-pa*, meaning "to invoke the gods." The indigenous pre-Buddhist religion of Tibet was known as *Lha bon*, "the invoking of the gods." However, Beckwith points out that Tibetan *bon* may actually come from a Sogdian Buddhist word *bwn* meaning

"Dharma." The close connections of ancient Zhang-zhung with the Sogdians, an Iranian-speaking people who dominated the Silk Route in Central Asia to the northwest of Tibet before the advent of the Muslim conquest of that region, has been pointed out by the Bonpo Dzogchen master Lopon Tenzin Namdak (oral communication). Many old Bonpo texts, such as the *Ma rgyud*, the Bonpo Mother Tantra, claim to have been originally translated from the Iranian language of Tazig (probably Sogdian) into the language of Zhang-zhung, a Tibeto-Burman dialect closely related to Tibetan. See Christopher Beckwith, *The Tibetan Empire in Central Asia: A History of the Struggle for Great Power among Tibetans, Turks, Arabs, and Chinese during the Early Middle Ages* (Princeton: Princeton Univ. Press, 1987).

39. According to Bonpo tradition, Tonpa Shenrab was not born in Western Tibet or Zhang-zhung, but in Tazig (sTag-gzigs), or Iranian-speaking Central Asia (modern-day Uzbekistan and Tajikistan), in the country of Shambhala, or Olmo Lung-ring ('Ol-mo lung-ring). Modern Western scholars have doubted the historical existence of Tonpa Shenrab, asserting that he is a mere myth, his hagiography being based on the Buddhist *Lalitavistara*. However, there is much material in the three biographies of this teacher, the *mDo 'dus*, the *gZer-myig*, and the *gZi-brjid*, that is demonstrably not of Indian Buddhist origin. Karmay admits the probable historical existence of Tonpa Shenrab as some sort of gShen priest in Western Tibet in the seventh century. The title Tonpa (*ston-pa*), "Teacher," is applied not to an ordinary teacher but to one who reveals the higher truth and founds a spiritual lineage and tradition based on that truth.

40. Srong-btsan sgam-po, 569–650 CE.

41. Gyer-spungs sNang-bzher Lod-po, the disciple of Je Tapihritsa, seventh-eighth century CE.

42. The *Zhang-zhung snyan-rgyud*, "the aural transmission from Zhang-zhung," was an uninterrupted oral transmission tradition of Dzogchen (*bka'-ma*), deriving not from India, as was the case with the Nyingmapas, but from the country of Zhang-zhung in Western Tibet and preserved in the Bonpo school. The other systems of Bonpo Dzogchen are Terma (*gter-ma*), or rediscovered hidden treasure texts, found in the eleventh century and later.

43. In the view of Namkhai Norbu Rinpoche, both the Nyingmapa tradition deriving from Padmasambhava, Vimalamitra, and Vairochana and the Bonpo tradition deriving from Tapihritsa and Gyerpungpa in Zhang-zhung represent genuine historical traditions of Dzogchen, nearly identical in content and method. He further hypothesizes that these two traditions, the Indian and the Zhangzhungpa, have a common origin in the mysterious country of Uddiyana (O-rgyan), which was adjacent both to Northwest

India and to Western Tibet, that is to say, in Eastern Afghanistan. See C. S. Upasak, *History of Buddhism in Afghanistan* (Sarnath, Varanasi: Central Inst. of Higher Tibetan Studies, 1990).

44. Khri-srong lDe'u-btsan, 742–797.

45. *Yang-dag-pa'i sems bon rdzogs-chen gyi skor.*

46. *rDzogs-chen sde gsum.*

47. *rDzogs-chen gyi ston-pa bcu-gnyis.*

48. These Twelve Teachers of Dzogchen (*ston-pa bcu-gnyis*), as listed by Dodupchen Rinpoche in his *Tantric Doctrine according to the Nyingmapa School* (Gangtok, Sikkim: Namgyal Inst. of Tibetology, 1975, pp. 31–32), are as follows:

1. sTon-pa Khye'u snang-ba dam-pa
2. sTon-pa Khye'u 'od mi 'khrugs-pa
3. sTon-pa 'Jigs skyob-pa'i yid
4. sTon-pa gZhon-nu rol-ba rnam-par brtse-ba
5. sTon-pa 'Tsho-byed gzhon-nu
6. sTon-pa gZhon-nu dpa'-bo stob-ldan
7. sTon-pa Drang-srong khros-pa'i rgyal-po
8. sTon-pa gSer 'od dam-pa
9. sTon-pa brTse-bas rol-pa'i blo-gros
10. sTon-pa 'Od-srungs bgres-po
11. sTon-pa mNgon-rdzogs rgyal-po
12. sTon-pa Shakya thub-pa (Shakyamuni)

At least one of these prehistoric teachers (number 9) is described as being a Sogdian (*sog-po*).

49. *Yang gsang rdzogs-chen snying-thig gi rgyud bcu-bdun.* These are the principal Tantras of the Dzogchen Upadesha Series.

50. mKhar-chen bza' ye-shes mtsho-rgyal. She was the Tibetan consort and companion of Padmasambhava.

51. *Man-ngag rgyab chos.*

52. *rGyud rab tu rgyas-pa'i man-ngag.*

53. *Zab 'dus man-ngag.*

54. *dKar-chag.*

55. Lha-lcan Padma-gsal.

56. *rNam-shes.* It is this ever-changing stream of consciousness that reincarnates, providing continuity lifetime after lifetime.

57. Padma las-'brel-rtsal.

58. *rGyud rab tu rgyas-pa'i man-ngag.*

59. *Brag seng-ge 'dra-ba.*

60. *Zab 'dud man-ngag.*

61. Dang-lung khra-mo brag.

62. Tshul-khrims rdo-rje.

63. Padma las-'brel-rtsal (1291–1315)

64. Myang Ting-'dzin bzang-po.

65. mChims-phu'i dge-gung.

66. dBu-ru zhwa'i lha-khang.

67. *bShad rgyud.*

68. *sNyan rgyud.*

69. 'Bro Rin-chen 'bar.

70. sBas bLo-gros bdang-phyug.

71. lDang-ma lhun-rgyal.

72. Zhwa'i mgon-po.

73. lCe-btsun Seng-ge dbang-phyug, eleventh-twelfth century.

74. *'Od lus.* According to Nyingmapa tradition, the Mahasiddha Vimalamitra never experienced death, but while still alive, he transformed his material body into a Body of Light, a process known as the Great Transfer (*'pho-ba chen-po*). He is thus able to manifest visibly to his disciples at any point in time and history and in a form of his own choosing.

75. *Kha-byang.* Complete cycles of hidden treasure texts generally possess such guidebooks. These are obtained by the Terton before recovering the main cache of hidden treasures.

76. *sDe-tshan lnga.*

77. *Zhal-'chems.*

78. *Rig-'dzin gyi 'das-rjes rnam-pa bzhi.*

79. *Srog snying.*

80. *Chos zab-pa'i gnad kyi mthar thug rnams.*

INTRODUCTION

1. This is the view of Namkhai Norbu Rinpoche, who in his approach emphasizes the nonsectarian nature of the Dzogchen teachings, although traditionally these teachings have been associated with the Nyingmapa school. Other Tibetan Lamas generally take a more sectarian stance, insisting on the exclusive association of Dzogchen with Nyingmapa tradition. However, Namkhai Norbu Rinpoche points out that the real meaning of the term *Dzogchen* is the Primordial State of the individual (*kun-bzang dgongs-pa*), and that, therefore, it does not represent just another sectarian viewpoint associated with a particular historical school. Again, with respect to Dzogchen, the term *lta-ba* means "a way of seeing" rather than an intellectual view or credo. In this context, direct personal experience is more important than precise philosophical formulation. The approach of Norbu Rinpoche here is reminiscent of that of D. T. Suzuki, who, in his writings on Zen Buddhism, tended to universalize Zen and project it beyond a purely sectarian context. For example, see his *Zen Buddhism: Selected Writings of D.T. Suzuki* (Garden City, New York: Doubleday, 1956) and *Zen and Japanese Culture* (New York: Pantheon, 1959). The claim that Dzogchen represents the highest teaching of the Buddha, and so forth, has offended some Western Buddhists, especially practitioners of Theravada and of Zen; but here we have simply repeated the traditional claim within the Nyingmapa school made from the perspective of their own particular classification of the teachings of the Buddha into the nine successive vehicles to enlightenment. Among the Nyingmapas in general, this claim is not employed in a polemical manner to attack and denigrate other Buddhist doctrines and traditions existing in Tibet. Of course, leading Lama-scholars of the newer schools, namely, the Sakyapas, the Kagyudpas, and the Gelugpas, do not necessarily recognize the claim the Nyingmapas make for Dzogchen being the highest peak of all the vehicles to enlightenment (*theg-pa'i yang rtse*). See Part Three, "Historical Origins of Dzogchen."

Again, according to Namkhai Norbu Rinpoche, the original Dzogchen texts in Tibetan, especially the Upadeshas, always pointed to the practitioner's immediate experience. They were composed in ordinary nonphilosophical language and were easy to understand. Philosophical argumentation was at a minimum. But the commentaries and expositions written in later centuries are much more difficult to read and much more complex in thought because scholars had their own philosophical biases and wanted to assert and justify their own points of view, usually at the expense of other scholars. Part of the effort of Longchen Rabjampa in the fourteenth century, for example, was to justify and defend the Dzogchen teachings from the accusations of heresy and inauthenticity made by certain Lama-scholars of the newer schools. He set about to cast Dzogchen, as he did in his famous *Theg-mchog rin-po-che'i mdzod*, in the very philosophical and scholastic format used at the time by scholars to expound systematically the Sutra and the Tantra traditions. He did this in order to make Dzogchen comprehensible, if not acceptable, to the mind-set of these same scholar-monks. The same was true of Jigmed Lingpa in the eighteenth century. There exists a similar tendency nowadays, in certain quarters, to translate Tibetan Dzogchen texts into an artificial language of neologisms and rarefied academic jargon, far removed from the ordinary language of everyday life. Perhaps the aim here is also to make Dzogchen acceptable as a serious philosophical system to modern academic intellectuals. But this does little service to those who actually desire to practice the teachings in this present life and social context. In terms of Dzogchen, we must first look to the essential meaning and communicate that, rather than to theories, speculations, and system-building. We must first grasp the principle, and, with regard to Dzogchen, the principle is that of an immediate intrinsic awareness (*rig-pa*), which is prior to and transcends the thought process.

In the traditional exposition of Dzogchen, it is implied that this quintessential state known as Rigpa is the same for all individuals, for all sentient beings whether they be human or nonhuman. Rigpa is the opposite of ignorance or the lack of awareness. This state of Rigpa is a pure, contentless, imageless awareness or sense of presence. Although it is often spoken of in exalted language, rather than being something mystical or otherworldly, the state of Rigpa is quite ordinary and immediate, belonging to this world of the here and now. It does not necessarily involve any occult phenomena or beatific visions. On the contrary, Rigpa represents the ground of all possible experience, ordinary and nonordinary, in this dimension or in any other dimension, including the Bardo, or after-death experience. Without Rigpa, to a certain degree, there would be no experience of anything whatsoever. Again, in terms of its intrinsic ordinariness, we are reminded of the treatment of Satori in the Zen tradition of China and Japan by D. T. Suzuki in his writings. Whether Rigpa is to be considered a mystical experience or not is a question of definition. In the Dzogchen tradition itself, Rigpa is not considered a mystical experience (*nyams*) or as a content of consciousness or even as a subjective state of consciousness. (See my *Self-Liberation through Seeing with Naked Awareness* [Barrytown, NY: Station Hill Press, 1989].) In any event, there exist many kinds of mysticism, and mystical experiences may or may not be the same for all individuals. Some scholars assert that they are the same (Vivekananda, Radhakrishnan, etc.), while others deny this and attempt to distinguish different categories of mystical experiences. (As an example of the latter, see R. C. Zaehner, *Mysticism Sacred and Profane*

[Oxford: Clarendon Press, 1957].) As for my own view, whether mystical experiences differ among individuals or whether they are ultimately identical for everyone, the interpretations of mystical states of consciousness, both religious and philosophical, certainly do differ, and these interpretations evolve and change over time for various historical and philosophical reasons. Thus, even if the ultimate mystical experience is beyond time, mysticism itself has a history, just as does any religion. With regard to mystical experiences generally, and here with regard to Dzogchen in particular, both of these aspects, the universal nonhistorical and the particular historical, must be appreciated.

2. I have prepared a translation of this collection of Bonpo Dzogchen texts in consultation with Lopon Tenzin Namdak, which we hope to see published in the near future. Selections from these translations may be found in *The Bonpo Bulletin* (Copenhagen, 1989–1991), and in my forthcoming book *Space, Awareness, and Energy*, to be published by Snow Lion.

3. Prahevajra or Prajnabhava Hevajra. See Part Three, "Historical Origins of Dzogchen."

4. These are the *thal-ba bcu-gsum* found in the *sGra thal-gyur*, the chief Tantra among the Upadesha class of the Dzogchen Tantras. The cosmology and cosmogony found herein and in other Dzogchen Tantras bear a certain similarity to the cosmology found in the *Avatamsaka Sutra*. A summary of this cosmology written by Dodrubchen Rinpoche, which I have translated under the title *Cosmology of the Dzogchen Tantras*, will be published in the future.

5. These matters I deal with a bit more extensively in *The Pure Melodious Voice of the Dragon* and *Cosmology of the Dzogchen Tantras* (forthcoming).

6. See the biography of Garab Dorje, Part Two.

7. Dakinis (*mkha' 'gro ma*, literally, "she [*ma*] who goes ['*gro*] in the sky [*mkha'*]" or "she who moves in space") are manifestations of energy in feminine form. A Dakini may manifest as a human being, usually a woman possessing spiritual knowledge and certain psychic powers, as a goddess, or as a spirit. Generally, Jnana Dakinis, or Wisdom Dakinis (*ye-shes mkha'- 'gro*), i.e., those who possess *ye-shes* or jnana (wisdom, knowledge, gnosis), are enlightened beings in feminine form. They are distinguished from Karma Dakinis, or Action Dakinis (*las kyi mkha'-'gro*), who are worldly goddesses, spirits, witches, etc. Although powerful and possessing occult knowledge, these latter still belong to Samsara and are therefore not enlightened beings. This question of divine feminine energy, the Dakini, I treat much more fully in *The Secret Book of Simhamukha* (forthcoming, Vidyadhara Publications) and in *The Dance of the Dakinis* (forthcoming).

8. Although many of these old Tantras were not included in the official Tibetan canon of scriptures known as the *Kangyur* (*bka'-'gyur*, "the translation of the Word"), they were later gathered together by Ratna Lingpa (1403–1479), Terdak Lingpa (1634–1714), and others into a large collection known as the *Nyingmai Gyud-bum* (*rNying-ma'i rgyud 'bum*). See Part Three, "Historical Origins of Dzogchen."

9. In this context divine pride (*lha'i nga-rgyal*) should not be confused with ordinary pride or egotism (*nga-rgyal*), which is a passion or negative emotion (*nyon-mongs-pa*, Skt. *kleśa*, literally, "defilement") and therefore represents ignorance. Nor should this divine pride be confused with the sin of Adam in the biblical myth, his pride here representing the desire to be God. By disobeying God's ordinance not to eat of the fruit of the tree of the knowledge of good and evil, Adam would set himself up as the virtual equal of God. This is not what is meant here; one is not desiring to become God. One's empirical personality and ego, which are limited and ignorant, are characterized by ordinary worldly pride or a sense of identity. This personality or ego is not God or divine. Nor does the spiritual pride of the would-be saint represent divine pride. Rather divine pride is a knowledge of, and acceptance of, one's innate enlightened nature or Buddha-nature and a sense of identity of one's purified (nonegotistical) consciousness with a divine energy or god-form (*yi-dam*, Skt. *devatā*) which is a particular manifestation of this innate enlightened Buddha-nature. This does not represent an inflation of the empirical ego to divine status, but rather a manifesting of one's innate being and potential in the absence of ego. At the commencement of sadhana practice, this empirical ego, as well as one's ordinary perception of one's immediate environment, is dissolved into the state of emptiness, or shunyata (*stong-pa nyid*). Then, in this state of imageless contemplation, which is characterized by both emptiness and luminosity, one remanifests oneself in a purified divine form known as the symbolic being, or Samayasattva (*dam-tshig sems-dpa'*). It is into this purified vessel that the higher energies of power and inspiration emanating from one's inherent enlightened Buddha-nature are invoked out of the infinite sky of the Mind, descending into this purified form of the Samayasattva, which has been constructed and visualized by the activity of the mind. These energies of inspiration or blessings present themselves in specific forms known as the Jnanasattvas, or knowledge beings (*ye-shes sems-dpa'*). Thereupon these two, the symbolic being and the knowledge being, merge into a unity, becoming one and inseparable (*dam ye dbyer med*). One then develops a sense of identity of actually being this unitary entity for the duration of the sadhana practice. And because of this sense of identity or divine pride, all of the powers and potentialities of this divine manifestation or god-form are actualized in one's experience. At least, this is the case for the adept or Mahasiddha. I treat this process of sadhana or tantric transformation (*grub-*

thabs) much more fully in *The Staircase to Akanishtha* (forthcoming, Vidyadhara Publications) and also in *The Secret Book of Simhamukha* (forthcoming, Vidyadhara Publications).

10. The Sambhogakaya is said to be characterized by five certainties (*ngespa lnga*) as to place, teacher, audience, teaching, and time. That is to say, the Sambhogakaya, in the guise of the Teacher Vajrasattva, manifests in eternity beyond time, in Akanishtha, the highest plain of existence, and nowhere else. Here he teaches only the highest, most esoteric, doctrines of the Mahayana and the Vajrayana to an audience consisting exclusively of great Bodhisattvas who have attained the seventh through the tenth stages (Skt. *bhūmi*) of their spiritual evolution. In contrast, the Nirmanakaya manifests five uncertainties with regard to place, teacher, audience, teaching, and time. That is to say, Nirmanakayas can manifest at any time throughout the dimensions of Samsara to various different types of beings possessing various different levels of intellectual development and spiritual maturation. The teachings that the Nirmanakaya expounds to these audiences depend on the circumstances, the needs, and the capacities of the individuals in question to understand.

11. Generally, the views (*lta-ba*) of Mahamudra and of Dzogchen are the same, but according to most of my Lama informants, they differ in some respects in terms of meditation (*sgom-pa*) and conduct (*spyod-pa*). See the Appendix of my *Self-Liberation through Seeing with Naked Awareness*, pp. 103–106.

12. In the past, this term has been erroneously translated as "heart drop," which makes no sense; properly "drop" is *thig-pa*, not *thig-le*.

13. Or to put it another way, the three essential points refer to the view, the meditation, and the conduct of Dzogchen that correspond to the three statements of Garab Dorje: the direct introduction to the state of Rigpa, having no doubts with regard to it, and continuing in that state with confidence.

PART ONE: THREE STATEMENTS THAT STRIKE THE ESSENTIAL POINTS

Commentary on "The Special Teaching of the Wise and Glorious King" by the Translator

1. See my *Self-Liberation through Seeing with Naked Awareness*.

2. See his *Theg mchog rin-po-che'i mdzod*, vol. VAM, pp. 75-84.

3. On this, the continuous practice of contemplation both day and night, see the text by Namkhai Norbu translated by myself in *The Cycle of Day and Night* (Barrytown, NY: Station Hill, 1987).

4. See the discussion in the Appendix of my *Self-Liberation*, pp. 81–87.

5. On how to practice the natural Clear Light in relation to sleep and lucid dreaming, see Namkhai Norbu, *The Cycle of Day and Night*.

6. For the Buddhist critique of mysticism, see the Appendix to my *Self-Liberation*, pp. 81-87, 96-103.

7. See the Appendix in my *Self-Liberation*, pp. 96-103.

8. On gnosis and wisdom, see E. Conze, *Buddhism: Its Essence and Development* (London: B. Cassirer, 1951) and E. Conze, *Buddhist Thought in India* (London: George Allen & Unwin, 1962).

Interlinear Commenatry to "The Last Testament of Garab Dorje" by the Translator

1. See Namkhai Norbu and Adriano Clementi, eds., *Dzogchen: The Self-Perfected State* (Ithaca: Snow Lion, 1995), pp. 37-41.

PART TWO: THE LIFE OF GARAB DORJE AND GURU SADHANA

Translator's Introduction

1. *Gangs ljongs rgyal bstan yongs-rdzogs kyi phyi-mo snga 'gyur rdo-rje'i thegpa'i bstan-pa rin-po-che ji-ltar byung-ba'i tshul dag cing gsal-bar brjod-pa lha dbang g.yul las rgyal-ba'i rnga-bo-che'i sgra dbyangs* (Kalimpong, 1967), chapter two, section III, entitled *Atiyoga'i skor*, fol. 119–142.

2. See Samten G. Karmay, *The Great Perfection* (Leiden: Brill, 1988) p. 225.

3. *sNying-thig ya-bzhi*, vol. 9, fol. 1–179, (New Delhi: Jamyang Trulku Tsewang and L. Tashi, 1970–71). The section translated here is from fol. 89–110.

4. Oral communication from Yangthang Rinpoche.

5. On the archetypes found in the lunar and chthonic symbolism of the Higher Tantras, that is, the Mahayoga and the Anuttara Tantras, see "Is Dzogchen an Authentic Buddhist Teaching?" in Part Three. Since this present book deals principally with the question of Dzogchen and not Buddhist Tantra or Tantra in general, I cannot go into the highly interesting dichotomy between the uranian and solar symbolism in the Mahayana Sutras and the Yoga Tantras and the chthonic and lunar symbolism of the Mahayoga and Anuttara Tantras. This dichotomy is also exemplified by the *Zhi-khro*, "the Peaceful and Wrathful Deities," described in the *Tibetan Book of the Dead*. On

solar vs. lunar, uranian vs. chthonic, etc., in general, see Mircea Eliade, *Patterns in Comparative Religion* (Cleveland: World, 1970), pp. 124–187. Also see my booklet *Wicca, Paganism, and Tantra* (Freehold: Vidyadhara, 1994).

The Life of Garab Dorje

1. According to the *Phug-lugs* system of astrology and chronology, the Parinirvana of the Buddha Shakyamuni occurred in 881 BCE. Here it is also said that Garab Dorje was born 360 years after the Parinirvana, that is, in 521 BCE. Elsewhere it is said that he realized the Body of Light some 544 years afterwards, that is, in 337 BCE. On the problem of dating Garab Dorje, see "Historical Origins of Dzogchen" in Part Three.

2. Aryadesha (*Phags-yul*), "the noble land," was the usual designation for India in Sanskrit Buddhist texts. The ancient name for Bodh Gaya, where Shakyamuni attained the realization of Buddhahood, was Vajrasana (rDorje gdan), "the diamond throne of enlightenment." This site represents the sacred center of the Buddhist cosmos, and all directions and distances are measured from here in yojanas. A yojana (*dpag-tshad*) is a little more than a mile. In Nyingmapa texts it is usually said that the country of Uddiyana lay to the northwest of Aryadesha or India, somewhere in modern-day Pakistan or Afghanistan. Some scholars, such as Giuseppe Tucci, would identify it with the Swat Valley in Pakistan. On the other hand, Upasak compiles the evidence for clearly locating Uddiyana in eastern Afghanistan. See C. S. Upadak, *History of Buddhism in Afghanistan* (Varanasi: 1990).

3. The Kosha or Koshana had human bodies and humanlike hands and feet, but with iron claws on the tips of their fingers and toes. Their faces resembled those of bears (*dred*). They could walk upright on two feet or run along on all four, and thus they resembled in their general appearance the Yeti, or wild man (*mi rgod*). (Oral communication from C. R. Lama.) It is uncertain whether the non-Tibetan word *koshana* has any relationship to the name Kushana, a non-Indian people of Scythian origin who once had an empire in the very region where Uddiyana was located. The Kushana rulers, foremost among them Kanishka, who lived around the time of Christ (78–102 CE), were patrons of the Buddhist religion, certainly of the Sarvastivadin school, but probably also, as tradition asserts, of Mahayana Buddhism. The great Mahayana master Nagarjuna composed an epistle to this king or his successor. Kanishka emulated the emperor Ashoka in his support, financial and otherwise, for Buddhism, but also in his toleration for other religions; his coins display, besides the Buddha, the images of the gods of Hinduism and Zoroastrianism, and also ancient Greek deities. See A. K. Warder, *Indian Buddhism* (New Delhi: Motilal, 1970) p. 345.

4. Uparaja (U-pa-ra-dza) is not a personal name, but a title meaning "a lesser king."

5. Dudjom Rinpoche has Sudharma for the name of this princess, which is proper Sanskrit. In the *'Dra 'bag* (see "Historical Origins of Dzogchen" in Part Three), she is called Praharini, and her father, the Uparaja, is identified as King Indrabhuti, which is probably a dynastic name for the rulers of Uddiyana.

6. The Pravrajya (*rab tu byung-ba*) is the ordination for a novice monk or nun, entailing 36 vows in the Tibetan tradition. The Upasampada (*bsnyen-par rdzogs-pa*) is the ordination for a fully ordained Bhikshu, or monk (*dge-slong*), with 253 vows to be observed, whereas a Bhikshuni, or nun (*dge-slong-ma*), has some 300 vows.

7. dGe-sbyor skong. Dudjom Rinpoche specifies that these were practices belonging to the Yoga Tantra.

8. Although not explicitly stated, it is implied that this mysterious white man is the Buddha Vajrasattva. In both the Yoga Tantras and the Anuttara Tantras, during the kalasha-abhishekha, or vase initiation (*bum dbang*), the individual empowerments of the Panchakula, or the Five Buddha Families (*rigs lnga*) are conferred. These empowerments transform the five skandhas, or impure aggregates of one's personal existence, revealing that, in actuality, they are the five Tathagatas, or aspects of Buddhahood (*rgyal-ba rigs lnga*).

9. The Maras (*bdud*) are black demons of relentlessly evil disposition, and the Brahmas (*tshang-pa*) are the gods dwelling on the higher mental planes of the Rupadhatu, or Form World. In the Hindu traditions found in the Puranas and elsewhere, Brahma is the name of the Creator God, but in the Buddhist context, Brahma is a generic term. The Gyalpo (*rgyal-po*), the Tsen (*btsan*), and the dMu (*dmu*) are native Tibetan names for different races of spirits.

10. A Nirmita (*sprul-pa*) is an emanation or a manifestation. A Buddha or other realized being is able to project many such Nirmitas simultaneously in an infinite variety of forms.

11. The Devas, or gods, address the infant Garab Dorje as their Teacher (*ston-pa*) and as their Protector or Lord (*mgon-po*), which indicates that he, as a Nirmanakaya Buddha or manifest enlightened being, is more exalted than even the gods on high. The title Lord or Natha (*mgon-po*) is also given to the Primordial Buddha Samantabhadra (Kun tu bzang-po), who is addressed in the Tantras as the Primordial Lord or Adinatha (*gdod-ma'i mgon-po*). Adinatha is also a title borne by Shiva in the Natha-sampradaya tradition of India, a Shaivite sect of Yogins. During the high Middle Ages, Buddhist

Mahasiddhas and Shaivite Yogins were in close informal personal contact. Some of them, like Matsyendranatha and Gorakshanatha, had both Buddhist and Shaivite affiliations. Their names are found, for example, in the Buddhist list of the eighty-four Mahasiddhas and in the Hindu lineage for Hatha Yoga.

12. The Devas (*lha*), the Nagas (*klu*), and the Yakshas (*gnod-sbyin*) are the worldly deities or spirits who inhabit the heavens, the underworld, and the surface of the earth, respectively. The Lokapalas (*jig-rten gyi skyong-ba*) are the deities who guard the ten directions of the universe against assault from the outside forces of chaos. In the east there is Indra, in the south Yama, in the west Varuna, in the north Kubera, in the southeast Agni, in the southwest Nirrita, in the northwest Vayu, in the northeast Ishana, at the zenith Brahma, and at the nadir Vishnu. These ten Lokapalas are found in a number of Buddhist mandalas, and the same list of ten deities appears in the Hindu Puranas.

13. A Pandita is a scholar knowing Sanskrit.

14. A Purohita is a priest of the Vedic tradition of the Brahmans.

15. The king recognized the young boy to be a Mahapurusha (*gang-zag chen-po*), a great personage, that is to say, an individual possessing the 32 major marks and the 80 minor characteristics of a Buddha or of a Chakravartin, a universal monarch.

16. The four types of birth are birth from the womb, birth from an egg, birth from heat and moisture, and apparitional birth. He circulated in the special realms of rebirth (*nye 'khor 'khor-bas*); these special realms (*nye 'khor*) are created by the individual's particular idiosyncratic karma, and their locations are various and uncertain.

17. *Ting-nge-'dzin la snyoms-par bzhugs-pa'i tshul bstan-pas.* Samadhi (*ting-nge-dzin*) here means the state of contemplation. Generally, *Samapatti* (*bsnyoms-par bzhugs-pa*), "remaining in equanimity," refers to the higher levels of abstract absorption in meditation, where one meditates without there being some concrete object of meditation.

18. The Tirthikas (*mu-stegs-pa*) are Hindus and other Indo-Iranian non-Buddhists. The sinful ways refer to the practice of sacrificing living animals.

19. Rather than two Dakinis, as indicated by this version of the story, Dudjom Rinpoche, according to C. R. Lama, appears to distinguish three Dakinis here: 'Jig-rten bde-ba'i ro dang ldan-ma, bDe-byed ser-mo, and Yon-tan mtha'-yas.

20. *Rang-byung rang-babs kyi yi-ge sprul-pa'i sku.* The terms *self-originated* (*rang-byung*) and *self-occurring* (*rang-babs*) both mean natural and unartificial. Stupas, Buddha images, works of art, books, inscribed letters, and so on,

may be Shailpa-nirmanakayas (*bzo yi sprul-sku*), that is, spontaneous manifestations of the Nirmanakaya in the form of art (*bzo,* Skt. *śilpa*) or other material objects.

21. A short lineage of transmission (*nye brgyud*) for the teachings is distinguished from a long lineage of transmission (*ring brgyud*). In the case of the former, the individual receiving it finds himself very close to the original source of the transmission, having a more immediate and direct access to the power or energy (*byin-rlabs*) of the teaching, without a long line of teachers and disciples intervening, as in the case with the latter.

22. The reference is to special sites which are source places (*gnas 'byung*) for the revelation of the Tantras, the esoteric teachings of the Buddhas. Another very important site for the revelation of the Tantras is the great cremation ground of Shitavana (*dur-khrod chen-po* bSil-ba'i tshal), the cool forest, which is near modern Bodh Gaya. Since in a cremation ground (*dur-khrod,* Skt. *śmāśana*), the human corpses are exposed or cremated, the Tibetan term should not be translated as "cemetery" or "graveyard."

23. Some Lamas interpret this as a Garuda.

24. The five sciences (*rig-gnas lnga*) are (1) the science of grammar (*sgra'i rig-pa*), (2) the science of rhetoric and dialectics (*tshad-ma'i rig-pa*), (3) the science of medicine (*gso yi rig-pa*), (4) the science of arts and crafts (*bzo yi rig-pa*), and (5) the inner sciences (*nang gi rig-pa*), that is, the spiritual sciences of Buddhism. The master's name Manjushrimitra (Jam-dpal bshes-gnyen) means "the friend of Manjushri," the latter being the great Bodhisattva of Wisdom and the patron of all the arts and sciences of civilization.

25. Here reference is made to the four stages in the development of vision (*snang-ba bzhi*) in relation to Thodgal practice. The Yogin may realize the rainbow Body of Light (*'ja'-lus*) through perfecting this practice. (See the notes to the *'Das-rjes* translation.) At the time when Garab Dorje transcended the fourth stage of vision known as the culmination of Reality (*chos-nyid zad-pa*) and thereby realized the Body of Light (*'od lus*), his disciple Manjushrimitra simultaneously realized the second stage of vision, known as the increasing of experiences (*nyams gong phel-ba*).

26. *sPrul-pa rang-bzhin gyis gnas byed-do.*

27. *Sems gnas-pa rnams la sems kyi sde / bya bral rnams la klong gi sde / gnad gtso-bo rnams la man-ngag gi sde.*

28. That is to say, the *sNying-thig,* or the Essence of the Mind teachings of the Dzogchen Upadesha Series.

29. A vishvavajra (*sna-tshogs rdo-rje*) is a double vajra or diamond scepter in the form of an equal-armed cross.

30. That is to say, these texts of the *sNyan-rgyud* and the *bShad-rgyud* were concealed as *gter-ma*, or hidden treasure texts, and placed in the custody of the Dakinis (*mkha'-'gro-ma*) and the Dharmapatis (*chos-bdag*), who would be their guardians and protectors.

31. *Ke'u-ri ma-mo brgyad*. The Matrikas (*ma-mo*), literally "the Mothers," are female nature spirits found in wild and awesome places. In particular, reference is made to a group of eight goddesses headed by Gauri (Ke'u-ri). They also appear in the *Tibetan Book of the Dead* and in certain mandalas of the Anuttara Tantras, such as Hevajra, as follows: Gauri, Chauri, Vetali, Ghasmari, Pukkasi, Shavari, Chandali, and Dombi. HVT I.iii. See David Snellgrove, *The Hevajra Tantra* (London: Oxford Univ. Press, 1959), vol. 1, p. 58.

32. A Makara (*chu-srin*) is a sea monster, at times said to resemble a crocodile, at other times resembling a dolphin with an elephant snout.

33. Anandakumara (Kun-dga' gzhon-nu) is a form of Bhairava, the terrifying aspect of the god Shiva. Residing in the cremation ground, standing amidst hosts of Dakinis and Matrikas, he superintends their bloody nocturnal rites.

34. *gSod-byed ma-mo*. Elsewhere, Durga is cited as their queen. Oral communication from C. R. Lama.

35. A Yogeshvara (*rnal-byor dbang-phyug*), "Lord of Yoga," is a master practitioner of the esoteric methods of the Higher Tantras. Such a master is engaged in various kinds of ascetic conduct of the Yogins (*rnal-byor-pa brtul-zhugs kyi spyod-pa sna-tshogs byed-pa*) prescribed in the Tantras, including Guhyacharya (*gsang-spyod*), "secret conduct." This refers to higher tantric practices, especially sexual yoga (*thabs lam*) done with a consort partner or Yogini.

36. *Ting-nge-'dzin skyong-ba la . . . snyoms-par bzhugs*.

PART THREE: HISTORICAL ORIGINS OF DZOGCHEN

The Problems of Historiography

1. See the introduction by Hendrik Kern to his translation of *The Sadharma-pundarika, or the Lotus of the True Law, Sacred Books of the East*, vol.21 (Oxford: Clarendon, 1909).

2. This is the assertion of Samten G. Karmay in his Ph.D. thesis *Origin and Early Development of the Tibetan Religious Traditions of the Great Perfection* (1986) at SOAS, the University of London, as well as in his recent book *The Great Perfection: A Philosophical and Meditative Teaching of Tibetan Buddhism* (Leiden: Brill, 1988). This contention is dealt with below.

3. On the Book of Enoch, also known as *I Enoch* and *The Ethiopic Book of Enoch*, see Jozef Tadeusz Malik, *The Books of Enoch, Aramaic Fragments of Qumran Cave 4* (Oxford: Clarendon, 1976). Also see J. C. Greenfield and M. E.Stone, "The Books of Enoch and the Traditions of Enoch," in *Numen*, vol. 26, 1979, pp. 89–103. The standard translation is that of Robert Henry Charles, *The Book of Enoch or I Enoch* (Oxford: Clarendon, 1912). On the Book of Daniel, see John Joseph Collins, *The Apocalyptic Vision of the Book of Daniel* (Missoula, MT: Scholar's Press, 1977). Also on the Daniel cycle in general, see Buckner B. Trawick, *The Bible as Literature: The Old Testament and Apocrypha*, (New York: Barnes and Noble, 1970) pp. 311–24.

4. The kingdom of Ugarit flourished on the north Syrian coast c. 1500 BCE. In 1930–31 at the site of Ras Sharma near the Syrian port of Latakia, a vast hoard of clay tablets was discovered containing alphabetic inscriptions in the Ugaritic language. This language was a West Semitic dialect closely related to later Hebrew and later Phoenician. Much of this extant Ugaritic literature and mythology prefigures the Hebrew literature of the Old Testament, c. 1000 BCE and later.

5. A similar process may be observed in the Western tradition. The oldest part of the Bible, the so-called "J" or "Yahwist Document," according to critical scholarship, dates from the reign of King David, c. 1000 BCE. In fact, it is believed that this document was actually commissioned by King David in order to justify and legitimize his dynasty and the monarchy he established over the Hebrew tribes, whereas previously the tribes had been ruled over by elected judges and not hereditary kings. But the J Document was not fabricated at that time solely in David's interest. It drew most certainly on oral tradition, that is, on Hebrew legends and even on pagan Canaanite mythology. But it also drew on earlier written texts no longer extant, for two of these prebiblical texts, the *Book of Yasher* and the *Book of the Wars of Yahweh*, are specifically mentioned in the Old Testament. It may even be that David had these sources and any other rival versions of Hebrew history destroyed, in order to leave the J Document surviving as the only official version of the history of the Hebrew people which culminated in the establishment of the kingdom of David. Then c. 700 BCE this J Document was reworked and combined with material deriving from the northern Hebrew tribes. This material was contained in the more systematic and elaborated E Document and is now largely found in Genesis and Exodus. This "E" or "Elohist Document" is so called because the principal name employed for the Hebrew god in the text is Elohim (the plural form of the name El, "god," the old Canaanite creator god), in contrast to the J Document of southern origin that uses the name Yahweh. During the reign of Josiah, king of Judah, in 621 BCE, a text now known as the "D Document" or Deuteronomy, consisting principally of rules relating to religious practices,

was inserted into the combined J–E text. This interpolated text is called the D Document. About 570 BCE, the so-called Holiness Code, the "H Document," was added to the above composite text as Leviticus 17–26.

Then, after the return from the Babylonian exile about 500 BCE, the priests and scribes in Jerusalem, under the leadership of Ezra, felt the need to consolidate and systematize the Hebrew traditions of law and history. They preserved the inherited material of the J, E, D, and H Documents, but edited them and added new material. These scribes were much under Babylonian intellectual influence, so that they tended to classify everything in terms of sevens— reflecting the Babylonian practice of classifying everything in heaven and earth in accordance with the seven astrological planets. They also added the Babylonian creation myth as Genesis 1, somewhat as a preface to the earlier Canaanite creation myth that we now know as Genesis 2. This priestly material is known as the "P Document." Then about 350 BCE, all of this material was edited once again and largely put into the form in which we find it today. In this way the canon became closed to the inclusion of any new prophetic material c. 150 BCE. All of this amply demonstates that sacred texts grow and become more elaborated with additional material over the course of time.

On modern biblical criticism and the significance of the five principal documents—J, E, D, H, and P—which enter into the composition of the Torah or Pentateuch, see Walter Beltz, *God and the Gods: Myths of the Bible* (New York: Penguin, 1983).

The Historical Existence of Garab Dorje

1. See, for example, Edward Conze, "Buddhism and Gnosis," in *Further Buddhist Studies* (Oxford: Cassirer, 1975), and Elaine H. Pagels, *The Gnostic Gospels* (New York: Vintage, 1981). I have also considered the problem in my *Mystical Illumination in Gnosticism and Buddhist Tantra* (unpublished).

2. A translation of this text will be found in Namkhai Norbu and Kennard Lipman, *Primordial Experience* (Boston: Shambhala, 1987) pp. 55–68.

3. On this, see Lipman's introduction and notes in Norbu and Lipman, ibid.

4. See the *'Brug-pa chos-'byung* (1575) of Padma Karpo ('Brug-chen Padma dkar-po) and the *mKhas-pa'i dga'-ston* (1545, 1565) of Pawo Tsuglag (dPa'-bo gtsug-lag phreng-ba).

5. Tulku Thondup, *The Tantric Tradition of the Nyingmapas* (Marion: Buddhayana, 1984) pp. 46–48; p. 191, n. 194.

6. *Phug-lugs* is the system of astrology and chronology based on the *Pad dkar zhal-lung*, a detailed commentary on the famous explanation of the Kalachakra system entitled the *Vimalaprabha* (*rGyud 'grel dri-med 'od*),

traditionally attributed to the legendary king of Shambhala, Kulika Pundarika (Rigs-ldan Padma dkar-po), c. 176 BCE. This commentary, more fully the *Padma dkar-po'i zhal-lung* (1447), was written by Phug-pa Lhun-grub rgya-mtsho (fifteenth century), with the assistance of his disciple mKhas-grub Nor-bzang rgya-mtsho (1423–1513). The latter wrote a number of supplementary works on astrology. The system of Phug-pa was adopted by the regent of the Fifth Dalai, sDe-srid Sangs-rgyas rgya-mtsho (1653–1705) in his famous encyclopedic exposition of astrology, the *Vaidurya dkar-po* (1687). From his time onward, the *Phug-lugs* spread throughout Tibet, completely replacing earlier astrological systems, such as the *mTshur-lugs* of mTshur-phu Don-grub 'od-zer.

7. See Anthony Kennedy Warder, *Indian Buddhism* (Delhi: Motilal, 1970) p. 44.

8. Namkhai Norbu and John Shane, eds.*The Crystal and the Way of Light* (London: RKP, 1986) p. 20.

9. Tarthang Tulku, *Crystal Mirror*, vol. 5 (Emeryville, CA: Dharma, 1977). His account of Garab Dorje is found on pp. 182–86 and this date on p. 328.

10. Namkhai Norbu and Adriano Clemente, eds., *Dzogchen: The Self-Perfected State* (London: Arkana, 1989) p. xii; p. 84, n. 3.

11. Norbu and Clemente, ibid. According to the *bsTan rtsis kun las btus-pa*, published in China, n.d., Garab Dorje was born in the wood-horse year (*shing glang / rdzogs-chen bstan-pa'i bdag-po dga'-rab rdo-rje khrungs*). Norbu cites this chronology and says that its source is the *Chos-'byung* of Patrul Rinpoche. Oral communication.

12. A. W. Hanson-Barber, *The Life and Teachings of Vairochana* (University of Wisconsin, unpublished Ph.D. thesis), Madison 1986.

13. *Tibetan Tripitaka*, vol. 81, n. 4554. This Sanskritization is pure conjecture on the part of D. T. Suzuki and other Japanese editors of this photo-reproduced reprint of the Peking edition.

14. H. V. Guenther in *Crystal Mirror*, vol. 3 (Emeryville, CA: Dharma, 1974) p. 86.

15. Sarat Chandra Das, *A Tibetan-English Dictionary* (Calcutta: Government of West Bengal, 1902).

16. A. W. Hanson-Barber also discusses the question of the Sanskritization of the name Garab Dorje, as well as the question of his date, in his article "The Identification of dGa'-rab rdo-rje," JIABS vol. 9, no. 2, Madison 1986, pp. 55–63.

17. On the two Manjushrimitras, see Eva Dargyay, *The Rise of Esoteric Buddhism in Tibet* (Delhi: Motilal, 1977) pp. 20 ff; p. 245.

18. Hanson-Barber, "Identification of dGa'-rab rdo-rje," p. 62, n. 25.

19. Translated in George Roerich, *The Blue Annals* (Calcutta: Royal Asiatic Society of Bengal, 1974) pp. 159 ff.

20. Benoytosh Bhattacharyya, ed., *Two Vajrayana Works* (Baroda: Oriental Institute of Bengal, 1929).

21. G. Roerich, *Blue Annals*, p. 552.

22. Hanson-Barber, "Identification of dGa'-rab rdo-rje," p. 59.

23. On Yantra Yoga, see Namkhai Norbu, *Yantra Yoga: The Yoga of Movement* (Naples: Shang Shung Edizione, 1982) (introduction in English and text in Tibetan); and also Namkhai Norbu and Oliver Leick, *Yantra Yoga* (Gleisdorf: Edition Tsaparang, 1988). Yantra Yoga (*'khrul-'khor gyi rnal-'byor*) is a system of movements, positions, and breathings associated with the practice of *rdzogs-rim* and *rtsa-rlung*.

24. See Dargyay, *Rise of Esoteric Buddhism*, pp. 42–43.

25. Giuseppe Tucci, *Travels of Tibetan Pilgrims in the Swat Valley* (Calcutta: Greater India Society, 1940).

Possible Historical Sources of Dzogchen

1. See E. Gene Smith's preface in *The Autobiographical Reminiscences of Ngag-dbang dpal-bzaṅ* (Gangtok: Sonam T. Kazi, 1969) pp. 1–19.

2. Tulku Thondup, *The Tantric Tradition of the Nyingmapas* (Marion: Buddha-yana, 1984) p. 164.

3. Tulku Thondup, ibid., pp. 54–67.

4. Eva Dargyay, *The Rise of Esoteric Buddhism in Tibet* (Delhi: Motilal, 1977).

5. See Helmut Hoffmann, *The Religions of Tibet* (London: Allen and Unwin, 1961) chap. 4, "Padmasambhava and Padmaism," pp. 50–65.

6. Dudjom Rinpoche, *rNying-ma'i chos-'byung* (Kalimpong, 1967) chap. 2, *sGrub-sde skor*.

7. Oral communication.

8. Giuseppe Tucci, *Minor Buddhist Texts*, part 1 (Rome: IsMEO, 1956).

9. This has been translated by Herbert V. Guenther in his *Jewel Ornament of Liberation* (London: Rider, 1959).

10. See his *Collected Works*, vols. 1–2. David Jackson briefly discusses this problem in relation to the occurrence of the symbols of the Garuda and of the lion cub with respect to instantaneous enlightenment and the delayed manifestation of enlightenment. See his article, "Birds in the Egg and New

Born Lion Cubs: Metaphors for the Potentialities and Limitations of 'All-at-once' Enlightenment," IATS, Narita Conference, Japan 1990, pp. 1–23.

11. Paul Demieville, *Le Concile de Lhasa* (Paris: Impr. Nationale, 1954).

12. On the *Bhavanakrama*, see Tucci, *Minor Buddhist Texts*, parts 1 and 2.

13. See Namkhai Norbu and Kennard Lipman, eds., *Dzogchen and Zen* (Oakland: Zhang-Zhung, 1984).

14. I have also dealt with this question in my article "Dzogchen and Ch'an" (unpublished).

15. See Per Kvaerne, "The Great Perfection in the Tradition of the Bonpos," pp. 367–92, in W. Lai and L. Lancaster, eds., *Early Ch'an in China and Tibet* (Berkeley: Asian Humanities, 1983).

16. For the traditional account of Gyerpungpa, see David Snellgrove and Hugh Richardson, *A Cultural History of Tibet* (New York: Weidenfeld and Nicolson, 1968) pp. 99–102. The principal texts of the *Zhang-zhung snyan-rgyud* have been published in India by Lopon Tendzin Namdak on behalf of the Bonpo Monastic Centre through the International Academy of Indian Culture as *History and Doctrine of Bonpo Nispanna Yoga* (New Delhi, 1968). There is an English preface by Lokesh Chandra. I have prepared my own study and translation of these texts, *The Oral Tradition of Zhang-zhung*, to be published in the future.

17. See Per Kvaerne, "Aspects of the Origin of Buddhist Tradition in Tibet," in *Numen* 19 (1972), pp. 30–40. Also see Namkhai Norbu, *The Necklace of gZi: A Cultural History of Tibet* (Dharamsala: LTWA, 1981) pp. 17–19.

18. See David Snellgrove, *Indo-Tibetan Buddhism* (London: Serindia, 1987) pp. 399–407.

19. See Tucci, *Minor Buddhist Texts*, and Snellgrove, *Indo-Tibetan Buddhism*.

20. See Norbu, *The Necklace of gZi*.

Four Early Texts Relating To Dzogchen

1. Namkhai Norbu and Kennard Lipman, *Primordial Experience* (Boston: Shambhala, 1987) pp. ix–x.

2. See Namkhai Norbu, *The Small Collection of Hidden Precepts: A Study of an Ancient Manuscript of Dzogchen from Tun Huang* (Arcidosso: Shang Shung, 1984). Preface in English, text in Tibetan.

3. Samten G. Karmay, *The Great Perfection* (Leiden: Brill, 1988) pp. 59–76.

4. *Tibetan Tripitaka* (Peking ed.), bKa'-'gyur, vol. 5, no. 451.

5. There exist two other English translations of this text based on the oral explanations of Norbu. See Namkhai Norbu and John Shane, eds., *The Crystal and the Way of Light* (London: RKP, 1986) p. xv; and also Namkhai Norbu and Adriano Clemente, eds., *Dzogchen: The Self-Perfected State* (London: Arkana, 1989) p. 48. Karmay's translation of the text is found in his article "The rDzogs-chen in Its Earliest Text: A Manuscript from Tun Huang," in B. Aziz and M. Kapstein, eds., *Soundings in Tibetan Civilization* (Delhi: Manohar, 1985) p. 281.

6. Karmay, *Great Perfection*, p. 176.

7. A complete transcript of Norbu's seminar on this text has been published as *Rigbai Kujyug: The Six Vajra Verses, An Oral Commentary by Namkhai Norbu Rinpoche*, ed. Cheh-Ngee Go (Singapore: Rinchen, 1990). Much of this same material is presented in the section entitled "The Cuckoo of the State of Presence," found in Norbu and Clemente, *Dzogchen*, pp. 45–83.

8. Sir Aurel Stein, *On Ancient Central Asian Tracks* (London: Macmillan, 1933).

9. Paul Demieville, *Le Concile de Lhasa* (Paris: Impr. Nationale de France, 1954) p. 176.

10. Karmay, *Great Perfection*, pp. 41–49.

11. See "The Jewel Ship" in Kennard Lipman and Merrill Peterson, *You Are the Eyes of the World* (Novato: Lotsawa, 1987).

12. See Samten G. Karmay, "A Discussion of the Doctrinal Position of the rDzogs-chen from the 10th to the 11th Centuries," in *Journal Asiatique* 1 and 2 (Paris, 1975) pp. 147–55.

13. See Eva Dargyay, "The Concept of a Creator God in Tibetan Buddhism," in JIABS, vol. 8, no. 1 (Madison, 1985) pp. 31–47; and also Eva Dargyay, "A Nyingmapa Text: The *Kun-byed rgyal-po'i mdo*," in B. Aziz and M. Kapstein, eds., *Soundings in Tibetan Civilization* (Delhi: Manohar, 1985) pp. 282–93. See also, Eva K. Neumaier-Dargyay, *The Sovereign All-Creating Mind: The Motherly Buddha—A Translation of the Kun-byed rgyal-po'i mdo* (Albany: SUNY, 1992). This book, which came out after my own book was completed in 1990, elaborates on the above articles.

14. Dargyay, "A Nyingmapa Text," pp. 282–93.

15. See the Appendix in my *Self-Liberation through Seeing with Naked Awareness* (Barrytown, NY: Station Hill, 1989).

16. Oral communication.

17. See Ken Wilber, ed., *The Holographic Paradigm and Other Paradoxes* (Boulder: Shambhala, 1982).

18. See my *Self-Liberation*.

19. Shantirakshita, for example, refuted the conventional Hindu idea of a Creator God from the Buddhist standpoint. See Ganganatha Jha, *Tattvasamgraha*, 2 vols. (Baroda: Oriental Institute, 1937, 1939) vol. 1, pp. 68–107, 132–38. Also see Kewal Krishan Mittal, *A Tibetan Eye-View of Indian Philosophy, Being a Translation of the Grub-mtha' Shel gyi Me-long of Thu'u bkwan bLobzang Chos kyi Nyi-ma* (Delhi: Manoharlal, 1984).

20. The *Hevajra Tantra* begins: "Evam māyā śrūtam ekasmin samaye bhagavān sarva-tathāgata-kāya-vāk-citta-vajrayoṣid-bhageṣu vijahara." This is translated by David Snellgrove as "Thus I have heard: at one time the Lord dwelt in bliss with the Vajrayogini who is the Body, Speech, and Mind of all the Buddhas." See David Snellgrove, *The Hevajra Tantra: A Critical Study* (London: Oxford Univ. Press, 1959), vol. 1, p. 2. However, what the text in both the Sanskrit and the Tibetan actually says is ". . . the Lord (Bhagavan) dwelt in the vagina (Skt. *bhageṣu*) of the Adamantine Lady *(rdo-rje btsun-mo'i bha-ga la bzhugs-so)*. . . ."

21. Dudjom Rinpoche in chapter two of his *rNying-ma'i chos-'byung*. The Sambhogakaya possesses five supreme aspects *(phun-tshogs lnga)* or five certainties *(nges-pa lnga)* of place *(gnas)*, teacher *(ston-pa)*, audience *('khor)*, doctrine *(chos)*, and time *(dus)*. For a translation of Dudjom Rinpoche's text, see Gyurme Dorje and Matthew Kapstein, *The Nyingma School of Tibetan Buddhism: Its Fundamentals and History* (Boston: Wisdom, 1991) vol. 1.

22. See my *Self-Liberation*. In "The Jewel Ship" of Longchenpa, it is explained how the practitioner reenacts this Primordial Act of emanation in the context of Guru Yoga. I have dealt with the clear parallels to this in the Western Gnostic tradition in my *Mystical Illumination in Gnosticism and Buddhist Tantra* (unpublished).

23. *bCom-ldan-'das* and *legs-ldan* are found in the *Mahavyutpatti* dictionary. Some verses from the Tibetan translation of the *Bhagavad Gita* are found in V. Bhattacharya, *Bhota-Prakasha: A Tibetan Chrestomathy* (Calcutta: University of Calcutta, 1939).

24. On Rinchen Zangpo (Rin-chen bzang-po), see Helmut Hoffmann, *The Religions of Tibet* (London: Allen and Unwin, 1961) pp. 115–18.

25. The *Svarodaya Tantra* belongs to the science Svarodaya Shastra, which deals with divination by means of breath. See S. Kannan, *Swara Chintamani* (Divine Breath) (Madras: Kanaan, 1967); and Swami Sivapriyananda, *Secret Power of Tantrik Breathing* (New Delhi: Abhinav, 1983).

26. Under the guidance of Namkhai Norbu Rinpoche, a complete English translation of this Tantra has been prepared by James Valby. The text has also been very differently translated by Eva Dargyay, *The Sovereign All-Creating Mind.* This book, which came out after my own book was completed in 1990, presents a feminist and theistic interpretation of the Tantra having little relationship to how the native Tibetan Nyingmapa Lamas understand it. I have replied to this theistic interpretation as expressed in her two earlier articles.

27. See David Lorenzen, *The Kapalikas and Kalamukhas: Two Lost Shaivite Sects* (New Delhi: Thomson, 1972) chap. 6, "Lakulisha and the Pashupatas," pp. 173–92. See also Pranabananda Jash, *History of Shaivism* (Calcutta: Roy and Chaudhury, 1974) pp. 35–60.

28. Jash, ibid., pp. 18–34. And on Titumular (ninth century CE) and his *Tirumandiram,* see Jash, ibid., p.89.

29. See Sir John Woodroffe and Pramatha Natha Mukhyopadhyaya, *Mahamaya: The World as Power: Power as Consciousness* (Madras: Ganesh, 1954).

30. On *ābhāsa,* see Lakshmi Nidhi Sharma, *Kashmiri Saivism* (Varanasi: Bharatiya Vidya Prakashan, 1972) pp. 112–25.

31. Kanti Chandra Pandey, *Abhinavagupta: An Historical and Philosophical Study* (Varanasi: Chowkhamba Sanskrit Series Office, 1963).

32. On Chinachara, see "Chinachara (Vashishtha and Buddha)," in Sir John Woodroffe, *Shakti and Shakta* (Madras: Ganesh, 1975) pp. 123–30.

33. See Namkhai Norbu, "Textual Introduction," pp. 1–9, in Lipman and Peterson, *You Are the Eyes of the World.*

34. See Norbu, ibid., and "The History and Structure of the *Kun-byed rgyal-po,*" pp. 79–87, in Lipman and Peterson, *You Are the Eyes of the World.*

35. Quoted in Karmay, "A Discussion of the Doctrinal Position of the rDzogs-chen in the 10th to the 11th Centuries."

36. See *Nges don 'brug sgra,* p. 464, in the *Collected Works of Sog-zlog-pa bLo-gros rgyal-mtshan* (New Delhi: Sanje Dorji, 1975) vol. 1, no. 5.

37. The possible Bonpo connections of the *Kun-byed rgyal-po* are particularly intriguing in view of the association of the Bonpo Dzogchen teachings found in the *Zhang-zhung snyan-rgyud* with the same Western Tibetan region in which the medieval kingdom of Guge arose. Also see Karmay, "rDzogs-chen in the Bonpo Tradition," pp. 201–05, in his *Great Perfection.*

38. See Sog-zlog-pa, *Nges don 'brug sgra,* p. 469. This citation is also quoted and translated in Norbu, "History and Structure."

39. *rNying-ma'i rgyud 'bum*, mTshams-brag edition, vol. 1, p. 220.3.

40. TTP, vol. 9, p. 126.5.2.

41. See Norbu, "History and Structure," pp. 86–87.

42. *bSam-gtan mig sgron* (Leh: S. W. Tashigangapa, 1974) p. 320. *Lhun gyis grub-pa'i ngang chen-po lta-ba ni / . . . sangs-rgyas dang sems-can dang / de'i spyod-yul ril gyi rang-bzhin ni / yong ye gdod-ma med-pa na tha-ma med-par lhun gyis grub-pa'i chos-nyid ngang chen-po'i rang-bzhin du lhag-ma med-par sangs-rgyas-so.*

43. *bSam-gtan mig sgron*, pp. 375–76. *Chos thams-cad gzhi ji-bzhin-par lta-ba ni / khyad-par du'ang ma nor-ba ste / de ci'i phyir zhe na / dngos-po rnams kyi de kho na nyid kha na ma bcos bslad-pa nyid pas atiyoga rdzogs-pa chen-po'o.*

44. Karmay, *Great Perfection*, pp. 99–101.

45. *mGur 'bum* (Sarnath: Lobsang Tsultim, 1971). The *mGur 'bum* has been translated into English by Garma C. C. Chang in *The Hundred-Thousand Songs of Milarepa* (New Hyde Park, NY: University Books, 1962).

46. For the traditional account of gNubs-chen sangs-rgyas ye-shes, see Tulku Thondup, *The Tantric Tradition of the Nyingmapas* (Marion: Buddhayana, 1984) pp. 152–53.

47. Personal communication. See also Karmay, *Great Perfection*, pp. 35–37.

48. *rJe-btsun thams-cad mkhyen-pa bai-ro-tsa-na'i rnam-thar 'dra 'bag chen-mo* (Leh, 1971). Besides this Leh edition, there is also an edition, published in Dehra Dun (1977), reproducing a Lhasa xylograph edition with a colophon by Dharmasimha (Khams smyong Dharma seng-ge).

49. *Bairo'i rgyud 'bum* (Leh: S. W. Tashigangpa, 1971).

50. *Chos-dbyings rin-po-che'i mdzod*, Gangtok, n.d., fol. 206b.

51. *Chos-'byung me-tog snying-po sbrang-rtsi'i bcud*, in *Rin-chen gter mdzod chen-po'i rgyab-chos*, vol. 6 (Paro: Ugyen Tempai Gyaltsen, 1979).

52. The text of the *'Dra 'bag chen-po* has been studied by Karmay, *Great Perfection*, pp. 17–37. See also Karmay, *Origin and Early Development of the Tibetan Religious Traditions of the Great Perfection* (SOAS Ph.D. thesis) (London, 1986); and A. W. Hanson-Barber, *The Life and Teaching of Vairochana* (Univ. of Wisconsin Ph.D. thesis) (Madison, 1986).

53. *'Dra 'bag chen-mo*, pp. 439–40.

54. Norbu and Lipman, *Primordial Experience*, pp. 3–5; pp. 55–68. Lipman also translated this account found in the *'Dra 'bag chen-mo*.

55. Karmay, *Origin and Early Development*, pp. 35–72.

Is Dzogchen an Authentic Buddhist Teaching?

1. See the *Nges don 'brug sgra* in *The Collected Works of Sog-zlog-pa blo-gros rgyal-mtshan* (New Delhi: Sanje Dorji, 1975) vol. 1, no. 5, p. 325. A portion from this text is cited and translated in Namkhai Norbu, "The History and Structure of the *Kun-byed rgyal-po*," pp. 78 ff., in Kennard Lipman and Merrill Peterson, *You Are the Eyes of the World* (Novato, CA: Lotsawa, 1987). Selections from 'Bri-gung dpal-'dzin's *Chos dang chos ma yin-pa rnam-par dbye-ba'i rab tu byed-pa* are quoted in this work of Sog-zlog-pa.

2. See the bibliography.

3. On the *Mahavyutpatti* and the *Madhyavyutpatti*, see Nils Simonson, *Indo-Tibetische Studien* (Uppsala: Almquist and Wiksell, 1957).

4. Oral communication.

5. The Sanskrit word *sandhi* means "junction, connection, union with, comprehension, totality, the entire scope of, the interval between day and night, twilight," etc., in M. Monier-Williams, *A Sanskrit-English Dictionary* (Oxford: Clarendon, 1956) p. 1144. On the writings of Rongzom Pandita, see *Selected Writings of Rong-zom Chos kyi bzang-po* (Leh, 1974).

6. *Tibetan Tripitaka* (Peking ed.), bsTan-'gyur vol. 83, no. 4726. On this text, see below.

7. *Man-ngag lta-ba'i phreng-ba zhes bya-ba'i 'grel-ba* in *Selected Writings of Rong-zom*, pp. 19–124.

8. Samten G. Karmay, *The Great Perfection* (Leiden: Brill, 1988) p. 138.

9. On the transmissions of the Upadesha from the master Tilopa to his disciple Naropa and in turn to Marpa, see Herbert V. Guenther, *The Life and Teachings of Naropa* (Oxford: Clarendon, 1963), and also Chögyam Trungpa and the Nalanda Translation Committee, *The Life of Marpa the Translator* (Boulder: Prajna, 1982). Karmay also agrees that Dzogchen was originally Upadesha relating to the *rdzogs-rim* practices of Mahayoga Tantra. In the earliest period it appears that there did not yet exist this classification into nine successive vehicles (*theg-pa rim dgu*), and so only later did Dzogchen come to be treated as a separate vehicle independent of Tantra. That this was the case is strongly suggested by the *Man-ngag lta-ba'i phreng-ba*. See Karmay, *Great Perfection*, pp. 137–74.

10. In *Tibetan Tripitaka* (Peking ed.), bsTan-'gyur, vol. 83, no. 4726, the Sanskrit title of the *lTa-phreng* has been reconstructed as *Rajopadesha darshana-mala* by D. T. Suzuki. But Karmay doubts the authenticity of this text, although not its antiquity; for he says, "No evidence can be gathered that it is of Indian origin inspite of its ascription to Padmasambhava" (*Great*

Perfection, p. 137). Karmay has studied and translated the text of the *lTa-phreng* on pp. 137–74. Also see Giuseppe Baroetto, *L'Insegnamento Esoterico di Padma-sambhava: Man-ngag lta-ba'i phreng-ba* (Arcidosso: Shang Shung Edizione, 1990).

11. Book review of Namkhai Norbu and John Shane, eds., *The Crystal and the Way of Light* (London: RKP, 1986) by Stephen Batchelor in *The Middle Way* (London), Winter 1987.

12. Jampa Samten, "Preliminary Notes on the *Phu-brag bka'-'gyur*: A Unique Collection of the Tibetan Buddhist Canon," IATS, Narita Conference, Japan, 1989.

13. *A Catalogue of the Manuscripts Collected by Sir Aurel Stein*, the Stein Collection in London.

14. *Sarvatathagata Tattvasamgraha* fragments: VP 367 II, 447 III, 417 I, II, III. *Durgati parishodhana* fragment: VP 531 I.

15. *Guhyasamaja Tantra* fragments: VP 438, VP 481, no. 583 XI. *Zhi-khro* texts: VP 332, VP 540, etc. See Kimuaki Tanaka, "A Comparative Study of the Esoteric Buddhist Manuscripts and Icons Discovered at Dun-Huang," IATS, Narita Conference, Japan, 1989.

16. In the early period, that is, before the eleventh century, only two schools of Madhyamika were known in Tibet (*dbu-ma rnam gnyis*): (1) the Sautrantika-Madhyamika (*mdo-sde spyod-pa'i dbu-ma*) of Bhavaviveka (sixth century) and (2) the Yogachara-Madhyamika (*rnal-'byor spyod-pa'i dbu-ma*) of Shanti-rakshita (eighth century). In the eleventh century the works of Chandrakirti (seventh century), in particular the *Madhyamakavatara Karika* (*dBu-ma la 'jug-pa*), were translated into Tibetan, and his Prasangika-Madhyamika philosophy became widespread and then predominant in all the schools of Tibetan Buddhism.

17. See Giuseppe Tucci, *Indo-Tibetica*, 4 vols. (Rome: Reale Accademia d'Italia, 1932–41).

18. See James Robinson, *Buddha's Lions* (Berkeley: Dharma, 1979); and Keith Dowman, *Masters of the Mahamudra* (Albany: State Univ. of NY Press, 1985).

19. See Sir John Woodroffe, *Introduction to Tantra Shastra*, 2nd ed. (Madras: Ganesh, 1952). Also see Ajit Mookherjee and Madhu Khanna, *The Tantric Way: Art, Science, Ritual* (Boston: New York Graphic Society, 1977).

20. This does not mean that Anuttara Tantra or Shakta Tantra is Satanism. Satanism belongs to an entirely different cultural and mythological context—a Christian one, but one where values and symbols are inverted with regard to conventional meaning. Moreover, medieval witchcraft, insofar as

it was ever organized as a cult, was more connected with the worship of the pagan goddess Diana (or similar goddesses) and with the Old European horned god, a fertility deity only later identified with the biblical Satan by theologians and churchmen. This is the thesis propounded by Margaret Murray. See her *The Witch-Cult in Western Europe* (Oxford: Clarendon, 1921) and *The God of the Witches* (London, 1934). This theory was popularized by Gerald Gardner, the founder of modern Wicca. See his *Witchcraft Today* (London: Ryder, 1954). The historical basis of the claims of the Murray thesis has been criticized by Elliot Rose, *A Razor for a Goat: Problems in the History of Witchcraft and Diabolism* (Toronto: Univ. of Toronto Press, 1989). But with respect to the Witches' Sabbat and the Chakrapuja, we do find the same archetype coming into manifestation, one that is antinomian and utterly antagonistic to the patriarchal establishment and its official religion. I deal with this question in more detail in my booklet *Wicca, Paganism, and Tantra* (Vidyadhara Publications, 1994). As for the sexual practices associated with Anuttara Tantra, in the days of the Mahasiddhas in India and at first in Tibet, they were practiced in the flesh and not just symbolically. But with the resurgence of puritanism connected with the revival of the monastic system in the eleventh century, these practices tended more and more to become symbolic only, as is almost universally the case nowadays. The Shakta Tantras are principally concerned with the worship of the Hindu goddess Kali, who represents shakti, or divine power (energy). See Sir John Woodroffe, *Introduction to Tantra Shastra*.

21. While residing in West Bengal for two years at Santiniketan and elsewhere, I had personal contact with the cult of the goddess Kali and have subsequently been able to compare this experience with others when I came into contact with Wicca and other neopagan goddess-oriented groups in the West. On neopaganism and the revival of the Goddess Religion in the West, see Margot Adler, *Drawing Down the Moon* (New York: Viking, 1979).

22. Thubten Jigme Norbu and Colin Turnbull, *Tibet: An Account of the History, Religion, and People of Tibet* (New York: Simon and Schuster, 1968) pp. 177–85; pp. 193–94.

23. On the career of Atisha in Tibet, see Alaka Chattopadhyaya, *Atisha and Tibet* (Calcutta: Firma Mukhapadhyay, 1967).

24. The Sanskrit manuscript discovered at Samye Monastery by Sakya Pandita was the *Guhyagarbha Tantra*. He compared this with the existing Tibetan translation from the early period and was satisfied with the accuracy of the latter. Sakya Pandita also obtained from Nepal a Sanskrit fragment of the *Vajrakilaya Tantra*. He translated this fragment, and it is now included in the *Kangyur* as the *Phur-pa'i rtsa-ba'i dum-bu'i rgyud*.

25. *Collected Works*, vol. YA (New Delhi: 1971) p. 990.2. This passage is quoted in Eva Dargyay, *The Rise of Esoteric Buddhism in Tibet* (Delhi: Motilal, 1977) p. 285.

26. *bKa'-'gyur dang bstan-'gyur gyi dkar-chag bstan-pa rgyas-pa*. Besides the above catalogue, there was compiled an abridged catalogue for the Kangyur alone. On the history of the editions of the Kangyur and the Tangyur, as well as the *rNying-ma'i rgyud 'bum*, see Namkhai Norbu, "History and Structure."

27. Herbert V. Guenther, *Buddhist Philosophy in Theory and Practice* (Baltimore: Penguin, 1971) pp. 13–23, 155–170, 192–202.

28. On this dharma theory and the method of philosophical analysis, see Edward Conze, *Buddhist Thought in India* (London: Allen and Unwin, 1962) pp. 92–116. An example of this method from the Madhyamika standpoint is found in "The Wheel of Analytical Meditation" (*Sems kyi dpyod-pa rnam-par sbyong-ba so-sor brtag-pa'i dpyad sgom 'khor-lo-ma*) by Mipham Rinpoche (Mi pham 'Jam-dbyangs rnam-rgyal rgya-mtso, 1846–1914) in Tarthang Tulku, *Calm and Clear* (Emeryville: Dharma, 1973) pp. 43–53.

29. On the *gzhan-stong* theory, see David Snellgrove and Hugh Richardson, *A Cultural History of Tibet* (London: Weidenfeld and Nicolson, 1968) pp. 179–80. On the continuing *gzhan-stong* vs. *rang-stong* controversy, see E. Gene Smith, Introduction, in Lokesh Chandra, ed., *Kongtrul's Encyclopedia of Indo-Tibetan Culture* (New Delhi: International Academy of Indian Culture, 1970). For a Kagyudpa approach to this theory, see Khenpo Tsultrim Gyamtso and Shenphen Hookham, *Progressive Stages of Meditation* (Oxford: Longchen Foundation, 1988).

30. On the Jonangpa sect and its suppression, see Snellgrove and Richardson, ibid., pp. 196–97; and on the struggle of the Gelugpas with the kings of Tsang, see pp. 183–95. On the intellectual position of the Jonangpas, see especially D. S. Ruegg, "The Jo-nang-pas: A School of Buddhist Ontologists according to the *Grub-mtha' shel gyi me-long*" in JAOS 83 (1963), pp. 73–91.

31. The three samadhis (*ting-nge-'dzin gsum*) are *de kho no nyid gyi ting-nge-'dzin, kun tu snang-ba'i ting-nge-'dzin*, and *rgyu'i ting-nge-'dzin*.

32. I have dealt with this process of sadhana or tantric transformation in my book *The Staircase to Akanishthha* (forthcoming). Herbert V. Guenther has also dealt with this question in his own way in his *Matrix of Mystery: Scientific and Humanistic Aspects of rDzogs-chen Thought* (Boulder: Shambhala, 1984) and his *The Creative Vision: The Symbolic Recreation of the World according to the Tibetan Buddhist Tradition of Tantric Visualization Otherwise Known*

as the Developing Phase (Novato, CA: Lotsawa, 1987). For a different but equally nontraditional view, see Alex Wayman, *Yoga of the Guhyasamajatantra: The Arcane Lore of Forty Verses* (Delhi: Motilal, 1977).

33. This is the special Dzogchen use of the term. In the Sutra system *thugs-rje* (Skt. *karuṇā*) means "compassion," which is the empathic feeling for the suffering of others.

34. See Edward Conze, *Prajnaparamita Literature* (Tokyo: Reiyukai, 1978).

35. See D. T. Suzuki, *Studies in the Lankavatara Sutra* (London: Routledge, 1968).

36. It may be noted that, unlike the Nyingmapa school, the Bonpo school has developed an intellectual defense of Dzogchen linked with logic and debate. Oral communication from Geshe Tenzin Wangyal Rinpoche. See the *Gal-mdo* (Dolanji: Tibetan Bonpo Monastic Centre, 1972). Anne Klein and Rinpoche are now preparing a translation of parts of this interesting text.

37. Edward Conze, *Buddhist Thought in India* (London: Allen and Unwin, 1962) pp. 195–96. By way of comparing Buddhism and Gnosticism, Conze writes, "The doctrine of the divine spark, which is our true Self, is indeed fundamental to both systems. For the Mahayana the innate essence of man's being is 'the celestial nature itself, purest light, *bodhicittam prakriti-prabhasvaram.*' In salvation the god within has united with the god outside. ... The 'self-luminous thought' which is at the centre of our being and has been overlaid by 'adventitious defilements' becomes in the Mahayana 'the embryo of the Tathagata'. . . . To see through to one's own 'Buddha-self' became the chief preoccupation of the Zen sect. The Manicheans likewise speak of 'our original luminous nature,' 'those around Basilides are in the habit of calling the passions appendages,' and 'in the *Poimandres* the ascent is described as a series of progressive substractions which leaves the naked true self.' Here Conze is citing quotations from Hans Jonas, *Gnosis und spaetantiker Geist*, vols. 1 and 2 (Gottingen: Vandenhoeck and Ruprecht, 1934, 1954). A portion of this work has been translated into English in Hans Jonas, *The Gnostic Religion* (Boston: Beacon, 1963). See "Buddhism and Gnosis" in Edward Conze, *Further Buddhist Studies* (Oxford: Cassirer, 1975) pp. 18–19; also n. 2 on p. 19.

38. See Edward Conze, *Buddhist Meditation* (London: Allen and Unwin, 1956) pp. 45–138; and also see Parawahera Vajiranana, *Buddhist Meditation in Theory and Practice* (Colombo: Gunasena, 1962) pp. 139–208.

39. See Thera Nyanaponika, *The Heart of Buddhist Meditation* (London: Rider, 1969).

NOTE ON THE TRANSLATION

1. See H. A. Jaeschke, *A Tibetan-English Dictionary* (London, 1881).

2. Sarat Chandra Das, *A Tibetan-English Dictionary with Sanskrit Synonyms* (Calcutta: Govt. of West Bengal, 1902) p. xi.

3. (Barrytown, NY: Station Hill, 1989).

4. (Moskow, 1986).

5. See Edward Conze, *Materials for a Dictionary of the Prajnaparamita Literature* (Tokyo: Suzuki Research Foundation, 1967).

APPENDIX: BRIEF BIOGRAPHY OF PATRUL RINPOCHE

1. On the Rimed Movement, see E. Gene Smith's introduction in *Kongtrul's Encyclopedia of Indo-Tibetan Culture*, pts. 1-3, Lokesh Chandra ed. (New Delhi: International Academy of Culture, 1970) pp. 1–78.

2. See E. Gene Smith's preface in *The Autobiographical Reminiscences of Ngag-dbang dpal-bzang*, late Abbot of Kah-thog Monastery, critically edited from three original Tibetan texts by Bya-bral Sangs-rgyas rdo-rje (Gangtok: Sonam T. Kazi, 1969) pp. 1–19.

3. See E. Gene Smith (1969).

4. See W. D. Shakabpa, *Tibet: A Political History* (New Haven: Yale Univ. Press, 1967) pp. 134–139.

5. See E. Gene Smith (1970).

6. See E. Gene Smith (1969).

7. On the Khyentse incarnations, see E. Gene Smith (1970), p. 74.

8. E. Gene Smith (1970), pp. 27–28.

9. *Dza dPal-sprul rin-po-che'i rnam-thar mdor bsdus* by Thub-bstan nyi-ma, found in *Khams khul mkhas-dbang rnams kyi snyan-ngag dper brjod phyogs sgrub* (Lhasa: Si khron mi rigs dpe skrun khang, 1987) pp. 10–16.

10. The region of rDza-chu-kha lies in northern Kham between the Myag-chu River in the east and the 'Bri-chu River in the west. It is largely a nomad area.

11. *rtsa-rlung* or *rtsa rlung thig-le'i rnal-'byor* "the yoga of the channels (Skt. *nāḍi*), winds (Skt. *vāyu*), and drops (Skt. *bindus*)." These are the esoteric yoga practices associated with the Higher Tantras.

12. rDzogs-chen Monastery, founded in 1685 by Padma Rig-'dzin, was the largest among the Nyingmapa monasteries in Eastern Tibet. rDzogs-chen shri seng chos-grwa was a famous college at that monastery.

13. The *Byams-chos*, "the teachings of Maitreya," are five texts belonging to the Yogachara school composed by Maitreyanatha (Byams-pa) and his disciple Asanga, namely, the *Mahayanasutralankara, Abhisamayalankara, Madhyantavibhaga, Dharmadharmatavibhaga,* and *Mahayanottaratantra.* "Madhyamaka" means texts by the masters of that school, such as the *Madhyamaka Mulakarika* by Nagarjuna, the *Catuhshataka Shastra* by Aryadeva, and the *Madhyamikavatara* by Chandrakirti. The "Abhidharma" means the *Abhidharmakosha* of Vasubandhu. The *Yon-tan mdzod* is Jigmed Lingpa's *magnum opus* on Sutra, Tantra, and Dzogchen. The *sDom gsum rnam nges* of mNga'-ris Pan-chen Padma dbang-rgyal (1487–1542) is a definitive treatment of vows at the levels of Hinayana, Mahayana, and Vajrayana.

14. Kah-thog Monastery in Kham was founded in 1159 and revived in the seventeenth century. It was the leading center of Nyingmapa scholarship in Eastern Tibet.

15. See E. Gene Smith (1969).

16. The *mKhas-pa shri rgyal-po'i khyad-chos,* or "Special Teaching of the Wise and Glorious King" is translated in Part One.

17. *rDza dpal-sprul rin-po-che'i rnam-thar mdor bsdus,* p. 16.

Selected Bibliography

BOOKS AND ARTICLES IN ENGLISH

Aziz, Barbara, and Kapstein, Matthew, eds. *Soundings in Tibetan Civilization*. Delhi: Manohar, 1985.

Conze, Edward. *Buddhist Thought in India*. London: George Allen & Unwin, 1962.

Dargyay, Eva. "The Concept of a Creator God in Tantric Buddhism." *Journal of the International Association of Buddhist Studies*, vol. 8, no. 1, Madison 1985, pp. 31-47.

—. "A Nyingmapa Text: The *Kun-byed rgyal-po'i mdo*." Barbara Aziz and Matthew Kapstein, eds. *Soundings in Tibetan Civilization*. Delhi: Manohar, 1985. pp. 282-93.

—. *The Rise of Esoteric Buddhism in Tibet*. Delhi: Motilal Banarsidass, 1977.

Dowman, Keith. *The Three Incisive Precepts of Garab Dorje; The Dzogchen Precepts of the Extraordinary Reality of the Glorious Sovereign Wisdom of Patrul Rinpoche; Patrul's Short Elucidation of the mKhas-pa shri rgyal-po*. Kathmandu: Diamond Sow, n.d.

Hanson-Barber, A.W. "The Identification of dGa'-rab rdo-rje." *Journal of the International Association of Buddhist Studies*, vol. 9, no. 2, Madison 1986, pp. 55-63.

—. *The Life and Teachings of Vairocana*. Univ. of Wisconsin, Madison 1986 (Ph.D. thesis).

Karmay, Samten G. "A Discussion of the Doctrinal Position of the rDzogs-chen from the 10th to the 11th Centuries." in *Journal Asiatique* 1-2, Paris 1975, pp. 147-55.

—. *The Great Perfection: A Philosophical and Meditative Teaching of Tibetan Buddhism*. Leiden: Brill, 1988.

—. *Origin and Early Development of the Tibetan Religious Traditions of the Great Perfection*. SOAS, London 1986 (Ph.D. thesis).

—. "The rDzogs-chen in Its Earliest Text: A Manuscript from Tun Huang." *In* Barbara Aziz and Matthew Kapstein, eds. *Soundings in Tibetan Civilization*. Delhi: Manohar, 1985. Pp. 272-82.

Kvaerne, Per. "Aspects of the Origin of Buddhist Tradition in Tibet." *Numen* 19 (1972), pp. 30-40.

—. "The Great Perfection in the Tradition of the Bonpos." *In* Whalen Lai and Lewis Lancaster, eds. *Early Ch'an in China and Tibet*. Berkeley: Asian Humanities Press, 1983. Pp. 367-92.

Lai, Whalen, and Lewis Lancaster, Lewis, eds. *Early Ch'an in China and Tibet*. Berkeley: Asian Humanities Press, 1983.

Lipman, Kennard, and Merrill Peterson, eds. *You Are the Eyes of the World*. Novato, CA: Lotsawa, 1987.

Norbu, Namkhai. *The Crystal and the Way of Light*. Compiled and edited by John Shane. London: RKP, 1986.

—. *The Cycle of Day and Night*. Translated by John Myrdhin Reynolds. Barrytown, NY: Station Hill, 1987.

—. *Dzogchen: The Self-Perfected State*. Compiled and edited by Adriano Clemente. Translated by John Shane. London: Arkana, 1989; reprint Ithaca, NY: Snow Lion, 1996.

—. *The Necklace of gZi: A Cultural History of Tibet*. Dharamsala: LTWA, 1981.

—. *The Small Collection of Hidden Precepts: A Study of an Ancient Manuscript of Dzogchen from Tun Huang*. Arcidosso: Shang Shung Edizione, 1984. (Preface in English, text in Tibetan.)

Norbu, Namkhai and Cheh-Ngee Goh, eds. *Rigbai Kujyug: The Six Vajra Verses, An Oral Commentary by Namkhai Norbu Rinpoche*. Singapore: Rinchen Editions, 1990.

Norbu, Namkhai, and Kennard Lipman, eds. *Dzogchen and Zen*. Oakland: Zhang Zhung Editions, 1984.

—. *Primordial Experience*. Boston: Shambhala, 1987.

Reynolds, John Myrdhin. *Self-Liberation through Seeing with Naked Awareness*. Barrytown, NY: Station Hill, 1989.

Roerich, George. *The Blue Annals*. Calcutta 1974; reprint Delhi: Motilal Banarsidass, 1976.

Shakabpa, W. D. *Tibet: A Political History*. New Haven: Yale University Press, 1967.

Smith, E. Gene. Preface. *The Autobiographical Reminiscences of Ngag-dbang dpal-bzang*. Ngagyur Nyingmay Sungrab Series, vol. 1. Gangtok: Sonam T. Kazi, 1969.

—. Introduction. *Kongtrul's Encyclopedia of Indo-Tibetan Culture*. New Delhi: International Academy of Culture, 1970.

Snellgrove, David. *Indo-Tibetan Buddhism*. London: Serindia, 1987.

Snellgrove, David, and Hugh Richardson. *A Cultural History of Tibet*. London: Weidenfeld and Nicolson, 1968.

Tarthang Tulku. *Crystal Mirror*. Vol. 5. Emeryville: Dharma, 1977.

Tucci, Giuseppe. *Minor Buddhist Texts*. Vol. 1. Rome: IsMEO, 1956.

Tulku Thondup. *Buddha Mind: An Anthology of Longchen Rabjam's Writings on Dzogpa Chenpo*. Ithaca, NY: Snow Lion, 1989. Reprinted as *The Practice of Dzogchen*. Ithaca: Snow Lion, 1996.

—. *Buddhist Civilization in Tibet*. London: RKP, 1987.

—. *The Tantric Tradition of the Nyingmapas*. Marion: Buddhayana, 1984.

Vostrikov, A. I. *Tibetan Historical Literature*. Calcutta: Indian Studies, 1970.

TIBETAN TEXTS

mKhas-pa shri rgyal-po'i khyad-chos by rDza dPal-sprul Rin-po-che. Tashijong, n.d. (xylograph edition).

rNying-ma'i chos-'byung by bDud-'jom Rin-po-che, 'Jig-bral ye-shes rdo-rje, Kalimpong 1967. Full title: *Gangs ljongs rgyal bstan yongs rdzogs kyi phyi-mo snga 'gyur rdo-rje'i theg-pa'i bstan-pa rin-po-che ji-ltar byung-ba'i tshul dag cing gsal-bar brjod-pa lha dbang g.yul las rgyal-ba'i rnga-bo-che'i sgra dbyangs*.

'Dra 'bag chen-mo. bsTan-rgyas-gling edition. Dehra Dun 1977. Full title: *rJe-btsun thams-cad mkhyen-pa bai-ro-tsa-na'i rnam-thar 'dra 'bag chen-mo*.

rNal-'byor mig gi bsam-gtan or *bSam-gtan mig sgron* by gNubs-chen Sangs-rgyas ye-shes. Leh: C. R. Lama, 1974.

Bi-ma snying-thig. Vols. 7-9 in *sNying-thig ya-bzhi*. Compiled by kLong-chen Dri-med 'od-zer, T. Tsewang and Jamyang, and L. Tashi. New Delhi 1971.

Zhang-zhung snyan-rgyud in *History and Doctrine of Bonpo Nispanna Yoga.*
New Delhi: International Academy of Indian Culture, 1968. English preface by Lokesh Chandra.

General Index

Index of Tibetan Texts and Terms